MUSLIMS AND NEW MEDIA IN WEST AFRICA

T0385014

MUSLIMS AND NEW MEDIA IN WEST AFRICA

PATHWAYS TO GOD

DOROTHEA E. SCHULZ

Indiana University Press
Bloomington and Indianapolis

This book is a publication of

Indiana University Press
601 North Morton Street
Bloomington, Indiana 47404-3797 USA

iupress.indiana.edu

Telephone orders   800-842-6796
Fax orders   812-855-7931

Library of Congress Cataloging-in-Publication Data

Schulz, Dorothea Elisabeth.
    Muslims and new media in West Africa : pathways to God / Dorothea E. Schulz.
        p.   cm.
    Includes bibliographical references and index.
    ISBN 978-0-253-35715-1 (cloth : alk. paper) — ISBN 978-0-253-22362-3
(pbk. : alk. paper) — ISBN 978-0-253-00554-0 (electronic book) 1. Islam—Africa,
West. 2.Women in Islam—Africa, West. 3. Islam—Mali. 4. Women in Islam—
Mali. I. Title.
    BP64.A38S38   2012
    297.082'096623—dc2

                                          2011025571

        1   2   3   4   5   17   16   15   14   13   12

To my mother, Dr. Gesina Schulz,
and my late father, Dr. Arnold Schulz.
And to "Gesina fitinin."

CONTENTS

PREFACE

"No, really, now you are losing it, Nanaaa." My long-standing friend Solo, a journalist of considerable renown in his hometown, San, pronounced the second syllable of my local name with a disapproving sigh before he continued. "Why should you be interested in these conservative Muslim folks who shout everywhere on the media that they alone are proper believers?" "Leave her alone," Fatim, Solo's older sister retorted laughingly, "why should she not try to understand what these Muslims are after? True, their preachers sometimes exaggerate, and all this body covering they exact from women is just outrageous. But those women I know, who meet in these Muslim women's groups, I find them convincing in their seriousness."

It was a hot and dusty afternoon in January 1998. We were sitting in Solo's courtyard in San, chatting and slowly consuming the typically highly concentrated, dark green and sugary brews of "tee chinois." I had just returned to San, a town in southwestern Mali where in 1994 and 1995 I had conducted a survey of radio reception, and was now eager to catch up on family news with Solo and his wife. Our conversation had been in a casual and light tone, until we reached the topic of my new research project. When I mentioned my plan to study the movement of Islamic moral reform that over the last years had gained a striking public presence in towns such as San, Solo, who had been leisurely leaning backward in his chair, abruptly bent forward and said, in an unyielding tone: "There is nothing to understand about these Muslim folks, these so-called rightful believers. They are dangerous. They bombard us with their radio lectures seven days a week. Their leaders want to usurp political power and transform society with their conservative, patriarchal morals. As for the many women who support them, I tell you: they only want to have their share of the Arab money that is distributed behind the scene; it's economic interest alone that makes them join the movement."

Alas, this was only the first of many disapproving comments on my new research topic. Over the following weeks and months, other long-standing friends and acquaintances were similarly negative in their responses. Although disappointing, my friends' dismissal of the Islamic reform movement also piqued my curiosity: almost unanimously, they explained its origins and success by its—alleged—external, "Arab" funding. The argument that "economic interest alone" motivated women to support Muslim leaders and their organizations whose conservative gender morals were detrimental to their own cause did not appear convincing. Too strong was its resemblance to the "brainwashing" argument frequently employed in depictions of "dangerous" religious sects in Western society. Also, although my friends frequently alluded to the key role played by audio recording and broadcasting in the propagation of Islamic renewal, it seemed that the transformative effects of these media for existing forms of religious practice and authority needed closer scrutiny. With these questions in mind, I approached several radio preachers as well as female leaders of the Islamic renewal movement to find out about their motivations. In San, in particular, the relatively novel and pervasive presence of signs and sound bites of Islamic piety in public arenas was striking, given that this town had historically never been a place where Muslim religious traditions and families had played an influential role.

This book is about Islamic renewal in West Africa, and about the particular, institutional, symbolic, and material forms it takes in urban arenas of southern Mali. It examines the understandings of religious subjectivity and authority articulated by those men and women who favor an Islamic moral reform of society and self, and analyzes the pivotal role that new media technologies play in these reconfigurations of conventional forms of religiosity. The book is based on eight intensive periods of field research in San, a market center of approximately twenty-five thousand inhabitants located between the Bani and Niger rivers. Here, at a dusty and busy intersection behind the central marketplace, several important roads intersect that connect trading towns in southern Mali and in Burkina Faso to the capital Bamako (to the southwest), and to towns located farther northeast on the road that ultimately leads to neighboring Niger. My research took place between July 1998 and July 2006, and lasted more than sixteen months. Though drawing intensely on research conducted in San, I sought to place my investigation in a broader politico-economic framework and to move beyond ethnographic approaches to the study of Islam in Africa that, based on research in one location, seek to draw far-reaching conclusions about wider societal, political, and religious ramifications and resonances. For this reason, I collected extensive comparative data in three old neighborhoods of the capital Bamako.

An important rationale for choosing San as my first research locale was that in this town, similar to Bamako and most towns of southern Mali, the majority of the population converted to Islam only during the colonial period. Islam, as a discursive tradition, was never as closely associated with the "spiritual economy" of an established Sufi order as in Nioro, Djenne, and Timbuktu. Much extant research on Islam in Mali has been conducted in these towns with a long history of Muslim erudition. My concern was to assess whether the insights drawn from these studies applied to the numerous urban and semi-urban areas of southern

Mali where Muslims, if they were present at all in the early days of colonial rule, had formed a—sometimes negligible—minority. Given the historically and politically marginal position of Islam in towns such as San—a marginality reflected in the absence of prestigious families of religious specialists—I was also curious to know how the present success of reform-minded Muslim leaders in these towns could be explained.[1]

Bamako, until the late nineteenth century an insignificant town on the border of the River Niger that gained importance only under French colonial administration, occupies a somewhat special position in the Muslim religious field. Yet Bamako resembles San in that, throughout its colonial history, it never constituted a stronghold for powerful clans of religious specialists. The success of Islamic revivalist trends in Bamako dates back to the 1940s, when it became a hotbed of reformist activities by a younger generation of Muslims whose challenge to conventional practices and credentials of religious authority was influenced by Muslim modernist trends in Egypt and the *hejaz*. Hence common to the situation in present-day San and Bamako is that, in the absence of a sufficient number of eminent religious specialists and scholars capable of controlling religious interpretation, both urban centers allow various Muslim reform discourses and activities to thrive.

Another chief reason to situate my exploration of Islamic moral renewal in San was that this town typifies other smaller towns of southern Mali, not just in its long-standing coexistence of Muslim and non-Muslim inhabitants but also in its multiethnic composition and the ways that these multiple social identities and religious affiliations played out in the political history prior to colonial rule. San, historically and still today a place where vectors of travel and trade intersect, formed a small settlement within a zone referred to as Bendugu ("meeting place") that was under the influence of the eighteenth-century kingdom of Segou. In 1898, a few years after the French colonial army had arrived in town (in 1891), San became the center of a *cercle*—the basic administrative unit of the French Sudan. The town was easily accessible by land and water, and served as a weekly market center. It was a transit point between the towns of Djenne, Segou, and the "kingdom" of Kenedugu (Sikasso) to the south. Because the town had a sizable share of "foreign" (*dunan*)[2] merchant families, the population of San and the surrounding area was far from homogeneous with respect to its ethnic composition; nor was it uniform in its response to the occupational powers. The (non-Islamized) Bobo and Bamana populations south and southeast of the town "stubbornly resisted" colonial occupation in the first two decades of French presence. The few Islamized Marka, Fulbe, and Djenneké[3] families, in contrast, who lived in San and a few villages of the *cercle* behaved in ways that made them appear "loyal" to the French *mission civilisatrice*.[4] Shortly before the turn of the twentieth century Christianity, too, had made its presence felt in the area, with Catholic, and later Protestant, missionaries starting to proselytize among the Bobo populations in the southeastern, and later western, part of the *cercle*. But in San the influence of Muslim families prevailed. The multiethnic composition of the population continued in the 1920s and after the Second World War, when labor migrants from the Dogon plateau and later from the regions near Koutiala established themselves in San and its adjacent villages to benefit from the market town's thriving cash crop production (mainly cotton, peanuts, and shea butter) (Mann 2006, 27–28). Over the following decades of colonial rule, more and more people in the area converted to Islam, but their religious practice remained mostly limited to performing the obligations of worship. The marginal role in formal politics played by Muslim religious specialists was perpetuated in San in the 1940s with the onset of the struggle for independence under the aegis of the two contending parties, PSP and US-RDA. The situation did not change substantially after Mali gained independence in 1960. Nor were there any indications, until the mid-1980s, of a greater presence of Islam in the form of schools, mosques, or social institutions.

When I moved to San in 1998, Islamic moral renewal marked its presence in the form of a thriving Muslim activist infrastructure and uncountable religious programs broadcast on two local radio stations. Within days, I made the acquaintance of several Muslim women and men who, through various mobilizing and preaching activities, sought to rally fellow Muslims around the cause of Islam. By far the most visible—and audible—presence of Muslim activism in San was effected by supporters of the charismatic preacher Shaykh Sharif Haidara whose interventions, mediated by radio and audiotape, have earned him nationwide acclaim. Haidara's disciples, the Ansar Dine, were the most effective in inviting "others"—among them myself—to their learning and social activities, with the express desire to convince us to break with our earlier lives and "move closer to God" (*k'i surunya ala ma*). Within a week I was invited to attend the learning sessions of the local Ansar Dine's women's group.

Islam's palpable prominence in San's public arenas, I soon realized, was in itself a sign of the significant transformations that had taken place in the years following the introduction of multiparty democracy. Much of the social unrest and political euphoria after the 1991 fall of President Moussa Traoré had faded away. The times were over when life in town was perturbed by clashes between governmental forces and groups of students and unemployed youth, who felt they did not benefit from the restructuring of the political apparatus. Opposition parties accused the ruling party ADEMA and President Konaré of manipulating the 1997 elections. In private conversations and radio call-in programs, young men poignantly expressed their disillusion with the promises of democratization that were not borne out. Yet one could also sense how profoundly the introduction of civil liberties had benefited people by allowing a great variety of societal initiatives and private media to thrive. The pervasive presence of Muslim activism was vivid proof of these new possibilities. It was in this lively atmosphere, suffused with sumptuous signs and sounds of Muslim piety, that I started my investigation.

Especially in the first months of my research I spent much of my time with supporters of Islamic moral renewal, participating in Muslim women's learning sessions as much as in their economic and socializing activities, for instance, during religious ceremonies and social events. Another initial concern was to gain insight into the motivations and educational and family background of prominent representatives of the renewal movement, men and women. Between September 1998 and October 2000 I regularly attended two Muslim women's groups in San two to three times a week, and, starting in February 1999, I participated in three Muslim women's groups in middle- and lower-middle-class neighborhoods of Bamako, whenever I was in town. Spending extended periods of everyday life with group members and leaders with whom I was more closely acquainted gave me a sense of the complexity of Muslim women's life situations, and offered insights into the ways individual Muslim women incorporate the teachings they receive into their daily negotiations and struggles. Conversations with these women, and with their children and husbands, helped me complement the information I gathered during formal interviews with male and female leaders of the renewal movement in San and Bamako. To gain a sense of the historicity of Islamic moral reform and of Muslim practice and conceptions of religiosity in this area, I conducted research in the Malian National Archives. To understand the conditions and expectations that inform the daily lives of professing Muslims, men and women, I conducted more than sixty semi-structured interviews in Bamanakan and French with men, adult women, and adolescents whose socioeconomic origins can be roughly located in the urban middle and lower-middle classes. My long-standing relationship with some of these people was reflected in, among other things, my receiving a local name, Nanaje. In addition to my audio and video recordings of Muslim women's Arabic teaching and of discussion sessions, I consulted extensively the various materials written in Bamanakan, Arabic, or French (such as religious pamphlets, instruction manuals, and Arabic literacy manuals). I transcribed numerous audio- and video-recorded religious broadcasts (such as sermons, religious ceremonies, and gatherings) with language assistants and discussed them with Muslim women and leading protagonists of the movement.

Similar to my experiences during earlier research in Mali, I found that being a woman researcher was an advantage in most situations. Gender segregation is not well developed in most regions of Mali, with women moving freely in the market and other public places, but it is generally more difficult for male researchers to access domains of female sociality and everyday life. Some male protagonists of Islamic moral renewal were reticent at first to enter into discussions or even to socialize with me, but, over time, many of them took a keen interest in my research and provided great help and generous support. Having conducted most of my previous research in rural areas of the Southwest (around Kita) and near Nara, a town close to the Mauritanian border, doing research on Islamic renewal in an urban environment posed unknown challenges. I insisted on living with host families, who, while considering themselves observant Muslims, were neither affiliated with nor supportive of the Islamic renewal movement. My housing situation created dilemmas for me vis-à-vis both my hosts and the Muslim women and men with whom I spent major chunks of daily life. My hosts found it difficult to understand why I would "hang out with these Muslim women" whose "conservative" attitude and dress style they derided and respected at the same time. The latter, on the other hand, felt that my staying with people not supportive of Islamic moral renewal rendered questionable my professed "interest in Islam." I remained convinced that my housing choices helped me straddle the requirements of emphatic research and disengaged analytical scrutiny; yet over the years I felt increasingly torn by my interlocutors' deep bewilderment, especially as it became evident to my Muslim women friends that their hopes to convert me to Islam would not materialize. My interlocutors' conflicting expectations became evident in daily snapshots and minute details. Until my last visit in San (April–June 2006), my apparel remained a source of incomprehension on both sides of the fence. The mothers in my host family in San, who had become close confidantes over the years and who could be described as "fashion-conscious," and several friends who worked for the two local radio stations continued to shake their heads in disbelief at my regular visits to two Muslim women neighborhood groups and at my gradual change in dress style. Over time I went from dressing European-style to wearing locally adapted robes to donning dresses that entirely covered my arms and legs as was expected in the Muslim circles in which I spent most of my time. Members of the Muslim women's associations, on the other hand, until my last visit, remained disappointed about my reticence to cover my hair and neck with a scarf outside the Muslim women's social events. They felt that although I regularly participated in their learning and prayer sessions, I lacked the proper Muslim ethical responsibility as long as I refused to comply with certain sartorial norms. I never managed to reconcile these conflicting expectations and to move with ease between these two different moral universes; my attempts to respond to and soften the bewilderment of my social entourage resulted in bizarre, sometimes comical, situations. I can only hope that, beyond these unresolved instances of miscomprehension between me and some of my closest confidantes in San, my book does justice to the complexity of their personal motivations and concerns, and to their responses to the dilemmas that shape their daily life-worlds. To maintain the privacy of the women, teachers, and women's groups whose gatherings I attended and with whom I established confidential relationships, I have changed their names and occupational identities, as well as the names of the neighborhoods where their groups are located.

Map of Mali and surrounding countries. *Courtesy of author.*

ACKNOWLEDGMENTS

Many people have contributed, directly or indirectly, to this book's development. It could not have been written without the input, patience, support, and humor of many people I worked with in San, Segou, and Bamako, and with whom I often established long-lasting ties of trust and friendship. Foremost, I thank the members of the Muslim women's groups and their leaders who, over all the years of our acquaintance and conversations, generously shared their views and concerns with me, taking me to their social events and patiently answering most of my questions. Key male leaders of the movement similarly showed an amazing willingness to discuss their critical views on society and politics. Employees from the national broadcast station ORTM, especially the members of the Bureau des Ulemas, as well as the directors and radio speakers of various local radio stations in San, Segou, and Bamako helped me immensely to orient myself in the complicated field of Muslim debate. Mory Soumano's unfailing logistical support and substantive intellectual input, and his insightful analyses into the micropolitics of Malian family life, proved crucial in understanding important aspects of the economic, social, and political setting within which Muslims' efforts to renew society and self need to be understood.

I also incurred an enormous debt of gratitude while working on various incarnations of this book during my nomadic years spanned between the two sides of the Atlantic. Foremost, I thank Harold Scheffler of Yale University and Jan Simpson for their long-standing friendship, intellectual input, and encouragement since my graduate years at Yale; Ute Luig of Free University of Berlin for contributing to the making of this manuscript, through the breadth of her theoretical and ethnographic expertise, and by offering me unwavering support during the sometimes stormy days at the Free University; and Jean and John Comaroff of the University of Chicago for their impressive intellectual inspiration and unfailing institutional support. Birgit Meyer's scholarship and intellectual generosity have been an endless source of inspiration. Next I express my gratitude to Annelies Moors for inviting me to spend seven months at the International Institute for the Study of Islam in the Modern World in Leiden; and to the Society for the Humanities at Cornell University for awarding me a one-year fellowship that allowed me to work full-time on the monograph. I particularly thank my former colleagues at Indiana University for a stimulating and collegial working environment that enabled me to complete the manuscript. Special thanks go to Maria Grosz-Ngaté, Nancy Levene, and Katie Lofton for their logistical and moral support.

Earlier versions of some of the chapters were presented at various conferences, workshops, and seminars at Leiden University, the University of Amsterdam, Free University and Humboldt University in Berlin, Dartmouth College, Cornell University, the University of Chicago, Columbia University, Indiana University, the University of Hannover, and the University of Frankfurt. I acknowledge the tremendous intellectual input of all the colleagues who on these occasions offered me critical feedback and helpful suggestions. For intellectual and moral support, I thank the many colleagues and friends whom I cajoled into reading different versions of the manuscript. Barry Hall provided swift and efficient copyediting work in times of emergency. At Indiana University Press, Dee Mortensen shepherded the book manuscript through the publication process with excellent advice and gentle efficiency, and Rita Bernhard did a first-rate copyediting job.

Passages of chapters 3, 5, and 6 originated in the articles "Drama, Desire, and Debate: Mass-Mediated Subjectivities in Urban Mali," *Visual Anthropology* 20 (1): 19–39; "Competing Sartorial Assertions of Femininity and Muslim Identity in Mali," *Fashion Theory* 11, nos. 2–3 (2007): 253–280; and "Promises of (Im)mediate Salvation: Islam, Broadcast Media, and the Remaking of Religious Experience in Mali," *American Ethnologist* 33, no. 2 (2006): 210–229.

I am grateful to my extended family, especially my sister Dr. Katharina Erling, for their practical support. Finally, and especially, I express my deep gratitude to Ulrich Thon for his enormous emotional, intellectual, and logistical support during the final phase of writing, and for often sacrificing his own interests so that I could complete this book.

I dedicate this book to my mother, Dr. Gesina Schulz, and to my late father, Dr. Arnold Schulz, with gratitude for everything they have given me; and to my daughter Dussuba Johanna who, with her thoughtfulness, vivacity, and wit, embodies what I enjoyed most about the women and men I worked and lived with in Mali.

MUSLIMS AND NEW MEDIA IN WEST AFRICA

Overture

Publicizing Morality: Islam's Female Face

In March 1999 I was granted an interview with the chairwoman (*présidente*) of the National Union of Muslim Women of Mali (Union Nationale des Femmes Musulmanes du Mali [UNAFEM]). The friend who introduced me, herself a member of the association's steering committee, explained that I had come to inquire after the "role played by Muslim women in exhorting Malians to return to proper Muslim practice." The *présidente,* a sixty-five-year-old woman who commands respect, listened to my friend with a serious air. She then stood up, walked over to a bookshelf, took out two videocassettes, and said, somewhat sharply,

> Here is a recording of the first conference organized by our association. Watch these cassettes and you will find everything there is to be understood about us. In it, we Muslim women tell the public about the important role of women in society's return to Islam. Everything about us, why we decided to don the veil and what our goals are, is explained in it, in detail. We made this recording with the goal of broadcasting it on national television, on the occasion of the next holy month, to explain to everyone in Mali, believers and those who are not, what our, the women's role is in this society, in reminding them of the need to return to the values of Islam.

It was not the curt nature of the *présidente*'s response nor its implicit expression of skepticism about my intentions that rendered this statement so significant. After all, throughout my research on Islamic moral renewal in urban Mali, I had become acquainted with such initial reservations. This reluctance was particularly marked among women who participated in the movement and who, at the initial stage of our acquaintance, saw in me the Western woman from whose "libertinism" they distanced themselves and against whom they defined a woman's proper place in the family. But no one before had so succinctly established a link between moral reform as personal endeavor and its significance to the wider Malian public. Also significant about the *présidente*'s explanation was that she described women's individual "reorientation" toward "the teachings of Islam" as a decision of "taking the veil." Her portrayal of Muslim women's objectives made "veiling" a potent symbol of individual religious "conviction" and of a broader move toward moral reform.

In San, which, as noted in the prologue, is a vibrant market town of about twenty-five thousand located between the rivers Niger and Bani in southwestern Mali, and in San's surrounding areas, the majority of the population converted to Islam under colonial rule. Starting in the 1940s, more and more people gradually adopted Muslim religious practice, clothing styles, and other habits of regulating social and cultural life.[1] In sharp contrast to these historical forms of Islamic presence stands what an astute observer of Malian politics called "Islam's new public face,"[2] that is, the palpable public presence of an infrastructure and iconography of Islamic renewal in contemporary Mali. Wherever one goes in San and Bamako today, one is confronted with an unprecedented public visibility of Islam that manifests itself in a multitude of symbols of Islamic piety, in numerous mosques and school buildings, and in oversized billboards declaring the presence of numerous Islamic welfare organizations. In its present appearances, Islamic renewal emerged in the 1980s under the influence of aid money from the Arabic-speaking world, particularly Saudi Arabia (Triaud 1988a; Brenner 1993b, 1993c).[3] It gained new momentum after the overthrow of President Moussa Traoré in 1991. With the introduction of multiparty democracy and the adoption of a new constitution granting civil liberties, various actors and interest groups have moved to the forefront of political life, along with the proliferation of decentralized media products and institutions, such as private press publications, local radio stations, and video and audio tapes. Among them are various Muslim actors and activists who publicly articulate their desire to reform public order in accordance with God's will.

Particularly remarkable about the Islamic renewal (Arabic, *tajdid*) movement, which distinguishes it from its historical predecessors, is its conspicuously female "face." More and more women in town organize themselves in "Muslim women's groups" (singular, *silame musow ton*) to learn to "read and write [Arabic]" and the correct performance of a Muslim's ritual duties, and to work together on curing society of its social and moral ills.[4] Since 1996 most Muslim women's groups have joined the national umbrella organization, the UNAFEM, the female branch of the national Muslim association AMUPI.[5] Members of the women's groups refer to themselves simply as "Muslim women" (Bamana, *silame musow*[6]), and thereby set themselves apart from "other women" (*muso tow*), whose lack of dedication to the cause of Islam is reflected, among other things, in the refusal to "don the veil" (*ka musòrò ta*).[7] The leaders of the Muslim women groups endorse male activists' call for a return to the original teachings of Islam during funerals and other events, and in sermons broadcast on local radio stations and audio tapes. Like the *présidente* of the UNAFEM, they assert that women are a pillar of the Islamic reform movement and, seemingly paradoxically, publicly express their conviction that the proper place of women is first and foremost in the family. This claim reflects a specific ethical sensibility which stresses the significance of religion to public life, and thereby challenges conventional understandings of the categories "public" and "private."

Of Pathways and Mediation

What is it about Islamic renewal that makes it appeal to diverse segments of the urban population? Why are so many women attracted by the call for a proper, Islamic way of life? The remark by the UNAFEM chairwoman hints at a primary response to these questions. Key in her account is the notion of a "pathway to God" (*alasira*), a term that synonymously refers to religion.[8] What inspires her and her fellow Muslim women's support of Islamic renewal is the desire to "move closer to God" (*k'i magre ala la*) and to overcome a sense of moral disorientation and alienation. The metaphor *alasira* indicates that these women conceive of their moralizing endeavor as a path (*sira*) that involves movement at once physical and ethical. What these women share is, first and foremost, the objective to achieve a "greater closeness to God" and to experience His presence in their daily lives; second, they jointly embark on the path to attain this goal, namely, through an unconditional "submission" (the literal meaning of Islam) to His will. The notion of "pathway" evokes yet other associations. Most notably it echoes conventional understandings of religious practice in this area of West Africa, understandings that are inflected by the Islamic mystical traditions (*tasawwuf*) and their dominant organizational form, the Sufi order or "path" (Arabic, *tariqa*). In these traditions, the notion of "path" refers to a specific set of spiritual and meditative exercises through which the spiritual leader (*shaykh*) of a Sufi order and his disciples seek to experience God's presence in the world. Beyond this most immediate resonance with long-standing religious conventions, "pathway" captures the multiplicity of ways that may allow a believer to achieve communion with God and to experience His presence as immanent. These "paths" are open to aberrance and failure. A believer cannot anticipate what she will see on her way and what challenges she will need to overcome. Only the goal, reaching closeness to God, is certain, as well as the confidence that other Muslim women engage in a similar search.

This book is about the various "pathways" chosen by supporters of Islamic moral renewal in urban Mali, among them numerous women from the middle and lower-middle classes, to establish greater closeness to God. It is also about the changes in the political, social, and economic environment over the last decades that make these different pathways, and the very idea of searching for closeness to God, appear as a desirable option. The pathways that supporters of Islamic renewal adopt do not center on a fixed set of spiritual exercises, as in the case of initiates of a Sufi order. Nor do they refer to a shared, uncontested, and consistent set of rules about how to lead a life as a proper Muslim. The pathways may involve discrepant and dissonant uses of objects, materials, and other means conducive to the experience of God's presence, such as a recitation of the Qur'an or, as in the aforementioned encounter with the UNAFEM chairwoman, a media product. Still, common to all these "pathways to God" chosen by participants in the renewal movement is that they foster a special bond between individual believers and God, by offering multifarious conduits to experience His presence in daily life. In this sense, all the pathways on which Muslim women and men embark ultimately involve a process of mediation.

Why should "mediation" be an adequate term to grasp the complexities of the "pathways to God" promoted by supporters of Islamic renewal? Broadly speaking, nothing works without mediation. Social life itself is deeply grounded in processes—and practices—of mediation.[9] Mediation processes are often (inter)personal and subjective. Conceived in a narrower sense, mediation denotes a movement or passage of an entity or datum from one location to another. Here its resonance with the notion of "pathway," so central to Muslim religiosity in Mali, is evident. After all, the traditional devotional exercises of Sufi Islam and the various "paths" chosen by supporters of Islamic renewal all center on a spiritual passage—that is, their spiritual itinerary is oriented toward an experience of God's immanent presence. Mediation also refers to acts of "bringing together" discrepant tendencies and interests, with the purpose of rendering them congruent, communicable, and mutually intelligible. A medium, put in the service of mediation processes, works to render an experience, a vision, or another form of sensuous perception immediate. In this respect, the modus operandi of a mass medium does not differ from any other mediation technique. If we follow this perspective, we can discern yet another striking congruence between "mediation" and the "pathway" envisioned by Malian supporters of Islamic renewal. If integrated into religious practice, a medium—and any act of mediation—serves to render experiences of the Divine palpable, and communicable. In fact, religion itself is predicated on processes of mediation (van der Veer 1995; de Vries 2002; Stolow 2005). The direction, passage, and outcome of these acts of communicating with the Divine are unpredictable. Media and mediation constitute "inherently unstable and ambiguous conditions of possibility for religious signifying practices" (Stolow 2005, 125). Herein, then, lies another resonance with the notion, formulated by many Muslim activists in Mali, that a true believer should concentrate his or her efforts on seeking to establish communion with God, however unpredictable the outcome may be.

The term "mediation" highlights the multiplicity of means through which believers may experience God's presence. It also points to the indeterminate and partly unexpected outcomes of these various acts of spiritual communication and connectivity. For all these reasons, "mediation" offers a suitable framework to understand the many promises the "pathway" narrative holds for supporters of Islamic renewal in Mali. To illustrate this point, let us take a closer look at the activities through which Muslim activists in Mali seek to achieve "closeness to God."

Understanding Muslim Women's Moralizing Endeavor

A guiding concern of Muslim women's group meetings is to learn to "read and write," as well as the correct performance of a Muslim's ritual duties. Their emphasis on the importance of Arabic literacy and ritual knowledge echoes the significance that earlier generations of Muslim reformists have attributed to religious education. Already in the 1940s reform-minded Muslim activists identified education as a key site for the making of proper believers. They created new opportunities for formerly marginalized groups, especially youth and women, to acquire literacy in Arabic and to learn the proper performance of Muslim ritual obligations.

That Muslim women engage in learning activities is thus not a new phenomenon. Still, until about thirty years ago, religious instruction remained largely the prerogative of women from privileged families of religious specialists or merchants. Most of these elite women found time for religious study once they had reached menopause. Novel about the current learning circles of Muslim women is that most participants are younger (married) women and come from the urban lower and middle classes.[10] Muslim women's learning groups thus reflect on a widening access to religious knowledge that started in the 1940s, under the influence of Muslim modernist trends in Egypt and Saudi Arabia (Kaba 1974; Brenner 2001). Muslim women's strong investment in religious education, and their reliance on various media technologies during their learning activities, illustrate the many parallels to processes found in other areas of the Muslim world. Here, too, broader access to educational facilities, combined with the adoption of various mass media, contributes to an unsettling of conventional religious authority and to a rejuvenation of Muslim reformist concerns. Another characteristic feature of these wider developments is that the "symbolic language of Islam" (Eickelman 1992) manifests itself in feminized forms.[11]

That the forms and objectives of Islamic renewal among Malian Muslims echo many of these broader, trans-regional trends is widely acknowledged by Malian observers, many of whom consider themselves observant Muslims. They look with suspicion at the public interventions of Muslim activists and their claim to promote the original and true teachings of Islam, and maintain that membership in a Muslim women's group is motivated by support in a financially precarious situation. Others, many of them secularist-minded intellectuals, fear that Muslim women's neighborhood associations serve "radical Muslims" to mobilize gullible voters to their challenge to Mali's secular constitution. To them, women's associational life is proof of the invigoration of Islamic "funda-mentalist" tendencies made possible by money from Saudi Arabia. Prominent among these critics are elite women who gained access to leading governmental positions under the presidencies of Alpha Konaré and his successor Amadou Toumani Touré, elected in June 2002. They dismiss the "patriarchal bent" of Muslim women's interventions as a backlash against recent, hard-won victories in gender equality.

All these critics are bewildered at Muslim women's support of conservative gender ideology and are incapable of explaining it. Their bewilderment echoes that of scholars who, puzzled by women who assume leading positions in "patri-archal" religious movements, ultimately cannot account for their participation in these movements other than as an indication of their role as "pawns" in the hands of male leaders (e.g., Marty and Appleby 1993a, 1993b; Hodgkin 1998, 210–212). In these accounts, there is a slippage between different levels of analy-sis, such as objectives and social forms of Muslim activism, and a tendency to conflate the intentions of religious leaders with women's individual motivations to join the movement. Moreover, these critics cannot adequately explain why Muslim women should choose knowledge acquisition as a principal conduit to the moral renewal of society and self.

Exploring the moralizing endeavor of Muslim women as a "path" they walk in order to experience God's presence in their daily lives is a powerful way to shed light onto the social and moral investments of Muslim women. Seen from this perspective, the significance that Muslim women in urban Mali assign to their joint learning practices can be understood, first, as local refractions of dynam-ics that animate current trends toward religious renewal in Muslim Africa and throughout the Muslim world; and, second, as an expression of a personal search for ethical self-improvement that, in itself, reflects on changing understandings of individual religiosity and responsibility (see Mahmood 2005). This book departs from views of women's mobilization around the cause of Islam as an indication of a fundamentalist backlash against modernity. It shows that Muslim women's organizational and learning activities are more adequately understood as one among several conduits through which these women seek to reorder personal and collective life in accordance with Islamic principles.

Zoning in on Muslim women's pathways to God grants us several insights. First, it gives us a more nuanced sense of the new momentum that "Islam," as a blueprint for social and moral order, has lately gained in Mali, by allowing us to scrutinize how the strategies and aspirations of different categories of activists interrelate with the life situations and motivations of individual members of the movement, and how this feeds into discrepant agendas within the Islamic renewal movement (see Brink and Mencher 1997, and Ask and Tjomsland 1998).[12] Here attention is warranted to possibly class-specific tendencies in women's "Islamic militancy."[13] But analysis will not be limited to this perspective, nor to one that highlights connections between Muslim women's ethical quest and their dilemmas emerging from economic liberalization. Second, conceiving of Muslim women's engagements as a search that privileges their relationship to God over their relationship to fellow human beings allows us to navigate the dangers of portraying female Muslim activists either as lacking a "liberal," progressive agenda or of characterizing their activism as a sign of women's "empowerment" or resistance agency. Religious activism may "empower" women to speak up in public, but this does not necessarily imply that their interventions have liberating effects in the sense envisaged in Western liberal political theory. Muslim women's social and public interventions may challenge the normative grounds not only of secular nation-state politics but also of Western feminist theory (Mahmood 2005, chap. 1). At the same time it is evident that Muslim women themselves explicitly associate their moralizing endeavor with notions of personal enlightenment and societal progress.

Focusing on Muslim women's desire to commune with God directs us away from the constraining or liberating effects of the Islamic movement, and toward the ostensibly self-improving—and in this sense progressive—implications Muslim women associate with personal and societal reform. The remark by the UNAFEM chairwoman highlighted her view of education as a principal means of self-advancement. Education enables a woman to build her own opinion and defend her views of a proper, Islamic way of life before a broader public, so as to "invite" other Muslims to join her moral endeavor. This felt obligation to extend one's moral calling to other Muslims reflects on the key significance these women attribute to pious self-cultivation in the ordering of collective life.

Redefining the Personal and/as the Political

How does the pathway to God chosen by female supporters of Islamic renewal differ from conventional understandings of religiosity? And how should we analyze the ethical sensibilities that inform this particular itinerary of moral reform? Some novel features of Muslim women's activism are evident, such as a marked stress on individual responsibility and the mass basis of expressions of female religiosity. Yet because of significant lacunae in the scholarship, both historical and ethnographic, on Muslim religious practice in the area, it is difficult to identify historical continuities in women's religious praxis. The existing literature on changing Muslim religiosity in Mali since the 1940s focuses on men.[14] Several studies on other areas of Muslim West Africa document women in religious leadership positions, but they tend to offer little information about religious practices of "ordinary" women.[15]

By exploring the "pathways" and attendant ethical concerns that guide the actions of supporters of Islamic renewal in Mali, this book attests to the diversity of religious practices in which ordinary believers, men and women, engage. With its focus on one particular group of Muslim women who play a leading role in Muslim activism in Mali, the book grants insight into how these women's activities reflect on recent changes in understandings of religiosity, individual responsibility, and the relevance of faith to everyday life. Female religious praxis, in Mali and elsewhere in Muslim West Africa, is the product of long-standing, transnational intellectual influences and their intertwining with local traditions of Islam.[16] The ethical concerns articulated by Muslim women in Mali place them in a broader field of competing Muslim viewpoints; they occupy an indeterminate space between Sufi-affiliated practices, authorities, and interpretations on the one side and, on the other, Muslims whose reformism borrows from trends in contemporary Egypt and other Arabic-speaking areas (Brenner 1993c).

An important lesson I took away from my initial encounter with the *présidente* of the UNAFEM was that female participants in the Islamic renewal movement consider the public practice of piety an important element of their pathway to God. Mariamu, the leader of a Muslim women's association to whom I was introduced in March 1998, clarified this view. With dignified restraint and pride, she promised to "help me with my interest in the teachings of Islam." She promptly added that being interested in the path of Islam was an either-or decision.

> Once you embark on the path to God, there is no middle
> ground, no halfway, no lukewarm adoption of Islam. Take

me, for example. Two years ago I decided to follow God's calling and to veil. This has completely transformed my life. Now, I do not present myself to anyone without attaching a headscarf, except for my husband.

Mariamu describes her "taking the veil" as an outward sign of her decision to embark on a path that would let her live in accordance with God-ordained principles. By singling out this particular act, Mariamu signals—to me as much as to the outside world—that her reorientation toward Islam is intricately related to her intention to render her conviction public.

The remarks by Mariamu and by the UNAFEM chairwoman illustrate a key argument of this book. The exploration of the ethical engagements of supporters of Islamic renewal requires us not only to focus on their personal quest for piety but also to examine how this quest is inspired by, and intersects with, a broader concern with moral degeneration, a concern whose pervasiveness in Malian society echoes a worldwide Islamic revival. Rather than examining female Muslim activism in terms of either an individual cultivation of the pious self (Mahmood 2005) or of religious/cultural identity politics (e.g. Moghadam 1994; Göle 1996; Hale 1997), this book stresses that the first analytical perspective makes no sense without the second. We can grasp the present appeal of Islamic piety only when we consider the broader transformations in the political, economic, and social environment, such as, in Mali, the new conditions for public self-expression since 1991, shifts in gender relations, and the permeation of everyday life by mass-mediated experience.

Mariamu's and the UNAFEM chairwoman's highlighting of "veiling" illustrates the need for such a combined analytical perspective on Muslim women's religiosity. In the scholarly (and popular) literature on women in Muslim societies, "the veil" has become synonymous with the invigorated force of Islam in a modern world.[17] To some, "the veil" symbolizes women's dedication to their role as mothers and wives, and indicates Islam's capacity to resist the morally corrupting influences of the West (Marshall 1984; see Stowasser 1994, 9–11). To others, women's veiling is the ultimate sign of Islam's oppression of women (see Watson 1994) and the dangerous, reactionary turn political Islam has taken in the Middle East, Africa, Western Europe, and North America (see Abu-Lughod 2002). A third body of literature, wary of the association of "veiling" with "women's subjugation," advances more benevolent interpretations of the liberating effects of "the veil" in allowing women to move freely in public arenas and pursue professional careers (e.g., MacLeod 1991; Mirza 2002).[18] These studies posit a link between dress practices and women's rights and status in society.[19] Much of the discussion implies that veiling refers to a uniform mode of dressing—without accounting for the regional and historical variety of dress modes that are labeled "veiling" and of the diverging significance that these dress modes bear, not only across countries and cultures but also within the same society.[20] Similarly problematic is the focus on veiling per se, and the assumption that women's religious practices or social positions can be ascertained by analyzing their dress (see Lindisfarne-Tapper and Ingham 1997, 11–12).

Yet even if scholarly preoccupation with veiling is problematical, my initial exchanges with the UNAFEM chairwoman and Mariamu forcefully demonstrate that it is impossible to deny the significance of this dress practice. Both women emphasized that they consider "donning the veil" an important element in their public practice of piety. Mariamu explained that her turn to Islam is intricately tied to her intention to render her conviction public. She does not separate the veil's significance in enabling a pious disposition from its expressive role in articulating her decision to her social entourage. Mariamu's choice of veiling as an act of public declaration is significant because this practice has spread among Mali's urban population only recently. Until the 1980s, wearing this kind of scarf (in addition to the turban, the conventional headgear of a married woman) was a marker of age, status, and, occasionally, of regional and ethnic origin.[21]

We need to take seriously Muslim women's concern with "modest dress." Rather than reducing veiling to an issue of identity politics, I consider its self-improving and symbolic role against the backdrop of transnational intellectual influences and consumer styles that draw on a long history of interactive constructions of veiling at the interface of "Western" and "Muslim" discursive fields (see Ahmed 1992; Chatty 1997; Schulz 2007a). Muslim women's decisions to "dress modestly," as well as other women's reactions to it, offer a window on people's conflicting notions of morality and on the particular ways in which such a morality may be sustained. The very act of referring to their apparel as "donning the veil" helps Muslim women to assert their place in a discursive field, in which transnational intellectual and stylistic trends intersect with competing local perceptions of Muslim propriety. This book follows Muslim women's view of "veiling" and of the self-enhancing and expressive functions this practice performs. By taking seriously their insistence on the personal and collective meanings of "modest dress," the book traces Muslim women's definition of the personal *as* political—and the revision of the relationship between the private and the public that this view implies.

Islam's Public Face

Islamic moral renewal in urban Mali is no isolated phenomenon in Africa; nor does it differ substantially from developments in the Middle East. In its transnational orientation, it connects Sub-Saharan Africa to Arabic-speaking areas of the Muslim world and thereby perpetuates centuries-old, transcontinental networks of intellectual inspiration and reform. Religiously inspired movements, such as the one captivating the minds and hearts of supporters of Islamic renewal in Mali, capitalize on the niches left by the postcolonial state's failure to secure basic services and moral orientation (see, e.g., Marshall-Fratani 1998; Dasgupta 2001). Their immense success points to the reconfiguration of relations between the state, society, and economics, and thus to the remaking of key parameters of state sovereignty (e.g., Sassen 1996; Scott 1997; Randeria 2007). In urban Mali, as elsewhere in Africa, these reconfigurations have been reinforced by political and economic liberalization.

Indicative of the shifting Malian political landscape over the past decades is the push of diverse Muslim actors into Mali's public arenas. Most of these Muslims belong to a category of actors whose authoritative claims are based on broadened access to religious learning and on new forms of sociopolitical engagement. Those activists who, since 1991, have fought for the introduction of religious parties are numerically and politically weak in Mali; yet they are decried by party and state officials as a "fundamentalist" threat. The fear these Muslims inspire reveals state officials' awareness that politico-administrative reform, since 1991, contributes to the political system's loss of credibility. As broad segments of the population deplore multiparty democracy as a weakening of central state power (Schulz 2001a, chap. 3), the government is unable to mount a convincing vision of the common good to inspire political order and collective identification. Muslims who call for a remaking of social life in accordance with Islamic norms threaten their secularist counterparts by framing their claims in the rhetoric of democratic participation and as a moralizing critique of society and politics that is intelligible to broad segments of the population.

Their highlighting of moral concerns could be taken as evidence of a historical shift from a "fundamentalist," political Islam of the mid-twentieth century to contemporary "neo-fundamentalist" movements (see Esposito 1994 [1984]; Roy 1994; but see also Göle 2002). But if we step back from a perspective that frames the issue principally as a religious challenge to secular politics,[22] we can see that the moralizing appeal of Muslim activists in Mali reflects a more substantial shift, namely, a shift in the political ends to which notions of a shared morality or culture are employed in contemporary politics. Along with the weakening significance of the nation-state as a reference point for constructions of community and belonging, there has been an upsurge of articulations of local particularity and partisan interests that are couched in ethnic/cultural or religious terms.[23] In Mali the turn toward "religion" or "culture" as the basis for one's claims to representation coincides with economic and political liberalization since the mid-1980s. Exploring the institutional, social, and symbolic architecture of the pathways chosen by supporters of Islamic renewal in Mali allows us, first, to understand the effects that neoliberal policy has generated in this national context (see Comaroff and Comaroff 1999; Ferguson 2006);[24] second, it allows us to appreciate how the pathways of Muslim activists, and the social, moral, and political investments that guide them, differ from Islamic revivalist movements elsewhere.[25]

How religion intervenes in public controversy, and the political and social dynamics it generates, needs to be examined, not presumed. Authors working on contemporary Muslim movements sometimes view them as indications of an emerging "Islamic counterpublic" that is conceived of as a site for oppositional politics (see Sreberny-Mohammadi and Mohammadi 1994), as a "conceptual space" (see Hirschkind 2001a, 2006), or as a distinct site of Muslim discourse.[26] This perspective is vital for an understanding of Muslim activists' concern with questions of public order and collective interest, and yet it risks reiterating a view of Muslim activism as being outside, and a challenge to, the sphere of secular politics. But as my first encounter with the UNAFEM *présidente* illustrated, the efforts of protagonists of Islamic renewal in Mali are geared toward *interacting with* state officials, politicians, and other political opponents in a shared domain of public intervention and representation.

As long as we refrain from conceiving the public as an "Islamic" one—or simply as a *site* of discourse—it is a powerful means of illuminating the social dynamics and appeal of "Islam" in Mali, and the structural transformations in the nexus between state and society that unleashed these dynamics.[27] "Public" refers to a sphere of discursive exchange whose features are to be understood by reference to modern state institutions and the capitalist economy, and thus render it distinct from various kinds of "audience."[28] But "public" also implies an imaginary body of people who, in their capacity as readers, listeners, and speakers, serve as recipients, participants, and makers and bearers of public opinion. As such, the public constitutes a "horizon for the organization of social experience" (Negt and Kluge 1993). Characteristic of the public is a particular quality of discourse that distinguishes it from discourse effected in more intimate settings. Lastly, the public is predicated on "publicity," that is, a quality of symbolic forms that results from and indicates their broader circulation.[29]

The notion of "public" is a useful tool for the analysis of Islam's new appeal in Mali because it allows us to combine an exploration of societal and institutional structures with an actor-oriented account of subjective experiences, motivations, and practice. "Public" centers attention on the historical transformation of state-society relations rather than reifying a state–civil society divide (see Lemarchand 1992). It compels us to interpret the new social and political relevance of Islam as an outcome of recent institutional transformations, while simultaneously drawing attention to the complex, colonial and postcolonial, legacy of contemporary social dynamics. "Public" is thus a good entry point to analyze different dimensions of Islam's new prominence in Mali, and to avoid interpreting Islamic renewal simply as a religious fundamentalist challenge to secular politics.

The Moral Negotiation of Gender Relations in Times of Economic Hardship

In the middle- and lower-middle-class neighborhoods of San and Bamako, signs and sounds of an invigorated Muslim piety are omnipresent. One way to understand the immense appeal of Islam is to view it as a blueprint for personal ethics, and as a moral idiom through which people assess and redress relations between the genders and generations in a situation of radical social and economic change. Amid two decades of economic decline, Malians, like most citizens of other African countries, face a situation in which the norms and obligations of patriarchal authority and control are losing their grip and validity. Current challenges to conventional forms and norms of social organization were initiated by migration and urbanization processes dating back to the colonial period, and accelerated in the late 1960s and 1970s. Economic liberalization, initiated in Mali since the mid-1980s, exacerbated these social transformations in rural and urban areas, partly by fueling fierce competition over the state's ever-shrinking resources. The dismantling of the few remaining areas of a social and educational infrastructure in the late 1980s fed into the alteration of intra-familial structures of labor control, responsibility, and decision making. Recent measures of market liberalization intensified this development rather than stopping it.[30]

Islam's new visibility in Malian social and political life, seen in the mushrooming infrastructure of Islamic welfare organizations financed by sponsors from the Arabic-speaking world, concurred with the breakdown of state-supported domains of social infrastructure since the mid-1980s. Still, and *pace* the explanations of secular-minded critics of Islamic moral renewal in Mali, Islam's appeal cannot be fully explained by "Arab money." External funding funneled into domains abandoned by the state may account for the thriving Muslim networks. But it does not explain why a particular, markedly conservative reading of "Islamic" gender roles becomes attractive to a growing number of women and men. To understand the moral magnetism of Islam, we need to relate the gender ideology proposed by Muslim leaders to broader debates about social and moral disintegration. These debates reflect on transformations in the political and moral economy of family life under the shadow of macro-societal economic changes. By relating the attractiveness of Islamic renewal to these structural transformations, this ethnography of Islamic revivalism contributes to new scholarship on the social and moral repercussions of economic liberalization in Sub-Saharan Africa (see, e.g., Campbell and Loxley 1989; Jacquemot and Assidon 1988).

Although it is difficult to generalize about the effects of the Structural Adjustment Programs on intra-household dynamics, the measures undertaken clearly alter existing divisions of responsibility and decision-making powers between husband and wife, and between the generations.[31] How do these changes in the responsibilities within urban households interlock with a reassessment of gender norms (e.g., Hodgson and McCurdy 2001; Hansen and Vaa 2004)? To respond to this question, it is important to move beyond a narrow focus on household economies and pay attention to the intertwining of political and moral economies. We need to situate an exploration of women's scope for maneuver in the context of broader changes in intra-familial control and decision making (see Ong 1987; Wolf 1992; Lamphere et al. 1993; Cairoli 1998). But as long as we focus on women, rather than on gender *relations*, it remains unclear how men and women negotiate their relationship by espousing and reworking stereotypical views of femininity and masculinity, and how they draw on a moralizing idiom to bargain their relations and responsibilities. A key concern of this book, therefore, is to analyze men's and women's moral negotiation of their relationships, and to relate these dynamics to the motivations underlying Islamic revivalism.[32] Thus an exclusive focus on women is inadequate. Consequently I pay considerable attention to how challenges to ideals of masculinity and male family authority affect women's and men's bargaining capacities in urban households.

Mass Mediation and Religious Experience

My initial encounter with the UNAFEM chairwoman pointedly drove home to me that the appeal Islam unfolds in Mali's urban arenas cannot be understood independently from the pervasive presence of media technologies and products. After all, before even speaking to me, she handed me the video recording of the first national UNAFEM conference as a first step to introduce me to key objectives and forms of Islamic renewal. The video recording served as a token of the instrumental role she and other participants in the renewal movement attribute to media technology in making their moral call known to a nationwide public. Later that day, after returning home with the videotape in my bag, I invited my longtime friend Brehima, himself an observant Muslim who keeps a critical distance from the renewal movement, to join me in watching my precious new acquisition. For a while we followed a stream of female speakers, elegantly clad in various all-white and all-black robes and headdresses, delivering their carefully balanced reflections on women's God-ordained duties to the female-only audience. Then Brehima suddenly turned to me and said:

> See, something is changing with Islam these days. In the mosque [i.e., during Friday communal worship] and at funerals, men may still think they are in charge of speaking. But look at all these women. Twenty years ago, it would have been unthinkable to have this gathering recorded and disseminated. Nowadays, it is women who speak up on behalf of Islam; they speak up on media; they listen to religious media as part of their daily entertainment; and no one can deny the role they play in reminding us of God's eternal will.

Brehima's remark powerfully captures the multiply constitutive role of media technologies for Islamic moral renewal. The innovation, Brehima surmises, resides not only in the new possibilities for dissemination that media technologies generate, that is, in their technical capacities and functions. Mass-mediated religion is in the process of merging with popular entertainment culture. Also novel is that a great number of women assume the role of authoritative speakers, and address and invoke female audiences. Media technologies, in other words, yield transformative effects for existing forms of religious authority, community, and (gendered) subjecthood. Media technologies are essential, not ephemeral, to the reconfiguration of the "pathways to God" that have been conventionally practiced in this area of West Africa. For this reason, the adoption of new media technologies by various actors, and the diverse, partly embodied acts of signification they generate, need to be interrogated as part of the changing social and material environment within which Islamic moral renewal is situated.[33]

How are the pathways to God on which supporters of Islamic renewal embark expanded or otherwise transformed through technologies of mass mediation? How is a believer's individual search for pious self-making inflected by an increasing mediatization of everyday life? A purely instrumentalist reading of the role of media technologies in Islamic renewal in Mali, such as a focus on how leading Muslim activists "make use" of media technologies for purposes of proselytism, would be an inadequate response to these questions. It would miss the complex transfigurations of conventional forms of religious practice and experience that media technologies set into motion, as well as their sometimes unexpected consequences. An instrumentalist reading of the "effects" of media is based on a view of communication as a unilinear transmission of a message with fixed meanings from source to destination. This view concedes recipients a purely passive role in assimilating an unchanging "message" (Stolow 2005, 124). But, as Brehima's remark suggests, media technologies foster, and are entwined with, more complex social and religious transformations. Women's new roles as speakers, their efforts to circulate media products in order to make their viewpoints known to a broader public, and the new opportunities for diverse appropriation by female listeners—all these are processes that an exclusively instrumentalist reading of media's effects would dismiss as interferences and yet are constitutive of Islam's new public relevance and appeal. Asking how mass mediation technologies inflect the particular modalities by which women move into public arenas adds a perspective that is of vital importance to recent studies of female public piety in the Muslim world (e.g., Deeb 2006; de Jorio 2009; Masquelier 2009).

As noted earlier, media and mediation entail inherently unstable and ambiguous conditions for religious signifying practices, for their integration into daily efforts of cultivating a pious self, and for their articulation with wider realms of religious belonging. The social, historical, and cultural specificity of mediation processes calls into question key tenets of Western media theory, especially its universalist claims about the effects, meanings, and social sites of media practices (e.g., Ginsburg, Abu-Lughod, and Larkin 2002; Larkin 2008). In view of the uncertainties and semantic instabilities of mediation processes, we need to study the actual media practices by various groups of "recipients" in order to understand what negotiations over meaning they perform, and how their signifying practices are constitutive of all processes of communication and mediation.

Media technologies themselves transport meaning in a double sense. They mediate meaning, and the physicality of specific communication technologies facilitates a range of acts of cultural signification that exist in a mutually constitutive relationship with the social formations where they take place (Morley and Silverstone 1990; Larkin 2008, chap. 5). This book departs from essentialist views of "the audience" and "consumption" that are based on the assumption of an unchanging relationship between the significance of specific media technologies and the social formations and spaces within which they are used (e.g., Allor 1988).[34] Because media technologies unfold their relevance in particular social settings, it is necessary to explore the "specific relationships of particular audiences to particular types of media content" (Morley and Silverstone 1990, 45).

Media practices in Mali require us to break with preconceived notions of the social forms that accompany "reception" of media messages, such as the view of the individual, atomized consumer/spectator as the subject of interpretation.[35] Such subject-centered approaches to media consumption are insufficient to illuminate Malian urbanites' media engagements, as well as other settings where a socio-centric perspective is needed to make sense of people's densely intertwined media practices (Spitulnik 2002; Schulz 2007b). This also requires us to consider the social and gender-specific relations of power and inequality that structure everyday life, not just the specific setting in which media are used and consumed (e.g., Bausinger 1984). What media consumption entails, and how it articulates to broader realms of everyday (social) experience and practice, needs to be explored. As we shall see, many Malian television viewers engage certain TV serials as a powerful way to assess and rework family dynamics. Moreover, their acts of media consumption include a variety of practices that, depending on particular genres, range from active engagement to more ritualistic modes. For this reason we need to do away with an exclusive focus on media texts and the related assumption that "reading" media texts is the most important form of media engagement.

Brehima's depiction of religious media as a form of "entertainment" points to yet another dimension of the intertwining of media and religious experience that is of central relevance for this book. His remark hints at the consumer culture within which all practices of media reception and signification are embedded, a culture that is conducive to particular religious practices and understandings. Clearly the Islamic renewal movement in Mali, and the revised understandings of religious practice it promotes, cannot be considered independently from an expanding media entertainment culture. By stressing this insight, this book departs from Hirschkind's (2006) account of cassette-sermon listening by male supporters of the Islamic revival movement in Cairo, an account that otherwise shares many concerns of this book. Hirschkind compellingly argues that male participants in the revival movement in Cairo integrate their media practices into conventional understandings of how to facilitate experiences of the Divine. Devout Muslims relate their listening activities to a tradition of ethical discipline that constructs pious hearing as an element in believers' cultivation of ethical sensibility. Although Hirschkind mentions that habits of listening to sermon tapes are influenced by popular entertainment media and styles of consumption, this is not his main concern. Instead, he situates audition practices within the wider ethical project of the Islamic revival and explains their significance from within a particular Islamic discursive tradition.

This book insists on the great significance of entwining dynamics of mass mediation, commodification, and religious experience for urban Mali. It argues that extending the analytical focus to male *and* female media consumers greatly enhances our understanding of the variety of ways media interlock with religious traditions and practices within and across different Muslim social contexts (see Larkin 2008). This perspective refutes generalizing assumptions about Islam as a religion, and about the relationship between scripture, doctrine, and religious practice (see Asad 1986; Bowen 1992). Highly relevant for this perspective is the distinct institutional and discursive context of Mali which has important implications for the ways that new media technologies affect conventional religious practice and subjectivity. Whereas in Egypt discursive traditions of Islam have been entrenched in society for centuries, Islamic disciplinary traditions are only loosely engrained in the social practices of the majority of Malian Muslims. The majority of the population in southern Mali converted to Islam only over the past eighty years, and language barriers restrict mass access to the foundational texts of Islam. As will become apparent, the implications of these differences are highly significant for a comparative anthropology of Islam. In the absence of widely articulated Islamic disciplinary traditions of ethical hearing in Mali, sermon-audition practices need to be understood in terms of their interlocking with other conventions of hearing and "forceful speech." By establishing important differences between the cassette-sermon audition practices analyzed by Hirschkind and those relevant for listeners in urban Mali, this book promises new insight into variations among regional traditions of Islam, and in the different ways Islamic ethical understandings intersect with market forces.

An investigation of the subjective repercussions of the interlocking of mass mediation, religious discourse, and consumer culture requires an analytical framework that, while making room for the diverse material and social environments into which new media technologies are adopted, simultaneously points to common structural dynamics shaping these adoption processes. In an early article on the entwining of mass media and changing modes of auditory perception, Adorno (1938) offered an incisive reflection on the implications of mass-mediated cultural production for everyday experience. His perspective offers a starting point for an understanding of how a media entertainment culture inflects circulation and consumption of religious discourse. According to Adorno, in contemporary industrial societies no act of cultural production or consumption can evade the logic of capitalist market production. Similar to King Midas's golden touch, the pervasive logic of the market transforms the character of art. It affects the ways in which artworks are performed and created, the manner in which they are consumed, and the consumers' perceptive capacities.[36] By emphasizing the market logic according to which Culture is produced and consumed, Adorno avoids technologically deterministic readings of the interplay between mass mediation and experience.[37] His distinction between the objective and subjective dimensions of the culture industry, and his emphasis on the novel character of the objective structures of mediation offer a good starting place for an exploration of mass-mediated religious discourse in Mali. This book argues that similar to the historical interlocking of religion and consumer culture in Western societies (Moore 1994), processes of commodification make religious discourse more central to Malian public culture. By the same token, the book interrogates the degree of commercialization of religious objects and discursive genres in Mali and, ultimately, shows that they do not proliferate according to the same totalizing market logic outlined by Adorno. The book therefore makes a special case for understanding the intertwining of religious experience with mass-mediation processes through sustained attention to the particulars of different social and historical settings.

The Structure of the Book

The book's subtitle, *Pathways to God,* points to several angles from which to interrogate the personal and collective resonances of Islamic renewal in urban Mali, and the broader transformations that generate its conditions of possibility. The notion of "pathway" centers on the long-standing roots of the understandings of religiosity formulated by supporters of Islamic renewal in Mali. It allows us to understand their moral endeavor as being in line with traditional religious practices, and not in terms of religious fundamentalism and radical otherness. By the same token, an exploration of the "pathways" chosen by members of the Islamic renewal movement prompts us to identify how their pathways diverge from conventional Muslim religious practices and modes of authority. The image of a "path" on which believers embark also captures a foundational idea of the Malian Islamic renewal movement. It is the idea that renewal can—and should—be effected through believers' individual search or "path" toward communion with God and, hence, through their personal itinerary of pious self-cultivation. Furthermore, "pathway," when applied to mass-mediated conduits toward experiences of the Divine, brings to our attention that mass-media technologies do not introduce a radical break into Muslim religious practice but help to expand existing conventions and practices of achieving closeness to God. To conceive of mass-mediated religious practice as one among several "pathways to God" that an observant Muslim may choose highlights the role of mass-mediation processes in revising and transforming established views and practices of religiosity. Finally, I use "pathway" to refer to the recent movement of Islam to greater public prominence in Mali's urban arenas, and to the wide appeal of Muslim activists' understandings of personal and collective moral renewal, as well as to retrace the transformations in the material, political, and social environments that sustain these reformulations of Muslim religiosity. Here "pathway" not only describes a physical movement, from realms of domesticity and intimacy to domains of public debate and interaction; it also hints at more complex transformations in gender-specific realms of religious debate, practice, and authority that underlie Islam's public role and visibility.

Chapter 1 introduces the main protagonists of Islamic renewal in Mali. Here I explore the implications of what Warner (2002) has identified as the "perplexing" quality of the public, a quality that results from the tension between the public's potential to construct itself as a unitary entity by invoking "the people," on the one side, and, on the other, the particular identities that such a body of "the people" always entails. I take a 2000 controversy over the reform of family law as a way to understand the implications of the tension-ridden quality of the public for political controversy in Mali, and for the chances of Muslim activists to mount a coherent and compelling vision of an Islamic moral order. I also use the law reform debate as a window onto the divisions that structure Malian public debate and the field of Islamic moral renewal, and that reflect on the history of changing power constellations, affiliations, and confrontations among Muslims since the 1940s. I interpret the new political momentum of Islam in Mali as the paradoxical result of the interplay between transnational networks of dependence and influence, and national struggles over the economic and symbolic resources of the state that have been exacerbated under conditions of post-authoritarian rule. Although legislative reform may have been prompted by "progressive" concerns, it opens up a field for conservative forces to mobilize popular discontent by contrasting an Islamic cultural autonomy to political dependence on the West. Thus, paradoxically, the internationally sponsored support for democratic values offers a new rallying ground for conservative oppositional forces and endows them with greater moral authority.

Chapters 2 and 3 move the exploration of the wide appeal of Islamic renewal from the level of national politics to that of interpersonal relations. By examining the material, social, and symbolic practices through which men and women in town reflect on, and rework, the conditions of their livelihoods, the two chapters prepare for the subsequent analysis, presented in the second part of the book (chapters 4–7), of the institutions and conceptions of religiosity that inform the activities of female supporters of Islamic moral renewal.

Chapter 2 examines the changes in the material and social environment of urban life since the late 1980s that were conducive to Muslim activists' push into public arenas. The focus here is on changes in the moral economy of gender and intergenerational relations in middle- and lower-middle-class families in town, and, through biographical sketches of several women and men, to tease out the emotional and material dimensions of their daily struggles to make a living. Shifting financial obligations between men and women, and between generations, create conflicting, sometimes paradoxical, demands for married men and women, and thus compound other social and normative repercussions of the economic liberalization measures implemented in Mali since the mid-1980s. From these disruptions of domestic moral economies emerge particular dilemmas that provide a fertile ground for a yearning for moral, rather than structural, reform. A particular form of response to these dilemmas, articulated by Malian urbanites through their "media talk" and media engagements, is analyzed in chapter 3. Here I focus on media engagements by Malian television audiences as a way to understand how urbanites, of different ages and socioeconomic backgrounds, make sense of the changing moral economy of family life. To consider the central relevance of these media engagements not only to supporters of Islamic renewal but also to a broad variety of television consumers is a key analytical step in contextualizing the social practices and ethical endeavor of Muslim activists within the broader social reality of urban everyday life. Media engagements constitute a central field of everyday symbolic and social practice in town, and they need to be analyzed as the simultaneous consumption of different media and broadcast genres that allow for various kinds of engagement. The responses of numerous urban Malians to soap operas and *telenovelas* offer occasions to assess, but also to rework, family dynamics. By documenting the immense interpenetration of the urban lived world (*Lebenswelt*) and of mass-mediated experience, the chapter serves as a preamble to my subsequent argument (in chapters 6 and 7) that the religious "pathways" chosen by many supporters of Islamic renewal are intricately related to mass-mediated forms of religious experience, practice, and authority.

Chapter 4 brings the analytical focus back to those Muslims in urban Mali who consider themselves supporters of Islamic moral renewal. It illustrates the particular forms of social organization on which Muslim women rely, both to pursue their individual search for pious self-cultivation and to claim greater collective relevance for their personal moral endeavor. By exploring the structures of mobilization that secure Muslim activists, men and women, in highly visible positions in public controversies, chapter 4 addresses a third dimension of Islam's palpable public presence, that is, its institutional foundations. Attributing special importance to the interventions of female Muslims and their leaders, the chapter portrays their initiatives as directly related to ongoing reassessments of gender relations. The advantages of such a multidimensional account of women's involvement in Islamic renewal trends reside in a departure from reductive interpretations of women's "interest" and "motivations," on the one side, and from a preoccupation with structural constraints that predetermine women's actions, on the other. Muslim women's "learning groups" and related structures of mobilization are deeply rooted in conventional forms and norms of sociality. But they also integrate impulses from transnational Islamic revivalist trends, especially in the marked emphasis on women's leading role in societal renewal, and on the importance of female learning. Drawing on insights from chapter 1, chapter 4 demonstrates that the conditions of possibility that allowed these structures of Muslim mobilization to emerge and flourish are the result of complex transformations in the articulation between the state and social groups since the mid-1980s. By tracing how these transformations were conducive to Muslim activists' move into Mali's public arenas, the chapter sheds light on the complex, partly unexpected ways in which the social institutions of Muslim activism at once challenge and reinstate the central importance of the state.

A fourth dimension of Islam's public prominence in Mali, discussed in chapters 5 and 6, concerns the changing notions of religious subjectivity that go hand in hand with the aforementioned shifts in the institutional and social foundations of public debate. Chapter 5 discusses the conceptions of religiosity that guide Muslim women's search for piety and illuminates how the "pathway to God" they advocate differs from conventional understandings of Muslim identity and proper religious practice. Muslim women's personal beliefs take shape in a wider social-historical field, where inner commitments must be manifested in a "public" sphere that they recognize to be of plural moral orientations. The chapter relates Muslim women's understandings of piety and collective responsibility to long-standing, transnational frameworks of spiritual and intellectual orientation, as well as to the broader transformations in understandings of learning, relevant knowledge, and personal responsibility. Muslim women's particular views of religious subjectivity are also demonstrated in chapter 6, where they are described as intertwining with revised understandings of religious experience, authority, and community, understandings that reflect the influence of a thriving, partly mass-mediated religious consumer culture.

Chapters 6 and 7 closely investigate the "pathways to God" in which mass-mediated religious experience and discourse play a significant part. Looking at these "pathways" from complementary angles, both chapters demonstrate how individual media technologies affect conventional forms of religious experience, community, and authority, and how these media technologies are in turn re-signified by religious practice. Because media technologies do not carry fixed procedural conventions of communication, the collectivities and forms of religiosity constituted by particular media technologies depend upon the ways in which these technologies link up with conventional forms of authenticating religious experience and authority.

Chapter 6, in particular, focuses on the Muslim movement Ansar Dine and its charismatic, media-savvy leader Sharif Haidara to detail the ways in which proliferation of mass-mediated discursive genres fuels reconfigurations of religious authority and community. These revised conceptions need to be understood in the context of the growing mediatization of religious products and the concomitant liberalization and diversification of a media market that, until 1991, had been under close state control. The resulting field of public discourse, which is shared by Muslims and their critics, is structured by new media technologies, a thriving religious consumer culture, and the diversification of credentials of religious interpretive authority. Chapter 6 demonstrates that the adoption of new media technologies in urban Mali adds further complexity to the inherently tension-ridden quality of the public (discussed in chapter 1), by transforming the ways "Islam" figures as a blueprint of moral and social order, in public debate and in controversies among Muslims.

Chapter 7 explores the media practices of individual members of the Islamic renewal movement to show the interplay between new media technologies, personal religious experience, and the shifting position of "religion" in public life. By illuminating how broadcast technologies enable perpetuation of conventional notions of religious leadership and yet, paradoxically, also advance the spread of more rational paradigms of leadership, the chapter affirms the complex trajectories of mass-mediated religious discourse. Members of the moral reform movement in Mali turn some media engagements into religious acts that transform everyday experience. But these practices do not replace conventional forms of religious expression, nor do they point to entirely novel conceptions of religious authority and spiritual power. They do, however, illustrate interconnections and convergences between newly adopted media technologies and long-standing conventions of validating spiritual authority. They therefore do not instantiate a "re-enchantment" of an allegedly disenchanted realm of public communication and everyday experience. Rather, acolytes appropriate certain technologies in ways that reflect on their belief in the presence of the supernatural in everyday life. To them, media technologies have the potential of extending, not reinserting, spiritual experience into an array of mundane domains. Mass mediation has become a pervasive feature of religious practice and experience in town, fundamentally affecting the social implications of the sacred in the world, the nature of intimate religious experience, and the operation of religious authority.

ONE

"Our Nation's Authentic Traditions": Law Reform and Controversies over the Common Good, 1999–2006

IN MARCH 2000 Malian national radio announced in daily news broadcasts that a family law reform proposal, prepared by legal specialists and representatives of civil society, was to be publicly discussed so as to ensure popular participation and support. The projected reform of the codification of family law (*Code du Mariage et de la Tutelle* [*CMT*]), the broadcasts explained, was part of PRODEJ (Promotion de la Démocratie et de la Justice au Mali), a project financed by a consortium of Western donors to improve the effectiveness and credibility of the judiciary, and to mend inconsistencies within the Malian legal code "in accordance with international standards."[1] The anticipated law reform generated vehement protest among Muslim religious authorities and activists who publicly condemned the government's endorsement of the Beijing platform as an attack on women's "traditional role and dignity" that ultimately threatened to undermine Mali's authentic culture, one "rooted for centuries in the values of Islam."[2] Yet the main targets of these Muslim leaders' wrath, and their main political adversaries, were women's rights activists who, in broadcasts aired on local and national radio and tacitly supported by the Family and Women's Ministry, dismissed their protest as an attempt by "conservative religious forces" to pave the way for reactionary influences from the Arabic-speaking world by mixing religion and politics. Clearly, behind obvious differences in ideological orientation, Muslim activists and their political opponents have several points in common. Speakers on each side acknowledge that the government's decision to reform Mali's legal and judicial system is the result of various international influences and support structures, on the one hand, and of local and national political processes, on the other. Agendas of Western donor organizations intersect and collide with the interests of sponsors from the Arabic-speaking world, but also with interest groups struggling to gain greater influence in the national political arena. Both parties also present women's dignity, and their rights and duties, as essential to definitions of the common good and of membership in the political community.

That each party casts questions of shared values and public order in a legalistic discourse that grounds political belonging in rights and entitlements echoes the ways that politics is realized throughout contemporary Africa and around the globe (Mamdani 2000; Shivji 1999; Englund and Nyamnjoh 2004; Werbner 2004, 263; see J. Comaroff and J. L. Comaroff 2000, 2004; J. L. Comaroff and J. Comaroff 2004). Imported together with other elements of the institutional and normative scaffolding of liberal democracy, Law has become a privileged modality of political intervention.[3] Throughout Africa this development manifests itself in a mushrooming infrastructure of legal practitioners and extrajudicial structures, and in a panoply of nongovernmental organizations (NGOs) that act as supervisors of governmental politics and as promoters of a "politics of recognition" (Taylor 1992) cast in terms of legal rights and entitlements.[4]

The thriving of a legalistic discourse in contemporary Mali illustrates how this particular modality of political praxis in the national arena is produced in a global arena of politics and finances. The Malian law reform also reflects on how inconsistencies and paradoxes inherent in the model of the liberal nation-state play themselves out in the multicultural state politics of contemporary Africa. The model of the liberal state, based on the principle of an impartial treatment of religious and cultural diversity, is currently challenged by a heterogeneity of identities (J. Comaroff and J. L. Comaroff 2004; J. L. Comaroff and J. Comaroff 2004, 2006). In Mali, these challenges are cast in a moralizing idiom that centers on "proper" gender relations and thereby draws on long-standing discursive conventions (Schulz 2001b). What has changed is that conflicting constructions of belonging are expressed in a discourse of rights and entitlements. Whoever employs this discourse supports, and yet is simultaneously exposed to, the trappings of this form of political intervention; the language of rights in which the politics of recognition are nowadays cast inflates the significance of the legal domain in resolving issues of political participation and, even more important, in bringing about economic and social equity (Tomasevsky 1993; Kuenyehia 1994, 1998; Ilumoka 1994; Shivji 1999).

The aim of this chapter is twofold. It provides the historical backdrop against which contemporary interventions by Muslim activists and leaders into public debate, and their diverse relations to the state, need to be understood. It thereby retraces the historical process through which Islam has recently taken a central position in public debates on the moral foundations of the nation. The chapter then examines the particular stakes and forms of the politics of recognition that manifest themselves in the 2000 law reform debate, and analyzes the unintended consequences these struggles generated. Muslim leaders, by framing their challenge to official constructions of political belonging in the language of religious rights, capitalize on, and hint at, significant changes in the position of religion in the moral topography of the nation. In their efforts to frame religious identity as a matter of personal rights and entitlements, they present Islam as beyond, and unaffected by, the realm of politics, yet simultaneously reclaim it as central to their ethical self-understanding. Islam, in other words, becomes central in a politics of religious and moral difference.

Calhoun (1998) has critiqued communitarianism for its assumption that the common good is substantively defined and exists prior to historically constituted communities. This view, he argues, fails to address whose actors' definition of the common good is made the normative basis of the political community, and where these actors are located in the social and political land-scape (see Mansbridge 1998). What a political community accepts as shared normative foundations is the temporary outcome of a historically specific power constellation. Prevailing definitions of collective interest may not be a matter of common acceptance but a sign of the exercise of sovereign state power (Asad 1999). Struggles between unequal opponents center not only on substantive definitions of collective interest but also on the very right to participate in its definition. This right is determined by one's location vis-à-vis state power, but it also depends on loci of power outside state control, such as religious author-ity, to which the government has to respond. How does the thriving legalistic culture in Mali empower particular interest groups—those that formerly could not partake in political processes but that now present themselves as bearers of certain cultural or religious entitlements—to seek public support for their visions of the common good? Why has Islam become such a powerful language of moral community, and why now? Answers to these questions will shed light on the ways neoliberal ideology translates into politico-institutional reform and, draw-ing on heavy financial and institutional support of Western donor organizations, generates unintended and paradoxical consequences.

Muslim Interest Groups and the State in Historical Perspective

Contemporary Muslim doctrinal disputes and competition over public recognition as representatives of civil society continue a long history of intra-Muslim controversy which, since the colonial period, has been fueled by the state's ambivalent treatment of manifestations and representatives of religion in Mali's public sphere. Rather than taking these ambivalences as a reason to deplore the discrepancy between the claims by the state to establish *laïcité* and its failure to realize this principle, my objective is to illustrate that, in the southern triangle of present-day Mali, historical attempts to articulate Islamic norms of public order and visions of collective interest were shaped by Muslim leaders' mutual doctrinal contestation, and by their differential positioning vis-à-vis the colonial administration.[5] Divisions among Muslims were reinforced by their unequal access to opportunities of travel and intellectual enrichment that were created by new technologies of transport and media and that intensified exchange with the Arabic-speaking world. The evolving "discursive capacities" of Muslims (Salvatore 1999) to formulate visions of public order and shape the moral topography of collective life were circumscribed, yet never fully determined, by colonial administrators' efforts to control institutions and leading representatives of Islam. These efforts manifested themselves in the domain of education and in the colonial regulation of an emergent sphere of public discourse (Brenner 1993c; see Launay and Soares 1999).

Controversy among Muslim scholars over questions of how to order the life of the political community in accordance with Islamic principles predates the colonial period in Muslim West Africa. In the eighteenth and nineteenth centuries, controversy often congealed in an interlocking of political and doctrinal dispute, as Islamic renewal took the form of militant jihad, and conformity with Islamic doctrinal prescriptions became a precondition for establishing political dominance. Disputes between Muslim leaders, often cast in a "Muslim discourse about truth and ignorance" (Brenner 2001, 133–144), highlighted questions of social justice, of authority in initiating a militant jihad and in ruling a theocratic state, and of the treatment of nonbelievers. Muslims' competition over leadership was also reflected in their conflicting assertions of scholarly erudition and of special, divinely granted esoteric capacities (Last 1974, 1992; Robinson 1985, 2000; Levtzion 1986a, 2000; Brenner 1988, 1992, 1997). These controversies constituted the historical context within which the establishment of three important Sufi orders—the Qadiriyya-Mukhtariyya, the Tijaniyya, and the Tijaniyya Hamawiyya—since the late eighteenth century needs to be understood. French colonial conquest deeply affected Muslim debate with respect to the contents of doctrinal debate and its forms of articulation. These changes reflected challenges to the sources of authority and of political legitimacy that emerged from the reconfiguration of sociopolitical and economic fields under colonial rule. Doctrinal controversy and shifting power constellations among Muslims were also fueled by the overlapping effects of various local, regional, European, and Middle Eastern institutional connections and influences.[6] Debates in the colonial French Sudan about Islam as a blueprint for social conduct had repercussions for broad segments of the population, as more and more people converted to Islam during this time. Muslim intellectuals of different orientations and educational background experimented with new institutions that were to enable modern Muslims to function in the social and political setting created by colonial rule and within the colonial and postcolonial political economy (Brenner 2001, 127–129; Triaud 2000). Still, in many areas, the Islamic civilizing traditions were of concern only to certain segments of the population until the 1930s and 1940s. The role of religious lineages as brokers between local producers and the colonial state was not nearly as important as it was in other West African countries, such as Senegal and Nigeria. Until the 1940s Muslims remained a minority in colonial French Sudan, except for some urban centers of religious erudition such as Timbuktu, Gao, Mopti, Djenne, Segou, and Nioro, that thrived under the influence of lineages associated with Sufi practice (e.g. Hanson 1996; Soares 2005).[7] In some towns, the influence exerted by these lineages originated in precolonial polities and expanded in the colonial era.[8] Particularly in the southern areas of Mali that became the post-independence centers of state administration and control, many converted to Islam only gradually.[9] To the majority of these converts, being a Muslim was a matter of group and professional identity expressed in regular worship (*zeli* in Bamana; from the Arabic *salat*), a particular dress code, and food restrictions (Launay 1992).

San is a good illustration of the dynamics unfolding in colonial areas where Muslims long constituted only a minority. The (non-Islamized) Bobo and Bamana populations south and southeast of the town resisted French intrusion and the canton chiefs established by the colonial administration during the first twenty years of occupation.[10] Until 1917, several insurrections were repressed with great bloodshed.[11] In contrast, the few Islamized Marka, Fulbe, and Djenneké families who lived in San—some of whom claimed adherence to the Qadiriyya—and a few villages of the *cercle* were considered "loyal" to the "cause of the French nation" while forming "isolated" islands of Muslim practice among a "largely animist population" steeped in "superstition."[12] Although colonial reports expressed apprehension at the increased numbers of people converting to Islam,[13] they assured administrative superiors in Bamako and St. Louis that there was no indication of a spread of "insurgent" ideas of pan-Islamism or of oppositional Muslim tendencies that were causing great concern in other areas of the French Sudan (e.g., Harrison 1988, chaps. 2, 5; Soares 2005, 51–60).[14] Over subsequent decades, several politically powerful families in San converted to Islam. Yet, as local administrators condescendingly observed, "the level of religious knowledge" among the converted remained "very low" and was limited to the performance of the daily prayers.[15] The limited spread of Islam in the area of San in the colonial period casts doubt on some claims formulated by proponents of Islamic moral reform, particularly their call for a "return" to the authentic readings of Islam. Others who participate in contemporary Muslim controversy today also appeal to a past consensus among the community of learned people (*ijma*) as the blueprint for present Muslim religious practice. This, too, is a somewhat nostalgic portrayal of past Muslim discourse. Throughout the colonial period, debates over ritual orthopraxy and the collective significance of Islam were shaped by actors with very diverging religious credentials.[16] Among them were religious experts, scribes, and leaders from lineages with close ties to the Sufi order. Labeled *marabouts* by the colonial authorities, they benefited from the prestige associated with their genealogical descent and scholarly erudition. They were often supported by French colonial authorities who considered them representatives of a traditional African or "Black Islam" (Monteil 1980; see Harrison 1988, chap. 6) capable of limiting the influence of "radical" local Muslim reformers and of intellectuals who, from the 1930s on, challenged established religious understandings by referring to a universalistic conception of Islam that bore strong markers of a Salafiyya reformist discourse gaining currency in the Arabic-speaking world at that time.[17]

Various other actors also played a part in these debates. Some of them lacked genealogical pedigree but became religious self-made men by combining their various political, moral, and economic ambitions. Among them were those who could be called "political prophets," that is, men who used their entrepreneurial skills to announce the immediate end of the world and mount attacks against the occupying powers.[18] Others were labeled "ambulant preachers" by colonial authorities, who closely monitored their travels and proselytizing activities across West Africa because they feared the Islamism associated with the emerging pan-Arabic movement in the Middle East.[19] Muslim scholars who preached under the tutelage of the colonial administration popularized understandings that placed special emphasis on the field of Islamic *adab* (Arabic, cultivation, manners). In so doing, they made this term central to their definitions of Islam as public norm, thereby partly reformulating the significance of *adab* (see Salvatore 1999).[20] The effects of Muslims' discursive interventions on common perceptions of Islamic norms depended in part on their relationship to the French colonial apparatus and administrators, and can therefore be seen as the paradoxical outcome of the administration's monitoring of Muslim scholars' proselytizing activities. By selectively supporting certain ambulant preachers, the colonial powers furthered a process in which Islam's role as blueprint for social and moral action became accepted by a steadily expanding constituency of believers.

A parallel development occurred in the field of education, where the French encountered an organized resistance from intellectuals whose reformist initiatives were a direct response to their own attempts to streamline the making of colonial subjects. Administrators labeled these Muslims *Wahhabi*, a still widely used, yet also contested, term that contradicts the self-understanding of these intellectuals as Sunnis or *ahl al-sunna wa'l-jama'a* (Arabic, "People of the Sunna and the community [of the Prophet]"), that is, those who observe the regulations and doings of the Prophet Muhammad. Conversely, their self-portrayal as Sunni is considered an affront by other Muslims, because it implies their dismissal as nonbelievers. From the early days of their presence in the *Soudan Français* in the late 1930s, the Sunni reformists, many of whom had spent time in Egypt, Saudi Arabia, or North Africa, articulated an idiom of Islamic awakening. Though they differed in their priorities and in the local, regional, and Middle Eastern intellectual currents from which they drew inspiration (Kaba 1974, chap. 1; Brenner 2001, 140–152), they all attributed primary importance to the foundational texts of Islam and the example set by the community of the Prophet and his companions, thereby embracing central tenets of Salafiyya doctrine.[21] Drawing on inspirational figures of Muslim modernist thought in the Middle East, the activities of these Muslim intellectuals—referred to by some as *Al-Azharis* because of their source of inspiration from Al-Azhar, the center of Islamic erudition in Cairo—were geared toward the articulation of an Islamic normativity in response to the institutions of the colonial state (Triaud 1986b; Brenner 2001, chaps. 2, 4). They provided a critical cornerstone to the traditions passed down by influential religious lineages, some of whose practices and beliefs they denounced as distortions (that is, as *bida' makrûha,* unlawful innovations) of the original teachings of the Qur'an and Hadith. By reforming institutions and pedagogies of Islamic learning and promoting Arabic literacy, they reworked conventional understandings of religious knowledge and prepared the ground for a more inclusive religious instruction. By insisting on a more immediate access to the foundational texts and on facilitating individual interpretation, they challenged not only traditional interpretive authority but also conceptions of spiritual leadership based on esoteric knowledge. Although in keeping with the conventional structure of doctrinal dispute, their teachings broke with established understandings of orthopraxy (Kaba 1974, chaps. 1–2; Brenner 2001, 142–146). Still, these intellectuals questioned not Sufi devotional practices per se but exploitative forms of religious patronage (Brenner 2001, 141–142; Launay 1992, chap. 4). They were fiercely opposed by established families of Muslim religious specialists and by colonial administrators who feared them as spearheads of a pan-Arab, radical discourse of Islamic renewal.

Throughout the French Sudan, the 1940s and 1950s witnessed the emergence of a heterogeneous field of religious activism that reflected the diverse attempts by Muslims to articulate Islam as a public norm and create new forms of social organization. Muslim activism was structured by crisscrossing and shifting alliances rather than by a clear-cut divide between French colonial administrators and Muslim scholars, as illustrated by the educational counter-reform movement, spearheaded by such renowned figures as Amadou Hampate Bâ (Brenner 2001, chap. 4). The counter-reformists opposed the Al-Azhari reformists' educational endeavor and promoted an "African," "tolerant" version of Islam, one that they, as well as French administrators who backed the movement, saw as amenable to the making of modern French Muslim citizen-subjects (Brenner 2001, chap. 3; Soares 2005, 211–214). Though largely unsuccessful, the counter-reform movement left a complex legacy for a Muslim discourse on civility and institutions of knowledge transmission.[22] It put into relief the ambivalent treatment of religion by French administrators who, by promoting an enlightened African Islam unthreatening to the colonial state, contravened the principle of laïcité (Brenner 1997).

The 1950s saw the rise to influence of a new generation of Muslim intellectuals intent on disclaiming religious practices endorsed by lineages associated with Sufi orders. This new generation resembled the earlier activists in emphasizing a universalistic Muslim orientation. Yet their striving for an authentic Islam was often more strongly aligned with the model of Islamic piety formulated under the influence of Wahhabi doctrine in the hejaz (Triaud 1986b). Some promoted a more locally or regionally rooted endeavor toward moral renewal. This was the case in San where reform-minded Muslim critics, and their vocal opposition to the most influential families of religious specialists in town created considerable rancor and uproar in the late 1950s (see below). In other towns, Muslim opponents of established religious leaders formulated a vision of proper life and religious orthopraxy that was more closely associated with a trader identity (Kaba 1974, chaps. 4, 5; Amselle 1977, 1985; Brenner 1993b). Many younger Sunnis thus differed from earlier defenders of a universalistic Islam in their emphasis on individual achievement and a frugal lifestyle, exemplified in their refusal to redistribute their wealth among their own kin. Instead, they invested their earnings in public endowments and an Islamic institutional infrastructure. Their abstinence from the conspicuous display of generosity in traditional life-cycle rituals generated antagonism among representatives of "traditional" Islam (Brenner 1993a, 71–77; 2001, 63, 131–133) and among older Sunni merchants. Echoing intergenerational tensions in other West African Muslim societies (Launay 1992; Masquelier 1999), these antagonisms found expression in the young Sunni merchants' adoption of a symbolism of Islam piety modeled after the dress code and bodily discipline promulgated by official Saudi Islam.[23]

The gradual merging of the two older Muslim factions into a religious establishment in the 1950s signaled a significant restructuring of the field of Muslim debate. The insertion of younger Sunnis who emphasized individual responsibility into this discursive field indicates that issues of personal accountability and salvation could now be posed and answered in new ways. Views about proper religious practice and the relevance of individual ethics to politics remained contested in pre-independence politics. None of the conceptions formulated by the different generations of Muslim reformists completely displaced earlier ones (Brenner 2001, chaps. 3, 4), and yet they left an imprint on local ethical understandings at the same time that many converted to Islam.[24]

In the decade preceding the country's independence in 1960, Muslim doctrinal disputes, refracted by shifting moral and political positions, gained poignancy from the competition between the two political parties, the US-RDA (Union Soudanaise du Rassemblement Démocratique) and the PSP (Parti Soudanais Progressiste). The ways in which the combination of religious and party affiliation played into existing alliances and power struggles among politically influential families varied considerably from one locale to another. Whereas the PSP was often supported by the colonial canton chiefs, as well as by religious families associated with the Islamic mystical traditions and by some older Sunni merchants, the US-RDA recruited many followers among those who could only gain from older elites' loss in power. Accordingly, though in some areas more than others, the US-RDA party's ranks were filled with people from less powerful segments of the population, among them inferior social status groups and younger Sunni businessmen. Muslim controversy occasionally took violent forms, as in the case of the "Wahhabiyya conflict" (*wahhabiyya kèlè;* Kaba 1974; Amselle 1977), that were craftily manipulated by colonial administrators to lend force to the PSP, the party deemed more supportive of the French *mission civilisatrice.* Here again, French colonial powers, far from maintaining neutrality toward religious groups, readily sacrificed the principle of *laïcité* to the higher goals of colonial domination. In San the complex intertwining of religious and party affiliation resulted in a shifting and ultimately equivocal constellation. Ousmane Sidibé, a Muslim preacher who in 1957 established himself as a vocal critic of Muslim leaders in town and of some ritual practices they condoned, drew initial support from families siding with the PSP. Over the years he and his followers were also courted by representatives of the US-RDA, yet neither of these political alliances became a stable factor in local politics.[25]

Throughout the French Sudan, representatives of leading religious families who had supported the PSP lost political terrain when Modibo Keita and the US-RDA won the elections for the municipalities and the Territorial Assembly in early 1957. The party owed its success to the brokering activities of younger Sunni merchants, but this alliance ended when Keita's regime started to implement its socialist state-directed economic development, a measure that threatened the merchants' brokering position between rural producers and urban consumers (Amselle 1985). The new socialist government sought to neutralize the influence of Muslim leaders on local politics and reconfirmed the French principle of *laïcité* in the new constitution, stipulating that any religion was to be treated as a purely private matter.[26] Defining national culture by its "unity in diversity," the regime declared religious and ethnic diversity irrelevant (Schulz 2001a, chap. 5). President Keita's government also continued with colonial educational policy by integrating some Islamic reformed schools into the public system while denying other Islamic educational institutions the same status (Brenner 2001, chap. 5). In reaction to these policies, Sunni merchants once supportive of the US-RDA sided with their former Muslim opponents to mobilize a popular opposition that was decisive for the overthrow of the socialist regime in 1968.

The massive changes in the sociopolitical, institutional, and normative parameters of colonial rule had equivocal effects on the contending Muslim factions that existed prior to independence. Muslim intellectuals' attempts to make an Islamic code of civility binding for the majority of the population remained limited.[27] This situation continued after independence, when these Muslims' efforts were periodically submerged but never fully vanished from the political landscape. Colonial Muslim activities thus laid the groundwork for a broader acceptance of Islam as a frame of reference for community constructions, particularly after the coup d'état of 1968 that brought Colonel Moussa Traoré and his military regime to power. Underneath the apparent continuity of Moussa Traoré's twenty-three years of military and (post-1979) single-party rule, politics changed in ways that enabled Islam to gain force as a compelling moral idiom and alternative to official constructions of belonging.[28] This development was the paradoxical outcome of Traoré's effort to ingratiate himself to powerful Muslim interest groups by granting them privileges—such as giving them more broadcast time than Christians—despite Mali's secular constitution. Such special treatment was part of Traoré's attempt to extend his control over the financial funds that local Sunni businessmen received from the Arabic-speaking world to invest in religious and educational infrastructure (Brenner 1993c; Schulze 1993). At the end of Traoré's rule, multiple ties of kinship and patronage linked party members to wealthy businessmen who made a point of publicly displaying their Muslim identity, thus contributing to Islam's visibility and discursive representation in a national arena (Amselle 1985; Triaud 1988a). President Traoré's creation of the national association of Muslims, the Association Malienne pour l'Unité et le Progrès de l'Islam (AMUPI) in 1985 consolidated state control over the religious establishment and its new opponents, many of whom graduated from institutions of higher learning in the Arabic-speaking world.[29] The new generation of *arabisants* (Otayek 1993) occupied leading posts in the state bureaucracy, thereby illustrating that their educational career had given them strategic advantage over representatives of traditional Islam and established families of Sunni merchants. By granting the competing Muslim factions representation in the AMUPI's steering committee, Traoré's government effectively minimized conflicts among them.

The Traoré regime's loss of credibility under the effects of neoliberal economic reform after the mid-1980s contributed to a widespread moral vacuum that heightened Islam's appeal as a credible alternative. As the regime grew increasingly corrupt, the exclusion of major segments of the rural population and the urban lower classes from access to state resources could no longer be denied. Investments by Arab sponsors for the construction of schools and mosques, and the Malian Muslim associations that distributed these funds enjoyed greater credibility among many illiterate and middle-class people than the development projects set up by Western donors. As a consequence of Traoré's favorable treatment, Muslim leaders were among the president's closest allies in 1989, when the oppositional Mouvement pour la Démocratie, created by Western-oriented intellectuals, organized civil unrest that led to the overthrow of President Traoré in 1991.[30]

President Alpha Oumar Konaré and his Alliance pour la Démocratie au Mali (ADEMA), the victor in the country's first democratic elections in 1992, favored a stringent interpretation of Mali's secular constitution and ostracized the so-called *intégristes*,[31] those who promoted stricter readings of (what they considered) an Islamic code of conduct and who called for the introduction of *shari'a*. Yet neither President Konaré nor President Toumani Touré, who followed Konaré in office in 2002, risked antagonizing prominent Muslim leaders whose political influence they both feared and depended on.[32] President Touré continues to endorse *laïcité* and multiparty politics, as well as projects initiated under President Konaré such as the campaign against female circumcision. Because he managed to integrate several oppositional parties into the government that repeatedly contested Konaré's presidency, parliamentary opposition has weakened considerably. As the government becomes a de facto single-party ruler, unofficial structures of mobilization have gained political momentum.

Since the introduction of civil liberties in 1991, divisions among Muslim leaders and interest groups have resulted in a panoply of organizations and in the institutional infrastructure of a decentralized public arena. The new opportunities for reaching illiterate segments of the population through local radio stations have allowed various Muslim actors to compete with representatives of traditional Islam and draw on novel means and registers to do so. These Muslim activists lack traditional credentials of religious authority but capitalize on their combined literacy in French and Arabic, and sometimes on their education in the Arabic-speaking world. They represent a new generation of "debating Muslims" (Fischer and Abedi 1990) that, for the past twenty-five years, has been on the rise throughout the Muslim world (Roy 1994; Eickelman and Piscatori 1996; Anderson 1999; Larkin and Meyer 2006). Their success in Mali reflects a general politico-moral malaise with the Western donor–supported establishment of participatory and plural democratic institutions. Some of the associations created by Muslim activists are steadily expanding into the rural hinterlands. They thrive under the guidance of men and women who belong to the political elite that lost their privileged access to state resources with the overthrow of President Traoré. Most of them are represented in the national Muslim association where they form uneasy and unstable alliances. Even if Sunni intellectuals with close ties to Egypt, Libya, and Saudi Arabia dominate the current directory board of the AMUPI, the organization is thought to represent a politically moderate wing of the Muslim camp.[33] Other Muslim organizations challenge the AMUPI's claim to represent the interests of all Malian Muslims and its conciliatory stance toward governmental politics. Among these contestants are the *intégristes,* mentioned above, who adopt a more radical position on the binding character of Islamic precepts. Though they experienced a major backlash in 1991, when the religious parties they sought to create were banned, they continue to call for the introduction of *shari'a,* usually without specifying its precise contents.

Other Muslim activists share the *intégristes'* concerns, particularly their denouncement of the government's irreligious orientation. Still, most of them distance themselves from the attempts by *intégristes* to radically alter the Malian constitution. Instead, they seek public influence by presenting themselves as moral watchdogs removed from politics. The movement of the preacher Sharif Ousmane Madani Haidara, whose media performances are analyzed in chapter 6, exemplifies the "third space" that some Muslim activists occupy. He mobilizes followers and fans from the urban lower and lower-middle classes through social welfare and solidarity structures that operate largely outside the realm of the state. The government's lack of credibility thus adds to the magnetism of leaders who invoke Islam as an alternative foundation of political community. Ultimately this situation leaves the government in a double bind. Having acceded power by referring to the procedural rules of multiparty democracy, President Touré's government needs to conform to a participatory mode of governance. Any official attempt to display and "perform" (Worby 1998) the pluralistic nature of the new democratic system, however, only reinforces the appearance of a weak government incapable of suppressing internal difference and establishing law and order (Fay 1995; Schulz 2001a, chap. 3; see Mbembe 1992). The disparity between the liberal state model and its inability to realize its democratic promises constitutes the backdrop against which present-day controversies over legal reform need to be understood. Also relevant for their understanding is the legacy of colonial jurisdiction.

Legislating the Family: Historical Antecedents

The Malian judicial system illustrates the heritage of a dual legal order established by French administrators and its underlying ambiguous construction of civic subjectivity. Prior to the French occupation of the Sudan, a variety of regional legal regulations and customary practices existed in the area of contemporary Mali. Islamic law (following the Malekite *madhab,* or "school") was predominant in the northern regions of Gao and Timbuktu. In areas where the majority of the population was non-Muslim and converted to Islam only since the early twentieth century, the regulation of conflicts followed local custom. The French dual judicial system of 1903 was based on two bodies of law for different categories of colonial subjects, thereby establishing a divide between citizens and the majority of the (mostly rural) population (see Mamdani 1996, 57–61).[34] French positive law, the *Code Napoleon,* was applied to the *assimilés.* The application of locally diverse customary laws to the rest of the population, although understood as maintaining "traditional" law and order, initiated complex reconfigurations of existing power relations within the family and among different social groups.[35] Both customary law (including Islamic law) and modern law were applied by French magistrates, with the assistance of advisers in local customary law.[36] In regions with a Muslim majority population, one of the two advisers was an expert in Islamic jurisprudence. The integration of these experts into the colonial apparatus sidestepped the influence of Muslim scholars, because colonial authorities deprived them of their discretionary power in regulating disputes over inheritance, land, and slave ownership, and reduced their role to that of assessors (Stewart 1997).

In spite of post-independence reforms, the legacy of a dual colonial judicial system is still tangible today, as seen, for instance, in the regional diversity of customary law and the considerable gap between legal regulations, on one side, and social practice and local legal norms, on the other.[37] This gap is most evident in the regulation of family matters. The *Code du Mariage et de la Tutelle,* in 1962, reflected the modernization agenda of the US-RDA party and its promotion of the nuclear family model.[38] Accordingly, the *CMT* was designed to establish the spousal relationship as the principal axis along which the transfer of services is negotiated. Article 36 of the code laid down the full civil capacities of married women, and Articles 4 and 10 regulated the minimum marriage age and the necessity of the wife's consent to the marriage. Articles 16 and 29 made official marriage registration obligatory. These measures imposed certain restrictions on kin-based elderly authority. Yet many prerogatives of husbands and older men persisted, respectively, over women and younger men, partly because legislative reform left most sensitive domains untouched, such as the regulation of inheritance. Also, actual legal measures were rarely enforced, such as the minimum age for marriage and the prohibition of forced marriage. Contradictions within the legislation thus continued to exist, such as the one between the guarantee of women's equal rights and full civil capacities (*CMT,* Article 36) and Article 231 of the *Code de Procedure Civile, Commerciale and Sociale* (*CPCCS*) that leaves the regulation of inheritance to customary conventions. The limitation placed on the size of the bride-price was generally disregarded, nor were punitive measures taken against elevated bride-price payments and arranged marriages, often of legal minors. Official marriage registration, although a legal requirement, remained the exception in a situation where institutional oversight was weak and many (male) officials were interested in maintaining a situation that was to their own advantage. This "policy of non-intervention" (Jalal 1991) of the ruling party often played into the hands of locally powerful kin groups.

Strategies of evasion further undermined the enforcement of state law in rural areas during the military and later civilian regime of Moussa Traoré and the UDPM (Union Démocratique du Peuple Malien). Yet even if people managed to keep family matters largely outside the purview of state power, local authority structures did gradually change, along with broader socioeconomic transformations. Wage labor, seasonal labor migration, and Western education of adolescents resulted in greater financial independence and the weakening of parental and kin authority. Related processes in town undermined the foundations of established marital power relations and male authority in family decisions. It is these changing family dynamics, and the conflicts they generate, that rendered the recent law reform debate so poignant and bitter.

The PRODEJ Project

Given that none of the earlier draft laws generated public controversy and media coverage comparable to that of the PRODEJ project, it is time to explore the stakes it held for different groups of supporters and opponents. Their reactions to the project reflect how Malians perceive the efforts of state and party officials to act democratically and affirm the capacity of the state to mend, by means of the allegedly supra-political means of the law, dissonances emerging from the heterogeneous composition of Malian society (see Comaroff and Comaroff 2004a, 191–192; 2004b, 538–539).

A cornerstone of PRODEJ was the organization of debates over the draft law, the so-called *Concertations Régionales,*[39] in which selected representatives of civil society were invited to participate. Yet, also celebrated as a milestone in participatory democracy, these *Concertations* remained restricted to urban areas. Here the permanent PRODEJ staff encountered widespread suspicion and thus shared the fate of earlier government-supervised and Western-funded campaigns, such as those against AIDS and female circumcision. Bystanders with whom I talked, many of them from low-income households with little or no schooling, denounced PRODEJ as another Western donor-funded project whose main rationale was to provide politicians and NGO leaders with additional income. The main problems with the Malian juridical system, they felt, was not legislation but the inaccessibility of the law and rampant corruption. As one interlocutor, a father in a lower-income household, said, "If you change the law on paper, it still remains paper law. Disputes are not resolved by paper but by [having the] means to impose force." This remark succinctly summarizes the perception that to face the Law in contemporary Mali is always an encounter with the state's exercise of its sovereignty and coercive powers (see Hansen and Stepputat 2005). The comment also captures many Malians' awareness that legalism, closely associated with Mali's state apparatus, has little potential to transform entrenched forms of social and political inequality that are, after all, an immediate result of the exercise of state power.

Intellectuals who were not involved in PRODEJ articulated a similar distrust of the proliferation of a human rights discourse and of legalistic forms of political intervention. They, too, insisted that the gap between legislation, its enforcement, and social practice constitutes the most fundamental challenge to the rule of law, apart from blatant corruption.[40] They viewed the law reform mainly as the government's effort to increase its respectability in the eyes of international donors attuned to the discourse of civil society and rule of law. These various apprehensions reflect an acute understanding of the ways that the changing agendas of international donors, and the broader shift toward a neoliberal paradigm of politics that these agendas reflect, are redirected by certain interest groups in Mali to bolster their positions in a national arena.

One interest group, composed of various women's rights NGOs (often subsidized by Western donors) and of representatives of the Ministry of Women, Children, and the Family (*Ministère de la Femme, de l'Enfant et de la Famille*), manifests the growing influence gained by a new female elite in the 1989 *Mouvement pour la Démocratie*, and their privileged access to governmental and international donor support under Presidents Konaré and Touré.[41] Although the Ministry of Women is the driving force of the PRODEJ reform, the project is formally under the tutelage of the Ministry of Justice, whose representatives are far less supportive of the draft law and favor instead a reform of the judiciary to improve its efficiency and reduce venal practices. The few magistrates and members of the Ministry of Justice who wholeheartedly support the reform do so mainly, as critics allege, because they expect to convert the public recognition gained through the reform project into more enduring kinds of assets. Whether or not these charges are justified, the propositions made by representatives of the Ministry of Justice during the debates reflected pragmatic considerations and a concern with maintaining the central administrative functions of magistrates, and hence of the state's interventionist powers. Notwithstanding the sometimes fierce competition between women's rights NGOs over state and international donor support (Schulz 2003b, 143–144), their respective leaders formed temporary alliances around the law reform project. Those invited to the public debate focused their efforts on women's conditions in urban areas and articulated compromises on which the different NGOs had agreed in advance.[42] Their prearranged provisos encapsulate how the interests of international donors intersect with and are reworked by governmental policy, on one side, and by certain segments of the political elite, on the other. Already noted is that many Western-oriented intellectuals dismiss the law reform as indicating a recent shift in an international regime of politics, and therefore of the country's ongoing dependence on the fads and neoliberal fantasies of international monetary institutions. The question, then, is whether the criticisms voiced by Muslim opponents can be read along similar lines.

During the debates, AMUPI spokespeople straddled the different positions represented in the association's steering committee, yet also clearly followed a pragmatic assessment of the current political situation.[43] Their propositions similarly entailed prearranged provisos on which the different AMUPI factions had agreed and that testified to their effort to present a broad Muslim consensus. Prior to the *Concertations Régionales,* leading Muslim authorities and activists launched a campaign in the private press and on *Radio Islamique,* the AMUPI's local radio station in Bamako. Their critique of the draft law primarily targeted its main proponents, the women's rights activists and the Family Ministry. Their public interventions plainly demonstrated their effort to engage, rather than withdraw from, the governmental reform project, and to shape it in line with their own concerns. During the *Concertations,* AMUPI spokesmen were supported by leading representatives of the national Muslim women's association UNAFEM, who framed their interventions as a defense of the dignity of Mali's Muslim women. Muslim critics of the AMUPI's close alliance with the state were not invited to the debate. Yet this did not prevent their most vocal representative, Shaykh Sharif Haidara, from criticizing the Muslim leaders present at the *Concertations* for their hypocrisy and political opportunism.

Although he questioned their credibility and erudition in numerous audio cassette recordings and local radio broadcasts, he never mounted an attack on the government, nor did he address substantive points of the draft law.

Representatives of the *intégristes* were less raucous in their protest against the proposed reform. A few warned against the imposition of foreign values that would alter the "fabric of our nation's Islamic traditions." Yet, although they claimed to confront a Westernized government, their criticism was mainly directed at the AMUPI and its failure to address "the most pressing concerns of Muslims." Thus, similar to Haidara, the *intégristes* framed their position as a question of who may legitimately speak on behalf of all Muslims, and thereby employed a discourse of truth and ignorance that historically generated and reflected divisions among Muslims throughout West Africa (Brenner 2001, chap. 6). Rather than revealing a substantive legal argument, the criticism of the PRODEJ project by these different Muslim opponents indicates that primarily at stake was the question of institutional power—that is, under what conditions would religious actors be allowed to participate in an allegedly democratic debate on the common good.

Contentious Claims: The 2000 Draft Law Debate

What arguments and controversies were generated by the 2000 draft law, and how did these reflect the divisions and alliances among participants and interest groups?[44] The fiercest debates occurred over the legislation of inheritance matters, mirroring the vicious conflicts that frequently emerge over these issues in rural and urban areas. These conflicts arise from contradictions between state law based on the model of the nuclear family and customary law which, regardless of regional variations, particularly regarding a married woman's access to land and inheritance, gives precedence to the rights of collateral relatives over descendants.[45]

Women's rights advocates pleaded for the codification of inheritance law as a way to strengthen the structural position of women who, according to Islamic and customary regulations, are either not entitled to an equal share of an inheritance or are denied any share at all. UNAFEM representatives emphasized the progressive spirit of Islamic law, which puts daughters in an advantageous position by awarding them a share equal to half of their brothers' inheritance, in contrast to customary regulations that treat women as part of the property inherited by collateral male relatives. Women's rights activists, in contrast, maintained that Islamic and customary law effected a systematic discrimination of women that contradicts the principle of equal rights for women and men and the "determination to promote women's rights" established in the constitution of 1992. The draft law proposed to settle inheritance matters according to the person's written will but always "within the confines set by the constitution,"[46] which implies that whenever a case is brought before a judge, positive law (and thus the equal treatment of women and men with respect to inheritance) will trump customary and Islamic conventions. The inheritance legislation thus signals the state's greater intrusion into family matters and the institutionalization of the nuclear family.[47]

AMUPI representatives, rather than substantiating how Islamic juridical principles of inheritance should become the basis of legislation, criticized the proposed legislation as an imposition of a culturally foreign legal code. Their interventions expressed their hope that the legislation would guarantee the validity of Islamic regulations and thus maintain established patriarchal prerogatives. Male state officials and civil society representatives kept largely silent on this issue but privately expressed their fear that this form of state intrusion would interfere with their own privileges. To them, the proposed inheritance legislation was the principal reason for the unpopularity of the draft law among many party and state officials, and for its ultimate rejection by the National Assembly.

The efforts of women's rights activists to impose compliance, by legal fiat, with the official registration of civil marriage (laid down in the 1962 *CMT*) was another hotly debated issue, partly because it touched on questions of institutional control over the issuing of official marriage records. Muslim activists and male representatives of the state administration jointly opposed the women activists who, in order to improve women's chances to claim financial support, proposed to increase the fines for noncompliance with official registration requirements.[48] AMUPI representatives dismissed this proposal and instead sought to expand their own leverage in the domain of marriage validation, maintaining that state recognition of religious marriage as equivalent to official marriage registration would close the gap between legislation and social practice. Ministry of Justice officials rejected their proposition, arguing that to invest representatives of a religious cult with the legal capacity of civil servants entailed a breach of *laïcité*. Implied in this argument was the fear that to grant Muslim authorities an official function would endow them with greater informal power than Christian religious authorities presently hold. State officials' refusal to admit any amendments triggered heated debates, demonstrating that questions of authority over marital relations and family matters play a central and emotionally charged role in defining relations between the state and "civil society." AMUPI representatives, in particular, framed the controversy as a confrontation between Islamic principles and a culturally foreign secular constitution. The actual debates suggested, however, that most participants were preoccupied with two kinds of social transformations directly affecting intra-familial authority structures that conservative forces, among them the AMUPI representatives, sought to halt. The first kind of transformation manifests itself in the weakening of elderly control over family decisions, a process directly related to young men's and women's greater financial independence from their parents. The second transformation is related to changes in power relations and mutual obligations between spouses, particularly among the urban lower and lower-middle classes where increasingly precarious economic conditions undercut husbands' authority.

Apprehension about the second transformation became even more pronounced in debates over the so-called obedience clause,[49] choice of residence, and choice of matrimonial form. Proponents of women's rights pleaded for legislative changes that acknowledged women's growing contribution to family subsistence and expanded female decision-making powers (see chapter 2). Not surprisingly, male government officials and AMUPI representatives, backed by journalists, endorsed legislative measures to counterbalance the erosion of family authority. Together they blocked the effort of women's rights activists to abolish the "obedience" clause. The result was a lukewarm compromise that left the clause in place but added a proviso: "obedience within the limits of the rights of women laid down in the constitution." Regardless of the improvement this qualification provided,[50] the debate over the obedience clause and its outcome reveals converging interests between intellectual men from opposing ideological and political positions. Although male government officials and AMUPI representatives claimed to be opposed to the clause on political, institutional, and moral grounds, their strategic alliances bridged the ideological divide they so vocally postulated.

Debates of the most contentious issues revealed not only a rift between the new Western-educated female elite and male state officials who temporarily sided with (female and male) Muslim defendants of male privilege and patriarchal norms. The controversies also highlighted the diversity in women's class-based interests. Women's rights advocates were preoccupied with the concerns of urban middle-class and upper-class women. Their interventions hint at the divide between rural women and those of a privileged, urban background, and at the exclusion of rural women from the public deliberation process. The class bias on which women's rights advocates operated was evident both in the issues they identified and the legal amendments they recommended. Solutions to prevalent bride-price malpractices and to women's lack of autonomy vis-à-vis their husbands were attuned to the capacities of urban women with a regular and independent salary. The position of women's rights advocates on issues of marriage validation, that is, their call for inflicting penal fees, similarly failed to consider how illiterate women could improve their chances to acquire written proof of their marital status.

Many UNAFEM spokeswomen, in contrast, addressed the distinct life situations of women from rural areas and the urban lower classes, pointing out that financial insecurity and a lack of social security networks renders urban lower-class women more vulnerable than other women in town.[51] They endorsed the AMUPI representatives' demand for investing the religious marriage with the status of a civil act, arguing that only an officially recognized proof of marriage status would strengthen a woman's position. Their approval of Islamic regulations of inheritance could be similarly read as an endorsement of the AMUPI official position. Yet it also illustrates that UNAFEM spokeswomen, to a greater extent than the women's rights advocates, recognized that rural women's right to inheritance would be improved by applying Islamic regulations. Clearly controversies over the draft law cannot be seen either as a struggle of women against a coalition of men and patriarchal norms nor as a crude class conflict. Rather, and similar to recent law reform in other Muslim-majority countries, the draft law endows women with new capabilities and responsibilities but also accentuates divisions among women.[52] UNAFEM spokeswomen have a similarly privileged background as their female opponents; they also differ from them, however, in their relations with the new political leadership, in the followers they mobilize, and in their conservative outlook on gender propriety that resonates with those of many middle- and lower-class women whose interests they seek to defend.

Another parallel to law reform projects throughout the Muslim world is that pragmatic considerations of mostly male state officials, magistrates, and representatives of civil society have a greater weight than ideological positions vis-à-vis issues of gender equality. Women activists and government representatives were confronted by an opposition of Muslim leaders and a broad spectrum of male intellectuals who claimed to represent the secularist orientation of the government, free press, state administration, and judiciary. Although hailing from different ideological quarters, these men drew on a shared, popular idiom of cultural authenticity to make sometimes contradictory claims about "culturally authentic" forms of law. They all tended to single out women's conduct as a rallying point for common political goals and as a prime terrain for social control.

Clearly the fissions emerging over the draft law cannot be reduced to a simple confrontation along gender or class lines or to a struggle between defenders of secularist political modernity and their Muslim adversaries who challenge the principle of *laïcité*. Instead, Mali's recent law reform debate brings into relief a diversity of struggles and the shifting alliances that together form a complex topography of interests and strategies that cannot be mapped onto a clear divide between secularism and religious fundamentalism. Rifts within the government and state administration that became visible during the debate refute generalizing arguments about the hegemonic or disciplinary project that "the" postcolonial state pursues with regard to law reform. Still, the proposed legislation of inheritance clearly hints at the interest on the part of state officials to promote certain social transformations and forestall others. The attempts by subsequent postcolonial Malian governments to regulate family matters illustrate that the state, in spite of its relative inability to enforce legislation, yields considerable power to undermine the legal and factual basis of kin-based structures of authority. Yet the relatively moderate changes proposed for the *CMT* also indicate the state's reluctance to interfere with some sensitive intra-familial matters. It is likely that the challenge to the law mounted by various interest groups will persist as long as a disconnect exists between the state-endorsed nuclear family model and kin-based institutions of authority and social control.

Muslim authorities' efforts to achieve greater autonomy demonstrates the continuing struggle between them and the government over the extent of state intervention and, by implication, over the legitimacy of the model of the "equidistant" laic state (Bauberot 1990, 1998; Barghava 1998). The government, vilified by certain Muslims as irreligious, is under constant pressure to fend off attempts by some Muslim groups to gain a foothold in formal institutions of family regulation, and to contain the influence Muslim authorities exert over people via media and patronage networks. Clearly there is a dialectical relationship between the precarious nature of the liberal state's foundations and its need to stage the legitimate nature of its institutions of governance.

Civil Gestures, Un-civic Exclusions: Whose Good, Who's Common?

By criticizing the government for its failure to realize the noninterventionist ideal of secularism, AMUPI representatives appropriate the model of a secular liberal state to justify their search for greater autonomy and to present this search as a defense of cultural particularity and a right to difference. They align themselves with, rather than challenge, the parameters of state politics. This strategy of appropriation and partial accommodation limits the effectiveness of their interventions, however, because they are obliged to accept compromises that will disprove their secularist opponents' charges that they contravene secular state politics. Also, although AMUPI representatives' search for public recognition is advantageous vis-à-vis competing Muslim interest groups, it also generates new conflicts, for instance, with the *intégristes,* who resent that the AMUPI's pragmatist political position undermines their principled opposition to *laïcité.* Moreover, the AMUPI's accommodation of governmental policy weakens its claims to defend a divinely ordained conception of the common good against the shifting demands of mundane state politics. Contrary to their insistence on the immutable nature of the common good, Muslim representatives formulated worldly and contingent readings of it.

The efforts of AMUPI speakers to gain control in the public arena illustrate another dilemma of Muslim interest groups that seek to maintain traditional prerogatives through state power. Because representation via party structures is foreclosed, they can gain influence only by adopting the role of civil society representatives. Yet, as became evident in numerous private conversations during the draft law controversy, neither the government nor Muslim opponents recognize the AMUPI as a legitimate representative of civil society. Muslim critics questioned the association's claim to speak on behalf of all Malian Muslims, and government officials and NGO activists see AMUPI representatives as religious forces, that is, representatives of Islamic values that clash with secularist state politics. Accordingly, in the final version of the draft law, the interests of the AMUPI were sidestepped or neutralized. The dismissal of the Muslim actors, along with the interests of the lower classes whom they often represent, as *Les Religieux,* religious interest groups, casts doubt on the staging of legal reform as a cornerstone of participatory democracy. Ultimately at stake are struggles over exclusion and inclusion, over who may or may not participate in public debate. These struggles pit Muslim representatives against Western-oriented intellectuals but also reproduce rifts within the topography of Muslim activism. Secularist-minded elites are keenly aware that they need to maintain a careful balance in these struggles of exclusion. As the example of Shaykh Sharif Haidara, documented in chapter 6, shows, a Muslim leader's marginalization in state-orchestrated debates may bolster his success in informal mobilization. Muslim interest groups' appropriation of governmental policy and participatory rhetoric is therefore only one among several strategies to gain public standing as a defendant of Islamic values.

As the 2000 law reform controversy illustrates, national processes, and specifically the transformation of alliances within civil society and the prominence of Islam as a new language of cultural authenticity, can only be understood by considering how national dynamics intersect with global neoliberal institutional reform. A proliferating, global legalistic culture, once it is adopted into national politics, encourages various social groups to enter the public arena and claim recognition in the name of their cultural rights and religious sensibilities. This process has paradoxical implications. In an era officially designated to realize post-authoritarian state politics, multiparty democracy, and a politics of legal intervention, political actors eagerly espouse the idiom of cultural/religious rights to gain standing in a public arena and mobilize a following. Yet, although Muslim actors and their Westernized opponents present their struggle as a confrontation between secularist and religious values, closer scrutiny of their arguments and interventions does not substantiate such a view. What ultimately emerged as a consensus of civil society during the debate primarily reflected participants' unequal chances to make their position heard in public.

The new political momentum of Islam in Mali is the paradoxical result of the interplay between transnational networks of dependence and influence, and national struggles over the economic and symbolic resources of the state that have been exacerbated under conditions of post-authoritarian rule. The government straddles two competing legitimizing repertoires: it employs the idiom of democracy, political modernity, and enlightened rule promoted by international donors. But to gain popular credibility, the government also draws on the language of cultural authenticity, and of Islamic tradition and morality. Although legislative reform may generate greater leverage for some women, it also opens up a field for conservative forces to mobilize popular discontent by contrasting an Islamic cultural autonomy to political dependence on the West. Thus, paradoxically, the internationally sponsored promotion of women's rights offers a new rallying ground for conservative oppositional forces and endows them with greater moral authority. Mali's present political conundrums are fueled by a long-standing history of intellectual and financial engagement with the Arabic-speaking world. Arab influence may have diminished in Mali since the late 1980s, but it still provides a reference point and moral orientation in a situation that many Muslims experience as socially and normatively insecure. These long-standing ties create a particular political legacy: they shape the conditions under which political actors mobilize a following in Mali and other Muslim majority countries of the region. Claims to particularity and recognition tend to be cast in a moralizing, religious idiom rather than in terms of ethnicity or cultural difference (see Bunwaree 2004; Hagberg 2004; Comaroff and Comaroff 2004a).

Was the staging of the law reform debate primarily an act of political posturing rather than an attempt to realize popular participation? The answer is yes but with qualifications. The setup of the law reform debate did not ensure widespread participation of possible critics. The criteria for exclusion and inclusion in public controversy were not open to debate but were implicitly defined and enforced by the political elite, a definitional act that constitutes an exercise of state power (see Asad 1999). My interlocutors' frequently expressed doubts about the ultimate realization of the draft law reinforces the impression that the display function of the PRODEJ, its symbolic role in appealing to the rule of law rather than creating it, was of primary importance. And my interlocutors' apprehensions proved to be well founded: until this day the draft law has not been approved by Mali's *Assemblée Nationale*.

TWO

Times of Hardship:
Gender Relations in a Changing Urban Economy

God is justice but it is hard to see where on this world his justice is done.

—FATHER OF NINE CHILDREN, SAN, APRIL 2000

Women do not marry to be free of sorrow. Life is sorrow and we ask God to help us accept it. What God decided for us is our destiny. Our husbands are not what we wished for, they are our destiny. We have to . . . endure the suffering they cause. God will help us to try and change their minds from time to time. For God is truth and justice. He tests my endurance by making me suffer. But it is not my husband who should make me suffer.

—AMINATA, MID-FORTIES, SEVEN CHILDREN,
BAMAKO, AUGUST 1998

FOR MORE THAN a decade *geleya* (literally, "heaviness," "difficulty") has been a recurrent trope in the daily conversations of urban middle-class and lower-middle-class families. *Geleya* refers to the emotional and material dimensions of the daily struggle to make a living; it also reflects many people's realization that "money affairs have become difficult" (*wari ko gèlèyara*), which burdens them with feelings of helplessness. To many urbanites, *gèlèya tuma* (times of hardship) also marks the onset of a particular era in Mali's recent history: the devaluation of the CFA franc by 50 percent on January 12, 1994, a measure executed as part of a broader program of neoliberal economic reform.[1] In the months that followed, most conversations I overheard reflected people's preoccupation with the social and moral repercussions of what was called a shortage in money (*wari dògòyara*). Older men and women maintained that the loss of morality and order resulted because "nowadays money can no longer be found" (*Bi bi de, wari te sòrò tugun*), and they deplored the fact that "patriarchal authority has gone kaput" (*Du fanga tinyèna*) because of children's "ingratitude" (*wali nyuman donbaliya*) and "lack of respect" (*u tè mògòw bonya*). Other adults identified marriage as the locus of family conflicts, maintaining that it "has become a matter of acquiring the *nasòngo* [literally, the price of the ingredients for the daily sauce]." Ultimately, many adults asserted, "it is the envy among women that creates endless strife within the family" (*Furu kèra nasòngo ko dòròn; nga a kòrò yèrèyèrè, o de muso ka nata ye*). Whereas this perception was shared widely by male youth, young women felt that their problem was not only a shortage of money but also of trustworthy, marriageable men. Dissonant as these accounts of present-day difficulties are, they reveal that people tend to mix reflections about the long-standing, socially corroding effects of money with the repercussions of recent economic liberalization. The comments reflect a widespread sense of crisis that goes beyond a materialist struggle for survival and cautions us to move beyond studies of the effects of Structural Adjustment Programs in urban Africa that assess hardship in the urban areas in purely material terms (see Salama 1998; see Lamarre and Miller 2000).

This chapter addresses the relationship between recent economic liberalization measures and urbanites' attempts to deal with the failure of the state to ensure the basic conditions of survival in town (see Riddel 1992; Sottas and Vischer 1995; Thomas-Emeagwali 1995; Hansen and Vaa 2004). The discussion is based on research in three locales characterized by a low level of infrastructure and a comparatively high rate of migrants:[2] a relatively new neighborhood in San and two neighborhoods in Bamako. A key concern is to understand whether the term "poverty" adequately renders the lived experiences of men and women and their sense of personal dignity, and what factors enable them to deal with the repercussions of economic liberalization. The situation of low-income families deserves special attention here because these are well represented in Muslim women's groups. This focus helps clarify how women and men maneuver networks of social security that have been affected across the socioeconomic divide, and how they make these networks fit the new expenditures and needs. The perspective also illuminates how changes in urban economies, especially in conventional institutions of social support, transform the existing ideology of gender inequality in ways that give women more choice (see Beneria and Feldman 1992; Afshar and Barrientos 1999).

Another purpose of this chapter is to understand the forms by which men and women in urban Mali assess and negotiate their interrelations, and the role a moralizing idiom of propriety plays in this process. Despite considerable advances in the anthropology of gender and feminist theory in the past thirty years, studies on Muslim societies are still haunted by the legacy of the early "anthropology of women" (Abu-Lughod 2002). Analyses of gender dynamics in Muslim societies in Africa are often preoccupied with women's "status" and assume a uniform gender ideology (e.g., Callaway and Creevey 1994; but see, too, Bernal 1994; Willemse 2001); they emphasize the extent to which women rework the constraints of their lives as intentional and self-empowered actors (e.g., Joseph 1980; Rassam 1980; Messick 1987; MacLeod 1991; Poya 1999). Even sophisticated rereadings of earlier accounts of women's alleged subordination in Muslim society primarily attend to questions of women's power and "resistance" (e.g., Abu-Lughod 1986; Boddy 1989; but also see Abu-Lughod 1990). I suggest that we allow for greater critical reflection on the specific analytical framework that should be brought to bear on the dynamics of gender relations and the remaking of particular ideologies of masculinity and femininity.[3] One should be mindful that the applicability of an analytical framework may depend, importantly, on the kind of questions one highlights. The second challenge is to account for the dynamics between spouses and determine how these dynamics are affected by factors such as the actors' social and economic standing, age, and individual personality and upbringing (see Potash 1986; Kerns and Brown 1992; Kandiyoti 1994; Wikan 1996).

The Social and Material Dimensions of "Hardship"

The location of a household and its social and material infrastructure are clear indicators of the position the family occupies, both in a metaphorical and material sense.[4] A characteristic pattern of income generation in the urban middle and lower-middle classes in Mali is the combination of different activities in the formal and informal sectors of the economy.[5] In middle-class households, male household heads are typically employed in the state bureaucracy or as teachers, state extension service agents, or nurses. Breadwinners in less well-off families make a living from various artisanal occupations (e.g., blacksmith, tailor, or carpenter) and often combine this with activities in the informal sector, such as small-scale trade in locally produced or imported food or consumer goods. Neighborhoods in Bamako are ethnically and socially heterogeneous, and reflect shifting patterns of rural-urban migration and changing economic trends within the capital. In these socioeconomically diverse neighborhoods, where numerous families make a living from various and often irregular sources of income, social success is indicated by the degree to which a household has access to electricity, piped water, and sewage and waste disposal systems. Indicators of economic achievement are different in San, where only a few households have access to electricity and basic elements of sanitation. Most families use petrol lamps at night, and those who can afford it run a television set with car batteries. Whereas Bamako may appear to be an alluring place of promise and an easier life, few opportunities to achieve a similar security of life and mind exist in San; all one can do is "cope" (*k'i jija* or *k'i debruye;* from French, *se debrouiller,* to find makeshift solutions) with what one has and what God gives. A modest living standard in San would, in Bamako, indicate that a family occupies a lower socioeconomic position and may have moved only recently to the capital.[6] There are more female migrants in the poorer strata of Bamako than typically is the case in smaller towns such as San. A disproportional, elevated number of poor migrant households are run by women.[7]

The size, number, and quality of homes are clear indications of a family's economic success. Houses are generally built with mud brick or cement and with metal roofs. An essential element of a courtyard's infrastructure is a brick wall–enclosed washing area and toilet (*nègène*). Because brick walls have to be repaired after each rainy season, it is a sign that a family lacks regular income or the support of migrant children when these walls are absent or of poor quality. In San, many families live in courtyards that they own and where they accommodate remote relatives and foster children, whereas in Bamako, many middle- and lower-middle-class families generate an additional income by renting out rooms to others. They content themselves with few bedrooms of limited size (approximately eight square meters) shared by two to seven people. Less well-off families live in rented spaces whose poorly maintained and jointly used infrastructure suffers as much from the indifference of property owners as from their incessantly insolvent tenants. In the three low-income neighborhoods of Bamako where I regularly attended Muslim women's learning groups, the majority of households I frequented had dysfunctional kitchen structures, where women cooked in the open air, unprotected against rain and sunshine. Even in more prosperous neighborhoods, partly broken-down walls and decrepit bathrooms were common.

Domestic life revolves around the *gaa* (*hangar* in French), a sitting area covered by wood to protect against sun and rain, where women pursue their household chores and socialize with visitors while keeping an eye on small children who play in its shade. As the prime space of hospitability, the *gaa* represents a family's social connectedness and achievement. Its absence triggers reactions from neighbors ranging from pity to malicious joy, and thus serves as a constant reminder of the intricate link between material deprivation and social failure. Wherever a *gaa* is missing, people sit in the shade provided by neem trees; in the course of a day, women, who usually socialize in the courtyard, follow the tree's wandering shade by moving their mats, little wooden stools, and chairs made of a metal frame and plastic strings. For men, the center of sociability is usually located outside the courtyard, either in front of the main entrance or at a specially designed site. A family's social standing is also measured by criteria other than material achievement. For instance, many members of Muslim women's groups who live in a state of relative deprivation nonetheless capitalize on a lively network of neighbors and peers. A primary indicator of a person's social connectedness is thus the extent to which he or she participates in networks of information exchange, mutual visits, and obligations. Popularity is assessed, for instance, by the frequency with which neighbors send small children to ask for little favors, for example, to borrow ingredients or utensils. Although these demands surely put a strain on a woman, they also testify to her integration into a network of mutual material, social, or moral assistance, and thus function as a bulwark against social death.

The Division of Responsibilities between Husband and Wife: Official Stories and "Hip Wrap" Versions

Divided Responsibilities

The distinction between public and private realms that emerged in Western European and North American societies in the eighteenth century does not conform to Malian social realities, even if public realms of communication in town bear characteristics that resemble those described by authors for eighteenth-century Europe. Local ideologies of gender difference map a normative scheme of gender inequality onto spatially segregated domains. Yet these female and male realms of action cannot be equated with a private realm of the family and a public domain of politics, as scholars working in the legacy of post-Enlightenment political theory claimed was the case in Western industrial societies (see Fraser 1992; Landes 1995; Weintraub and Kumar 1997; see also Comaroff 1987). The private as a realm of personal conviction, intimate sentiment, and interaction occupies a minor place in everyday life and is essentially relegated to the bedroom. The *gaa* or veranda is the place of legitimate sociality. No one spends even a few minutes with a guest or family member in his or her bedroom, a place reserved for sleep, sexual intercourse, and illness. On those rare occasions when people withdraw to a bedroom, it is clear that they are having an exceptionally important conversation that they want to keep secret.

Men are associated with the outside (*kènèma*) world where politics and economic affairs are conducted. A woman's place is at home, within the courtyard (*du*), yet her confinement to the courtyard is not absolute, even in areas where the influence of Islam reinforced the spatial separation of female and male activities. Women are omnipresent in the streets and the market, but they usually go out in groups of married women or, in the case of girls, with peers, often in the company of a young male relative. Because expectations are strong that a decent woman should spend as little time as possible outside the family, it is relatively easy for a husband or mother-in-law to reprimand a woman for freely "wandering around" (*yaala*) and spending time outside the courtyard, a reproach that implies the charge of promiscuity.

A woman's two principal vocations are matrimony and motherhood, and the success of her children in life contributes to her social and moral standing as much as her respectful demeanor vis-à-vis in-laws and seniors does. Compared to the honor/shame moral codex prevalent in Latin American, Caribbean, and Mediterranean societies, metaphors of female promiscuity and "natural" male sexual predation are less prominent in Mali. Still, norms of propriety do apply double standards, as they blame women for arousing sexual fantasies in men whereas men are considered to be sexually predatory "by nature." But men, too, are punished for committing adultery, and often more severely than women. The flip side of this double standard is that, although patriarchal norms of female propriety render a woman an easy target for admonition and control, acquiescence to these standards may become a source of influence. Early on in a woman's marriage the practice of virilocality, and the daily, emotionally charged, and burdensome interaction with her mother-in-law and sisters-in-law, gives her few reasons to feel at home. In her role as a wife and daughter(-in-law), she is in a position of dependency on men and submission to the directives of seniors; in the case of divorce she will have to return to her parents' home and leave her children behind. Over time, however, women are expected to establish themselves as permanent members of the family by creating an atmosphere of trust and solidarity (*badenya*) between them and their children. These relations of beneficial mutual dependence eventually allow a woman to exert influence through her children and over her daughters-in-law (Brand 2001; Roth 1994; Roost-Vischer 1997; see Potash 1986; Boddy 1992; Lambek 1992), if necessary by pitting them against the offspring of her co-wives.

The capacities of older women to make their voice heard within the court-yard, mostly in matters concerning the children's education and performance of household chores, is paralleled by the infamous "(hip) wrap power" (*taafe fanga*) adult women are said to have in the bedroom. The *taafe* wrap covers a woman's womb and thus the source of her powers: her capacity for procreation, her sexual attraction, and her ability to snub her husband's advances. Men allude to it whenever they seek to justify why they alone should decide on family matters. Many women readily concede that a wife is capable of turning family life into hell by combining her sexual attraction with her influence over her children. Other women, however, tend to dismiss the relevance of *taafe fanga* for family decisions. The extent to which wives actually capitalize on their *taafe fanga* depends on individual idiosyncrasies, as well as on the particular power constellation among co-wives and in-laws. This suggests that one should view assertions of the existence of complementary gendered realms as a conceptual ordering rather than as a blueprint for possible praxis. There are reasons to suspect that the gap between discursive representations of gender-specific roles and actual practice is widening under the influences of global economic transformations. As many men have to face a lack of work opportunities, women are forced to extend their activities beyond what is commonly seen as requisite female activity. Women differ in how ingeniously and imaginatively they draw on notions of female virtue to lend moral weight to their activities outside the household.

A Patriarchal Bargain under Stress

Similar to the discrepancy between the norm and praxis of gender-specific realms of influence, conventional views of the gendered division of financial responsibilities do not fit the exigencies of the current situation. In town, and increasingly so in rural areas, this lack of fit is most readily seen among the lower classes, but it is also evident in middle-class families. In rural southern Mali, women usually find opportunities to gain an independent, albeit limited, income. Marriage entitles them to small, individual plots on which they grow peanuts, cotton, and ingredients for the daily meal, and to call on the labor force of male in-laws. From family fields, men provide the staple food—mostly millet but in some areas rice and corn—and meat or fish occasionally. No husband has the right to use his wife's personal budget or labor product. Although women are responsible only for providing the ingredients of "the sauce" (*na*) that accompanies the daily staple food, they often do more, particularly in times of food shortage. They use their labor product to nurture an exchange network of favors and gifts that stretches beyond the confines of the husband's family, and to which they resort in situations of penury or intra-familial conflicts. A woman's capacity to mobilize this larger, partly kin-based, support network is key to how responsibilities will actually be divided between her and her husband, and between the generations.

In town, by contrast, the gender-specific division of labor and responsibilities is largely a matter of negotiation *between* spouses. Families who recently migrated to town suffer more from their inability to rely on a large support network than families with a longer-standing urban residency. As reflected in popular adages, the ideal husband is one who "makes [the family] live" (*balo*) by covering all its needs and providing his wives with a daily allowance, the "price of the sauce" (*nasongo*). Women are expected to find additional sources of income to satisfy their and "their children's little needs" (*olu den'w ka musaga*). This division of responsibility is an ideal to which men *and* women aspire. Whether they are capable of realizing this norm depends as much on individual choices and necessities as on external circumstances beyond their control. But with the implementation of the structural adjustment measures in the mid-1980s, chances to earn a regular income have diminished for men from these segments of the urban population. Many couples manage to maintain their middle-class living standard, but with the shrinking of the public sector and the lack of income sources in the formal economy, maintaining this standard requires greater support from wives and junior migrant workers (see Lachaud 1994). These changes affect conventional views of masculinity and male responsibilities.

"Du Fanga Tinyèna," "Family Authority Has Gone Kaput"

What modes of exemplary conduct are commonly expected from men, and what is now happening to these standards? Connell's (1995) view of coexistent hegemonic and subaltern norms of masculinity offers a useful entry point to address these questions,[8] as does Kandiyoti's (1994) distinction between age- and status-dependent ideals of masculinity. By emphasizing the polyvalent and contingent character of masculinity, I argue, we may gain a nuanced understanding of the role masculinity ideals play in the ways that adult men and women negotiate the terms of their interaction.

Predominant views of adult masculinity are closely related to the conventions that regulate the relations between the generations in rural households. Men in their role as heads of the household are in charge of family resources and their redistribution. Family fathers can expect that wives and children will cater to their whims, offer them drinking water, serve food, and respond to their demands at any time. As a correlate to their unchallenged authority, men are expected to adopt dignified behavior that commands "respect" (*bonya*) from juniors and women, and manifests itself in a rhetorical and emotional restraint, controlled facial expression, and physical self-discipline. These norms of embodied "dignity" (*dambe*) put men under psychological pressure and permanent scrutiny by male peers with whom they entertain relations of simultaneous camaraderie and competitiveness. Interactions between men of unequal status, such as between fathers and sons, are ruled by expressive restraint rather than verbal explicitness. Still, although juniors should heed a father's command without further ado, negotiations between juniors and seniors do take place, but most often through the intervention of a third party (either the father's peer or a woman of senior status).

I already mentioned that a woman pays a heavy toll for the influence she holds late in her life, as she needs to comply with the rules of female propriety until her children are grown. Senior women, in particular, view such standards of conduct as unalterable tradition that, although not fair, ensures social stability and moral orientation within the family. They justify their endorsement of patriarchal norms by relating it to their own experiences, and see submissiveness and patience as capacities that, deliberately acquired, are signs of moral strength and emotional self-control. Yet even if many female interlocutors, at least those "in their prime" (Kerns and Brown 1992), agree that acquiescence is central to female propriety, the existence of this norm tells us little about why and to what extent women of junior status accommodate it.

Deniz Kandiyoti (1988) coined the term "patriarchal bargain" to explain why women in Middle Eastern Muslim societies comply with patriarchal norms of female propriety, even if they go against their personal sense of dignity. She argued that women may adopt a code of conduct even if it contravenes their own (short-term) interests, because they consider it the price they have to pay for their husbands' and male relatives' protection and material support. Kandiyoti's suggestion that long-term considerations play a role in women's compliance with patriarchal norms of gender is pertinent to the situation in many urban households in Mali. Although women's compliance should not be reduced to strategic considerations, my interlocutors' reflections on their domestic situation do suggest that they view docile conduct as a possibility to enhance their bargaining position. I frequently heard a woman enumerate the physical and emotional toll paid in dealing with an irritable husband and his preferential treatment of other wives. Yet the same woman would then assert that "only endurance [*munyu*] puts a woman in a position where she might request support in situations of difficulty." This means that a woman's acquiescence to her marital duties puts a husband under a moral obligation that, though not directly enforceable, grants the woman a realm of normative protection that is sanctioned by the immediate social entourage.

To view marital relationships as dynamic arrangements in which women seek to create or enhance bargaining power allows us to move beyond conventional yet deceptive assumptions of women's oppression under the yoke of (Muslim) patriarchy. To assess the theoretical implications of this analytical perspective, we must contextualize the notion of "bargain" by setting it against the background of changing household economies. Only then can we understand how increased economic insecurity affects the relations between husband and wife, between junior and senior members of the household, and the bargaining position of women. Let us, then, return to people's accounts of *gèlèya* in town and explore in more detail the material, social, and moral insecurities that they associate with this term.

Elders' Greed, *Nasòngo* Disputes, and the "Shortage of Men"

In many urban households, daily life is permeated with more or less open confrontations that place women in opposition to their husbands and structure relations between co-wives, peers, and friends. These disputes reflect the uncertainties emerging from shifting responsibilities between spouses and from an eroding sense of mutual obligation between the generations. Most quarrels arise over financial contributions, particularly to the "price of the sauce" (*nasòngo*), that is, the daily meals. Another source of conflict is the discrepancy between people's financial situation and their yearning for greater individual freedom, a yearning sustained by media images and consumer goods. Given the often painfully experienced economic scarcity, and the limitations on people's choices this engenders, these desires typically go unfulfilled (see Ferguson 2002).

These conflicts color people's perception of everyday life and configure their "horizon of experience," a horizon of what is imaginable and feasible (Negt and Kluge 1993). Spatial confinement within the courtyard makes it difficult for people to evade this conflict-ridden atmosphere. Their sense of psychological and emotional pressure emerges in daily conversations about conflicts between family members and between friends or neighbors. Because relatives and friends can play a mercurial role in these conflicts, for instance, by providing emotional support to a woman or by pinching her lover, women (and men) eye each other carefully over an extended "probation" period before becoming confidants. These insecurities congeal in people's frequent complaint that "marriage has become a difficult affair" (*konyo kèra baara ye*).

Marriage is essential in becoming a "complete" woman (*muso dafalen*) and a "real man" (*cè yèrè*), that is, in gaining full adult status and achieving a certain economic independence. Although the capacity to procreate is important for both men and women, marriage as a step toward *legitimate* procreation is more essential for women. Unmarried women, therefore, are often torn between their desire to marry a partner of their own choosing on the basis of mutual affection and the risk of missing the opportunity altogether of becoming a socially, physiologically, and morally "complete" (*kika*) woman through marriage. After some hesitation, many discard their expectations of a romantic relationship and instead discern the advantages of becoming their husband's favorite (*baaramuso*) among his many wives.[9]

Notwithstanding the desirability of being a married woman, marital life exposes women (and men) to a range of conflicting interests and expectations. Dominant standards of gender propriety grant men more choice by authorizing them to exercise control in marital matters and, if necessary, impose their will by force. But men must also be accommodating in order to respond to the tensions emerging between their spouses and own kin, tensions that are structurally embedded yet also result from the different expectations that men and women have toward marriage (see Rebhun 1999, chap. 9). Even if a woman's marriage is strengthened by the support of her relatives and in-laws, she may experience material and emotional vulnerability that is often compounded by an atmosphere of disappointment and subliminal resentment in her new homestead. Whenever a woman has to share her husband with co-wives or lovers, occasions for conflict multiply. Arguments, which sometimes become physically abusive, arise between her and her husband, and between her and those who compete with her over the husband's financial and emotional attentions. Against this backdrop, the concern of adult men with marriage that "becomes a *nasòngo* affair" and with women who are devoid of love appears in a new light. "They don't like people, they like things, they are only after money" (*U tè mògò fè, u bè fen de fè, u bè wari ko dòròn de*) is a common refrain. These complaints illustrate men's fear that their inability to provide for women and offspring undermines a central pillar of adult masculinity and patriarchal power.

Women, too, tend to blame other women for the erosion of trust, friendship, and love. Their competition over material contributions from suitors and husbands, and over the advancement in social standing these favors effect, fuels a spectacular occult economy and manifests itself in numerous anecdotes among friends and neighbors about "immoral" and "envious" women (Schulz 2001b, 2005). Older women often deplore the "lack of love" expressed by their daughters-in-law and (occasionally) their daughters.[10] Young women, in turn, challenge the "greed" of their critics, an accusation that hints at their resentment of their own economic dependency and of senior in-laws' status and control. The envy reigning among women thus cuts across the generational divide and reflects a pervasive sense of shortage in opportunities of income generation, social networking, and control.

The flip side of male youth's observation that "marriage is a matter of money" (*furu ko kèra wari ko de ye*) is the complaint by younger women about "men's slowness" in choosing a marriage partner (*cew ka suman, u tè furu fè*) and about a "shortage in men." These grievances point to young men's reluctance to marry at the conventional age, a result of their lack of financial autonomy, but also reveal their reticence toward the constraints that this change in their life-cycle status would entail.[11] All these tropes of the envious and unfeeling woman, sauce price disputes, and dishonest men, then, allow people to address their material and emotional insecurities through a moralizing assessment of their own and the other sex. That unmarried women feel particularly vulnerable under the current circumstances was brought home forcefully by Mariam, a program coordinator of a local radio station in San. In late February 2000, on a walk home from a preparatory meeting for International Women's Day, we were deeply immersed in assessing our color and cut preferences for the costume that members of the local women's association to which Mariam belonged planned to wear on that occasion. As we passed by some market stands, a vendor of beignets intercepted us in a pleasant manner and wrapped up several extra-large beignets for Mariam to take home to her children. As we moved on, I casually asked Mariam whether this was a friend of hers. Her reaction was a silent, sardonic smile. Once we had reached her home and finished lunch, she responded to my question by reflecting on the nature of female friendship.

> The woman who gave me the beignets did not do it out of friendship. Envy and calculation is on her mind. She wants me to aggrandize her reputation over the radio. People speak badly about those whom they envy for their popularity. Since I have started working at the radio, everywhere people greet me whom I have never met. Every day, people come to visit me. Others spend hours gossiping on how many gifts I receive [from suitors]. Some friends have turned their back on me because they envy me. They don't even talk to me anymore. The nature of true friendship is that a friend is pleased about your popularity. . . . Nowadays, in these times of hardship, friendship has become a difficult affair. Even women who once were close friends envy each other for their popularity, for friends who become their [material] support, for a husband, and for a reputation.

Mariam's comment highlights the central importance of sociality to a person's sense of dignity. "Popularity," the ingredient of social attraction, can be translated into material assets and other forms of value. Publicity is another social asset from which a sense of personal worth and dignity is constructed. "Popularity" and "envy" constitute two poles between which individuals navigate to achieve social and moral standing among peers and neighbors. Envy is popularity's most dangerous challenge, as it unravels a person's capacity to convert social attractiveness into material favors.

The Revision of Marital Obligations in the Era of Economic Liberalization

Current economic reality makes it difficult for men and women to keep their budgets and responsibilities separate. The maintenance of separate financial responsibilities depends on a household's capacities to minimize the effects of an erratic income. Thus the current economic situation has the severest consequences for lower-class households with few (working) adults and teenagers. Families that were affected by the shrinking of the state bureaucracy in the late 1980s are often able to minimize the resulting economic repercussions because of the diversity of income sources on which they relied. Among low-income groups, in contrast, high rates of unemployment and the small profit range for many informal economic activities render men's contributions unreliable. Consequently, the number of women who are the main breadwinners has risen significantly over the past fifteen years.[12] To cover extra expenses, these women call on the support of their kin, their grown children, and, although with varying success, on in-laws. Simultaneously, they often seek to uphold the appearance of their husband's patriarchal authority. As some of them hesitantly admitted, they regularly pass on their earnings to their husband so that he might keep up the impression that he was the main provider. In helping him save face, women argued, they paid their husband "their due respect," an expression that suggests that they are under substantial normative pressure to uphold their share of the patriarchal bargain. But in some cases it was also evident that women's clandestine support of their husband gave them a greater weight in family decisions, for instance, with regard to their children's school enrollment.

Among the most destitute segments of the urban population, men and women are pushed into informal economic activities characterized by a high level of "self-employment," a euphemism that conceals the vicious circle and extreme psychological insecurity that people face in their day-to-day struggle to make ends meet.[13] Because they have almost no access to credit and product supply, their economic activities yield meager and unpredictable returns. Also, their activities are untaxed and unofficial, and therefore exceedingly vulnerable to state agents' extortion strategies. What happens to marital relationships under these conditions, when husbands are no longer capable of fulfilling their share of the conventional patriarchal bargain? The coping strategies of women with whom I interacted regularly show that, in spite of their diverse economic situations, attempts to counter the effects of recent economic insecurity are rather uniform. This suggests that economic standing alone cannot explain the variety of effects of economic liberalization on urban households.

Taking over Responsibility

I do not live, I simply survive.

—Female head of household, forty-nine years old, fourteen maternities, thirteen living children, Bamako, September 1999

Teltscher has recently criticized studies on informal economies for ignoring the great variety of economic actors who operate in this sector (Teltscher 1992; see de Miras 1987; McCormick 1996). Also, because most authors focus on manufacturing activities in the informal sector, they disregard trade as a major source of income. As a result, many authors do not investigate the diverse determinants establishing socioeconomic difference among operators in the informal sector. Drawing on data from urban Ecuador, Teltscher argues that socioeconomic hierarchies among operators of the informal economy result from their differential access to capital and products, and less so from exploitative wage labor relations. These mechanisms of stratification are also at work in the informal Malian economy; they explain the range of income opportunities open to women of different economic standing.

Women opt for particular trade opportunities and items according to the availability of starting capital and the seasonal availability of food. As in other African contexts (e.g., Lachaud 1994; Sheldon 1996), women frequently switch back and forth between different trades according to fluctuations in seasonal demand; they also expand their activities to those that are more profitable. In the absence of a clear-cut socioeconomic hierarchy, one can distinguish between three "ideal types" of female actors. The first are highly successful businesswomen who engage in long-distance trade of cloth, kitchen utensils, and other goods, and who rely on other employees. Because their profit margins are impressive (Vaa, Findley, and Diallo 1989), they have much in common with the famous "Nana Benz" of Ghana and other West African countries. These women access a variety of trade networks, often in domains in which women have a long-standing presence, such as in the long-distance commerce conducted by women in the triangle Bamako-Dakar (via railway) and the Gambia (Lambert de Frondeville 1987; Lambert 1993). The case of Thérèse, a friend of mine since 1992, illustrates the high profit this commerce generates. In 1997, after the sudden death of her husband, a successful merchant whose business had regularly taken him to the United States, Thérèse realized that her in-laws offered only limited support for her and her five children. Until then "just a housewife," she embarked on several trips to France and Belgium where she sold locally dyed mud cloth shirts and, in return, bought toiletry items for Malian upper-class women. She then gradually expanded her business to other West African countries, especially Ivory Coast, Ghana, and Benin, where she bought various items for African migrant consumers in France. When I last met Thérèse at a baptizing ceremony in February 2004, she arrived with her driver in a Mercedes Benz, and stunned visitors, family, and friends by the lavish gifts she bestowed on the newborn's grandmother. When I asked her whether she intended to remarry, she retorted, with a broad smile, that this "would jeopardize her children's economic situation." Cases such as Thérèse's are unusual in that her new economic autonomy did not trigger marital conflicts; other successful businesswomen, in contrast, suffer from the ambivalent implications of their economic prowess for their relations to their husband and mother-in-law.

Other women entrepreneurs are successful in domains that are relatively new for women. Among them are wives and sisters of well-established Muslim traders who use their husbands' connections or their own family ties to North Africa and Saudi Arabia to embark on long-distance trade in religious paraphernalia and highly sought-after Arab-style fashion accessories. Among these women are leading protagonists of the Muslim renewal movement who, for reasons of propriety, rely on daughters or other female relatives to conduct business in the Arab world. These women's ventures breed conflicts between the generations because they endow their junior partners with financial responsibilities that give them greater economic autonomy and weight in family affairs. Senior women traders sometimes lament these side effects, but they believe the advantages exceed the drawbacks. Most notably, their trade increases their capacity to compensate the effects of the tightening of the labor market, a process they describe as a "shortage in [making] money." In some families, the abilities of women entrepreneurs to compensate for their husband's lack of income are so substantial that the repercussions of structural reform are hardly felt.

The second type of female entrepreneurs, the "restauratrices de la nuit," have fewer opportunities to cope with financial hardship (Rondeau 1989; see Diouf 1981). They prepare and sell food at bus or railway stations, or in the market, from mid-afternoon until late at night. These women form a category of traders whose substantial starting capital allows them to gain an income equal to that of a high school teacher (about 50,000 FCFA per month).[14] Women engage in this trade to cover daily expenses or because they want greater economic autonomy for themselves and their children. In contrast to these women, the third type of economic actor comes from families that cannot rely on a predictable income and struggle to make ends meet. Because these women have little or no starting capital, their available economic niches are limited, and their earnings are unpredictable and extremely low.[15] They produce goods for immediate consumption, such as handicrafts and ingredients or processed food, such as grilled meat, beignets, and grilled and salted peanuts, sold in front of their doorways or by a child walking door to door. Another possibility is to resell "en detail" vegetables and fruits purchased for a low price from a benevolent patron, an activity of last resort because it offers little return. A more profitable activity that also requires a greater investment is the sale of embroidered or tie-dyed cloth. Many members of the Muslim women's associations I attended in

San and Bamako engage in this kind of trade to generate a starting capital for more profitable ventures.

More so than the two other types of economic actors, women from the lowest strata of the urban population frequently shift between different economic activities. They often need loans from peers and friends to start a business; those who failed to repay their debts in the past are reluctant to ask for loans for fear of further damaging their credibility. Their search for makeshifts solutions[16] and their dependency on those in their social entourage who "feel compassion" create feelings of helplessness and shame (*maloya*). This situation, once a distinctive sign of low-income groups, has spread dramatically since the 1980s and affects people across the range of lower-middle-class households (Rondeau 1989). Women describe this situation as one of poverty, *faantanya,* a term that refers to financial penury and the feelings of sorrow and shame that accompany it. The term also conveys the fear of being unable to reciprocate and act as a social being by offering basic tokens of hospitality. As Aicha, a woman in her mid-thirties from San, expressed it,

> What I learned in the years of my hardship is that a person alone is nothing in this world. God is my witness, Nanaje, this was a hard lesson to learn. . . . God the Merciful knows the heavy toll I pay. Look at me. Before, I used to go out and socialize. But now that I cannot reciprocate people's gifts, . . . I stay at home. You feel such shame if you only receive.

Whereas "poverty," understood as economic deprivation, applies first and foremost to low-income families, people across the socioeconomic divide feel menaced by *faantanya*'s shadow. *Faantanya* encapsulates the imminent threat of social death that comes with one's inability to return gifts. As we shall see, the ways that women of different economic backgrounds cope with this threat depend on their and their family's economic standing and, importantly, on the quality of kin and peer support.

"One Person Alone Is Nothing in This World": Women's Search for Security

How do women from destitute households experience their situation, and what strategies do they develop to achieve material and emotional security? Women in the low-income neighborhoods in San and Bamako offered me strikingly similar accounts of their circumstances. The following account is by Ina, a woman from the Badialan Muslim women's group in Bamako.

The event that marked me for the rest of my life was the illness of my husband and, after that, his death. This changed my life from one day to the other. . . . All our income had been spent on medicine, this is what made us poor. . . . The children had to quit school. . . . When I think about my situation I no longer want to live, I no longer want to do anything. Look at me, I do not even plait my hair or put henna on my feet. I do not live, I simply survive. My belief in God is what keeps me going. . . . I know that screaming and crying doesn't help. . . . Wherever I look, there is no way out. I cannot change destiny, I can only abide by it. But God can change things. A couple of weeks ago, people were celebrating the Mawlud. I had been awake all night asking myself, we do not even have something to eat, how can we celebrate our Prophet's birthday? Then the son of my benefactor [i.e., the family for whom she occasionally does the laundry] came and gave me 1000 FCFA to buy rice and make *seri* [rice soup] for my children. . . . As long as God is on our side, there will always be a tomorrow. We will always find some makeshift solution.

Women like Ina have few choices. Still, like other women, she invokes "God's help" in depicting her situation as one of material hardship but not of *faantanya*. In response to circumstances that exclude any prospect of generating a regular income, they seek to build a support network constituted by kin, in-laws, and friends, as much as their meager means of reciprocation allow them to. Adopting the argument that women's economic networks are more important than men's for maintaining a family among the urban poor (see Vaa, Findley, and Diallo 1989; Chant 1999; Iken 1999), we need to explore the social network within which women operate in order to fully understand women's strategies for generating security. How do these de facto household heads mobilize support, and what are the limits, both financially and morally, to their reliance on a support network?

Whereas rural society is structured by an elaborate economy of gifts, favors, and obligations among kin and in-laws, in town reliance on kin varies with the particular family constellation, economic background, and individual preferences. Whereas more middle-class families practice the norm of primary kin reliance, poorer families are unable to realize this norm. Many women resort to an imaginary "pecking order" of relatives and friends whom they ask for gifts of "compassion" (*hinè*), sometimes without their husband's knowledge. They are often reluctant to ask their in-laws for help, because in-laws are quick to ridicule them about their husband's economic failure. Some give up on their in-laws altogether and turn to their own relatives for occasional support, even if they risk "being insulted" (*nenini*) by them as well. All this places a heavy strain and psychological pressure on women and their relatives.

Labor migration usually results in a transfer of wealth from the city to the countryside (Institut des Sciences Humaines 1984; Findley 1994; Fall 1995), but this trend seems to be slowing down among the urban poor. In many cases, it even brings about a reversal in the direction of flow and in the obligations between generations.[17] Although it is assumed that children should provide for their parents, widespread unemployment makes it difficult to meet this expectation. Families living on the brink of subsistence are most seriously affected by their children's inability to provide for them. Aissata, a woman around sixty years of age who, together with her husband and co-wife's family, lives in an extremely poor household in San, put it this way: "In these times of hardship, things have changed. . . . Children no longer work for their parents. Many of them give what they can, but they are helpless. This is what creates much concern for me.[18]

Women habitually articulate their sense of entitlement vis-à-vis their children, and they do so regardless of the child's gender. But they count especially on their daughters' emotional attachment, reflecting the pattern of mother-daughter relationships in rural society that are based on close emotional bonds and mutual obligation. Mothers' frequent assertion that they "prefer girls to boys" also suggests that norms of intergenerational dependency make it easier to morally oblige a daughter than a son. Women's repeated emphasis on their daughters' importance to them seems to contradict their frequent allegations that younger women are "selfish" and "envious." Yet both assertions delineate models of behavior open to daughters. Only daughters who offer their mothers "support" are considered to pay them their due respect (*bonya*). Whether this support comes as material or emotional aid, daughters across the socioeconomic divide most often labor to respond to this moral obligation. But what happens to women who cannot rely on the support of children?

Beyond the Family: Exchange Networks among Peers

Authors have argued that, in contrast to Malian rural society where networks of social and economic security operate on notions of kin solidarity, in town networks of extra-familial support prevail (Vaa, Findley, and Diallo 1989; Fall 1995). I found that in the lower-class neighborhoods of San and Bamako many women expand their security networks and engage in various forms of reciprocal aid but that peer networks are their primary source of support only in some cases. One reason for this is that many women in my "study group" seem to be in a more precarious situation financially than the women Vaa and colleagues (1989) worked with.[19] Careful analysis is thus needed of women's differential coping strategies by relating them to differences in family composition, personal preferences, and socioeconomic standing. Although differences in income are important in delimiting women's choices, my claim is that socioeconomic background interacts in complex ways with other factors and should thus be examined.

Similar to informal economies in other African contexts, credit savings associations are important institutions of mutual support among urban women. These associations, called *tonw* (singular, *ton; pari* in French), are created by women who regularly socialize and share a similar age, socioeconomic background, and intra-family status.[20] Group members make regular contributions that range from daily to monthly installments and are collected by the elected leader, the *tontigi* or *pariba* (Projet Urbain du Mali 1984, quoted in Vaa, Findley, and Diallo 1989, 343).[21] The collected sum is accessed by each member in turn, who will use it to start an economic operation or repay debts from previous activities. The rotating funds thus enable women to embark on more capital-intensive operations that promise a higher return. Women across the economic divide participate in a *ton,* yet because only those who can regularly contribute are accepted, women from the most destitute strata of urban Mali generally do not take part in them. Of the twenty-five women of this background with whom I was more closely acquainted, none participated in a *ton.* Several had once been a member but dropped out because they were ashamed of their limited financial funds—yet another expression of *faantanya.* Others chose not to join a *ton* not out of fear or shame but because they had heard many stories of the misappropriation of *ton* funds. Thus women from poor families are often ambivalent toward *tonw,* just as they are about extra-familial support networks. If credit savings associations appear too risky for women with limited resources, or if the prospect of gaining access to an association is foreclosed, what forms of support do they create?

While considerations of finances and decency limit a woman's reliance on extra-familial support, most women from economically dysfunctional families "entrust" themselves in one way or another to the help of peers and friends. But the ways that women resolve their ambivalent feelings regarding peer cooperation differ greatly. Some prefer to rely on (irregular) kin support rather than on the compassion of neighbors because they are ashamed of their incapacity to reciprocate. Others prefer to call on kin for greater sums and in cases of emergency but rely on peers for small gifts such as food or meager amounts of money or services that help their social network. Their occasional exchange of gifts and favors can therefore be seen as an important strategy for generating security. Credit associations should therefore be regarded as only one, that is, the most formalized, institution of mutual support that allows women to create revenue out of little or no capital. Women who engage in the occasional exchange of favors and money refer to these donations as "gifts," suggesting that they consider this exchange a morally and economically important transaction, similar to the Maussian notion of a "gift."[22] Even women who do not regularly take part in "gift" networks feel that these favors are central to their sense of moral personhood because they generate long-term relations of mutual dependency and trust; for some, they are the last resource on which they may capitalize.

Women who live under more economically secure conditions engage in various structures of peer support, because they strive for a certain level of economic independence from their husband. This is so mainly because a woman's ability to provide for her kin is central to notions of moral personhood that define a "good" daughter as one who is generous and responsive to her relatives' demands. Thus the participation of these financially more fortunate women in exchange networks can also be seen as a response to the repercussions of economic liberalization. Financially secure and insecure women alike feel that gift exchange "play[s] an important part in helping people to cope with everyday demands and shifts of fortune" (Vaa, Findley, and Diallo 1989, 256). To all these women, extra-familial support facilitates a certain autonomy on which they capitalize to different effects, depending on their family situation.

Men's Discursive Regulation of Gender Relations

How do men respond to these developments, particularly to the challenge that women's greater autonomy poses to patriarchal family authority? If we consider their narrative constructions of personal experience as one form of response, we see that men, similar to women, combine two moralizing idioms: one concerning envy and the other the scarcity of means. Married men associate these phenomena with life in town and with a situation of "generalized envy" in which men compete over professional success. As a close friend, a carpenter in San, expressed it, "Life in town is not easy. Everyone wants to have the position of his neighbor. Envy rules all relations. People envy each other for their success and their popularity."

In men's narratives, the subject of moral disorder is almost without exception female, even if men are the principal protagonists. All these accounts offer reflections on the corrosive effects of money on social relations and on the "love" and moral obligation that should bind people together. The immoral woman, one who spurns love and "is only after money," is held responsible for whatever men consider the pernicious effects of urban life (Schulz 2001b). Unmarried younger men, many of whom are in poor financial conditions, are often the ones who most explicitly blame women for the degradation of moral standards. For instance, a neighbor in San, Sheikene, whose work as a driver earned him between 500 and 1,500 FCFA a day, blamed "girls" for the fact that he dropped out of school and had subsequent difficulties finding a well-paid job; these "girls," he claimed, were ultimately "just prostitutes" (*sunguruba*) who lured him into spending his money on them. He added,

> Any woman can be bought with money, only the sum varies with the category she belongs to. Usually it costs between 500 and 15,000. Uh, women are expensive. . . . For some, it is possible to get a woman just by dressing up. She will come with him . . . and count on his promise to give her some money the next day. Thank God, right now women are cheap because they need money to buy fabric, shoes, and *meshi* [artificial hair] [for the holiday *selicinin* marking the end of Ramadan].

This narrative pinpoints the ambivalences of desire and disdain that young men, short of money, experience vis-à-vis lovers and future wives. "Greedy girls" are the motor of social disintegration, and of rivalries between men to which Sheikene makes passing reference. A proper woman, in contrast, acts out of "love" and gratefully accepts whatever a man gives her spontaneously. By contrasting money-mediated relations to a disinterested gift exchange based on "true love," my interlocutor claims that women's search for money is at the root of their own dilemmas. This portrayal resembles the ways in which the Catholic societies of southern Europe and Latin America define female propriety by contrasting sexual promiscuity ("whore") and self-restraint ("madonna"), but it also includes a discourse on money and its destructive powers.

The contrast between non-monetary gift exchange and money-mediated forms of social interaction pervades many people's accounts of social change, not just those by young men. Young women apply it in their complaints about dishonest lovers, other women's "envy," and the shortage of men; older people's irritation with the "selfishness" of their juniors reflects a similar preoccupation with money as a corrosive force. All these accounts echo widespread tendencies in contemporary Africa and Latin America to hold money accountable for the erosion of moral, socially binding values (e.g., Taussig 1980; Weiss 1996; see Parry and Bloch 1989). Yet, significantly, they also share an inclination to feminize social and moral disorder (Schulz 2001b; Dilger and Luig 2010). Although the gender dynamics on which they reflect are historically specific, people's discursive representation of insatiable women puts current conflicts in a timeless framework and lends this explanatory scheme an indeterminate and unlimited validity. The *passe-partout* applicability of this moralizing idiom may explain why female immorality is so widespread in accounts of the disruption of moral and social reproduction throughout postcolonial Africa.

Men's opprobrium of "insatiable women" reveals their fears that they will no longer keep women "in check," particularly those for whom school education opens the door to economic independence and a stronger sense of individuality. Listening to conversations among young men, I was often struck by the vehemence with which some denounced educational and other reforms that would give girls new opportunities for social advancement. I found that local radio call-in programs were another site where male youth voiced their apprehensions. One evening in San in March 2000, for instance, a weekly call-in program staged a live debate on the question of female education. Prompted by the radio speaker's fictional account of a girl in sixth grade whose parents forced her to quit school and get married instead, several young men arrived at the station to offer their point of view. The first studio guest criticized the parents' decision as short-sighted, as it foreclosed their daughter's chances for professional advancement. But the second speaker wholeheartedly endorsed the parental decision, arguing that early marriage was "a woman's ultimate vocation" (*furu de ye muso dambe ye*). He was supported by a third studio guest who claimed that his expertise as a tenth-grade schoolteacher qualified him for a judicious assessment of the disadvantages of secondary school education for girls. His main objection against higher education for girls was, he added, that

> a woman who received some education or even a degree
> from some place in Europe, . . . will try to win the upper
> hand in her marriage. She . . . will take advantage of [her]
> . . . higher education to control the husband. No wonder
> that parents refuse to send their daughters to school. They
> fear that their girls will not find a marriage partner, and God
> is my witness, I myself would never choose such a woman.

The irony that a schoolteacher adamantly rejected female education escaped the notice of all the studio guests. As the program continued, I left the studio and joined the radio director and the teacher in front of the radio station. They were scandalized by my remark that the studio guests' emphasis on women's striving for control was one-sided. To convince me that my skepticism was entirely misplaced, the director volunteered a "true" story that had been broadcast on his program earlier that year. The story's truthfulness, the director observed, was substantiated by the great interest it had generated among local listeners. As I listened to the narrative, I was struck by its resemblance to stories I had been told by younger men on other occasions that reflected their concern with eroding patriarchal authority structures.

The director's story recounts the trials of "Maiga," whose infatuation with "Oumou," a poor girl from the neighborhood, leads to his ultimate demise. Exploited and deserted by Oumou, who is transformed from a poor yet beautiful girl to one of the most highly educated women of the country, Maiga is imprisoned and, upon his release, ends up in the hands of another woman who cheats on him. Similar to the studio debate and to other personal-interest stories broadcast on local radio, the anecdote identifies women's education as a path toward moral laxity and the destruction of orderly gender relations. A woman's independent income directs a final blow to a man's superior position. The story thus intertwines the narrative elements in men's accounts of recent social and economic change: it establishes a causal connection between women's economic self-reliance, greater autonomy from family control, sexual promiscuity, and betrayal. That such anecdotes are popular among various male audiences, among them the educated elites, illustrates the widespread apprehension about a process that, since the early 1990s, has allowed women to move into the highest echelons of political power. This narrative scheme, far from merely serving men as a way to make sense of their current dilemmas, provides men with a blueprint for action, for keeping women and daughters "in check."

Certainly male accounts of their dilemmas are not uniform. Among my closest acquaintances were several men who maintained that others' complaints about rebellious women primarily revealed their own fears about their loss of authority. Modibo, with whom I had frequent discussions in San, offered a frank assessment of men's dilemmas.[23]

> Nobody can imagine what a man feels who is unable to do what his own father used to do for his family. People say the problem is *faantanya* [poverty], but I say, it is shame [*maloya*]. Before, fathers were afraid to be discredited by children who misbehaved. Nowadays, fathers fear being humiliated by their sons . . . who struggle to provide for the family. Before, it was the behavior of others that put shame on you. Now it is yourself. And it is not wrongdoing, it is that you do *nothing* which makes you feel ashamed. Even worse, formerly you kept it to yourself when your children shamed you so that neighbors would not know what your children did to you. Nowadays, you depend on your

children's confidentiality. You hope that they will not tell others what you failed to do. The world is put upside down. Sons are expected to respect their fathers, but I ask you: for what reason [should they respect them]? How can they be men with a sense of dignity, if their fathers cannot walk upright because they are so embarrassed?

As Modibo suggests, fathers constantly fend off attempts by juniors, as well as by wives, to "nibble away" at their patriarchal authority. Notably Modibo speaks of his sons, not his wives, as the principal source of his shame. He suggests that fathers define patriarchal control as much through their relation of "care" for the younger generation as through their marital relations. His perspective calls into question the tendency of some studies to define patriarchy as primarily a relationship between men and women. This raises the question as to whether key claims of the new "Men's Studies" are applicable to urban settings in Mali and throughout contemporary Africa (e.g., Seidler 1991, 1992; Segal 1993; Brod and Kaufman 1994; Connell 1995; MacInnes 1998). Rather than argue that masculinity per se is "in crisis," we need to explore what particular pillar of patriarchal authority is undermined. In urban and rural Mali, patriarchal family authority is weakened because, Modibo suggests, many fathers are no longer able to accumulate wealth, by their own work and that of their juniors, and to redistribute it down through the generations. Adult men rightly fear that their loss of control weakens established patriarchal ideology and norms. But their frequent complaints about the greed of children and women are ambiguous. They resent the economic and moral obligations that weigh on them because they often do not have the means to meet these expectations. At the same time their denouncement of women's rebelliousness reveals that there are advantages to keeping women and juniors economically dependent because this maintains fatherly control. Fathers' loss of control is not a new phenomenon, nor is it limited to urban areas. Still, recent economic liberalization measures invigorate processes that facilitate economic independence of the young and affect broader segments of the urban population.

It remains to be seen how adult men's failure to meet the terms of the patriarchal bargain will affect current ideals of masculinity. Rather than claiming that these ideals are changing irreversibly, it seems that men across the socioeconomic divide reassert and simultaneously redefine adult masculinity by comparing it to an imaginative past moral order. Adult men and adolescents react to the erosion of entrenched ideals of male superiority by placing the blame on women's search for independence and lack of propriety. They identify the relations *between* the sexes as the main problem, even if they uneasily acknowledge that their difficulties derive as much from conflicts between the generations as from wives and girlfriends. Their preoccupation with female (im)morality should prompt us to more rigorously develop "gender studies" into an exploration of both genders and of the differences among men along several axes.

The Mixed Blessings of Greater Female Responsibility

This chapter treated power constellations in urban households as resulting from an ongoing process of "bargaining" and signifying practices, effected at the intersections of gender, generation, changing socioeconomic positions, and multiple, sometimes religiously inspired, blueprints for normative evaluation. Regardless of the socioeconomic standing of individual women and their families, the structural adjustment measures yield equivocal results for women's choices. Economic liberalization has forced women into new fields of responsibility and self-reliance, yet it simultaneously puts them under additional pressure to comply with norms of female propriety.

The ways that women respond to these novel opportunities and challenges depend on various factors, among them the particular power constellations within their family as well as their individual personality and upbringing. Women feel considerable pressure to straddle various needs and expectations, and to constantly improvise solutions to both material and normative constraints and demands. Anxieties emerging from the need to juggle the positive and negative aspects of greater financial responsibility are particularly marked in low-income households. The variety of strategies that women make use of vividly illustrates the coexistence of contending paradigms of femininity. Competing ideals of female propriety and accomplishment are generated and assessed in various personal interactions and intimate settings. Their mobilization in public arenas, sometimes fueled by political controversies and new media platforms, provides women with multiple occasions to reconsider and circulate views of self-esteem and personal worth in a dialectical process of individual and social, public and intimate articulations of ideals of femininity and moral personhood.

To conclude, I offer some reflections on women's sense of personal worth by returning to questions raised earlier in this chapter: What are the moral dimensions and women's subjective experiences of "poverty"? How does being in a state of "poverty" affect women's self-perception and self-esteem, as well as their bargaining position vis-à-vis their husbands? Many women from low-income households do not feel stigmatized or excluded. Only a few should therefore be considered "poor" in Salama's conception of subjective poverty, inasmuch as they feel incapable of meeting common standards of female responsibility. The majority of the women, in contrast, display a marked sense of dignity and of being in control of their life. By emphasizing women's sense of self-worth, I do not mean to minimize the anxieties they are exposed to; nor do I mean to downplay the gravity and precariousness of the situation in which women from low-income households find themselves. There is no way to adequately render the vulnerability and extent of suffering that goes with the daily experiences of these women. The few quotations I provided from my interlocutors cannot, by any means, capture how deeply grieved these mothers are about the persistent lack of means to care for their beloved ones and to ensure a better future for their children. Thus, although it is a mistake to describe "poor" women as helpless, we should be careful not to idealize women's often desperate survival tactics as instances of women's self-directed agency. My portrayal of the restrictions imposed on women's possibilities of capitalizing on their powers of reproduction points to the limitations of an analytical perspective that stresses women's capacities for deliberate choices. These are strong reasons to move beyond dichotomous assumptions that portray women as either subdued by patriarchy or economic conditions, or as imaginatively subverting existing economic and social inequalities.

THREE

Family Conflicts:
Domestic Life Revisited by Media Practices

Assessing Mass-Mediated Subjectivities in Urban Mali

When I lived in San in 1999, I found that passionate debates arose in my host family each night as soon as the evening's television serial began. The family and visitors would excitedly gather around the television set to comment on the drama unfolding on the screen. On Friday nights and weekends the streets of San's usually animated city center looked deserted shortly before 10 PM, the hour at which the telenovela *Rose Sauvage* started. Fervent supporters of Islamic moral renewal also organized their evenings around installments of televised family drama. These media consumers' intense engagement with television drama reflects the increasing permeation of everyday urban life with mass-media products and with mass-mediated forms of experience.

Departing from earlier generalizations about the culturally homogenizing effects of mass-media consumption, recent scholarship has drawn attention to the room mass media offer for creativity and partial appropriation, depending on the institutional context in which media products are produced, circulated, and interpreted (e.g., Manuel 1993; Wilk 2002). Even in cases where global television genres are produced under state supervision, consumers' interpretations often collide with, rather than conform to, the meanings projected by media producers. Media signification practices may vary with spectators' positions along a rural-urban continuum (e.g., Abu-Lughod 2005, chaps. 1, 2; Wilk 2002; Das 1995) and simultaneously reveal local schemes of interpretation (e.g., Liebes and Katz 1990; Allen 1995). The global circulation of American consumer culture thus seems to produce both universal commonalities and new local differentiation (e.g., Featherstone 1987); further, consumers position themselves in contingent ways vis-à-vis the West or "modernity" *tout court* (e.g., Miller 1992, 1995b; Abu-Lughod 1995). In many areas of the non-Western world, moreover, the popularity of Indian Bollywood movies and Latin American telenovelas rebuts assumptions of mass media's homogenizing effects that implicitly oppose an ideology-producing West to an uncritically consuming non-West (e.g., Penacchioni 1984; Larkin 1997). Televised media serve as blueprints for spectators' diverse desires and for their explorations of the paradoxes of social conventions emerging from local constraints and opportunities (e.g., Fuglesang 1994; Gillespie 1995).

Recent scholarship on consumption emphasizes the centrality of consumer culture to personal experience and the objective structures of capitalist production. Mass consumption, scholars argue, reflects at once an extension of the range of commodities and a reorganization of the form and content of symbolic production and everyday practice. Consumption becomes central to the performance of an identity articulated through consumer styles that establish and reproduce socioeconomic difference.[1] Jameson (1984), Harvey (1989, 2006) and Postone (1999), however, are more guarded about the relation between consumption and identity. They maintain that the alleged primacy of consumption to contemporary identity reflects on the restructuring of the global economic order that leads to increased dissociation of the places of production from those of consumption. The growing number of people who see their spending power shrink can only imaginatively participate in a cosmopolitan world where identity is predicated on consumption (see Comaroff and Comaroff 2000; Ferguson 2002). These different perspectives on the relevance of consumption form the starting place for my exploration of Malian urbanites' enthusiastic involvement with televised drama. My intention is to reconstruct the reflections and forms of engagements that the broadcasts prompt, as well as the kind of modern subjectivity they thereby create. I also seek to understand the high regard for American family drama among Muslim women, a regard that contrasts with their critical attitude toward Western culture. A first step toward breaking with conventional "othering" assumptions about the relation between Muslim faith and social life may be to consider the possibility that Muslims in search of moral renewal do not differ substantively in their media engagements from other urbanites (see Abu-Lughood 2002; Mamdani 2004).

To explore the subjectivity revealed in urbanites' emotional and self-reflexive engagement with media products means to stress the culturally and historically determinate nature of public subjectivity that varies with particular technologies of mediation and the institutional context in which dominant models of semiotic mediation and political community are embedded (Lee 1993). An important inspirational source for this analysis is Anderson's (1991 [1983]) and Habermas's (1990 [1962]) different perspectives on the link between modern nationhood and a particular form of (political) consciousness and subjectivity (see Schulz 2007b).[2] Yet, contrary to these authors' privileging of a discursive model of public interaction, and to Habermas's pessimistic account of public subjectivity under conditions of mass-mediated consumer culture, we should explore, rather than assume, the historically specific forms of public subjectivity that emerge in Mali at the nexus of new media technologies, commercialization processes, and a post-authoritarian political climate.

As various ethnographic and historical studies remind us, Habermas's stark contrast between critical debate and consumption might not be applicable in non-Western contexts.[3] Habermas's emphasis on the rupture introduced by market-mediated cultural production took up the arguments made by Lukács (1967) and Adorno (1938) that, in fully industrialized societies, any form of cultural production reifies in aesthetically compelling form the existing social relations of inequality; cultural consumption is thus fully subject to the logic of the market and the rationale of generating capitalist surplus value. Leaving aside the question of whether this gloomy view does justice to the multiple forms of public subjectivity in Western industrial societies,[4] a crucial insight of Habermas and other Frankfurt school theorists still applies, namely, that it is not the form or technology of mediation per se that carries certain political implications; rather, it is the coming together of media technologies with a particular context of market-mediated culture and politics. Habermas's perspective thus remains relevant inasmuch as it helps understand how the logic of an expanding capitalist consumer culture restructures individual consciousness, social relations, and cultural production, and how these changes affect existing notions of political subjectivity and public intervention (see Postone 1992). This perspective promises important insights into the nature of public subjectivities in the postcolonial world (see Salvatore 1998; Meyer and Moors 2006; Schulz 2006b, 2007b).

To assess the ways that media engagements in contemporary Africa are dictated by the logic of the market, we need to explore the existing structures of production and distribution and analyze their effects rather than take them for granted. Also, it is not self-evident that Malian media consumers share the characteristics of the Western consumer-spectator whose self-understanding revolves around notions of individual choice and difference. This chapter therefore examines the forms of engagement that "debate" and "consumption" entail in urban Mali and the public intervention they facilitate.

Media Practices in Urban Mali

Anthropological investigations into media consumption in the postcolonial world have opened up new conduits for assessing the complex implications of mass-mediated entertainment culture. Studies of small or decentralized media have revised earlier generalizations about the distorting effects of the cultural industry, and thus depart from the pessimism of both early Frankfurt school theorists and those who associate media technologies with Western institutions and values.[5] The downside of the focus on "small media" is that, by hailing their transformational or participatory potential, one risks technological determinism and overrating the subversive potential of these media, such as their capacity to establish alternative or counter-publics (e.g., Manuel 1993; Sreberny-Mohammadi and Mohammadi 1994; Eickelman and Anderson 1999). The studies also demonstrate the need to differentiate between different media and their effects, which depend on the ways that institutions of the state or commerce control their production, circulation, and consumption. Because mass-media consumption is embedded in a commercial entertainment culture, a thorough anthropological investigation is needed of the market institutions in which mass-mediated culture thrives in particular national contexts (e.g., Mankekar 1999; Rajagopal 2001; see Armbrust 1996). I therefore start with a sketch of the institutions and the degree of commercialization of cultural products in Mali, as well as of the urban middle- and lower-middle-class setting in which broadcasts are consumed.

Television consumption is a recent phenomenon in Mali.[6] Reception of national television, created in 1983, remained limited to Bamako and other towns in Mali's southern triangle until 1995, when heavy investments by Western donor organizations expanded television reception to the far north. The massive influx of low-cost, battery-run television sets from southeast Asia contributed to the steady growth in the use of mass media over the past two decades, even in smaller towns of Mali's remote regions.[7] In Bamako the reception of satellite television broadcasts from Saudi Arabia, Morocco, France, Senegal, Guinea, and the United States is no longer restricted to the economic and political elite. In San and other smaller towns, by contrast, few households have the equipment necessary to receive international television channels. National television thus continues to hold almost exclusive monopoly over television broadcasting. Watching television involves diverse modes of engagement. Whereas people generally chat during the broadcasts of presidential speeches and more or less attentively follow the evening news, the soap operas and telenovelas (*filimu*) prompt many people to abruptly end their conversations and follow the events on the screen. Apart from a few African films, most television programs are imported from Europe, the United States, and occasionally the Far East. Among the most popular national productions are music videos featuring Malian pop stars, which are broadcast in between programs and during weekly music shows and comprise about 75 percent of all music broadcasts.[8]

The widespread attention devoted to national television does not necessarily indicate a widespread appreciation of its programs but might reflect, instead, a lack of competition from other television channels. In smaller towns such as San, people's motivation to switch on television is often prompted by boredom. As daily life follows a slow, monotonous pulse, the *filimu* become the object of avid debate because they provide the metaphors that form "a major constituent of daily thought and action" (Morley and Silverstone 1990, 48). The *filimu* also structure the spatio-temporal organization of daily life: people organize work and leisure so they can follow their favorite serials. Although the serials draw spectators from all ages and educational backgrounds, individual preferences are age-dependent.[9] Although television consumption has recently intensified, radio is still the principal source of media entertainment. Local radio stations mushroomed in urban Mali after 1992 and enjoy wide appeal because they create new sites and forms of local communication and sociality (Schulz 1999b, 2000). Because the local stations broadcast in local languages, devote more time to local music and oral culture, and are more responsive to listener input, they present a challenge to the national radio which has started to adopt a more listener-friendly format.[10] National radio nonetheless has the widest coverage and programming variety because of its superior technical equipment, professional expertise, and support from international organizations.

The logic of capitalist marketing, which Horkheimer and Adorno (1972) identified as determining consumers' subjectivity in industrial societies, is not pervasive in Mali. Mass-media entertainment permeates quotidian urban life, but its impact remains limited at a national level; national television and local radio reception is much more widespread in the southern triangle of Mali than it is in the north; and in many remote rural areas, national radio is not available year-round. Even in urban settings, where individuals have greater access to commodities, the effects of mass-mediated aesthetics and commercial entertainment are constricted. Televised media production only partly follows consumer demand. Audio cassette production, which is the most important sector of the media entertainment market, has been impaired by the availability of pirated music. Few alternatives to television and radio exist, although video and tape recorders have increased consumers' choices. To better understand the commercial character of individual media products, we need to assess the media technology and institutional apparatus that enable their dissemination, and examine whether their production is centrally controlled, follows the logic of market demand and competition, or is informed by different trajectories and motors of dissemination.

The last ten years witnessed a steady increase in television advertisements for Malian and Ivorian products. These commercials are targeted at the same groups as are addressed in national soap operas in Egypt, India, and various African countries (e.g., Abu-Lughod 1995; Armbrust 1996; Mankekar 1999;

Schulz 2002). As with serials, advertisements promote the ideal notion of the middle-class nuclear family whose identity is defined by the products the family consumes (see Abu-Lughod 2005). The gap between the advertised imagery and the actual lives of most consumers is so blatant that it often seems to discourage spectators from even mimetically engaging with the advertisements. Given that spectators relate much more passionately to television serials and pop music clips, we can assume that these broadcasts are more important for the inculcation of consumerist norms. Although the broadcasting of these media products does not follow the dictates of the market, they nonetheless enhance the logic and appeal of consumer culture. They present, though in a highly abstracted form, existing social relations of inequality (see Lukács 1967). Local radio broadcasting, too, only partly follows the logic of market competition. Because funding through listener support and commercials barely exists, most radio stations, except those sponsored by international organizations, barely sustain themselves. Their lack of equipment and professional training, combined with listeners' limited spending powers, makes it hard for them to compete through innovative programming (Schulz 2000). Finally, in contrast to countries such as India and Egypt, where serials produced under the aegis of the state are subject to certain market competition (e.g., Mankekar 1999; Rajagopal 2001; Abu-Lughod 2005), television serials in Mali are usually imports.[11] Still, Mali's television serials are players in a culture of consumerism. Without addressing a specifically Malian consumer-citizen, they help advertise cosmopolitan imaginaries and lifestyles, and invite viewers to engage with television imagery and "message," and with the medium's materiality, prestige, and ideology.

Imagining Other Worlds, Making Sense of Everyday Life

> In your land, in Europe, people no longer care about human beings. What counts for us is people: who lives with whom, who fights against whom; whether women get along with each other or not; . . . who gets the greatest share of the father's inheritance and so on. But ultimately, you white people and we share the same concerns. That's what the filimu are about and that's why I like watching them.
>
> —RETIRED SCHOOLTEACHER, BAMAKO, DECEMBER 2003

Such comments vividly illustrate that Malian television consumers, far from uncritically consuming global media images, approach them selectively to relate them to their own lifestyle. They endorse claims of media theorists who, critical of blanket denouncements of media consumption, emphasize audiences' active participatory role. Yet as much as I share these authors' desire to "rescue" consumers from sweeping allegations of their passivity, these authors' emphasis on audience activity raises several thorny questions. The notion of audience "activity," despite its popularity and occasionally contentious existence (Seaman 1992), lacks "a thorough, systematic definitional analysis" (Gunter 1988, 109) and has been used to refer variously to intentionality, selectivity, involvement, or interpretational autonomy. Also, contrary to what is sometimes suggested, those who actively appropriate media may reproduce stereotypical or hegemonic understandings of society rather than subvert dominant power and gender relations.

A closely related methodological question concerns the kind of data scholars draw on to analyze the meanings consumers ascribe to programs. Whether we study media engagement in a foreign society or at home, we always bring our particular class- and identity-generated presuppositions to bear on the answers we elicit. Also, our involvement with media images and messages partly occurs at a visceral level that is only partially open to self-reflective articulation and argument. We therefore cannot rely exclusively on consumers' accounts of their interpretations but need, instead, to consider the range of spontaneous emotional-gestural and verbal responses we witness.[12] Finally, rather than assuming generalizations about "the" audience, the diverse media responses of different categories of viewers should be analyzed, even if this, too, has its own interpretive problems (Morley and Silverstone 1992; Fiske 1989, 1994; see Livingstone 1998, 244). The challenge here is twofold. First, scholars need to interpret audiences in a situationally contingent manner without limiting themselves to the collection and reporting of individual statements. The difficulty one faces is how to draw broader conclusions and discern systematic patterns of engagement from particular viewing situations and the comments of individual spectators (Abu-Lughod 2005, 19–25). Second, instead of analyzing the diversity of media practices based on preconceived distinctions between consumers, we should generate these categories of media consumers according to the ways that they engage media productions. To categorize viewers in a contextually sensitive way, we need to focus on the meanings they construct and systematically relate these to their locations in the broader field of social difference and inequality.

This leads me to a final analytical question: How does one balance a conventional scholarly preoccupation with media content with an analysis of the institutional setting and horizon of experience that molds the meanings attributed to media messages? Debra Spitulnik (2002) has recently critiqued "subject-centric" approaches to reception by maintaining that the significance of media consumption does not necessarily reside in individuals' interpretation of media content. She calls for an approach that situates the reception of media messages in the range of social domains and experiences that shape people's media practices. The challenge is to understand the significance that certain groups of television spectators in Mali attribute to the television serials by addressing their social locations of media engagement. But to pay particular attention to the meaning spectators ascribe to *filimu* does not imply that people's engagement with media content exhausts the significance of these practices.

I often watched the television serials with my host families, yet Muslim women were my most frequent viewing companions. I soon realized that it made little sense to mark off the media practices of members of the Islamic moral reform movement from those of other television consumers, since the former group watched the serials with similar keenness, although sometimes for different reasons. The widespread enthusiasm for soap operas and telenovelas shows the importance of situating media interpretations within the broader social context and of taking into account the common experiences shared by those in the Islamic moral reform movement and other urbanites. Daily life, for them all, involves a tension between a need for greater autonomy and responsibility, and the normative order of patriarchal authority and family membership. Family conflicts, and the feelings of insecurity and vulnerability that they elicit, make people resort to various remedies to rework their social environment (Schulz 2001b, 2005). Whatever the remedy, however, all agree that conventional forms of mutual obligation and solidarity are being threatened, and it is this existential menace to the social bases of quotidian life that informs people's involvements with televised family drama.

Between Distance and Identification

Appadurai (1996) and Castells (1996) argue that transnational media institutions and images instigate historically unprecedented possibilities and practices of imagination constitutive of current processes of cultural globalization. The notion of imagination certainly has great appeal, but it leaves unanswered the question of what dynamics are generated by practices of imagining and how these dynamics are affected by media technologies. Studies of the interplay of imagination, interpretation, and Western media exports suggest that the meanings attributed to particular images and soap opera plots are highly variable both between and within cultural settings. Yet whereas most authors stress audiences' capacity to reinterpret selectively, they do not always agree, or even reflect, on what particular aspect of a media image viewers assess and make sense of. Some base their reflections on spectators' evaluations and interpretations of a film's story line and moral (Liebes and Katz 1990; Allen 1995); others focus on the consumer goods displayed in films and soap operas, and discuss how this imagery serves as a symbolic repertoire for media consumers to locate

themselves in the contemporary world (e.g., Miller 1992, 1994). Neither a preoccupation with plot nor a focus on Western consumerism displayed in the *filimu*
is fully adequate to understand the telespectators' differential forms of engagement. Spectators differ considerably in the weight they attribute to different
aspects of a serial's story, and the elements of a televised narrative they privilege
points to systemic variations in their life situations and social positions. Their
patterned responses emerge not from specific interpretations but from multiple dimensions of the visual and aural television narrative. Their responses
also reflect the specific preferences of different groups of viewers that can be
loosely associated with age and social status. Telespectators' engagements with
soap operas in Mali render problematic the assumption that globally circulating American serials inspire uncritical identification across different audience
segments. I often overheard adult men deploring young people's indiscriminate
admiration for soap operas, which, they felt, illustrated youth's moral indifference and "aping" of American culture. Yet, although male and female youth are
often passionate fans of the prime-time American soaps—in marked contrast
to their parents' preference for telenovelas—their engagement with these films
shows that they do not wholeheartedly embrace or imitate what their heroes
and heroines do. Rather, they both identify with and feel distant from the soap
imagery, and passionately discuss their heroes' dilemmas as a way to reflect
on their own ambivalent positions vis-à-vis the adult world and its normative
expectations. Serials thus reflect but also encourage disagreements between the
generations, because they lend visible and "debatable" form to mutual allegations of (deficient) moral motivation and character. This insight also applies to
younger members of the Muslim women's associations. Their admiration for,
and reservations toward, a heroine's self-assertiveness differed from the reactions
of other young women only inasmuch as they took the heroine's willfulness as a
starting place to reflect on their own difficulties in convincing their mothers to
join their ethical quest. Hence television viewers construct themselves as specific
consumer-subjects through a double process of media involvement: by engaging
different dimensions of the serials and by engaging in debates about the effects
these serials have on developing moral subjects. Here we see one implication of
the imagination practices that are generated or facilitated by the global spread of
"mediascapes" (Appadurai 1996, chap. 2). Media circuits, institutions, and technologies that invite viewers' involvement with media products insert themselves
into existing structures of local difference and contestation, and thereby create
opportunities for the reassertion and reformulation of local understandings of
moral responsibility and personal autonomy.

That acts of imagination or fantasy (Meyer 2003) offer viewers opportunities to adopt specific modes of assertiveness, apprehension, and self-constitution

as consumer-subjects also comes to the fore in media practices by women of advanced age and status. Married women eagerly debate a *filimu's* visual details, and thereby assign it a significance that transcends the story line. They avidly discuss dress, interiors, and demeanor as tokens of a fashionable and "civilized" feminine lifestyle, one they variously associate with Bamako, with more "advanced" neighboring countries, or with France (Schulz 2007b). Their spontaneous engagement with the *filimu* plots suggests that the serials give them an opportunity to view themselves as belonging to a cosmopolitan world; at the same time, however, their comments reveal an acute sense of their marginal position in the world of consumption. Their imaginative, though ambivalent, location in a broader community of equal-minded women parallels the fantasy practices engaged in by their self-designated others, that is, by members of Muslim women's groups, even if the latter attribute an entirely different significance to the serials.

The Muslim women with whom I regularly watched television often stressed the *filimu's* educational benefit. As a member of the Ansar Dine women's group in San, a woman in her mid-thirties, put it,

> Watching these women in the *filimu* gives me great comfort and courage, (because) I no longer feel alone. I observe these young women [and] how their dreams of wealth and success falter. This makes me understand that, regardless of what you own and what you are striving for, women everywhere have the same problems.

This statement condenses Muslim women's preoccupation with the edifying effects of watching *filimu*. Their interest in moral edification lets them distance themselves from other women whom they pity as being "corrupted by a greed for things." Those so criticized would, in turn, ridicule Muslim women for their conservative attitude and for not knowing about the consumer goods thought key to a cosmopolitan lifestyle. We may conclude, then, that the *filimu* world lets viewers place themselves in a local context of difference among women, a difference that is framed as a matter of moral distinction or sophistication. As with controversies between adolescents and their fathers over questions of a soap opera's value, adult women's involvement with serials becomes an intricate part of their daily assertion of particular social and moral positions.

The responses by my male interlocutors, household heads, and married sons similarly suggest that *filimu* act as a mirror of one's own daily experiences and attempts at self-positioning.[13] Rather than emphasize the different, exotic nature of the world depicted on TV, these men, many of them intellectuals, stressed how much the telenovela world resembled their own. Even if the characters live somewhere else on the globe, they argued, they have to tackle similar problems most of which arise from conflicts among friends and relatives. Most men stressed the moral superiority of telenovelas, which, as one of my steadiest viewing companions, a schoolteacher in his mid-forties, said, "address issues of proper conduct in ways that distinguish them from . . . what you see in *Amoureusement vôtre*, where almost everyone has been in a you-know-what-I-mean relationship with everybody else." This rather common perception among married men puts them in a similar position as other television consumers, thereby diminishing the significance of professional and educational differences between them. Married men further along in their lives as husbands and fathers similarly distinguished between *filimu* not so much on the basis of their regional origin or the cultural world they depicted but according to their moral message. Likewise, in the courtyards of the Muslim women, family fathers sometimes took issue with the prime-time soaps for the sexually promiscuous world they depict and expressed a preference for the telenovelas. Whenever I asked them what, in their view, was the origin of the problems depicted onscreen, they argued that these problems were a result of "human nature." This response suggests that, like other men, male supporters of Islamic moral renewal are preoccupied with the morally edifying aspects of the serials.

The similarity of the responses to the *filimu* by those who consider themselves true Muslims, as well as by others, reveals a shared framework of evaluation that is only partly accessible to conscious articulation. Male and female participants in the Islamic movement were usually surprised when I asked whether they saw a contradiction between their regular consumption of soap operas and their denunciation of the immorality depicted in these series. In response, they affirmed that the *filimu* offered valuable moral lessons precisely because they depicted questionable behavior and love relations. Regardless of the multiple consumer-subject positions constructed through the engagement with televised media, all positions are predicated on the field of imaginative practices made possible by telenovelas and soap operas. The *filimu* allow viewers to reconsider their positions and offer various solutions so they can identify the one most fitting to their situation. This finding supports Ang's interpretation of an audience's engagement with the American television show *Dallas:* the polysemic and ambiguous nature of the show's messages allows spectators to inhabit a fantasy world where divergent aspirations and viewpoints are possible (Ang 1985, 49). Divergent interpretations not only establish and resonate with heterogeneous subject positions within a family, but also within broader social divides such as those pitting different Muslim positions and identities against one another. That spectators, regardless of their cultural and regional context, not only read their own meanings into the text of the soaps but also highlight the soaps' educational value echoes the insights of Liebes and Katz's (1990) cross-cultural study of soap opera reception. The inclination of viewers to privilege the familiar over the strange in soap operas and telenovelas, that is, their tendency to view them as a realistic portrayal of personal dilemmas, is not a peculiar feature of Malians' engagement with television. What appears specific in the Malian case (though not unique to it [see Das 1995; Larkin 1997]) is the way that spectators take what they see on television as an entry point into debates on personal relationships and the moral status quo of Malian society. This may explain why there are no substantive differences in the moralizing assessment of professing Muslims and other television consumers, both of whom engage televised drama in a similar manner. And regardless of the Muslim or secularist standpoint they might otherwise adopt, they do not draw on television series to emulate Western stereotypes or lifestyles. Instead, they make eclectic use of some elements, such as events, persons, and consumer goods, to perpetuate a local discourse about the unsettled relations between the generations and sexes, and about what they perceive as an intensifying crisis of their moral universe.

Malian viewers' involvement with *filimu* also illustrates that, contrary to what has been suggested by defenders of a "strong model" of audience activity (e.g., Fiske 1987), these media products do not offer an unlimited field of free association and interpretation, despite their polysemic nature. This finding places Malian television viewers on an equal footing with consumers of mass media and their realm for audience activity in the West. As Hall (1980) has suggested, there is always room for negotiation or opposition to the dominant interpretation intended by the producers of media texts. Nevertheless, these readings operate within a circumscribed horizon of experience that makes possible some lines of interpretation and forecloses others. The discussion that follows further substantiates Hall's postulation that the "decoding" of media messages in Western societies can be brought to bear on our understanding of media experiences in postcolonial Africa. Certain narrative elements of a television series channel spectators' reactions by evoking in them a sense of déjà vu and thus encourage them to take particular, often emphatic, positions toward the series' protagonists. The molding of interpretations by certain textual features does not preclude that viewers' readings are also inspired by, and predicated on, the social locations and daily struggles and concerns of particular groups of spectators (see Livingstone 1998, 218).

The Soapy Dilemmas of Family Life

Since the early 1980s scholars have moved away from earlier assumptions in communications research and literary theory—most notably the assumption that the "text" equals its reception. They made the audience their subject of inquiry (Fejes 1984; Lindlof 1988) and illustrated the diversity of interpretations within and across audiences and specific cultural settings. Some drew on Raymond Williams's (1991) critical reading of Gramsci's notion of hegemony and addressed audience reception as a set of socially embedded practices that yields multiple and potentially contradictory results (Hall 1977, 1980; Bennett, Mercer, and Woollacott 1986). In this they departed from the dominant ideology thesis on which predominant structuralist Marxist models of media hegemony had been based (Abercrombie et al. 1980). Fiske posited an autonomy of individual interpretation, yet followed Hall (1980) in arguing that dominant or preferred readings can reproduce hegemonic, commonsensical understandings of social order and hold greater social power than aberrant or oppositional readings (Fiske 1987, 1989). Others went further in their search for resistant readings. While maintaining that the range of interpretations is limited by textual constraints, they stressed the viewers' interpretational autonomy and attributed a great degree of creativity to their media engagements (Morley 1980, 1986; see Gunter 1988; Seaman 1992).

It seems that adopting the preferred reading viewpoint is methodologically more promising, even if its vague formulation can lead to misinterpretations (Hall 1994; Livingstone 1998, 245–248). The idea that a preferred reading coexists with less privileged readings allows us to explore the degree to which media texts generate systematic, patterned responses. It also highlights the fact that particular readings are defined not only by textual constraints but by the viewers' social locations (Ang 1994; Corner 1995). Malian urbanites' patterned media practices are generated not only by a narrative framework but by their shared horizon of experience that structures preferred readings of telenovelas. These readings are not shared by all in any particular audience; nor may they be supported by the majority of spectators across audiences. Rather, the preference for one interpretation resonates with dominant normative assumptions which, in turn, depend on consumers' particular locations in a field of social and economic difference.

Geraghty (1991) differentiates between the narrative structure of British and American soap operas by noting differences in the types of conflicts and solutions presented to female spectators. American soaps are "patriarchal dramas," because they center on the father's attempts to keep control of the family business and relations. Women are generally represented as a threat to family order and patriarchal control of succession and family property; they are at the origin of family discord, constantly moving in and out of the family via marriage, adultery, or divorce. British soap operas, on the other hand, are "matriarchal dramas," where women are portrayed as central moral authorities and directors of the family business. Family membership and control are not at stake. The source of family dynamics are extra-familial or social difficulties, such as unemployment, that the family needs to resolve. Geraghty's drama classification helps make sense of the déjà vu feelings that television viewers in Mali unanimously expressed when they identified the struggle between the generations as the central source of conflict in urban life and the driving force of the soap world. Still, Geraghty's opposition of matriarchal to patriarchal dramas is not fully congruent with social reality in urban Mali, where most tensions that structure daily life arise at the nexus of overlapping and competing allegiances that constitute an indeterminate field of conflicts. In addition to the matrifocal bonds between children and their mothers (who compete with their co-wives), age hierarchies among siblings play a pivotal role in creating relations and feelings of attachment. The widespread popularity of the telenovelas could result from their depiction of overlapping vectors of dependency and sentimental attraction, which resonate with spectators' own experience that their dilemmas arise from the *tension* between various axes of moral obligation.[14]

A leitmotif that spectators readily identify with is the central position of women in power struggles and conflict resolution. In their role as lovers, wives, and mothers, women appear as both a threat to, and guarantor of, the social order. This televised depiction of women mirrors the dominant portrayal of women as both custodians and destroyers of moral integrity that, as chapters 1 and 2 discussed, dominates local media productions and public debate. Another narrative element to which Malian spectators can easily relate is the complex structure of continually shifting relationships and the myriad patrimonial and matrimonial ties between protagonists and the ways they feed into rightful versus allegedly illegitimate claims to inheritance. Most television viewers acknowledge the familiarity of these conflicts by relating them to the bitter competition (*fadenya*) that exists between half-siblings and the affection and solidarity (*badenya*) ruling relations between full siblings. The frequency of disagreements around love relations is another point that reconfirms spectators' perceptions that "the *filimu* people are just like us." Their emphasis on the familiarity of the *filimu* problems might at first appear puzzling, because conflicts in urban marriages center on other matters such as obligations of material and financial support. Yet beyond this superficial difference, *filimu* and spectators *frame* social problems in similar ways. Predicaments are presented as purely ethical issues, not as the result of structurally entrenched power inequalities. Therefore the familiarity of soap opera narratives partly derives from their capacity to suggest ethical and individualizing solutions to dilemmas that arise from socio-structural constraints (Schulz 2001b). And because women are central to their narratives (as actors and emblems of the moral status quo), soap operas offer women the material to imagine themselves as self-directed, autonomous persons in a world of new and urban lifestyles.

In studying the reception of non-Western media products in Northern Nigeria, Larkin (1997) argues that their popularity among different consumer segments hints at the existence of parallel modernities, an imaginary space situated in cultural and normative realms located outside the conventionally established divide between a world of (local) tradition and (Western) modernity (see Gaonkar 1999; Sreberny 2000). I suggest that the reactions by Malian viewers to television series imported from the United States and Latin America both reconfirm and complicate these interpretations. Earlier I provisionally identified different categories of consumer-subjects that emerge from their engagement with specific narrative elements of televised dilemmas. No person or spectator group takes a univocal or fully consistent position vis-à-vis the world represented on television; rather, in their moralizing assessment of the *filimu*'s protagonists, spectators move in and out of empathic identification. Their remark that the protagonists "have the same problems we have" does not indicate their full-fledged identification with the plots and actors. Their claim to a commonality of experience refers, instead, to other patterns and objects of identification. And although spectators are acutely aware that soap operas and telenovelas are produced and set in America, they do not couch this distinction in terms of geographical or cultural difference. Supporters of Islamic moral renewal resemble other spectators in this respect. Although they decry the corrupting effects of money and (occasionally) Western culture, they draw pleasure from soap operas that capture these cultural influences. What, then, is the difference between the interpretations of Malians with whom I followed television serials and those made by consumers of Hindi and American films in Northern Nigeria (Larkin 1997)? Whereas Nigerian consumers explicitly differentiate between Hindi films and Western soaps, urban Malians do not see the world of soap operas as radically different in moral terms; people rarely claim that the world of telenovelas is closer to their own than is the world depicted in American-style soap operas. That such apparent discrepancies in interpretation exist even among different Muslim majority societies of West Africa shows the importance of considering the socially and historically specific trajectories informing media practices in individual societies of postcolonial Africa.

An Emergent Metatopical Space?

In his recent discussion of the "social imaginary" and public subjectivity that underlie modern Western polities, Charles Taylor (2002), following Habermas and Warner, characterizes the modern public sphere as a metatopical space that is ontologically and normatively distinct from previously existing topical common spaces. Topical common spaces were momentary social and spatial formations in which people came together around particular practices, objectives, and concerns. The modern public sphere, in contrast, is metatopical because it provides its members with a "framework that exists prior to and independent of their actions" (Taylor 2002: 115). Modern public subjectivity rests upon certain preconceived notions of a moral order that makes possible the emergence of a new form of being together. Taylor's perspective offers a valuable entry point for a parallel inquiry into modern public subjectivities in the postcolonial world. He raises questions about the normative underpinnings and imaginations that inform the subject positions of those who partake in public communication in Mali. Thus he allows us to query the view of Habermas and earlier Frankfurt school theorists on how mass-mediated, commercial culture impinges on people's capacity to relate the relevance of mass-mediated culture to their daily experiences and sense of self. What are the ideals of common good and "being together" that are presupposed and created in the course of Malian urbanites' consumption of mass-media products? Where do supporters of Islamic moral renewal figure in these imaginings of moral community?

Clearly the view of consumer passivity that Adorno and Horkheimer (1972) offered in their *Dialectics of Enlightenment* does not capture the ways that Malian urbanites engage with imported television series. The *filimu* allow them to assume the position of debating subjects, not only in the immediate context of television consumption but in various everyday settings. Youth, for instance, often allude to episodes from the parallel world of television to engage in socially sanctioned communication with parents. It is disrespectful for a youth to address shameful topics in the presence of seniors, and therefore allusions to episodes from a television serial offer both a discreet and commonly shared expressive repertory. The same practice also applies to relations between peers; friends console each other in difficult situations by suggesting a solution similar to one recently recounted on television. Far from being a passive process, television consumption is an active engagement that extends beyond the television-viewing context. Consumption-as-debate also underpins viewers' involvement with other programs. Women and girls, for instance, passionately engage music broadcasts that feature nationally and internationally renowned (mostly female) pop singers who combine different regional musical styles and instrumentation with the emblems of an international, Euro-American consumer orientation. The great popularity of the songs among women across the socioeconomic divide derives not only from the conventional gender ideology most songs articulate but also from the way singers convey aesthetically compelling images of cosmopolitan, yet authentic, African womanhood. Women and girls spend hours gossiping about the singers' recent professional successes, assessing their attires and discussing possibilities of purchasing such outfits for themselves (Schulz 2002, 2007a). They thus assume the role of debating subjects by positioning themselves within a local debate on female morality, cultural authenticity, and cosmopolitan lifestyles.

Members of Muslim women's groups are critical of the fan culture surrounding the pop stars. They sit through broadcasts of pop stars' musical performances without paying much attention to them and with no desire to discuss their private affairs. When I asked some of these women why they were so little interested in or even dismissive of these programs, they pointed to their obligation as respectable Muslims to disregard the whimsical desires and moral disorientation that pop stars embodied. As with *filimu,* televised music programs prompt supporters of Islamic renewal and other women to situate themselves and their mutually conceived others in a hierarchy of moral distinction or consumerist refinement.

Local radio broadcasts, closely intertwined with a commercial entertainment culture, contribute to the institutional foundations of a new public subjectivity. Talk-radio programs, highly popular among the urban youth and married women, allows listeners to combine their reception practices with modalities of public intervention that resonate with long-standing conventions of managing personal reputations and entertainment (Schulz 1999a). These programs thus blur the line between broadcast production and consumption as separate processes performed by different actors. By participating in broadcast debates, listeners who may have known one another before but are set apart by daily routines are drawn together into one audience, one "community of sentiment" (Schulz 2000; see Appadurai 1990). Supporters of Islamic moral renewal favor certain radio programs for the same reason they appreciate some television serials, for their educational value. They regularly listen to broadcasts featuring local oral culture and religious debate, and stress that their engagement with these broadcasts sharpens their capacity for critical self-inspection. Around these various radio programs, a local moral public comes into being, together with a new form and awareness of public togetherness. This public sociality extends beyond singular topical debates and is characterized by a greater communicative immediacy and the novel quality of commonly shared knowledge. Characteristic of this sociality is a sense of shared space-time or "public intimacy" (Schulz 2002), a perception Anderson (1991 [1983]) famously described as the precondition for imagining a broader collectivity and a distinctive feature of modern polities.

Although the analysis has focused on discrete media, it is important to remember that all signification practices take place in an inter-medial space.

In other words, media consumers make sense of individual media products by drawing on background knowledge constituted by different media. Television series and talk-radio programs together form an inter-medial topical site that provides consumers with the material to assess their everyday experiences and situate themselves in a broader constituency of consumers. It would be misleading, therefore, to associate media users' engagement with a specific communication technology with one particular kind of subject position and public intervention, as intimated by authors who stress the importance of visual mediation for public culture. This insight is not new. Thirty years ago Fabian (1978) showed that urban popular culture in Zaire thrives at the interface of different media and arts. Recent attempts to counterbalance Habermas's and Anderson's privileging of the discursive risk overrating the extent to which a particular mode of mediation changes the character of the public subjectivity. Individual technologies of mediation need to be assessed in terms of their connection with commercial institutions and with the social institutions and power relations within which they are mobilized. The various, crisscrossing modes of media engagements that punctuate Malian urbanites' daily experiences are part of a set of non-discursive practices and social institutions through which a shared realm of moral consideration is gradually emerging. Because of its unstable, fragmentary character and its confinement to urban and semi-urban areas, it can be characterized as a metatopical space in the making, meaning a space that is perched uneasily at the interface between a semi-commercial, state-dominated entertainment culture and incipient institutions of a new public sociality. What, then, is the potential of this public sociality?

Video Screenings:
The Mirroring of Consumption and Production

Thus far, analysis of media engagements in urban Mali has focused on television and radio, communication technologies whose effects are often studied by separating production from consumption practices (but see Hebdige 1979; Spitulnik 1993, 298). This analytical perspective, I will demonstrate, does not exhaust the range of forms of public intervention facilitated by media technologies in Mali. The multiple uses of video technology in Mali illustrate that the usefulness of the analytical divide between production and consumption depends not only on the kind of media technology but also on the specific genres it disseminates. An important implication of this finding is that one and the same technology occasions multiple forms of media practices (Spitulnik 2002, 338).

Malian "Home" Videos

The thriving local video-film industries in Ghana and Nigeria illustrate the astounding potential for creativity that this technology affords, as well as its capacity to lend expression to issues of social transformation and political legitimation (Meyer 1998; Haynes and Okome 2000; Wendl 2004). The Malian video productions I analyze differ from these film productions both in content and in the forms of sociality that animate them. Malian "home videos" document family celebrations, mainly weddings, which are among the most important public occasions for the promotion of family and individual prestige. They circulate through unique channels, are predicated on a distinct social organization of media engagement, and generate specific audiences. Because the video recordings celebrate and recycle the economic and social power of the families tied together in marital union, they are looked down upon by supporters of Islamic moral renewal, who denounce the videos, like the wedding celebrations they record, as vain consumerism. My analysis of wedding videos therefore draws exclusively on the media engagements of other Muslims. Exploring specific activities related to the joint production and consumption of wedding videos allows us to delineate certain loci of public debate that are facilitated by the circulation of decentralized media productions.

Wedding videos are produced by professional filmmakers; they circulate among extended family members and close friends, and along ties that reach into Malian expatriate communities in West Africa, France, and the United States. Since the early 1990s, when the first video production studios opened in Bamako, these enterprises have multiplied at breathtaking speed. Yet because of its cost, video production is limited to families with substantial income.[15] The growing popularity of the video-enhanced display of a family's social prestige and wealth resonates with urbanites' rising expectations of the kind of hospitality that the families of the bride and groom should demonstrate. The host family's financial burden is increased when praise singers (*jeliw;* singular, *jeli*) show up and invite hosts and guests of high repute to remunerate them generously for the praise they bestow on them (Schulz 1998, 1999a). As the number of *jeli* singers increases at a wedding, so, too, does the appearance of the host family's generosity and popularity. Social pressure to display one's status in a costly wedding has become so excessive in recent years that many families of low-income background resort to specialists other than *jeliw* to entertain guests and family. The advantage of this new arrangement is that the performers, generally members of Muslim women's groups, receive payment that is more predictable and modest than that of a *jeli*.[16]

Wedding videos reserve extra room for scenes deemed particularly important, such as the moment after the wedding banquet when the gifts bestowed on the bride and her family are shown to neighbors, friends, and relatives. A *jeli* speaker lifts up each gift for public validation and describes in great detail its value and origin. This celebration of generosity, high status, and moral obligation is witnessed by many and may last for hours. For weeks after the celebration, female invitees will assess the value of the presents and the celebration's cost. They will discuss the noteworthy people on whom the *jeliw* bestowed their praise, the amount the singers were paid, and whether the singers' attendance adequately reflected the host family's moral reputation. Other scenes documented in the video include the preparation of the bride for the event, the nightly festivities before the marriage, the civil ceremony, visits to the bride's and groom's families, the public entertainment in the afternoon, and the concluding ceremony. Arguably, however, the video's climax is the scene after the banquet, when prominent family members and invitees display their social prestige and wealth by delivering speeches and presenting gifts to the host family and to *jeli* speakers and praise singers.[17] There is a clear correlation between the social importance of guests and family members and the amount of footage devoted to them. The video production team is expected to reserve extended periods of time to depict "people of importance" (singular, *tògòtigi*). The more prestigious the venue, the more time should go into this depiction. Because of the videotape's time limit, foregrounding important people's celebration requires that the camera team cut other scenes, usually those featuring people of lesser importance.

The Doubling of Agency and Perspective

The first screening of the video recording transforms the actual wedding ceremony into a second real-time event by extending the festivity's social relevance into the present. As soon as rumors spread that the video has arrived, friends, neighbors, and relatives literally invade the family home of the bride. Crowds of chatting and giggling friends, most of them women, gather and comment on almost every detail of the video performance, comparing it to other weddings and their video replays. Central objects of scrutiny are the bride's wedding attire, the attire of her classificatory mothers (singular, *denba*) who play a central role in the wedding ceremony, and the appearance of other close relatives. Comments on the groom's appearance play a comparatively minor role.[18] Although the videos seem to render only the superficial (in the double sense of the word) dimensions of wedding ceremonies, the viewers' reactions suggest that the visual recording manifests the inner qualities of the participants, such as their dignity, social power, and ability to attract followers. Central to viewers' assessments is whether the representatives of the two families exhibited dignified demeanors and attire, and whether the *jeli* paid them due respect by "making their name great." Spectators scrutinize the patrons who distributed gifts and try to decipher the amount of money given to the *jeliw*, very often by moving closer to the television screen and touching it. Their careful appraisal of individuals' enactment of their reputation is facilitated by the lengthy passages that producers, in anticipation of their clients' interest, devote to certain individuals. The video narrative and its appreciation thus reveal the close connection that spectators establish between social rank and its visual enactment. The recording *performs* the actual creation of social eminence through its visual replay. Viewers' perception of the protagonists' inner qualities rendered visible by the recording illustrates how images, beyond their apparent illusory character, reveal hidden realities and thereby mediate between inner and outer worlds (Robins 1996, 168). There are also resonances between Malian viewers' assumptions about the social powers of dignified people that video technology visualizes and the intricate ways that occult forces are made visible by video technology in Ghana (Meyer 2003). The screening of a wedding video effects a doubling of perspective and agency. Viewers who attended the wedding now see themselves—and one another—in the replay of the video. They evaluate one another's capacities as actors enacting their own dignity. A meta-commentary on self-display emerges where spectators reflect on one another's conscious mise-en-scène, which in turn reveals the participants' awareness that they acquire the status of performers through the dual process of video recording and viewing. The meta-commentary illustrates that, in videotaped weddings, processes of production and consumption cannot be neatly separated but exist in a mutually constitutive relationship. Malian wedding videos thus show the cultural specificity and variability of practices associated with individual media technologies (see Ginsburg et al. 2002).

The adoption of video technology in urban Mali for the purpose of telescoping individual prestige to a wider audience demonstrates that new technologies, rather than necessarily generating institutional change or determining the direction of social transformation, may help perpetuate longer-standing practices and institutions. Wedding videos serve the performative assertion of social rank that follows long-standing styles of persuasion. Videotaped encounters between praise singers and their patrons magnify the social implications of this discrete event. Videos make possible the re-presentation and prolonged consumption of central emblems of prestige and dignity and thus play a crucial role in the assertion and validation of social prominence. In this process, conventions of enhancing prestige are reconfigured and partly adapted to new technological realities. The central role of *jeli* singers and speakers in unmediated wedding ceremonies derives from their function as "ventriloquists," as they magnify and broadcast their patrons' names to a wider audience. Video technology takes over, but does not fully replace, the function of the *jeliw*. Videos broadcast the enactment of dignity to a wider constituency but because the circulation and reception of Malian wedding videos involve neighbors and family members, some of whom live overseas in immigrant communities, the videos go hand in hand with newly emerging forms of sociality that do not fit a neat distinction between public and intimate realms. It is impossible to neatly separate acts of producing and consuming dignity in wedding videos and to relegate consumption to the private realm. This insight calls for a reassessment of the kind of publicity that characterizes these settings: videos circulate in, and are constitutive of, a semi-public realm that can be called an "intimate public." This public differs in scope, particularistic outlook, and moral sensibility from a broader (partly state-orchestrated) realm of public debate. Nonetheless, it partakes in the formation of a broader metatopical space by feeding into a general awareness of a common time-space and of shared experiences and concerns.

The continual restructuring of relations between husband and wife, and between the generations, analyzed in the preceding chapters, is embedded in and understood through people's daily media engagements in town. These intertwining processes can be grasped in their complexity when analyzed alongside the nature of the public, and of public subjectivity, to which Malian urbanites' engagement with different media and broadcast genres gives rise. The intercommunicative nature of the Malian public appears partly as a result of different, coexisting media that allow for various kinds of engagement. Although, for contemporary Africa, there is some validity to the thesis of the Frankfurt school that cultural production is increasingly penetrated by the logic of the market, it does not exhaust the social and expressive potential of mass-media technologies. In Mali, a partly commercial, mass-mediated entertainment culture allows media users to assume positions as debating subjects that are at variance with both subjectivities presumed in Habermas's model. Malian urbanites are neither critically debating political subjects nor uncritical consumers. The discrepancy between model and Malian realities results from the different degree to which the production of mass-mediated culture in Mali follows the dictates of the market and from the distinct forms of sociality that engagements with some media formats, such as wedding videos and talk-radio programs, presuppose and reproduce. The Frankfurt school theorists' view of mass-media users as uncritical consumers does not fit a situation in which the majority of the population remains marginal in a global world of consumption, even if their imaginary access has been facilitated by a liberalization of the media landscape.

A similar lack of fit exists with Baudrillard's (1970) thesis of the simulacrum, namely, that the visual sign form permeates everyday life to an extent that the sign and signified can no longer be distinguished. Such immaculate merging of signifier and signified is stalled by the fragmentary nature of visual consumer culture in Mali and, arguably, throughout Sub-Saharan Africa.

The result of a half-hearted commercialization of entertainment culture is a mixed-type citizen-as-consumer. This type combines the imported ideal of citizen-as-critical-participant (that is, a member of a democratic civil society) with a view of individuals as subjects of autocratic yet legitimate power. This partly consumerist, partly critical public subjectivity complicates prevalent views of the nature of political subjectivity in urban Africa. It suggests that, although we witness the emergence of a metatopical space characteristic of nation-states in Western Europe and North America, this space may differ not only in its conventions of sociality, modalities of communication, and location compared to a coercive and autocratic state but also in the political subjectivity it allows its citizens to adopt.

A learning session in a Muslim women's group. *Photo by author.*

A public prayer session led by a leader of a Muslim women's group and her assistant. *Photo by author.*

The leader of a Muslim women's group. *Photo by author.*

FOUR

Practicing Humanity:
Social Institutions of Islamic Moral Renewal

■ ■■■■■ ▶ ◆ ■■ ◀ ◆ ■■■■■ ▶ ◆ ■ ▶ ◆ ■ ▶ ◆ ■■■■■

> "Hademaden" *means "child of humankind," it means to be a*
> *human being in the truest sense of the word. To "do* hademad-
> enya*" means to practice humanity; to follow what God told you*
> *to do, to act with prudence, compassion and generosity towards*
> *others; in other words, [it means] to be sociable; because one*
> *person alone is nothing in this world.*
>
> —Kadiatou, San, April 2000

WALKING ON SUNDAY mornings in Bamako's popular neighborhoods of Badialan, Hamdalayye, and Lafiabougou, nestled along the River Niger on the old side of town, visitors are hit by dissonant sensory impressions. The air is filled with the sounds of gourd drums, feet stamping the city's red, dusty soil, and women's high-pitched religious chanting. Dressed in all-white attire, women slowly and majestically move in broad circles as they celebrate the *rites de passage* of individual families with religious song and dance performances. The sheer number of people drawn in by such festivity causes it to spill out into the space in front of the hosts' courtyard. On these public streets, women's invocations of the pleasures of duty, self-restraint, and moral excellence compete for attention with the piercing, electronically magnified voices of *jeli* wedding singers whose performances are taking place only a few courtyards away and drawing an audience that is quite different in composition and attire: at the weddings large crowds of young men and women of all ages show off their fancy clothes and jewelry to friends, acquaintances, and relatives.

There is not much opportunity to have a conversation during these festivities, and any attempt to do so is drowned out by the spectacularly attired *jeli* singers who yell their praises at potential patrons while circling with measured, evocative body movements. Meanwhile, Muslim women in their mid-twenties to mid-forties continue to dance in slow circles, praising the Prophet's deeds, local saintly figures, and moral examplars. Their hours-long performance is interrupted only by the electronically magnified voice of their group leader, an older woman sitting in a chair slightly above the dance square who punctuates the performance with short sermons. Those in attendance rejoice by clapping their hands and humming melodies. Meanwhile bystanders, usually youth and middle-aged women, eye the Muslim women, at a respectful distance, with curiosity but also bewilderment. Whereas most keep their thoughts to themselves, inevitably some adolescents, less observant of local norms of dignified behavior, giggle and whisper to one another, surreptitiously pointing to the Muslim women's dress and bodily demeanor. One occasionally overhears disgruntled remarks about the Muslim leader's moralizing reflections, remarks questioning the sincerity of the Muslim women's attitude by hinting at the monetary compensation they will receive in return. Yet, by and large, these complaints are muffled by the sensual vigor of the entire performance. These celebrations form part of the bi- or tri-weekly social activities engaged in by Muslim women. Together with the various male Muslim associations, the Muslim women's groups form the backbone of contemporary Muslim activism and constitute the social infrastructure through which Islam, as a moral idiom and a way of life, has recently gained new public prominence in urban Mali.

Female religious associations have been mushrooming since the mid-1980s in contemporary Mali and throughout the Muslim world (e.g., Nageeb 2004; Mahmood 2005; al-Mughni 1996). They are among the most pervasive and visible signs and structures of Islamic renewal, yet scholars of Islam in Africa have only recently begun to pay close attention to these structures of mobilization and to women's motivations for joining these associations (see Otayek 1993; Gomez-Perez 1991, 2005; Hodgkin 1998; Kleiner-Bosaller and Loimeier 1994; Miran 1998, 2005; Soares and Otayek 2007). The inadequate consideration of women's entry into these movements in Sub-Saharan Africa mirrors scholarly analyses of "political Islam" that tend to misapprehend the nature of female religious activism by viewing Muslim women merely as followers of male leaders (e.g., Roy 1994; Eickelman and Piscatori 1996; Beinin and Stork 1997; Esposito 1998 [1984]; but see Kamalkhani 1998; Nageeb 2004; Mahmood 2005). Certain scholars have recently begun to correct this perspective on different West African societies by focusing on the ethical sensibilities that inspire women's support of Islamic moral renewal (see LeBlanc 1998; Augis 2002; Alidou 2005; Janson 2008; Masquelier 2009). But the point is not simply to gain deeper insight into the motivations and concerns of these women. If we want to understand the novel roles and aspirations that religious movements claim in contemporary African politics, particularly after the demise of authoritarian single-party rule, an analysis of personal motivation and subjective experience must be complemented with an inquiry into the institutional infrastructure of religious revival. Indeed, a powerful way of discerning the social ramifications of the renewal movement in Mali is to explore the political locations of female *and* male Muslim activism, and the forms of sociality in which female activists, in particular, ground their interventions (see Glew 1996; Renders 2002; Weiss 2002.). Rather than merely complementing an earlier focus on male networks with one on female structures of Muslim activism, the task is to understand women's *differential* integration into these structures, and the views of ethical self-development that prompt women from very different backgrounds to join the movement.

Locating Islamic Moral Renewal

In the literature on the role that religion has assumed in post-authoritarian African politics, a curious disjunction exists between portrayals of Christian and Muslim organizations. Authors tend to highlight the anti-authoritarianism and progressivism of (mostly mainstream) Christian churches in challenging despotic regimes and bringing about democratic change (e.g., Bayart 1993; Gifford 1995, 1998). Muslim groups, on the other hand, are often studied as defenders of religious, anti-secularist values and are thus denied membership in a secular civil society, even though they resemble Christian groups in their institutions of socializing and their potential to transform society from within in the contemporary context of neoliberal restructuring. The normative presuppositions of this analytical perspective, which classifies some groups as democratic, progressive, and liberating and others as potentially anti-democratic and anti-modern, often remain implicit.[1] Perhaps most problematic about the preoccupation with the alleged threat Muslim organizations pose to a secular political order is that it misses an essential point about the way that politics in Muslim Africa has been conducted in the past. In numerous Muslim African societies, religious networks operated not as a threat to secular state politics but were, in fact, constitutive of it (see Loimeier 1997, 2003). The classification of Muslim activism as a religious threat to secular politics also risks concealing the immense heterogeneity of actors and doctrinal positions that inform Islamic revival in Mali and elsewhere. A way out of this narrow perspective is to examine the specific relationship of coexistence, contestation, or mutual co-optation with state institutions that Muslim movements have established historically.

Understanding the reasons why religion has so visibly gained in appeal in African politics since the late 1980s pushes us to examine the ways that religious groups politically mobilize, how they connect to state institutions, and how the particular nature of these connections, as well as the logic of the affiliation between group leaders and ordinary members, affects the terms on which they make their influence felt (see Joseph 1997). Assessing continuities and changes in these patterns of mobilization allows us to contrast them with earlier patterns of religious sociality, on one hand, and with religious associations in other areas of West Africa, on the other, and thus to attest to the diverse ways religious organizations insert themselves into wider political fields throughout Muslim societies in Africa (see Evers Rosander 1997, 1998; Strobel 1976; also see Meyer 2004; Fourchard et al. 2005).

One way to elucidate how the moral reform movement's internal dynamics derive from its location in a translocal field of influences is to address them through the concept of extraversion. Gifford (1998), Englund (2003), and Meyer (2004), following Bayart (2000), employ this concept to understand the spectacular thriving of Christian churches in an era of global religious idioms, media, images, and institutions, and to explain people's motivations to join these groups. African Christians' strategies of extraversion, they argue, are geared, importantly, toward material improvement and gaining access to financial and institutional support generated from transnational sources. Extraversion thus forms part of a local repertoire of strategies to respond to degrading economic conditions. I suggest that we push the analysis one step further and use "extraversion" to pinpoint new processes of internal differentiation (for instance, based on gender and age) that occur *within* local or national religious movements as a result of their presence in transnational structures of economic enterprise and spiritual salvation. Taking up "extraversion" in this way illuminates how the differential insertion of Malian Muslim women and men into national and transnational networks of religious patronage establishes, reproduces, and potentially transforms relations of inequality not only between men and women but also between women themselves.

Religious associations form the institutional backbone of the renewal movement in Mali. They do not fit a neat classificatory opposition between formal and informal organizations but display different degrees of institutionalization (see Lindisfarne 1997). They are rooted in a long-standing matrix of religious sociality associated with Sufi orders and influential religious clans, but also with groups initiated in the 1940s by reform-minded Muslims that challenged the hegemony of established religious clans by providing alternative structures of religious mobilization in the context of the colonial "civilizing" mission. Muslim associations in Mali also resonate with forms of grassroots mobilization that are mushrooming throughout West Africa and the wider Muslim world, and that address themselves to women and to disenfranchised segments of the urban youth. In Mali so far, mobilization has largely been directed toward married women and, to a lesser degree, men (Hock 1998). Their associations are integrated into wider networks of informal influence that connect their leaders to state and party officials. Thus, although variously portrayed by their critics as instances of a "patriarchal" or "fundamentalist religious" threat to political modernity, the political locations of these Muslim associations indicate that they are the product of recent social and political alliances.

Clear parallels exist between the associational infrastructure of Islamic renewal in Mali and other mutual support structures that, since the colonial period, helped rural migrants assimilate into a vibrant, highly mobile urban society (e.g., Little 1965; Meillassoux 1968). Commonalities between these different urban networks exist with regard to both organizational structure and the conceptual framework and discursive repertoire that inform their practices. Members express their shared interests not only as a matter of mutual financial support but also as conviviality, and they frame their associational activities in an idiom of traditional solidarity.[2] Muslim associations and other present-day urban support groups also occupy a similar socio-institutional space, as they intervene in social realms from which the state has withdrawn or in which it never successfully operated, and thus create a framework for people in search of mutual financial, emotional, and political support.

In contrast to most support groups that emerged with urbanization and have always been structured along kinship, neighborhood, or ethnic lines, Muslim associations cut across these divides. The Muslim groups mobilize not only urbanites but also foster patronage ties that stretch from urban benefactors to the rural hinterland, and that offer services and infrastructure in the realm of schooling that the state fails to provide. Moreover, as members of the Muslim associations never fail to point out, their combination of moral and material concerns distinguishes them from historical predecessors, as well as from other contemporary support structures such as the credit savings associations created in the wake of the Structural Adjustment Programs in the mid-1980s (e.g., Ardener and Burman 1995). That members of Muslim associations cast their socializing activities as a matter of traditional solidarity, conviviality, and enjoyment (*nyanaje*) is highly significant. They feel that their associational activities are in line with, and justified through, conventional norms of urban sociality. And they would reject any claim that they propose a "religious" alternative—or threat—to these conventions.

Another distinctive feature of Muslim associations in Mali is their integration into a parallel economy of political patronage and trade opportunities that promises members easier and more profitable access to financial and political resources. This intertwining of religious activities and patronage structures, which is not a novel phenomenon, places the Muslim associational infrastructure in continuity with long-standing economies of entrepreneurship and patronage in which Muslim traders were central actors (Amselle 1977; Levtzion 1986b; McDougall 1986; Launay 1992). Villalon (1995) argues that in Senegal a characteristic feature of the Muride Sufi order, and a principal motor for its astounding success since French colonial rule, was its capacity to bind religious leaders and their disciples into an "economy of affection" based on reciprocal moral and material obligations. This argument can be extended to contemporary Mali. The close interlocking of religious and strategic political considerations manifested in Muslim associational activities does not signal a recent politicizing of religion nor, for that matter, a dilution of true religious conviction by political or economic interests. Urban Muslim associations invigorate long-standing conventions that facilitate the intertwining of religious and political success and leadership in West Africa.

A string of events in 1997 and 1998 powerfully illuminated how Muslim associations in town operate within and structure forms of religio-political patronage. In 1997 a wealthy expatriate with close ties to high-ranking ADEMA government officials bought a plot of land on the banks of the River Niger, on the outskirts of Bamako. His intention was to build a restaurant for the wealthy expatriates who lived in close proximity. In early 1998 he took initial steps to eject several Fulbe families, a predominantly Muslim group of cattle herders and farmers that lived as squatters on his new property. This turned into a showdown between some ADEMA government bureaucrats and leading representatives of the AMUPI. Threatened by expulsion, the Fulbe squatters capitalized on their connections to a nearby *medersa*—an Arabic-language private school—financed by Saudi sponsors (whose identity was never disclosed to me) via a Malian Muslim association. One of the key founders of this association, and the chief mediator between it and its Saudi sponsors, was an influential member of the AMUPI steering committee who entertained close relations with President Konaré. He brought the affair to the president's attention and settled the conflict in the interest of his protégés. Not only were the Fulbe officially granted the right to stay on a small strip of the terrain, but in May 2006, when I last visited the site, the construction of the restaurant had barely begun and there were indications that this was not going to happen soon.

The episode illustrates the structure and logic of Muslim associational life and the often indeterminate dynamic of membership mobilization. The Fulbe plaintiffs did not need to formally join the Muslim association initiated by the AMUPI representative to call on his assistance. Certain gestures of deference and involvement, such as sending some of their children to the association-sponsored *medersa*, sufficed to signal that they willingly entrusted themselves to their benefactor's protective powers. Both parties' recognition of their interaction as one of enduring mutual obligation crystallized in the decision of several squatters to join their benefactor's Muslim association shortly after he had settled the dispute on their behalf.

The central role that prominent representatives of the Muslim moral reform movement play as patrons echoes Simone's account of the influence religious leaders hold in urban Senegal. Their influence, Simone argues, derives from their ability to manage networks that operate across various spatial and sociopolitical divides in town. Certain religious clans in Senegal wield a power unparalleled by Muslim authorities in many other West African urban settings. Yet in urban Mali, too, religious leaders act as power brokers largely because of their capacity to "affect various kinds of social articulation across administrative and morpho-logical divides" (Simone 2003, 236). There are slight variations between Mali and Senegal in the type of religious patrons who mediate access to state institu-tions,[3] even if in both countries religious leaders draw on genealogical prestige as well as on credentials such as Arabic literacy, international contacts, and, occa-sionally, employment in the state administration. But the logic and protocols of patronage are ultimately the same.[4] A similar logic informs the networking activities of Mali's rural dwellers. Their allegiances to urban-based benefactors or a Muslim association manifest themselves in the mosques and *medersa* school buildings that have been mushrooming in many semi-urban areas over recent decades. Rural followers, too, frame their relationship to the religious patrons whose beneficiaries they become as a matter of entrusting them for "protection" (*jigi;* literally, "hope," "support"). Rural male youth, some of whom attended a traditional Qur'anic school or *medersa,* enthusiastically gravitate toward these urban benefactors and the opportunities for spiritual, educational, and material advancement that their Muslim associations offer. Their status as juniors excludes them from positions of authority and decision making within the family; further, as rural dwellers, they tend to remain marginal in networks that operate along kinship relations and common origin, which are the ties that link rural families to the urban administrative-political centers. The double disenfranchisement of young men is an important reason for their eager response to the opportunities that Muslim activist networks provide.

The most successful example to date of Muslim activists' efforts to spread their influence to the countryside is the charismatic preacher Sharif Haidara whose group of followers, the Ansar Dine,[5] played a role in the draft law debate analyzed in chapter 1. Having full confidence in Sharif Haidara's capacity to "fix things" (Simone 2003, 237), villagers use their ties to him in Bamako whenever they need support in local conflicts over business transactions or with represen-tatives of the administration. Ties of religious and commercial-entrepreneurial patronage that link rural beneficiaries to Haidara and his followers in Bamako are facilitated by intermediaries, most of them merchants and teachers at local *medersa*s. These religious and commercial networks resemble the patronage connections to Muslim traders that emerged with the colonial market (*la traite*) (Kaba 1974, 1976). The religious structures of support offered by prominent figures in the Islamic renewal movement, therefore, do not signal the corruption of a purely religious motive by the logic of commerce. Rather, their associations allow followers and benefactors to combine social, religious, and moral considerations by fusing protection with charity.

The moral dimension of their associational activities is highlighted by Muslim activists who, referring to the image of a joint "pathway to God," claim that their gatherings follow a distinctive ethic of mutual assistance and joint spirituality that endows them with a credibility that other urban associations have long since lost. Amina, a highly respected member of the Ansar Dine women's group in San and a close confidante, once succinctly described how the moral preoccupations of her Muslim women's group contrasts with the self-interested and materialistic orientation of other women's groups:

> "The world is corrupt, Nanaje," she said, "and the poor [*fantanw*] suffer most. . . . If you are a sensible person, you keep away from these associations [*tonw*]. Participation in these groups only creates trouble . . . [T]hese women do not come together . . . because they want to live together as true human beings [*hademadenw*], but because they are guided by economic interest. . . . The political associations [*politiki tonw*], they are the worst. As soon as elections approach, . . . all kinds of presents are distributed among members, . . . so many women join these groups. But once the politician [who sponsored the group] has lost the elections or the [group's] *présidente* keeps the presents for herself, women quit the group and turn to a more successful politician. . . . Our association is different, it is for women who have few means and who need to count on others' steadiness. We . . . make up for the support that our relatives cannot provide, . . . in the name of God, the Merciful, and thus protect each other from feeling ashamed.

Amina's rebuttal of *politiki* groups is directed against the ends to which "politiki people" use patronage ties and their opportunistic pursuit of personal advantage. Institutions of religious sociality promise greater reliability because they implicate ordinary group members and their leaders in a dense fabric of shared moral concerns and of obligations with predictable outcomes. But even if Amina and her fellow Muslims define their own search for moral renewal in opposition to immoral *politiki,* they engage and do not avoid it. They practice their authentic expressions of Islamic solidarity in those areas of public sociality where issues of sociopolitical and moral import are debated because it is here that they might convince others to join their search for moral renewal.

Whereas Muslims, such as Amina, plead to counter Malian society's moral erosion with Islamic charity, their opponents, most of them secularist-minded critics close to the new political elite of the 1990s democratization process, deny Muslim activists this humanitarian role and dismiss their interventions as misguided by religious fervor and external—mostly Saudi Arabian—capital and influence. Strikingly, these Western-educated intellectuals do not consider the initiatives by Muslim activists on an equal footing with the Western donor–funded development projects, although these projects resemble the Muslim initiatives in their purpose and organization (Alliman 1984/85; Brenner 1993a, 67–74; see Renders 2002).

The point is not that Muslim activists' claim to an ethically inspired mission should be salvaged by a truthful public representation. Rather, the dynamics of Muslim activist infrastructure reveal that Muslim activists and their opponents both go astray. Muslim associations are a potpourri of at least three patterns of sociality: first, institutions of Islamic proselytizing (*da'wa*) that, with funding from Arabic donors, have extended their influence throughout Sub-Saharan Africa since the late 1970s;[6] second, conventional local forms of patronage; and, third, organizational features of the civil society institutions funded by Western donors after political liberalization of the early 1990s.[7] The group called the Association of the Servants of God (Association Serviteurs d'Allah) illustrates the novel mix of associational forms and rationales. The group was initiated and funded by the late Al-Bekayye Kunta, a descendant of a prestigious religious clan and the former ambassador to Saudi Arabia and Morocco, after his retirement in the early 1990s. In a conversation with me in August 1998 Kunta explained that his objective was to promote Islam among Muslims who had "suffered from Western imperialism couched in the cloak of humanitarian aid." Kunta had initiated "self-help projects in support of various segments of the urban poor." He stressed that his association was an ethically superior alternative to Western donor–dependent development projects that "only inspired individual enrichment and egotism." Yet contrary to Kunta's disparaging remarks about Western aid projects, structural similarities between them and his charity services are evident. Kunta conceived his aid measures without consulting with those whom he had singled out as beneficiaries. Similar to the ambivalent emphasis by Western donors on self-reliance, sustainability, and the import of foreign expertise, Kunta's association offers support for individuals to set up independent economic enterprises, yet at the same time perpetuates financial dependency. Kunta's association also faces the problems of Western aid projects that encourage the creation of parallel sectors of employment and the marketing of products. As Kunta's charity services come to resemble Western development projects, the norms of reciprocity that inform conventional religious patronage networks are altered, because benefactors such as Kunta lose some of the normative hold over their beneficiaries. For instance, in a project sponsored by Kunta's association, several young men and their spouses were offered a plot of Kunta's personally owned land to prevent them from slipping into delinquency, prostitution, and other semi-legal activities.[8] Kunta's combination of charity services and agricultural labor repeated a historical pattern of economic and religious organization throughout the West Africa Sahel, a pattern that also materialized in the labor units (singular, *daara*) organized by the Muride order and in other religious associations (*daaira*) in Senegal (Coulon 1983; Villalon 1995, chap. 5; Evers Rosander 1997). Kunta framed his humanitarian interventions as an expression of Islamic charity and his desire to realize Islamic principles of compassion, yet, as I realized during my stays with his clients, they held contradictory attitudes about their relationship to Kunta and the obligations this implied. On the one hand, they portrayed their daily labor as part of the life trajectory that, as proper Muslims, Kunta enabled them to pursue. On the other, they also sought to take advantage of Kunta's generosity as much as they could, occasionally insinuating that Kunta "exploited" their "cheap labor" by "keeping the profit to himself." That they clandestinely sold off parts of the harvest to generate additional revenue suggests that, while these clients articulate the ideal of Islamic welfare and "trust," their considerations and practices resemble those of Western aid recipients.

Kunta's humanitarian projects mirror the associational structures created by other Muslim activists. They all encourage the fusion of religious patronage, client-based and redistributive considerations, and a logic of individual profit maximization that, ultimately, subverts the trust and mutual obligation implicit in patronage relations. Also typical for the associational structures is that they benefit from connections to international and national "benefactors," which, as Kunta exemplifies, often result from one's former employment in the state bureaucracy. Connections to the state administration or the political regime of former president Traoré facilitate one's success as a prominent defender of Islamic moral renewal. There is some truth, therefore, to critics' allegation that Muslim activists' search for an "extra-parliamentary following" is actually an attempt to make up for their lack of official power. Still, there is clearly a mutually constitutive relationship between the close ties that Kunta and other leading activists cultivate with current governmental officials, on one hand, and their reputation and related capacity to mobilize a large following, on the other (Villalon 1995, 88). If the logics of patronage and redistribution are central to the functionality of the parallel economy that Muslim leaders establish, why do they seek public recognition as associations? Should their endeavor to "go public" (Lee 1993) be seen as a search for notoriety, as some of their critics allege? What kind of recognition do Muslim activists fight for?

In an analysis of new, increasingly transnational forms of social, cultural, and economic integration, Lipschutz (1992) proposes a typology of networks that generate what he calls a "global civil society." He distinguishes between movements that either operate against the state, aim to reform the state, or ignore the state or operate outside its reach. Lipschutz's typology relates to networks that operate on a transnational scale, but his distinction between groups according to the position they take in relation to the state is also helpful to clarify key parameters of orientation and intervention that characterize Muslim activism in Mali. The networks created by Muslim activists appear to conform to Lipschutz's third category: they operate not against the state but outside and parallel to it. This classification, however, cannot do justice to the close ties between proponents of Islamic moral renewal and the political elites. Muslim associations derive much of their political force from their capacity to bridge divisions between state and non-state actors and institutions. They thereby successfully inject themselves into the center of Malian state politics. The complex positioning of Muslim activists thus illustrates that there are no clear dividing lines between state officials and groups that claim the status of an emergent civil society. Even if the relations of Muslim leaders with state officials and politicians vary, none of them operates fully outside the state's reach. This insight has two important implications. First, there is incongruity between the actual sociopolitical locations of Muslim activism and the rhetoric of a "civil society against the state" that is espoused by representatives of the movement. Second, the multiple links between state institutions and the structures of religious activism cast doubt on scholarly analyses that interpret contemporary religious revival as a reaction to disciplinary state power and thereby reify notions of a monolithic, hegemonic state.

Muslim leaders' enormous talent to straddle informal networks and the realm of state politics should prompt us to reconsider their critics' resentments and allegations. Many officials in Presidents Konaré's and Touré's governments denounce the Muslim activists' propaganda in private conversations, but they avoid challenging Muslim activists too openly. Politicians' guardedness is evident, for instance, in their dealings with the national Muslim women's association, UNAFEM, and its leaders, some of whom once occupied top government posts under President Traoré. Since the creation of the UNAFEM in 1996, its steering committee has organized several conferences for which it mustered the government's financial and institutional support, to the surprise of many.[9] A striking illustration of the government's careful handling of the UNAFEM leaders was that they implicated Adam Bâ Konaré, the outspokenly secularist-minded wife of former president Konaré. The political leadership's deep ambivalence toward leaders of the renewal movement, which this governmental support revealed, was not lost on political observers. Several journalists expressed a deep uneasiness not so much with Bâ Konaré's conference participation but with the government's attempts to at once accommodate and contain Muslim activists' informal ties to the state. Officials from the Ministry of Women, on the other hand, deplored that Madame Bâ Konaré's decision had greatly enhanced the UNAFEM's public standing. Their criticism brings to light yet another dimension of the alleged confrontation between secular politics and religious fundamentalism: the competition among elite women from different ideological camps. Female politicians are acutely aware that Muslim women, in their public enactment of propriety, are more successful in securing popular support than most of their political opponents. Muslim women, by publicly distancing themselves from the indecency of secularist *politiki* women, capitalize on their higher competitiveness in this domain. And they use their authority in neighborhood politics to influence public opinion and build up pressure groups on behalf of certain politicians from whom they expect favors in exchange.[10]

The debate over Madame Bâ Konaré's conference participation illustrates that neither the claims of Muslim activists nor those of their critics can be explained by a neat opposition between a "religious" and a "secularist" camp. Muslim activists are divided among themselves and occupy different positions on governmental politics. Considerable competition exists between some activists and representatives of the traditional families of religious specialists; they all seek to mobilize popular support at the neighborhood level in order to gain a stronghold in national politics.[11] In view of its heterogeneous nature, Muslim activism should be cautiously accepted as an analytical category, as it refers mainly to a common motivational structure, ethical sensibility, and shared vision of the pathway that leads to a moral renewal of society and self. This vision of a pathway draws inspiration from a reformist impetus that, supported by intellectual trends from Egypt and Saudi Arabia, made its influence felt since the 1940s (Brenner 1993a, 71–72, 1993b; see Kaba 1974; Niezen 1990). The politics of recognition in which activists engage is characterized by considerable competition between leaders whose authority derives from their birth into established families of religious specialists; activists whose endeavor to transform society and self is inspired by intellectual trends in the Arabic-speaking world, especially Egypt and Saudi Arabia; and, finally, religious leaders with diverse credentials and highly variable abilities to attract a following and who are constantly at risk of failure.

Muslim Women's Associations

What kind of institutional infrastructure do female supporters of Islamic renewal choose for their joint pathway to God? Muslim women's groups (singular, *silame musow ton*) typically operate in neighborhoods and draw women who seek Arabic literacy and knowledge of ritual precepts. Like countless grassroots organizations that emerged after the end of authoritarian rule in 1991, most Muslim women's groups are registered as associations under the aegis of the national Muslim women's association—UNAFEM—to be formally recognized as part of civil society. The literature on women's associational life in Muslim societies often centers on issues of power and gender inequality, and on the potentially liberating capacities that these groups offer women to rework patriarchal control in the domestic domain (e.g., Shaheed 1995; Chatty and Rabo 1997). But attempts to counter power inequalities may not be women's central motivation to join these groups. How do members of Muslim women's groups in Mali describe and construct the moral and spiritual architectonics of their group activities, and how do they relate them to other aspects of daily life?

The significance of female associations for the Islamic renewal movement has broad theoretical relevance. As Boyd and Last (1985) observe in their historiography of female Muslim practices in West Africa, the role of women as religious actors has been understudied. Because scholars of Islam conceive of religious practice in a narrow sense, much research has focused on written texts, doctrinal debates, and male religious authorities at the expense of activities engineered by women (see also Constantin 1987; Coulon and Reveyrand-Coulon 1990).[12] Following Triaud's (1985) call for attention to the role of religious brokers[13] in the institutionalization of Islam in Africa, Boyd and Last propose a two-pronged approach: to recover the historical contribution of female Muslim scholars for whom some documentation exists; and to distill the significance of women who, though not engaging in religious education or scholarship, mobilized fellow believers and created the social infrastructure necessary for the fulfillment of religious duties. The relevance of Boyd and Last's perspective for an understanding of Muslim women's contribution to Islamic renewal in Mali is evident. It redirects scholarly attention to activities that, although not pertaining to worship and scriptural interpretation, are nevertheless relevant to believers' self-understandings *as* religious subjects. Their perspective also prompts us to inquire into historical continuities and discontinuities in women's religious practices, and in the significance of these practices for collective religious life.

Villalon (1995, 149–150) has cautioned against interpreting the current blossoming of Muslim women's groups as an indication of a recent Islamic "revival," or rise in religious fervor. Still, the sheer number of Muslim women's associations, as well as their greater visibility in Mali's urban landscapes, appears to be novel. Compared to Senegal, religious associational life in Mali, especially in the southern triangle, was relatively little developed historically, partly because it was less intricately linked to the social organization and political power position of Sufi orders. Mali's thriving Muslim associations do indicate recent structural transformations in the landscape of Muslim authority and activism (see Gomez-Perez 1991, 2005; Mbow 1997; Loimeier 2001; Augis 2002; Renders 2002), even if, heeding Villalon's suggestion, we should not regard Muslim associational life as a mere product of political liberalization. Nor can the alleged resurgence of Muslim activism be fully explained by influences from the Arabic-speaking world. What needs to be elucidated are the continuities between these associations and their historical predecessors, as well as the dynamics that facilitated the associations' rise at this historical juncture, characterized, among other factors, by the influence of a transnational Muslim missionary effort.[14]

Comparative literature on Muslim women's structures of socializing suggests that differences in form and historical origins can be seen as the result of the divergent actors, institutions, and normative practices through which Islam gained a foothold in different regions of East and West Africa (see Strobel 1976; Askew 1999). Muslim associations in Mali, particularly those addressing women, emerged more slowly than in Senegal, Nigeria, and Niger, where Muslim associations geared toward education became constitutive features of urban life by the 1920s, in the context of growing urbanization induced by colonial rule.[15] Most Mali associations appeared in Bamako and Kankan, then the newly emerging centers of this region of colonial French West Africa, initiated by reform-minded returnees from Saudi Arabia and Egypt who aimed to provide an alternative to colonial education.

Silame jama, the first Muslim women's association in what is now present-day Mali, was created in 1958 by Haja Binta Sall, shortly before the country gained independence. Born into a family of prestigious Muslim scholars from Kayes, Binta Sall studied at her father's Qur'anic school. But only late in life, when she returned to her family after her husband's death, was she able to devote all her time to Qur'anic studies. Binta Sall's second marriage to a well-known Muslim cleric from Senegal brought her to Bamako, where, considered harmless by colonial administrators, she continued her Qur'anic studies and passed on her knowledge to other women. After her return from a second pilgrimage to Mecca in 1958 (her first was in 1956), she founded Silame jama, an association of married, wealthy women whom Haja instructed in Arabic and ritual practice. Her reputation grew as her female followers created local groups of Silame jama in Kayes, Gao, Segou, and Mopti. One reason why Haja's association found the support of male authorities in the midst of fierce struggles among Muslims was her reputation as a learned woman who scrupulously followed Islamic etiquette of motherhood and marital companionship, but had been courageous enough to undertake the pilgrimage to Mecca twice, a feat considered extraordinary for a woman. After two more pilgrimages to Mecca, Haja Binta Sall settled in Medina. In her absence, the Silame jama transformed into a *haja ton* (from *ton,* association, and *Haja* (or *Hadja*), the honorific title of a woman returnee from the *hadj,* pilgrimage), that is, into a group of Hajas who met to commemorate their endeavor. Women who had not undertaken the pilgrimage began to stay away and the group lost its original educational impetus (Sanankoua 1991b).

Haja Binta Sall's story underscores that until recently religious erudition and leadership was a career path open to few women from mostly privileged family backgrounds. Only at an advanced age could these women spend their time with religious study and a pious life withdrawn from daily matters. Only women who defended conservative values and limited themselves to domains of knowledge considered proper for women were allowed to engage in religious education and proselytizing. Herein the career options for female religious erudition in the French Sudan resembled those of the wives and daughters of upper-class men in Northern Nigeria, as well as members of respected religious clans in Senegal (Sule and Starratt 1991; Coulon and Reveyrand-Coulon 1990; Boyd 1989, 2001; Umar 2001; see Dunbar 2000).

Until the 1970s, regular gatherings of Muslim women were a rare phenomenon, limited to a few towns. Since the mid-1980s, however, neighborhood-based associations of Muslim women have proliferated at breathtaking speed. Whereas some are based on loosely organized networks, the majority have been created with the financial and institutional support of women who enjoy great prestige at the neighborhood level. These leaders—referred to with the honorific title *hadja,* or *tontigi* ("group leader," *présidente* in French)—feel that helping fellow believers will give them additional spiritual merit (*nafa*) and contribute to the moral rejuvenation of society.

These groups differ from their historical predecessors in their social bases and age composition. From the late colonial period to the 1960s, female religious associational activities were largely an affair of well-off wives of wealthy merchants and clerics who found time to devote themselves to Islamic studies later in life. Nowadays many of those who participate in Muslim neighborhood activities come from the lower strata of urban populations and are younger, married women. The organizational structure of the groups and their objectives also differ from their historical predecessors in the nature and scope of their activities, and in their forms of mobilization. The organizational terminology of many groups, such as the functions of the *présidente, secrétaire général,* and *trésorière,* indicates that they draw inspiration from Western, donor-funded, grassroots organizations. All these groups cut across social status hierarchies and distinctions based on regional or ethnic origin. Their explicit denial of social differences distinguishes them from their historical predecessors but, more important, from the conventional types of religious associations in neighboring Muslim-majority countries. The latter are, at least in Senegal, linked to Sufi social organizations, where their ideals of human intercession in religious salvation and of genealogical prestige play decisive roles in structuring the hierarchical relations within these urban- or rural-based religious groups (see Villalon 1995, chap. 4; Evers Rosander 1997, 1998).

The explicit dismissal of social distinctions as articulated in Muslim women's associations in Mali does not foreclose the performance and reproduction of status differences. As chapter 5 will demonstrate, hierarchies between ordinary members and group leaders are established and reconfirmed through quotidian symbolic and material practices that reinforce the persistent validity of authority credentials to which female leaders historically laid claim. For the moment, analysis centers on the socio-institutional basis that enables, and is structured by, the reproduction of inequalities between group members and their leaders. Social hierarchies *among* Muslim women can be understood by considering group leaders' and ordinary members' differential location in a network of national and transnational religious patronage. This brings us back to the concept of extraversion taken up by some scholars of contemporary Christian movements to explain the thriving of religious networks in a globalizing world of symbolic repertoires, spiritual experiences, and economic enterprise. As noted earlier in this chapter, processes of extraversion should be further specified to illuminate what new dynamics of internal differentiation, such as differences in gender, age, and educational background, shape religious movements at local or national levels as a consequence of their entry into transnational structures of economic enterprise and spiritual salvation. Specified in this manner, the concept of extraversion illuminates how Muslim women's and men's differential participation reproduces but also potentially transforms relations of inequality between men and women, and between women themselves.

The high tides of foreign-sponsored Islamic welfare infrastructure and educational projects have been over for more than a decade. Whatever the background for the decline in international funding is, even in the heydays of foreign *da'wa* intervention in Mali, most institutional support was directed to and administered by male recipients.[16] This pattern has not changed. Yet, as Aissatou, one of the female leaders willing to discuss the matter with me, complained, "the donations we once received from our benefactors to help fellow Muslims has become erratic, and only God the Merciful knows when to count on them again."[17] As this suggests, international and national sponsors are usually men, and female group leaders are recipients of financial contributions that are unpredictable.[18] Ordinary group members, on the other hand, are in no position to approach donors directly.[19] Female group leaders, because of their intermediary positions between group members and national and international sponsors, form the crucial nexus of extraversion between transnational influences and local members' aspirations.[20] They access networks through male relatives and in-laws who maintain trade connections to Arabic-speaking areas of the Muslim world or, having themselves spent years abroad, may draw on long-standing forms of cooperation with foreign business partners. Some group leaders cannot rely on kin-mediated access to foreign sponsors; however, their influence at the neighborhood level allows them to solicit a Malian benefactor with ties to commerce and state administration. A prerequisite for a group leader's access to local and international sponsors is therefore her capacity to mobilize fellow Muslim women, a capacity that is mutually constitutive with her moral reputation. Her relationship to local or international sponsors does not entitle her to regular contributions, but she is in a privileged position to tap into networks that *may* prove helpful in gaining institutional and financial support.

Over the past thirty years Muslim women's groups drawing on historical conventions of religious sociality have marked a far-reaching social presence of Islam in urban Mali. The entry of female institutions of Islamic renewal and of male structures of activism into a field of transnational ties, intellectual influences, and symbolic references has paradoxical consequences. The movement's transnational orientation and locations generate new conditions and terms of intervention in the national arena, yet also contribute to the reproduction of two trajectories of inequality. One is the unequal position of male and female initiators within the moral reform movement that is as much a precondition as a consequence of women's and men's differential insertion into local and transnational religious patronage networks. The second is the reproduction of the social and economic hierarchy between leaders and group members, a hierarchy that only few supporters of the movement may forego. Even the insertion of female leaders into the national and international field of religious patronage, and the advantages they may draw from this privileged position, are brittle. The precarious nature of their brokering position is important, because it sheds doubt on frequent rumors, spread by their government critics, that Muslim women's leaders use their brokering position mostly for their personal benefit. There are examples of women who relied on benefactors to receive grants to study at institutions of higher religious learning in the Maghreb, and who, after their return, played a vocal role in the renewal movement; but these women, who usually come from privileged social backgrounds and are still unmarried, are not the same as the (older) leaders of Muslim women's groups. Understanding the dynamics within the renewal movement by looking at these women's differential insertion into the landscape of political and religious patronage should not be mistaken as an attempt to *explain* the existence of Muslim women's groups. It would be misleading to reduce the raison d'être of Muslim associations to the participants' short-term material interests. Such interpretations fail to elucidate why the endeavor to learn and gain knowledge in ritual matters has become key to Muslim women's mobilization. Their educational impetus offers a good point of entry to expand our understanding of the aims toward which Muslim women's acts of extraversion, no longer understood as guided by material interest alone, are directed.

Relevancies of Learning

Although Muslim women's group activities comprise an array of ritual celebrations, ranging from the organization of public worship and sermon sessions to the celebration of holidays such as the Prophet's birthday (*mawlud;* Arabic, *mawlid an-nabî*), Muslim women call their groups "learning groups" (*kalani tonw*). Explanations I received in this regard were unanimous: "learning" (*kalan*) was the prime "benefit" (*nafa*) of their activities; to learn "about Islam" and to learn to "read and write" would rescue them from their current state of ignorance and help them "move closer to God." Clearly more is going on here than issues of gender inequality, women's status, and their alleged attempts to subvert patriarchal gender ideologies. The groups promise opportunities for personal enlightenment in a situation where women are ambitious for self-improvement through learning but face a lack of opportunities to participate. Chapter 5 further addresses this self-civilizing sensibility of Muslim women. It illuminates how the new importance of Arabic literacy and the institutions to acquire it go hand in hand with the reformulation of religious subjectivity, for embarking on the path to God implies a new understanding of individual responsibility and the relevance of faith. Grasping the subtle changes involved in the reformulation of religious subjectivity requires us first to appreciate how Muslim women relate literacy in Arabic and knowledge of ritual requirements to notions of personal salvation, moral accomplishment, and religious orthopraxy.[21]

Most female leaders have rudimentary Arabic literacy and lack the ability to interpret the written sources of Islam. They often hire a *karamògò* to teach Arabic and instruct group members on their ritual obligations, while limiting their own role to dispensing occasional lessons on proper conduct in ritual and everyday settings. Women use the word *kalan* to denote "reading," as well as "learning" in a broader sense, and thus reflect the legacy and cultural capital of Arabic literacy in the region (see Wilks 1968; Loimeier 2002, 121–122). At the same time, by choosing the term used for the evening adult alphabetization classes set up by Western donor organizations, women demarcate their activities from traditional forms of Islamic learning.[22] When Muslim women refer to their gatherings as "learning/reading groups," this implies a close association of reading with notions of individual and societal improvement. Their high estimation of the capacity to read and write results from the intermingling of diverse notions of valuable knowledge with a Western schooling pedagogy that revolves on notions of enlightenment and progress. Women's emphasis on Arabic literacy thus suggests that they develop a locally specific sensibility that is at once modern, sophisticated, and ethical.

Muslim women's learning groups resonate with contemporary movements throughout the Muslim world that, in their effort to combine personal and societal reform, mobilize disenfranchised youth and women of varying ages, and make education a priority. Westerlund (1997, 323) observes that these movements' investment in educational infrastructure indicates that their political project and call for a return to the spirit of the Prophet's community of followers is not a reaction against modernity but an active engagement with and locally specific reformulation of it (see Roy 1994, chap. 3; Hodgkin 1998, 222). Though we should keep in mind that the stress on education and individual enlightenment does not mark these movements as something new (see Kaba 1974), Westerlund's observation is helpful to grasp the complex sensibility that inspires Muslim activists' present educational efforts. Their sensibility is reflected in the concern not only to gain knowledge in Islamic precepts but to render it relevant to everyday life. The importance Muslim women attribute to Arabic literacy and the acquisition of ritual knowledge reveals a long-standing shift in the significance of personal faith that started as early as the 1930s and increasingly made Islam a blueprint for public order and individual self-development. Simultaneously, however, the learning activities of Muslim activists reflect and refract the legacy of older traditions of acquiring knowledge and the high prestige of Arabic literacy in Muslim West Africa.

From the early centuries of Islamic presence in the West African Sahel and Sahara, literacy was restricted to lineages of Islamic scholars and scribes. The social basis of Islamic erudition was broadened with the politically motivated Muslim movements of the eighteenth and nineteenth centuries and the role that Sufi orders played in their emergence. Yet literacy and knowledge in Islamic jurisprudence and related religious sciences remained key markers of social distinction and cultural capital (Hamès 1997). In colonial French Sudan, education in religious and worldly matters became a vital site of confrontation between the colonial administration, Muslim "traditionalists" (Brenner 1993a, 67), and a younger generation of reformist Muslims. This latter group was inspired by reformist trends in Cairo and developed the *medersas* in response to colonial schooling policy in the 1950s and to the concomitant eclipse of the relevance of traditional Qur'anic schooling. In Francophone West Africa, the goal of Muslim reformists to preserve Muslim culture and knowledge led to a readjustment of the curricula, spatial organization, and didactics of traditional Qur'anic schooling and the transmission of Islamic knowledge (Stewart 1973; Launay 1992; Brenner 2001). Out of the collision of two different systems of schooling emerged new notions of relevant religious knowledge, along with an increased intermingling of different paradigms of learning (see Eickelman 1992). The principal aim of traditional Islamic education, namely, the initiation of a child into the status and bodily demeanor of a fully responsible believer, was dislodged, but never replaced, by a new emphasis on the acquisition of daily relevant skills and knowledge (Loimeier 2002). Because education was already central to the endeavor of Muslim reformers in the colonial period, particularly in their confrontation with established Muslim authorities, two important questions arise: What are the novel features of present-day Muslim educational activism, and where do they manifest themselves in Muslim women's learning activities?

Paradigms of Learning

On those bright, exceedingly hot afternoons in February 1998, when Amina, a respected member of the Ansar Dine women's group in San, took me to their meetings, we rode on her motorbike to the meeting place, the family courtyard of three group members. We arrived at about 2:45 PM to find that most of the thirty-five to fifty women present were already sitting on mats in the very large courtyard of an obviously affluent host family. We greeted the *karamògò,* a man in his early thirties with a non-imposing, almost shy, demeanor and a calm voice. He always welcomed me in a restrained but polite manner, often commenting approvingly on my persistence in attending the learning sessions. Over the months of my attendance I was very grateful to Amina and several of her friends for helping some of the older women overcome their initial reserve when I visited. Gone, too, was the mix of guarded distance and giggling curiosity that some of the younger women displayed in my presence. Even appreciative comments on my headscarf had become less frequent. Women made room for me on the mat not far from the *karamògò* so that I could follow his teachings closely, whereas Amina took a place farther away, on another mat. There she was immediately surrounded by a crowd of women all eager to share some news, a clear sign of her marked popularity and influence.

Group meetings passed in what appeared to be a fixed sequence of events. Women's chattering faded as soon as the *karamògò* welcomed them and spoke the *duwawu* (the benedictions), after which the "repetition session" started. In these sessions, about twenty women were summoned by the *karamògò* and, one after the other, they sat in front of him to repeat the passage from a *sura* that was the day's lesson. Women who had newly joined the groups (myself included) were asked to recite the *shahada*. These individual recital sessions followed a rigid protocol in which the *karamògò* looked straight into the eyes of the woman whose performance he was evaluating, while she, complying with the norms of modesty and respect for a male superior, kept her eyes fixed on the floor and spoke softly. The *karamògò* delayed his judgment, whether criticism or encouragement, until the woman had ended her performance. At about 4:00 PM, after jointly performing the *alasa* (the afternoon prayer), the *karamògò* lectured on how a proper Muslim woman should behave in her daily life or at special events. His lecture sometimes extended into another learning period where women repeated the rules of conduct their teacher had just explained. Before the *karamògò* closed the meeting (at about 5 PM), again by speaking the benedictions, there was a moment for group members to make announcements: about baptizing ceremonies, women who could no longer attend, or planned travels to Bamako. After the teacher's official dismissal, many women hurried home to start cooking, while others lingered to chat about recent social events.

Muslim women whose group meetings I attended stressed the usefulness of "learning to read Arabic" and contrasted it to the assets of Western schooling: literacy in Arabic opened "new opportunities" that were, in many ways, more edifying than the knowledge they could have learned in the adult alphabetization programs that some of them had attended. Even if these programs helped to improve a woman's material situation, it left her in a state of ignorance and moral destitution, and reinforced her remoteness from God. Given that only few of these women ever received formal school education, it might seem remarkable that they unanimously claimed that "learning to read the Qur'an" was preferable to the knowledge transmitted in Western schools. But although these women see a clear-cut division between secularist Western schooling and religious education, their actual efforts at ethical self-improvement follow a more complicated trajectory.[23] My regular attendance at group meetings made me realize that much of the women's time is spent not necessarily on acquiring Arabic literacy but on memorizing passages of *suras* relevant to proper ritual performance. Also, during learning sessions as well as informal conversations,

Muslim women and other supporters of Islamic moral renewal frequently express their disapproval of certain features of traditional religious learning. They take particular issue with Qur'anic teachers who make a living by sending their disciples to beg for money and food, and thereby echo the concern voiced by many secularist critics.[24] What emerges from their considerations on how to form proper Muslim subjects is that supporters of Islamic renewal view their own learning groups as part of a trajectory that allows them to navigate both the morally complacent Western literacy schooling and a traditional Qur'anic schooling that no longer fulfills the goal of creating ethical subjects.

The shifting, even ambiguous, position that supporters of Islamic renewal occupy in the national field of Muslim doctrinal debate is reflected in women's dissociation from the dominant secularist/materialist paradigm of personal success, on one hand, and that promoted by established families of religious specialists, on the other. By referring to themselves as proper Muslims, and emphasizing their learning activities as a distinctive mode of moral subjectivation, Muslim women simultaneously claim membership in a homogeneous category of rightful believers *and* assert their own special position. That education continues to be a battleground where competing Muslim understandings of proper practice and religious subjectivity are asserted and expressed is seen in the diverse activities of the various women's groups (Schulz 2008a).

Muslim women such as Amina do not view their learning activities as a conduit toward material advancement, and thus as a trump in their quotidian struggle for survival; they do, however, associate the acquisition of Islamic knowledge with notions of improvement and renewal, and thus as the pathway that leads them to God. "Being instructed" in religious and ritual matters becomes a marker of difference. The intricate connection between Islamic education, status hierarchy, and upward social mobility is not a novel phenomenon. Throughout West and North Africa, status enhancement was a career pattern built into traditional institutions of Islamic learning (e.g. Wilks 1968; Eickelman 1978, 506–508; Hamès 1997; see Berkey 1992, 62–70). What distinguishes these historical forms of social advancement from the current forms is that until the late 1930s erudition in the religious sciences was often identified with specific families of religious experts. Nowadays, in contrast, partly because of the transformation of the institutional context, access to religious education is no longer a family privilege but follows, to a greater extent than before, from individuals' decision to strive for moral and intellectual growth.[25]

The methods and contents of women's learning sessions and conventional Qur'anic schooling resonate in many ways. Muslim women's circles are instances of peer learning, a feature characteristic of traditional higher-educational institutions.[26] Both models prioritize correct ritual practice and the memorization of *suras* essential to ritual performance over reading and writing skills. At different times and places throughout the Muslim world, initiation through memorization was the only form of knowledge pupils acquired in primary education (see Eickelman 1978, 507–508; Sanankoua 1985; Brenner 1997, 2001; Mommersteeg 1991; Berkey 1992; Tamari 1996, 2003; Hames 1997; Reichmuth 1994, 2000; but see Wilks 1968). In traditional Islamic learning institutions in Morocco, for example, the memorization of a few *suras* was the first step in a more extensive curriculum. Only at a very advanced stage did disciples learn to apply *suras* to specific situations, critically debate passages, and weigh different scholarly opinions. In Western Sudan, the aim of initial learning stages was also the memorization of important *suras*. Most disciples only attended for a few years and never acquired full Arabic literacy.

Besides these similarities, women's learning activities are also strongly indebted to the reformed Islamic educational pedagogy of *medersas*. This pedagogy, which developed in the 1940s as an element of an emerging "rationalistic episteme" (Brenner 2001, chap. 8), combines traditional forms of knowledge acquisition with new didactics and media such as blackboards, chalk, paper, and pencils. Women's learning activities also draw on Western pedagogies and notions of relevant knowledge, as illustrated by their portrayal of their activities as an acquisition of "reading" skills and in their tendency to combine memorization, recitation, and debate. Rather than practicing the conventional method of simply repeating the *suras*, women, in discussions with teachers, frequently question their meaning, as well as the rationale of the rules of conduct their teachers articulate. This means that group members actually evaluate and interpret the teachings they receive, rather than simply memorizing and absorbing them. On these occasions some women students, usually those respected for their exemplary demeanor, deferentially but doggedly engaged their teachers on questions regarding the usefulness and applicability of certain duties of Muslim women. Questions pertaining to fertility control and a woman's demeanor toward her mother-in-law elicited passionate responses from group participants and a subtle probing of their teacher's reasoning. For instance, when Ansar Dine women in San asked their teacher whether Islam authorized abortion and fertility control, they listened patiently to his descriptions of the punishment awaiting a woman in the afterlife if she tried to interfere with God's will in this domain. After the teacher had exhausted the examples illustrating the pains of hellfire, one of the women in the group, who had been employed for years as a nurse in the local hospital, spoke up. In a soft voice and with her eyes downcast, she began with the teacher's own proposition that God favored the life of all children over their death, and involved him in a dialogue that finally led him to agree that the practice of birth control was a woman's best means to ensure her own and her children's well-being. The teacher appeared visibly unsettled by the dialogue and by the other women's murmurings of approval, and he quickly brought the session to a close. To interpret the nurse's intervention as an act of resistance to patriarchal control over women's bodies would miss an essential point. The nurse emerged as victorious in the exchange precisely because she had remained within the terms of interpretation and debate sanctioned by what the teacher presented as "proper Islam." Group members might differ in their acceptance or challenge of their teachers' lectures, but they share the conviction that their primary goal is to "learn the rules of Islam." Knowledge about Islam is intellectually appropriated through debate.

That Muslim women's educational aims included a blend of different learning paradigms is also reflected in how Muslim women represent their learning activities to a wider public. Shortly after I had been introduced to the *présidente* of the national organization, UNAFEM, she described the goal of Muslim women's gatherings in ways that revealed the influence of the Western educational ideal of reading-as-understanding. As she put it,

> [Muslim women] come together to learn to read the Qur'an because . . . it is our duty as women to defend our understandings of the holy Qur'an. Nowadays, in a situation of ignorance and denial of God's will [*jahiliya*], it is women's duty to form their own point of view and orient others towards the path to God. Because once you stand in front of your creator, you have to answer for what you did with your life. You have to justify your refusal to be rescued from the depths of ignorance and immorality.

Contrary to the Islamic tradition of learning God's Word by memorization and recitation, the *présidente* emphasizes women's knowledge and *understanding* as a prerequisite to independent judgment. A woman's capacity to form her own opinion is the basis for her self-improvement as a morally responsible person. The *présidente*'s preoccupation with a believer's individual responsibility hints at a process of redefining useful religious knowledge: only by combining ritual knowledge *and* religious argument will Muslim women be able to defend their specific views of the pathway that leads one to God, and thus to social and personal renewal. This view reveals a changing sensibility and understanding of religious subjectivity. Muslim women's eagerness to invest in religious instruction indicates that religious knowledge has left the restricted realm of schools and moved into a more accessible arena of reflection and debate. The significance of religious instruction, therefore, is concomitantly changing as education comes to embody the promises of—and path toward—ethical self-improvement.

The changing notions of learning and knowledge that inform the *présidente*'s statement are the underside of the democratization of Islamic interpretational knowledge and its greater availability to women since colonial times. This development extends beyond Mali and West Africa. Kamalkhani (1998) found that the activities of educational circles created after the Islamic revolution in Iran are characterized by a similar interweaving of conventional Qur'anic memorization, new learning content, and new practices, such as women's rehearsal of the methods and contents of preaching. Here, too, women's greater access to Islamic learning was the prerequisite for their claim to participation in debates over the significance of Islam to collective social and personal life. Although local conditions may favor the coexistence of knowledge paradigms in different ways, they are part of broader transformations throughout the Muslim world that have allowed supporters of Islamic moral renewal to gain public prominence over the past thirty years (Eickelman 1992).

Even if the development in Mali indicates a transformation that affects the Muslim world at large, one can discern specific changes in Islamic learning practices both locally and historically. Several factors establish distinctive trajectories within North and West Africa, for instance. A variation of the hybrid character of Muslim women's learning activities in Mali is seen in Morocco, where the transformation in the transmission of Islamic knowledge paradigms reflects a complex interweaving of continuities in normative conceptions of knowledge and changes in the institutional framework of transmission. Substantial transformations in the social context of learning and the development of new teaching techniques in Morocco over the past century were triggered by, among other factors, the integration of institutions of higher Islamic learning into the colonial schooling system. Despite these profound changes, Eickelman (1978) argues, there are long-term continuities in the norms of the immutability of religious texts and knowledge transmission.[27] This differs from the learning activities among Malian Muslim women, whose emphasis on scrutiny and individual opinion making points to competing conceptions of valuable religious knowledge. The coexistence and intertwining of these different conceptions of valuable knowledge have been generated within a new institutional context of learning.[28]

A comparison with learning groups that are rapidly expanding in urban Ivory Coast highlights variations in the groups' efficiency in spreading Arabic literacy. LeBlanc (1999; see Miran 1998) identifies the associations of adolescents as among the most important operators in the spread of Arabic literacy and the conception of a new Muslim identity that draws on intellectual trends and symbolic registers from the Arabic-speaking world (LeBlanc 1999; see Miran

1998). Muslim women's learning groups in urban Mali do not play a significant role in spreading Arabic literacy partly because their activities remain limited in time, scope, and efficacy. But their groups do fulfill a key role, parallel to the one LeBlanc identified, in providing a space for socializing and displaying personal responsibility, as well as fulfilling the new ethical roles that women claim for themselves. These roles and the social effects of women's activities mark important differences from the attempts of earlier generations of reformers to make education central to societal renewal.

The views on education formulated by Muslim activists, both women and men, are best understood as resulting from three influential factors: first, intellectual and institutional trends, transmitted mostly from Egypt and Saudi Arabia, that are locally identified as "Arab Islam"; second, institutions and discourses of Western aid agencies; and finally, local conventions of Islam whose basis in "traditionalist" (Brenner 1993b: 67) authority competes, but also overlaps, with the new credentials on which some Muslim activists draw. Whereas the objectives articulated by Muslim activists may be novel in part, their active adaptation of intellectual trends from the reaches of the Muslim world to local ways of accommodating socioeconomic and political change perpetuates long-standing conventions of active incorporation.

The Relevance of Ritual

Muslim women devote much of their time during group meetings to the essentials of ritual practice and to memorizing passages from *suras* that are essential to the proper performance of these ritual obligations. A key question is whether the preoccupation with correct ritual observance simply perpetuates its historical importance in this area of West Africa, or does the stress on proper ritual conduct signal a new development? It is difficult to resolve this question because of the scarcity of written documentation on female ritual practice since the colonial period. From the necessarily skewed oral accounts I gathered, it is almost impossible to discern clear continuities in women's religious knowledge and practice.[29] What appears certain, however, is that until the 1950s, except in the few urban areas with a long-standing, strong presence of Muslim religious clans, only a minority of women performed Muslim obligations of worship, simply because broad segments of the population converted to Islam only in the late colonial period, the 1940s and 1950s. Women often followed their husbands and sons in converting to Islam; once converted, their practices remained largely limited to individual worship and participation in ceremonies such as the celebration of the Prophet's anniversary (*mawlud*). Knowledge of the obligations of worship, as well as a pious lifestyle, remained a privilege for most women and a marker of elite status. In other words, even if proper ritual conduct was historically of central importance in local Muslim traditions, few women were in a position to fulfill their obligations of worship. This situation changed only gradually, from the 1960s on.[30]

Against this historical backdrop, Muslim women's keen interest in the specifics of ritual suddenly makes sense. Proper ritual conduct and knowledge of what constitutes a religious obligation outside the sphere of worship (*ibadat*) marks the path on which a woman must embark in her search for "closeness to God." This project of ethical self-improvement does not imply substantial changes in actual ritual practice, but it does involve a rethinking of the *relevance* of ritual conduct to everyday and collective life; for even if some forms of ritual engagement may have changed over the past forty years, these changes are not what make Muslim women's activities so unique. Essential about Muslim women's investments in ritual prescripts and in adopting a truly Islamic code of conduct is that they, as well as the men who teach and defend these rules, confer a central significance to it. Becoming a proper Muslim, walking on the "pathway to God," involves a conscious effort to renew one's moral fiber and embodied pious practices. Muslim activists' stress on proper ritual conduct is also related to their engagement with a new political environment that, since the 1990s, has at once enabled and generated the need for the public assertion of difference and particularity. Muslim interest groups articulate this particularity through claims to ethical distinction and express it, among other registers, through women's embodied action. Even if the structure of ritual performance may not have transformed substantially, what has changed is its significance, along with the political setting in which it is enacted and understood.

Women's eagerness to learn proper ritual behavior suggests a conception of personal faith that implies a shift in emphasis to public demonstration, a shift closely related to women's emphasis on personal responsibility. These women consider their search for closeness to God a matter of personal conviction and not a function of one's family background. Thus they maintain that adherence to Islam needs to be professed not only in communication with God, as the testimony of faith (*shahada*) implies, but before an audience of diverse-minded people. This trend toward individual responsibility, a driving momentum of the Islamic renewal movement, is particularly relevant to women, and not only because of their prior exclusion from institutions of traditional (higher) learning. Remaking oneself as a proper Muslim woman is no longer mediated through family affiliation, through male kin, in particular, but is a matter of individual initiation and conviction.

Muslim women's communal prayer is thus not a traditional ritual in any simple sense. Some of its features, such as the semi-public though confined setting of the courtyards in which Muslim women meet to pray and the sheer number of women who participate, signal its new relationship to public urban life. A similar privileging of publicity is evident in women's tendency to move more of their celebrations during the *mawlud* into zones of public visibility such as the squares surrounding mosques. These alterations in the setting of ritual reveal women's preference for a greater visibility over secluded individual prayer and a stronger valorization of a public and group-enacted religiosity.

Also key to Muslim women's self-understanding is a stronger emotional and ethical identification with a group of equal-minded believers whose support becomes more important than kin ties. This orientation also illustrates that women's preoccupation with ritual does not signal a return to an earlier authentic life modeled on the original community of believers, with all the denial of historicity this return implies (Roy 1994). Muslim women's performance of ritual aptly illustrates their efforts to render their moral call public and relevant to communal life. They may understand the code of female propriety they formulate as a matter of returning to traditional Islamic norms, but that they address the necessity of "returning" indicates their responses to alterations in the fabric of social and political life. All this illustrates the key role they give themselves in societal renewal. Highlighting personal responsibility, they attribute a central relevance to women as agents and as subjects of Muslim religiosity and reform, not just in their role of public symbols of piety.

The emphasis supporters of Islamic renewal placed on public demonstrations of proper religiosity lends substance to Roy's (1994) suggestion that "neo-fundamentalist" Muslim movements are distinct from earlier fundamentalist movements with their often anti-secularist and anti-statist agendas (see Esposito 1998 [1984]; but see Loimeier 2003; Kleiner-Bosaller and Loimeier 1994). Although this conceptual distinction is pertinent for contextualizing these movements, it drops the investigation where key questions regarding women's involvement only begin to emerge. The ways in which Muslim women in Mali make their presence felt in public refutes the tendency to portray female participants in religious movements as pawns of male activism. Women mold the face of the movement by reformulating conventional views of the relevance of Islam to one's individual life and sense of self, and to collective well-being. Autonomy from male authorities is certainly not their driving concern, but this still makes them agents of Islamic renewal who do more than merely pose as symbols of, or a projection screen for, male activist agendas.

Muslim women's activities within the moral renewal movement raise doubts about the proposition that these should be read as resistant or contestable reactions to dominant gender ideologies and relations (MacLeod 1991, 1992; Weix 1998; Gerami and Lehnerer 2001; Nageeb 2004). This interpretation risks ignoring that Muslim women consciously subscribe to the gender ideology dispensed in the teachings. Muslim women are self-assertive agents of Islamic renewal, but this does not necessarily imply that their practices aim at resistance (see Mahmood 2005, chap. 4; also see Asad 2003, chap. 2). Rather Muslim women, as in other contemporary Muslim movements, play an important role in asserting—and reformulating—the significance of religious knowledge and practice to everyday life (Kamalkhani 1998).

Becoming a Respectable Muslim

Muslim women such as Amina articulate their sense of particularity by contrasting their own ethical improvement with the opportunistic pursuit of material advantage by *politiki* groups and credit savings associations. Arguing that their activities are economically disinterested, they emphasize the morally supportive effects of group membership that help counterbalance the feeling of vulnerability that results as much from their status as Muslim women as from their lack of financial means and family support. Examining Muslim women's gatherings exclusively through the lens of women's search for knowledge risks underestimating these social and moral concerns.

The prospect of joining networks that extend beyond one's immediate social group is an important motivation for women to engage in this form of female socializing.[31] Their sense of vulnerability was conveyed by Halimatou, a woman I met at a women's group in Bamako-Badialan: "God told us that one of our principal duties is to treat the other as a 'child of humankind' [*hademaden*]. That's why whenever we Muslim women meet, we practice *hademadenya*. We care for each other and encourage each other to treat others in this fashion, too. We need not feel ashamed." Halimatou's reference to *hademadenya* grants us an intimate insight into the reasons that motivate women from destitute families to join a Muslim association. Studies that explain women's participation in Muslim groups as motivated by economic deprivation or to gain upward mobility posit too simplistic a link between socioeconomic standing and material and symbolic practice. Halimatou maintains, instead, that women who are confronted daily with the threat of social stigmatization empathize with women who have similar experiences. They receive gratification and comfort from their religious affiliation, which extends beyond any immediate material gain and is distinct from spiritual fulfillment. Concomitantly, the forms of religious sociality in which group members participate lend meaning to their sense of vulnerability and their search for emotional and moral security. Halimatou's observation that there is no need for feelings of shame among equal-minded Muslim women points to another dimension of the solidarity that, she feels, pervades the groups. There is a strong expectation that women should adopt a standard for dressing and behaving modestly that all members can share and that, for instance, does not impose on them the need to impress one another with generous, but ill-afforded, signs of hospitality.[32] Here we see how women's understandings of Islamic renewal, and thus their view of "Islam," generate the actual structures that render their daily experiences meaningful. Muslim women make sense of their own situation by turning their fear of material or social marginality into an Islamic ideal; this ideal, in turn, shapes the particular social forms through which they pursue their project of ethical self-making.

Female support networks draw on long-standing conventions of female socializing in urban and rural Mali (e.g., Grosz-Ngaté 1986; de Jorio 1997). Evers Rosander (1997, 106–107) observes that throughout West Africa belonging to female associations is vital for a woman's personal success, allowing her to experience herself as embedded in a field of social relations and hence as a "complete" woman. Through this form of conviviality, very often mediated through vertical and horizontal structures, a woman is able to realize herself as a social person (Schulz 2001b, 2002). Muslim women's associations seem to be particularly attractive to women who, partly because they are the primary bread-winner, feel under considerable pressure to conform to conventional norms of female decency. They differ importantly from other women's groups, such as the *tontine*s (credit savings associations), because they provide not only material support but also a space of emotional and normative protection. Muslim wom-en's frequent, spontaneous expressions of gratitude about socializing with other women who, similarly, "have *hademadenya* on their mind" vividly illustrates this protective dimension. They share not only moments of spirituality and joint ritual practice but also the daily experience of being relegated to a frequently ridiculed minority because of their fervent belief that they should declare their faith in public arenas and personal interactions. In Muslim women's groups, two modes and senses of collectivity converge: local conventions of sociability and mutual support together with the collective endeavor of a transnational move-ment toward moral renewal. This collective, socializing momentum materializes in activities beyond weekly group meetings. Informal visits allow women to share the limited leisure time they have with other women who also need to bal-ance the often conflicting expectations of family and associates. In marital and family conflicts, Muslim women's groups offer moral protection, as the leading group representatives, by virtue of their special status as respectable Muslims, may exert moral pressure on bickering mothers-in-law or advise husbands to act as "proper Muslims" and treat their wives fairly and with compassion. Muslim women also have a say in neighborhood politics, because even if their group activities and viewpoints are derided by outsiders, critics will nevertheless agree that Muslim women's activities are a sign of their spiritual dedication and collective attitude. All this suggests that because of their credibility, their emotional and social support is often more authoritative and effective than that offered by other women's groups. Ai'see, another Ansar Dine woman from San, summarized this dimension of group sociability:

> Life has become difficult for women in town. The problem is that many women aggravate their difficulties . . . and augment each other's load by envying others for the little they have achieved in life. They do not realize that their situation is not the result of a person's doing. It is God who gives and takes what we have. The same is true for women's life in the family. We cannot change the destiny that God has chosen for us. But we can try and talk men into giving up some of their arbitrariness. Because, God is my witness, Nanaje, men are selfish nowadays. They have no mercy for their wives. When we discuss a member's problem and decide to intervene on her behalf, we do this in the spirit of God, who told us that envy, lies and conflicts are vices we must fight, rather than nurture in our hearts. We go and tell the men what our duties are, what their duties are, that God allowed men to have several wives only if they treated them with impartiality; that patience is a virtue God exerts as much from men as he does from women. And men do listen to us, by God. [giggles] If they don't, other people will scold them for deserting the path to God.

Although more and more men do not allow their wives to join credit savings associations because of their history of mismanagement, a husband cannot keep his wife from joining a Muslim women's group without the risk of being denounced as a "bad Muslim" who interferes with his wife's attempts "to move closer to God." Most women I talked to felt that they would ask for the support of fellow Muslim women only if difficulties persisted and they considered leaving their husband's families (an act strongly criticized by Muslim women). But belonging to a women's group is in itself an asset to a woman's bargaining position with regard to in-laws or her own kin. Muslim women's gatherings thus constitute a normative shield, even if disapproving observers regard them with ridicule. Being part of a network of "proper Muslims" promises security and protection. Although it requires women to adopt a code of conduct that, to many outsiders, appears reactionary or repressive, this compliance with a conservative gender ideology opens a new opportunity for self-assertiveness and makes women less vulnerable to insults and insinuations from neighbors and kin.

In their effort to apply God's will to their daily lives, relying emotionally on like-minded women is more important than a woman's relationship with her husband. This resonates with Mahmood's (2005, 174–180) observation that a woman's decision to join the Islamic revivalist "mosque movement" in Cairo is not prompted primarily by the conflicted, emotionally charged relationship with her husband. Instead, Muslim women highlight gender differences and complementariness, rather than equality, a perspective that calls into question the preoccupation of numerous studies on women in Muslim societies with the power relations between men and women.

Trading the Islamic Way?

Muslim women often distance themselves from other women whose "excessive" preoccupation with money, they argue, contrasts with their own efforts to make a decent living, by which they mean to work on one's personal self-improvement and to ease the daily problems for themselves and fellow group members. Critics of Islamic renewal, on the other hand, also refer to "money" to rebuff the "purely economic motivations" of Muslim activism. By contrasting economic interest to religious motivation and presenting both as mutually exclusive goals, such critics miss the kernel of Muslim women's joint income-generating activities. Still, their interpretation deserves closer scrutiny, because it helps elucidate an important dimension of Mali women's participation in Islamic renewal and adds nuance to scholarly controversies over the nature of contemporary religious movements.

Critics' charges against Muslim activists are curiously echoed in some studies on the invigoration of religion in the era of economic liberalization. MacLeod (1991) and Marty and Appleby (1993a, 1993b) explain the popularity of religious movements among destitute strata of the population, especially urban unemployed youth and lower-class women, by the new possibilities and symbolic repertoires for social advancement that these movements offer. In critique of this argument that assumes a direct link between religious revival and the degradation of economic and social life since the 1980s, Mahmood (2005, chap. 1) and Asad (1993, 2003) question the assumption that religious practices are necessarily motivated by material interest; they maintain that such a framework is inspired by the motivational logic of Christian religiosity (see, too, Robbins 2007). By implication, according to this argument, authors who study non-Christian religions should be wary of the genealogy of the conceptual frameworks they apply. The same critique also applies to studies that interpret the thriving of new global Christian movements as the result of the economy of salvation they proclaim, in other words, by positing the close interlocking of religious idioms with the new possibilities for economic enterprise that became possible with economic liberalization (e.g. Marshall-Fratani 1998; Maxwell 1998; Comaroff and Comaroff 2002).

Mahmood's and Asad's call for a more self-reflective, critical engagement with analytical frameworks is pertinent here. But by emphasizing the nonmaterial motivations of those who engage in ethical renewal, one risks creating an opposition between material and ethical considerations that renewal-minded individuals may not share. The conceptual contrast between economic motivation and a spiritual search forecloses an understanding of the historical forms of religious practice and organization in Muslim societies in Africa. The broadly documented male and female Muride organizations in Senegal are the most notorious examples of the intertwining of Muslim economic enterprise with religious and socializing activities. The history of Islam in West Africa has also been deeply interwoven with the activities of merchants whose long-distance trade networks were crucial to the integration of Muslim practices into local culture (Cruise O'Brien 1971; Stewart 1973; Kaba 1974; Amselle 1977; Willis 1979; Launay 1992). Although the propagation of the Islamic faith occurred in several historical thrusts and through different patterns of rural and urban integration, there was never a contradiction between the spiritual quest and the economic interests of those who spread the faith (Levtzion 1986a, 1986b). On the contrary, as McDougall (1986) demonstrates, the economic success of the Kunta clan allowed them to exert considerable political and religious influence in the rural Sahara between the seventeenth and nineteenth centuries. As a clan of religious experts (*zawaya*) associated with the Qadiriyya order, their involvement in salt trade led them gradually to expand their activities as mediators and wealthy businessmen. Along with the Kunta's expanding trade connections, Islam's social organization changed. Centers of Islamic learning moved from towns to the countryside where they integrated into pastoral ways of life, with the result that religious affiliation acquired new important economic and political functions. The collection and redistribution of wealth, organized through the relation between disciples and *shaykhs,* was no longer centered on schools and mosques. This illustrates that Islam's spread was facilitated by the commercial activities of its agents and simultaneously enforced trade networks by grounding them in an Islamic ethics of mutual moral obligation (Vicor 2002).

Detailed accounts of Muslim women's commerce in West Africa are scarce, with a few notable exceptions: studies on merchant women in Northern Nigeria and Niger, and Muride women in Senegal. The studies of these women suggest that, in contrast to Muslim men's long-distance ties, women's trade activities were confined to local networks of trust and exchange (Schildkrout 1983; Coles and Mack 1991; Callaway and Creevey 1994; Evers Rosander 1997; Cooper 1997). Because these studies focus on particular historical periods, they cannot provide detailed insight into transformations in the social organization of female trade. The absence of similar documentation for the region that is present-day Mali makes it difficult to judge the novelty of Muslim women's trade activities. Sanankoua (1991b) does mention Muslim women's economic motivations, but she situates them in a context of what she terms the "banalization of pilgrimage," meaning the commercialization of activities related to the pilgrimage to Mecca. Her claim, which rests on the assumption of a recent shift toward the commercialization of religious culture in Mali, needs to be substantiated through a historical assessment of continuities in Muslim women's commercial activities. Sanankoua's implicit dismissal of women's economic initiatives as a distortion of pure religious motivation also raises the question of how the women themselves view and validate their activities.

Risk and material scarcity hover over the daily lives of many Muslim women. Their religious associations provide them with an informal network that facilitates a variety of income-generating activities, ranging from musical performances and entertainment to ritual teaching sessions for prospective pilgrims. They yield only a small return, considerably smaller than for men, but women are keen on pursuing them. The money gained in this fashion is not expressly dubbed as revenue. Women in all groups regularly pay small membership fees, and they jointly perform services that enable them to increase their group funds. The women's group in Bamako-Badialan whose activities I followed between 1998 and 2006 specialized in dancing and singing religious songs during weddings and other family ceremonies.[33] Thanks to the musical talents of several group members and the prestige of the leader, Hadja Bintou, the group gradually attained the status of semiprofessional entertainers. Over the years of my acquaintance with this group I stopped paying informal visits on Sundays or Thursdays, because I would not find them at home but in someone else's courtyard where, under Hadja Bintou's aegis, they would "provide entertainment" (*njanaje*) for their hosts' visitors and relatives. Families inviting "Hadja Bintou's women" maintained that this form of entertainment was at once decent and affordable, and thus more acceptable than what professional wedding singers provided. Hadja Bintou was very selective in accepting invitations, which added to her reputation as a respectable leader and to her host family's status. As a sign of special approval, Hadja Bintou graciously granted her female hosts the favor of performing religious songs the night before the wedding ceremony, as well as in the afternoon following the civic marriage act. She occupied a place of honor, seated in a comfortable chair next to the dance floor, both hands clasped around a microphone and alternating with a younger assistant in the role of lead singer. Other Muslim women performed the vocals and leaped up time and again to dance to a particularly compelling song. The length of the performance varied according to the hosts' requests, lasting somewhere between two hours and an entire day. Upon request, the group would bring their own recording equipment; the recording that resulted was then considered the property of the host family, and the technician would make copies to distribute to special guests. These performances resemble the services offered by professional weddings singers, but Muslim women refer to their performances as a service inspired by religious solidarity and compassion (*hinè*). Accordingly, the money Hadja Bintou receives from the group's hosts (which, it was assumed, would be added to the group's savings[34]) was never presented as a payment but as an alm (*saraka*).

Critics of these performances claimed that they indicate a broader development which they described as a general "shortage of money" in town. In their view, which echoes Sanankoua's account, the growing demand for Muslim women's semi-commercial performances should not be taken as an indication of a newly emerging ethical sensibility; they are more of a low-cost version of the expensive ceremonies in which *jeli* singers play a central role and that are restricted to affluent families, notorious for their conspicuous display of wealth. But supporters of Muslim women's celebrations maintain that the performances are not only modest but offer entertainment that older invitees, in particular, consider more edifying and valuable.

Hadja Bintou's group illustrates how Muslim women may engage in an urban economy of religious assistance while presenting their activities in the rhetoric of religious devotion, compassion, and mutual support. The language of pious support also extends to the networks within which Muslim women are commercially active. Women talk about these networks as a preferential form of generating money because they are based on mutual understanding and trust. They do not present their commercial endeavor as a specifically Islamic way of trading, but they often assert that they prefer to conduct business with group members who have compassion. "Islam" is invoked as a common frame of reference and emotional assurance. To conduct business together means not to engage in speculative and secretive activity but to capitalize on one's trust in God and fellow believers.

Women often benefit from the chatty atmosphere at the end of the learning sessions to offer informally, and "for a special fee," processed food ingredients and goods such as "proper" dress items, religious paraphernalia, imported fabric, and homemade beauty aids. Because buyers need to have confidence in the seller's credibility regarding the quality of the goods, their purchase from group members enhances a common sense of belonging and bonding. Other women use group meetings to sell goods that have been purchased through long-distance connections with other towns in southern Mali as well as neighboring countries or France. Still others use the women's groups to sell homemade products provided by their sisters and mothers in other towns. Women who belong to the Ansar Dine association in San regularly ask their husband's permission to leave for Bamako for the celebration of religious holidays, which allows them to personally transfer (at a lower cost) many goods from Bamako to Segou, Koutiala, San, and other places reachable through the road between Bamako and Mopti. Ansar Dine is also a notable example of the long-distance relations and high level of security that some of these commercial networks offer. Male members deal in products through a long-distance trade network spanning national borders into Bouaké, Kankan, and Abidjan, and also connecting Ansar Dine members to followers in France and the United States. Female acolytes of Sharif Haidara buy from one another and from other members' husbands and relatives, all of whom belong to the same patronage network.

All these business transactions by members of the Islamic renewal movement are grounded in agreements ensuring reciprocity and mutual obligation, with Islam as the common normative framework. Their economic activities do not dilute religious values and practices but emerge as a constitutive element and condition of belonging to a group of "proper Muslims." Reference to Islam creates trust and appears as a guarantor of the longevity and stability of social circuits of exchange that are otherwise easily destabilized. Critics who blame Muslim activists for their economic motivation do have a point insofar as activists fall back on long-standing affinities between networks that focus on Islamic erudition and those that generate income. Economic motivations, however, do not preempt other objectives but do solidify some of the collective spirit and sense of belonging inherent in Islamic moral renewal. Religious devotion and moral self-improvement go in tandem with a search for financial and emotional security. A Muslim woman in urban Mali can become a moral person in the fullest sense only by participating in ritualized forms of socializing *and* income-seeking strategies.

Islamic moral renewal in Mali thrives on the intertwining of female and male structures of religious sociality and patronage. These structures reveal and feed into the tension-ridden dynamics relating different fields and sources of power in the national political arena. Changes in the material, institutional, and economic conditions of public controversy, supported by neoliberal economic reform and political liberalization, have generated new spaces of action and (re)articulations between the state and particular interest groups within Malian society. These developments facilitate changes in common understandings of the relevance of religion to daily life and politics. The activities of Muslim women, their attempts to extend their moral call to a wider constituency of believers, are indicative of these developments. Their activities blur commonly accepted boundaries between public and domestic settings, and between gender-specific realms of proper practice. Their moralizing efforts are fueled by their experiences of the contradictory demands and constraints that neoliberal reform has generated for many women in urban middle- and lower-middle-class households. The anchoring of their activities in long-standing conventions of sociality explains the enormous appeal of Muslim women's call for renewal and their capacity to articulate the moral apprehensions of a broad range of followers. As structures of sociality, learning, and mutual support, women's religious associations allow women to claim wider relevance at the interstices of domestic, semi-public, and public settings, and to initiate new nodes of articulation between society and the state. As such, female Muslim activism can be seen as a particular modality of politics from below that aims not at political protest but at the transformation of the personal and social.

The objectives that Muslim activists formulate are inspired by three sets of influences: transnational Muslim reformist trends and *da'wa* efforts; institutions and discourses of a developmental state and of Western aid agencies; and local debates over proper Muslimhood that pit representatives of a (heterogeneous) religious establishment against a younger, often intellectual generation of Muslim critics with new credentials of leadership. Because they recombine these influences in different ways and to different degrees, individual groups, teachers, group leaders, and ordinary group members may highlight different objectives and thus occupy divergent positions within the landscape of Islamic renewal. They all contribute to religious activism, even if their activities reverberate differently throughout society.

Boyd and Last's (1985) call for recognition of female religious actors in Muslim societies in Africa can therefore be taken one step further. Given the breadth of involvement in the Islamic renewal movement by women of different socioeconomic standing, a broader definition of religiously relevant practice is needed. Also needed is the acknowledgment of a new dynamics of stratification *among* women that has resulted from their differential integration into a landscape of national and transnational ties and influences. Although the transnational orientation and locations of the renewal movement support new conditions of intervention in the national arena, they also contribute to the reproduction of two trajectories of inequality. One is the unequal position of male and female initiators within the moral reform movement, which is as much a precondition as it is a consequence of women's and men's differential immersion in local and transnational religious patronage networks. The second is the reinforcement of the differential socioeconomic standing of leaders and ordinary group members, a closed universe of social hierarchy that only a few privileged supporters of the movement may avoid.

Important as these material and political considerations are that inform the activities of Muslim associations, they should not be seen as lessening the import of these groups' integration into national patronage structures and religious transnational networks nor should their efforts be viewed as having been guided by short-term materialistic considerations. These interpretations not only ignore the historically close intertwining of notions of spiritual and material salvation; they also fail to explain why the effort to gain knowledge in religious matters has become key to Muslim women's activities and mobilization. Muslim women's educational endeavors offer an entry point to expand our understanding of the aims of Muslim women's practices of "extraversion." Muslim women's eagerness to civilize themselves through the acquisition of knowledge relevant to their ethical quest is consistent with a long-standing agenda of Muslim reformism. But their learning activities are also novel, inasmuch as they reflect a new sensibility and understanding of religious subjectivity. Religious knowledge has left the restricted realm of schools and moved into the more accessible arena of generalized learning. At the same time the significance of religious education is changing. "Learning" integrates the different ethical, material, and social concerns that inform Muslim women's pathway to God, as it embodies the promises of ethical self-improvement and more immediate access to the written foundations of Islam, and thus the possibility to live one's faith without relying on the intercession of religious experts. As much as Muslim women emphasize a sense of sharing and collective responsibility, their institutions of religious sociality also support their individualizing and civilizing drive for self-development.

The political locations of Muslim activist structures in Mali contradict a perspective that assumes clear divisions between state and civil society. Leaders of the renewal movement derive their effectiveness in mobilizing followers from the intricate ways that they balance their close relationship to state actors and institutions, on the one hand, and the need to operate partly outside state control, on the other. No wonder, then, that Muslim activists' complex integration into the national landscape of politics yields paradoxical results. In this respect, contemporary Muslim activism is consistent with practices and rationales that have long structured state-society relations in Africa. This insight is not new (Lemarchand 1992; Bayart 1989), but it indicates how difficult it is to generalize about the effects of religiously inspired movements on nation-state politics. In Mali, as in other countries in West Africa, Muslim activists derive their political weight from their capacity to create points of articulation between state and nonstate actors and institutions (see Villalon 1995; Kane 1997). By seeking access to state institutions, they validate the state's importance to collective life while challenging its normative monopoly. This, then, is one of the paradoxical effects of Islam's new public role.

FIVE

Alasira, *the Path to God*

"WE WILL ALL die one day, my daughter. What will you tell your Creator once you stand before Him? How will you justify your wrongdoings in life? How will you justify your disregard for God's truth, for Him who found so many ways to show you the right path?" With these words, Hadja Bintou, the leader of a Muslim women's group in Badialan, a lower-class neighborhood in Bamako, opened our first conversation in 1998 after the initial introductions had been made. With a gesture of impatience, if not indignation, she brushed away my mumbled effort to respond, and continued, "To live means to search for the path to God, and to return to the original teachings of Islam, that's the truth, plain and simple."

Alasira, the path to God, demarcates the horizon that, according to Hadja Bintou, frames all human doings, desires, and destinations. To choose the path to God means to return to the authentic teachings of Islam. *Alasira* thus signals a turning point in the truest sense of the word. Similar views of *alasira* are reflected in the teachings of other women leaders and male teachers. Here, *alasira* serves as an umbrella term for the various activities, concerns, and sensibilities that inform and animate their project of personal moral transformation.

This chapter looks at the areas in which Muslim women intervene in order to realize their quest for ethical improvement and at the same time contribute to their collective well-being.[1] Only by paying close attention to the pious practices through which women hope to "embark on the path to God" and become virtuous Muslims can we comprehend the modernizing project that these women pursue, one that articulates specific ideas about female religious subjectivity. These ideas are not entirely novel, but they gain new significance under contemporary political conditions that at once facilitate and create a greater need for women to articulate their moral and social aspirations in a public arena.

In investigating the ethical sensibilities that motivate Muslim women's search for closeness to God, we must navigate several difficulties that restrict scholarly understanding of these women's participation in reform movements throughout the Muslim world. It is important to recognize that, rather than conceptualizing piety as the exclusive result of individual practice (Mahmood 2005), female Muslim religiosity is constituted at the interface between, on one side, individual women's attempts to cultivate certain virtues and, on the other, the meanings that others attribute to the women's activities, claims, and attire. Here I want to emphasize that the current socio-political context, especially reconfigurations of the conditions for articulating an Islamic normativity in the national political arena, has important effects on women's religiously inspired actions. As a consequence, Muslim women's religiosity cannot be conceived independently of its public manifestation or of the need believers have to enact their faith before a broader, more normatively diverse constituency (see Deeb 2006).

The approach proposed here differs from studies that investigate how women who join various social and religious movements address and challenge the political institutions and ideological foundations of nation-state politics. The literature on the emblematic role of Muslim women in Islamic revivalist movements (Saktanber 1994; Göle 1996), identity politics (e.g., Moghadam 1994; Hale 1997) and nationalist projects (e.g., Kandiyoti 1991b; Chatterjee 1993) posits that the policing of women, their rights in the family, their scope of public maneuver, and their religious orientation gains a symbolic function in the politics of cultural authenticity; women's apparel, in particular, takes on unprecedented political and symbolic salience. Although I agree with this interpretation, I suggest that the focus on identity politics is too narrow. Deserving of closer scrutiny is how women's personal motivations and efforts to cultivate a pious disposition intersect with broader social transformations that emerge at the interface of the institutions and rationalities of state power, on the one hand, and transnational intellectual trends, institutional configurations, and communication flows, on the other.

In contemporary Mali the interaction between Muslim women, and between Muslim women and male supporters of the moral reform movement, is an important field in which inter-subjective meanings of Muslim piety are created. What interests me are the distinctive characteristics of the conditions and forms of Muslims' public interventions in Mali. This inquiry comes close to studies that, from divergent analytical standpoints, examine forms of Muslim public reasoning in the context of postcolonial state politics, but it does not search for distinctively Islamic positions and discursive engagements formulated by the proponents of Muslim reformist trends (Hirschkind 2001a, 2006; Göle 2002). Chapter 1 demonstrated that leading figures in the Malian movement for moral renewal had diverse positions and practices, and therefore diverse adjustments to the institutional and normative framework of multiparty democracy. There is no point in studying Muslim forms of religiosity in Mali as manifestations of particular discursive traditions, independent of the sociopolitical conditions of Muslim women's existence.

This raises the question of how Muslim women situate themselves, through their views of a good Muslim's social and ritual obligations, in a field where local preoccupations intersect with intellectual influences, especially from the Arab Muslim world and Western societies. These dynamics must be understood accurately so that one can assess distinctive features of contemporary reformist Muslim movements in West Africa and their implications for women. Different waves of West Africa's Islamic reform or renewal (*tajdid*) since the nineteenth century can be distinguished; one distinction is the degree of success with which reformists entered into alliances with or were co-opted by state actors and institutions (Loimeier 2003). The late 1970s and early 1980s heralded an era of reformist activities more explicitly conceived as a challenge to secular nation-state politics. Representatives of these new reformist trends were often trained at higher-educational institutions in the Arabic-speaking world, particularly at Al-Azhar. The diverse goals, activities, and class origins of different Muslim reform movements reflect the different local, regional, and trans-regional influences these movements incorporated (e.g., Otayek 1993; Brenner 1993b; Loimeier 1997, 2001; Kane 2003; Miran 2005). But recent reformist movements also share a number of concerns. Among them is the denunciation of local practices that emphasize human intercession instead of a believer's direct relationship to God. Also characteristic are reforms directed at mass education and a more inclusive canon and new structures of mobilization oriented toward segments of the (primarily urban) population such as youth organizations and the women's groups described in the preceding chapter. The crucial question is how to situate Muslim women in this complicated picture of divergent readings of Islam that cannot be mapped neatly onto an opposition between Sufi and reformist positions (see Triaud and Robinson 2000).

Recent scholarship on women's participation in West Africa's Muslim reformist movements argues that Muslim educational reform supports a new educational elite—and a Muslim elite consciousness—that draws on literacy in Arabic as well as in the language of state bureaucracy (Miran 1998; LeBlanc 1999; Alidou 2005). Where Islam historically had a greater stronghold—for example, in Senegal, the Gambia, and northern Nigeria—women's Islamic education facilitated new spiritual and consumerist identities. The support among women for Muslim reformist trends is related to intergenerational family dynamics, especially between mothers and daughters (Reichmuth 1996; Augis 2002; Janson 2008). The adoption by younger, unmarried women of a reformist identity, it is argued, expresses their endeavor to formulate a modern and cosmopolitan Muslim orientation separate from a traditional Muslim identity by calling for a stricter adherence to the rules of Islam. One mode of articulating this modern Muslim identity is to reject Western consumerism and to appropriate central emblems of an Arab Muslim identity.

As important as these studies are, they cannot explain why married women support trends toward Islamic moral renewal, nor do they examine the controversies *among* proponents of the renewal movement resulting from their divergent appropriations of regional and transnational reformist trends. But such analyses are important for understanding the moral reform movement in contemporary Mali that has its broadest support among middle-aged, married women, many of whom have no formal education, incomplete knowledge of French, and only limited access to intellectual trends in the Arab world.

What do Muslim women make of the conceptions of religiosity that emerge and circulate in Mali, often influenced by intellectual trends in Saudi Arabia and Egypt? How do they integrate the new emphasis on ritual orthopraxy and personal dialogue with God into their daily activities, experiences, and social interactions. These complex dynamics need to be understood in detail in order to comprehend the local debates that are triggered through these appropriations, the issues they highlight, and the processes of differentiation within the reform movement that they foster.

Continuities and Changes in Female Religious Practice

Social institutions of Muslim activism in urban Mali, although drawing on a new social basis and innovative ways of articulating political aspirations, are grounded in long-standing conventions of sociality and religious organization and patronage. To grasp both the historicity and potentially novel character of Muslim women's religiosity, we need to investigate their activities and claims beyond the realm of education, and interrogate their emphasis on individual responsibility and religious virtue. Is it possible to read their concern with personal improvement as a reflection of local conceptions of religious authority and virtue, as well as transnational intellectual trends?

Muslim educational reform in the 1940s, if it affected women at all, remained limited to urban areas. Until the 1970s, female believers' knowledge of Arabic, ritual matters, and religious doctrine was restricted to women with privileged (urban) family backgrounds. Those who gradually converted to Islam practiced their faith through the regular performance of certain iconic practices, such as ritual worship (*seli*) and the adoption of a particular dress code. Muslim ritual was as much a religious observance as a statement about one's minority identity (Launay 1992).

Even if religious erudition remained restricted to few women, this did not prevent some from becoming highly educated. Accounts of the period between 1930 and 1950 testify that some women excelled as models of piety. Today their tombs are centers of regular devotional visits (*ziyara*) and ceremonies by female and male devotees.[2] Leading a life withdrawn from the pressures of public opinion and worldly matters, and devoting oneself to self-improvement and the study of religious texts, was an ideal to which many women aspired but one that only the economically privileged could realize. That a life led in seclusion is still considered a desirable option is illustrated by the respect paid to contemporary female figures in leading Sufi religious clans in Senegal (Coulon and Reveyrand-Coulon 1988). The veneration of women as exemplars of female piety illustrates—similar to the notion of "path"—that it is misleading to assume a clear divide between Sufi-related practices and other forms of religiosity. The practices derive from shared commonsense convictions, such as a belief in the esoteric forces inherent in God's spoken word and in the importance of human intercession between individual believers and God (Brenner 2000). How do these long-standing conventions and ideas manifest themselves in the ritual activities of supporters of contemporary Islamic renewal?

One area of religious practice to which women have historically made a crucial contribution still plays an important, if controversial, role in claims to ritual orthopraxy and proper Muslimhood: the veneration of the Prophet and locally renowned saints through religious songs considered exhortative and edifying (Cissé 1992:175–176; Evers Rosander 1998).[3] The songs, which laud God, the Prophet Mohammed, and his companions as well as individual members of the local religious community, give women a visible and audible presence during the *mawlud* and other religious ceremonies. But the very performance of these songs also generates heated debate among women participants in the Islamic renewal movement. Some consider the performance of these songs a good work that generates additional "merit" (*nafa*), whereas others, in an effort to claim a true Sunni identity, denounce these practices as impure and hence unlawful. These conflicting claims about the orthodox nature of acts that could be read as a veneration of religious leaders, illustrate that women adopt ambiguous and shifting positions on practices commonly associated with established religious authority. These forms of religiosity have been denounced by reformist Muslims as "unlawful innovation" (*bid'a*)[4] since the 1940s. Among them are values and practices linked to Sufi Islam and its hierarchical organization of authority and spiritual privilege; various customary practices and functions associated with rites of passage (for example, naming ceremonies, weddings, and funerals); the belief in the performative powers of the Divine word, its mobilization in the form of ritual invocations and recitations, and its translation into devices of Islamic medicine—in short, a range of procedures that derive from Islamic esoteric knowledge (Brenner 1993a:65; Schulz 2005). Whereas some Muslim women's groups unequivocally denounce these practices as *bid'a,* the majority is more conciliatory toward them and occasionally engages in them.

The Ansar Dine, which is part of the Islamic renewal movement, exemplifies this complex, tension-ridden dynamic. Although Shaykh Sharif Haidara's followers refer to him as their "spiritual guide" (*dine nyema*), at the same time, paradoxically, they endorse Haidara's denouncement of certain practices associated with a Sufi leader, such as the bestowing of generous alms in return for a divine recompense (*baraka,* blessing) or additional spiritual benefit (*baraji*). In other words, although Haidara's followers reject conventional hierarchies in religious authority and practice, they believe that guidance by a leader with special divine blessing is of crucial importance for individual spirituality and salvation. Here again we see the continued relevance of religious forms that stress the necessity of human intercession and in the scholarly literature are often associated with "Sufi Islam." These diverse forms of religious engagement rather than indicating a neat shift toward a new conception of legitimate leadership reflect the coexistence of different, somewhat opposed views of religious authority and their respective foundations. Taken together, they form a complicated and contested topography of Muslim religious practice and ritual orthopraxy.

Soares (2005) proposes a similar argument with respect to Nioro du Sahel, a historical center of Tijaniyya and Hamawiyya influence. Here, many younger people no longer entertain close links with local Sufi leaders; they see doctrinal or ritual differences between the various Sufi orders as irrelevant and prefer to define their religiosity by establishing a direct relationship—via prayers—to the Prophet. Traditional lineages of religious specialists still maintain informal political influence and play a role in conventional customs such as name-giving ceremonies and funerals, but Sufi affiliation has lost its *social* relevance (Soares 2005, chap. 7). Although Soares's argument about the weakening significance of Sufi affiliation is germane, one wonders whether it applies to women's historical experiences. Research is needed to assess whether Sufi affiliation has ever had the same significance to Muslim women and, if so, to which women in particular. If in the past many Muslim women did not define their religiosity through their affinity with a Sufi path, then their present-day indifference to Sufi affiliation and doctrinal debate would not signal a recent shift in religious practice.

With this caution in mind, we should question the assertion of female leaders such as Hadja Bintou that their project of moral renewal is based on a return to Islam's original teachings. Do the teachings dispensed by female leaders to their followers indicate, as they claim, a departure from conventional conceptions of religiosity? Chapter 4 showed that Muslim women yearn to gain basic literacy in Arabic, a knowledge of the passages of *suras* necessary for ritual requirements, and an awareness of the "rules of Islam" (*silameya sariyaw*)—that is, an inventory of religious duties and additional, optional good works. This interest, and the implicit assumption that women can acquire Islamic knowledge and build "their own opinion" (*i yèrè ka famuyali còyò la*), goes against conventional views of women as dependent on men for achieving religious knowledge. Very often, however, Muslim women's understanding of the intricacies of religious interpretation remains limited. Participants in women's learning circles are generally eager to debate the significance of certain *suras* to their everyday life, but they largely accept the teachings of male *karamògòw* and of female leaders who, in turn, build their religious opinions on instruction they receive from men. Thus a slightly paradoxical process is at work. Women's eagerness to teach, engage in, and articulate Islamic normative readings of issues of collective interest indicates that they have a novel conception of their contribution to society's moral transformation. Tension persists, however, between the central role to which they aspire and their low position in the hierarchy of religious knowledge and authority. Similarly, as we shall see, because of Muslims' emphasis on the public enactment of a pious disposition, the conduct they promote both matches and transgresses conventional norms of female propriety.

Embarking on the Path to God

My research between 1998 and 2006, as noted, included regular participation in the learning sessions of a Muslim women's group in Badialan-Bamako that had been initiated by Hadja Bintou, the leader whose reminder of God's eternal judgment marked the beginning of this chapter. Women gathered in their leader's courtyard three times a week to improve their Arabic literacy skills and learn about proper ritual performance. The attendees, most of whom work in the informal economy, are between twenty-two and forty-five years of age. Some are female household heads and struggle to keep their families alive. Only a few of the women earn a regular salary as low-rank employees in private businesses. Their attire hints at their lower-middle-class background: they combine their large and colorful robes, made of relatively inexpensive fabric, with additional, equally colorful prayer shawls wrapped around head, neck, and shoulders. The leader of the group, Hadja Bintou, in contrast, wears only white attire. Formerly an influential state official under President Traoré, she began five years ago to pay a teacher, a graduate of Al-Azhar in the early 1990s, to dispense Arabic lessons to her "students" (*kalandenw*). As expected from a respectable Muslim woman beyond menopause, Hadja remained in her living room when the male teacher delivered his lectures. When, in his absence, she took over the teaching sessions, her performance was quite impressive. I was often awestruck by how she established her social standing by simply settling into a broad armchair placed beside the mats on which the women crouched. After waiting for the women to stop chatting and become attentive, she would softly exhort her students to absorb the moral advice (*ladili*) she had to offer. Today, she would tell her listeners on these occasions, she felt compelled to "elucidate the nature of a true Muslim woman's calling," that is, the ways a woman's desire to move closer to God should manifest themselves in her proper behavior at home and in the marketplace.

The subjects Hadja Bintou broaches reflect her own preoccupations and correspond in topic and narrative style to the sermons she delivers in a weekly local radio program. As a way to introduce today's topic, she raises a series of questions that her students, depending on how long they have participated in the group, are variously predisposed to answer. Certain questions are answered readily, for example "What is the appropriate behavior of a woman?" or "Why does it matter that a proper Muslim woman moves and behaves in a particular manner?" Other questions requiring knowledge of the textual sources generate greater hesitation, such as "What rules of conduct and apparel did the Prophet set in his teachings?" or "What can we learn from the Prophet's wives in this respect?" Students listen to Hadja Bintou's words attentively with a mixture of curiosity and respect, and murmur expressions of acceptance and responsiveness. After Bintou concludes a teaching session by reciting the benedictions (*duwawu*) and inviting the attendees to perform the afternoon prayer (*alasa*), the atmosphere in the courtyard becomes lively. The learning session ends promptly and unceremoniously, as attendees, chattering among themselves, gather their belongings, readjust their dresses, headscarves, and prayer shawls, and hurry home to prepare the evening meal.

Central to Bintou's teachings is the enumeration of the requirements for leading the life of a good Muslim woman, first and foremost, the proper performance of the daily prayers; in Bintou's view, a woman should perform at least four prayers a day as a way of "paying respect to God and his will." She frequently relates regular prayer to eschatological concerns, arguing that worship serves as a template to ensure "God's angels' intervention on behalf of believers on the last judgment day." Bintou identifies obedience to the husband and in-laws as a second path toward salvation: "God asks a woman to have patience [*munyu*, endurance]. A woman fighting with her husband is no good. If you think you need to fight your way through, God will show you that this leads nowhere, [that] it only results in distance from Him and thus in despair." Finally, Bintou stresses the need to act with modesty (*maloya;* literally, "a sense of shame," decency, humility) through one's bodily comportment: "whether you have decency or not is evident in the way you dress, speak, sit down, and walk. To dress modestly means first and foremost donning the veil. Whoever dons the veil while interacting with strangers and performing the prayer will be surrounded by the angels who will intervene on your behalf so that your prayer will be received favorably by God."

On a special request, Bintou specifies the occasions and modes of performing bodily propriety, whether a woman is alone—"even when she is at home, doing her work in the kitchen, especially when she thinks that nobody is watching her. For God the Almighty is everywhere and he judges your conduct"—or is interacting with men other than her husband—"always lower your eyes, never look him in the face, for this is how a woman acts out her humility: in the interaction with her in-laws and relatives. Only a woman who knows how to behave within the family can be considered a proper Muslim." A similar direct link between a correct state of mind and its bodily enactment is established when she exhorts women to manifest their sense of shame: "it is your bodily comportment that is the site of virtue and of vice, so you need to be in control of your body. You may pray as much as you want. The way you walk, sit, and move will always disclose that your mind is still caught in vice and distraction."

Hadja Bintou's advice illustrates the intellectual and emotive impetus behind Muslim women's eagerness to acquaint themselves with the rules of proper conduct. This impetus deserves special attention, because it helps enrich scholarly investigations of women's participation in West African Muslim reformist endeavors. The literature explores individual women's motivations to join a movement, but it also raises the question of how, behind women's assertions to return to purer and more authentic Islamic practices, new understandings of religious practice and responsibility emerge (Hodgkin 1998; Augis 2002; but see Janson 2008).

When Bintou admonishes her students that they must undertake all daily actions in a spirit of orienting themselves toward the Divine message, she defines religiosity not merely by acts of worship but by deeds that are at once religious and social. Furthermore, by positing a neat distinction between real Muslim women and others who only pretend to submit to God's will, Bintou proclaims another central tenet of Muslim women's activism: that personal moral transformation is to be effected through the reworking of one's cognitive and emotional patterns *and* bodily routines. Society's moral rejuvenation needs to start from individual transformation that is largely manifested through the inculcation of embodied norms that are acquired by practicing bodily restraint, self-control, and the cultivation of virtue. The body becomes the central site of a disciplinary intervention. "Choosing the path to God" means more than the accurate performance of ritual. It includes the cultivation of a certain spiritual and emotional disposition.

Hadja Bintou's preoccupation with proper posture can be seen as a simple reiteration of ritual orthopraxy, on which Muslim debate in West Africa has been centered repeatedly over the past two centuries (e.g. Triaud 1986b; Launay 1992; Brenner 1993a; Loimeier 1997; Hanretta 2003, 50-78; Kane 2003). An example is the controversy over the correct posture for praying that emerged in the 1940s, pitting traditional religious authorities against activists who saw themselves as defenders of the purer, Sunni form of religious practice (see chapter 1). Proper ritual practice, conceived of as a moral obligation, served as a backbone for the contested construction of proper Muslimhood. Similar to debates in other areas of the Muslim world reflecting Muslims' engagements with colonial modernity, being recognized as a true believer was closely linked to the proper embodiment of faith more than to a specific set of beliefs (Starrett 1995; Bowen 1997).

The parallels between these earlier preoccupations with bodily performance and Bintou's teachings are evident. Scarce attention has been paid, however, to the possibility that behind the continual controversies over proper ritual posture, the relationship between disposition and bodily performance is being remade. Bintou's teachings hint at processes of reformulation that reflect the influence of actors with ties to Egypt and Saudi Arabia but also to localized dynamics and controversies. By underscoring the significance of personal feeling and conviction, Bintou engages an individuation process facilitated by recent educational reform, changes in religious authority structures, and transformations in urban economies. By stressing the impossibility of separating acting, feeling, and knowing in one's search for closeness to God, she expresses an ethical sensibility that results from the recent merging of educational paradigms previously discussed. These changes in religious subjectivity are also evident in the precise ethical capacities that leaders of the moral reform movement exact from a proper Muslim woman.

Hadja Bintou identifies two principal elements of female piety that both need conscious and persistent cultivation: *maloya* (humility, modesty) and *munyu* (patience, endurance). Her explanations of *maloya* echo the standard view that a woman's decency should be measured according to her chastity and respectful, controlled bodily demeanor toward husband, in-laws, and people superior in age and social rank. *Munyu* designates the capacity for steadfastness, constancy, and an abiding responsiveness to other people's arbitrariness. Whereas from a Western feminist perspective these instances of female submissiveness and tolerance could be interpreted as an index of patriarchal domination, Bintou and others consider these qualities a hard-won personal achievement which, despite much personal effort, is ultimately granted by God.

The connection Bintou makes between the proper ritual and personal transformation has striking parallels to how participants of the Cairene mosque movement, a prominent manifestation of female Islamic revivalism in contemporary Egypt, conceive of religious virtue. Mahmood (2005, chaps. 3, 4) argues that women's deliberate cultivation of a pious disposition involves the combined training of one's bodily, affective, and cognitive faculties through repetition. Far from extraneous performances of certain requirements, these repetitive acts enable women to develop a specific ethical sensibility. This view of personal virtue does not establish a divide between being religious and acting religious. By habituating themselves to this sensibility through recurrent bodily practices, the disposition becomes permanent and is *spontaneously* enacted. According to Mahmood, this particular appropriation of the Salafi-Sunni reformist tradition by members of the mosque movement in Cairo hinges on the bodily inculcation of an ethical attitude.[5] Cognition and emotion require deliberate formation to become the ground from which the right ethical disposition can emerge. Prominent among the aspirational virtues are the desire to pray, the capacity to fear and love God, and the unconditional submission to His will. Though ritual worship is crucial, other religious duties and good acts, through repeated disciplinary practice, allow women to develop a pious disposition. Submission to God's will, Mahmood (2005, chap. 4) stresses, is not a sign of passivity but of an actively sought ability.

The parallels between Malian Muslim women's self-disciplining efforts and the practices by participants in the Cairene women's mosque movement attest to the long-standing, close intellectual ties between these two areas of the Muslim world. Clearly the objectives formulated by female supporters of Islamic renewal in West Africa are strongly inspired by the concerns expressed at centers of religious erudition in the Arabic-speaking world. Yet Muslim women's moral quest in contemporary Mali should also be read as distinctively local and at times divergent reformulations of these transnational intellectual influences. This insight is hardly novel, but it prompts questions as to exactly how Salafi-Sunni-inspired readings are integrated into local discursive traditions and what new controversies these appropriations generate.

In her lectures Bintou highlights the rewards and punishments that await humans and direct their course of action. Obedience to God's will, she argues, is ensured by believers' fear of God's punishment, and she cites women's hope for recompense as the major incentive for her compliance to God's will. Although Bintou reminds her students of their individual responsibility for salvation, she places less weight on self-transformation. The Egyptian mosque movement, in contrast, stresses the need to strive for a new emotive and embodied state of mind. Whereas Bintou makes fear part of a carrot-and-stick strategy to convince her followers of the advantages of proper conduct, members of the Cairene movement establish a different relationship between emotions and devotional practices. These women seek to cultivate the desire for a greater closeness to God by engaging in disciplinary practices that generate a greater love and fear of God (Mahmood 2005, chap. 4). Although not all teachers and female leaders emphasize punishment and reward as much as Hadja Bintou does, her position is widely shared, especially among group leaders who were taught by male religious authorities trained at local institutions of Islamic learning. These male teachers, who do not have the same training in Arabic and religious interpretation as their opponents do, deliver their lectures in an authoritarian, top-down fashion and are reluctant to engage in conversations about their teachings, preferring simply to cite rules. Few of them seem to be interested in enhancing women's deeper understanding of God's will. Their authoritarian attitude sometimes influences female leaders who studied with them. Their students often wish for more interactive modes of lecturing, but standards of decency prevent them from openly expressing their disappointment. As a consequence, they often debate the meanings of individual lessons among themselves before venturing to ask their *hadja* or male teacher for clarification.[6]

The few female leaders who favor more responsive, interactive modes of learning also stress inner motivation, rather than punishment, as an incentive for personal transformation. These women represent a younger generation of female leaders who are fluent in Arabic from travels abroad or because their education was financed for them. One of these women is Hadja Maam, the second wife of a wealthy businessman and initiator of a Muslim women's group in Missira, a neighborhood where many state and party officials and other affluent families lived until the early 1990s.[7] Like Bintou, Maam rarely intervenes directly in the learning activities of the women who gather regularly in her courtyard. When she does, the topics of her lectures resemble those of Bintou. The major difference is that Maam privileges the emotive and attitudinal dimensions of ethical self-making. The following excerpt from a lesson, recorded in September 1999, reflects Maam's approach as well as her responsiveness to students' inquiries.

> Some of you asked me how to interpret the advice I had given in last Friday's radio sermon. T. G. [the radio director] asked me to explain the significance of Islam to women. So I told you how women should make the rules of Islam relevant to their daily life. Women should strive to realize them in their daily life. It is not only the daily prayers to which I refer here. Certainly, praying to God is the first and final expression of

our submission to God, and a woman who is serious [in her desire to become a true Muslim] should never, ever neglect it. This is what distinguishes Muslim women [*silame musow*] from other women [*muso tow*]. But if I say that prayer makes a Muslim woman a true believer [*dinamògò*], I do not mean that praying is enough.

Women, listen carefully: it is the right attitude [*kè ko nyuman*] that counts. You should pray with the right mind, with your mind set on understanding God's will. And with a heart that is free of any wish, other than the one of obeying God's will. This is the comportment that God expects from a woman. It gives merit [*nafa*] and is the only way that leads to God. It is as important as prayer. True prayer, too, is the path to God and to spiritual benefit. The comportment required of a woman is patience [*munyu,* endurance]. Be acquiescent and abiding! Show your steadfastness in matters of family life, in moments of great temptation, when you would like to create trouble and to say [to your husband] "I don't agree with you, you are wrong." Only if you control yourself in many places and in many situations, if you [are ready to] endure unjust treatment, then your willingness to submit to God becomes true [*k'i yèrè di ala ma, a bè kè*]. The second virtue you need to practice is modesty [*aw kan ka min kè a finalan, o ye maloya ye*]: your modesty shows in the ways you act, dress and move around in public, and speak to people.

After a respectful silence, a woman deferentially addressed a matter on which she and other participants could not agree: "But, Hadja, what do you mean by the 'many places and situations' where our 'eagerness to submit to God's will becomes true'? Is not our eagerness true? Are we not told to follow the prescriptions for a good Muslim life?" To which Maam responded gravely,

There are many acts that should demonstrate your piety [*ka kè silame dafalen ye;* literally, "that makes you a complete Muslim"]. These acts prove the difference between a true Muslim woman and another woman; the latter may assert that she knows "religion" [*dina*] but from her behavior, you see that she is not a real believer. A true Muslim woman works on her behavior, with all her mind and heart, in her interaction with people. Do not engage in gossip or back-biting. Do not spend your time pointing your finger at others and saying "such-and-such did this-and-that." God detests such doings. But what is worse, what should cause you pain in your heart, is this: anything you do against another person prevents you from moving closer to God. It shows that you have been unable to submit to His will. It shows that you do not fear His punishment. It shows that you fail to love Him and His command.

Similar to Bintou, Maam highlights a woman's responsibility for self-improvement and contrasts Muslim women with "other women." Also like Bintou, she extends the relevance of pious conduct beyond the realm of immediate religious matters to relations in and outside the family. It is tempting to interpret the emphasis on the collective relevance of personal ethics as another influence of twentieth-century Sunni-Salafi reformist thought, but the stress on the social dimensions of pious conduct also has long-standing intellectual roots in this area of West Africa (Brenner and Last 1985; Boyd 1989; Sanankoua 1991b; Cooper 1995; Evers Rosander 1998). Significant departures from Bintou's rule-oriented advice are evident in Maam's assertion that rules should not be followed for their own sake but to facilitate ethical transformation, as well as in her appeal to women's reasoning capacities (*hakili*) and sustained self-monitoring. By reminding her students of their ability to reason independently in religious matters, Maam invites them to develop a capacity for critical discrimination. Both leaders' divergent exposition to reformist currents in the Arab world are also manifest in the different level of importance they attribute to fear in the process of ethical self-development. According to Mahmood, intellectually oriented members of the Cairene mosque movement cultivate fear as a motivational force that helps them develop virtuous qualities (2005, chap. 4). Bintou's teachings, in contrast, as my initial encounter with her illustrated, present the fear of Divine punishment not as a productive emotion but as something to avoid. Maam, on the other hand, believes that fear plays a positive role, even if her views on that matter are less elaborate than those of Mahmood's interlocutors. This became evident, for instance, when she responded to students' queries about the characteristics of a prayer "that reaches God" (*min be se ala ma*).

Prayer is the major path that leads to God. But praying and praying with the right mind is not the same. For a prayer to reach God, you need to make it an act that changes your inner self [*fò a ka bò i yèrè dusunkun de la, fò a ka yèlèma don i ka kokètaw la*]. Only then, if God sees your desire to change your attitude, will he receive your prayer favorably.

Bintou's and Maam's teachings constitute opposite poles of a spectrum of local re-readings of reformist thought propagated in Egypt and Saudi Arabia. Despite evident discrepancies between Bintou's "rule-oriented" and Maam's "disposition-oriented" approaches, both blend a "rationalist" paradigm (emphasizing understanding and self-monitoring) with local religious conventions. Distinctions between these reformulations of translocal intellectual trends can be explained by taking a closer look at the different social and educational backgrounds of the two *hadjas*.

Hadja Bintou's limited Arabic-language skills were achieved through private lessons with a *karamògò* trained at a higher-educational institution in Syria, but most of her knowledge stems from sessions with a locally trained teacher. As noted, Bintou held an influential administrative position under President Traoré. Following his fall from power in 1991, she has maintained close relations with leading members of the national Muslim association, AMUPI, and exerts considerable influence on neighborhood politics. Her relatively affluent living conditions, improved by the regular remittances she receives from several children in Canada and France, add to her prominent social status. Because Bintou's professional life was devoted to working in state institutions and facilitating exchange with Western donor organizations, she had no occasion to spend extended periods of time in the Arabic-speaking world. Bintou was a founding member of the UNAFEM but has withdrawn from active participation because of personal rivalries with members of the steering committee. Whereas Bintou builds much of her influence on her privileged ties to state officials and politicians, Maam owes her leading position in the UNAFEM to her wealthy family background and business ties to the Arabic-speaking world, as well as to her Arabic literacy skills and religious education. Although her husband initially preferred that she retire as much from public life as his first wife does, she convinced him that her activities were in the service of God. With his permission, Maam has been a respected and self-assertive but junior member of the UNAFEM's steering committee since 1999.

The two leaders' different educational backgrounds is reflected in the diverse readings they propose. The degree of their Arabic literacy seems particularly crucial, confirming the interpretation of authors working on Muslim reformist trends in Ivory Coast (LeBlanc 1999; Miran 1998, 2005). Their divergent viewpoints also derive from their respective personal agendas which are related to, but not determined by, their social standing, age, position in the field of religious patronage, and integration into translocal exchange networks. Another factor that has recently deepened the generational divide between older and younger *tontigiw* and rendered more complex the discrepancies among the kind of teachings female leaders formulate is the new policy of the national broadcast station (since 2003) that, for the first time, allows women to speak regularly on its religious programs. Officials have thereby adapted to the trend established by local radio stations. Women who sermonize on local radio are usually representative of the older generation of (locally) trained women leaders; those on national radio and television, on the other hand, are younger women educated in Egypt and the Maghreb. Their teachings tend to resonate with the disposition-oriented approach formulated by Maam. The diversity of interpretations articulated by different erudite women pinpoints an incipient development that reinforces the generational divide and competition among female leaders and preachers of different educational backgrounds. Once religious education became available to women from a broader range of socioeconomic backgrounds, not only has the basis of traditional interpretive authority been undermined but new lines and forms of competition among women have been engendered.

If we return to the convergence between the "rationalist" paradigm (Brenner 1993a) of Cairo's Salafi-Sunni-inspired reform movement and the focus on individual understanding by leaders of Mali's moral reform movement, significant differences can be detected in the ways that women translate this rationalist emphasis into practice. The differences result from the respective traditions of Islamic practice and thought, as well as from the differential educational and institutional context of female Islamic revivalism. Most Muslim women in Mali, because of their limited interpretational knowledge, have no authority to debate the meanings of particular texts. The *hadjas* of the women's groups rarely feel qualified to make authoritative statements about the interpretation of certain passages. When I occasionally asked them for clarification, they referred me to their teachers or other "more knowledgeable men," arguing that their role consisted only in "rallying women" around the search for closeness to God. This is an important contrast to the Cairene mosque movement, which, according to Mahmood, thrives on women's substantive religious arguments as well as on the eagerness with which attendees, not only teachers, assume an active role in expressing their opinions on worldly and spiritual matters. These differences arise because of the women's divergent educational and linguistic backgrounds and the fact that familiarity about proper ritual has until a few decades ago been less entrenched among women in urban Mali than in Cairo. This insight can be qualified by exploring reasons for the differences from the self-assertiveness of female supporters of reformist trends in neighboring countries who otherwise share many of the preoccupations of Malian Muslim women (LeBlanc 1999; Augis 2002; Alidou 2005). These differences seem to be related mainly to the women's varying age and educational backgrounds. Female disciples in Senegal and Ivory Coast belong to an upwardly mobile, francophone, intellectual middle class. In Senegal, in particular, the movement is rooted in a new generation of university students who are adamant about engaging in controversial debate. Many members of the moral reform movement in Mali, in contrast, have little, if any, Western education.

How do Muslim women resolve the discrepancies between the personal disposition–oriented interpretations and rule-oriented approaches in their daily activities? Only a few women I met favored the approach to reform based on one's disposition adopted by Maam. Most participants prefer a rule-oriented attitude toward questions of how to become a good Muslim, largely because it is the most commonly promoted approach. They relate knowledge of social obligations and ritual requirements to eschatological issues, and express a pragmatic attitude toward the "benefit" (*nafa*) and divine reward (*baraji*) they hope to gain. Fear of hellfire and other punishments plays a decisive role in Mali, whereas the participants in the Cairene mosque movement view the triad of "fear, hope, and love" as a complex of motivational forces that inspire a positive desire to realize God's will rather than a passive subjection to God's punishment.

One way to appreciate how Muslim women appropriate the teachings of their group leaders is to examine more closely the different viewpoints on devotional prayer (*seli*) that group members and leaders formulate. Their different views give us a sense of their divergent understandings of how personal piety should be achieved and, once again, demonstrate how the heterogeneous positions that make up the moral reform movement are formulated at the intersection of local and translocal influences.

Controversies over the Significance of Devotional Prayer

Salat, the act of worship, has recently been described as the most important common denominator of Muslim religious practice (Bowen 1989), despite procedural variation and the absence of a fixed semantic core.[8] In the area roughly covering present-day Mali, the regular performance of *salat* (or *seli* in Bamana) as a "visible sign of the proper performance of the code of the sunna" (Launay 1992:117) has historically served as the most prominent indicator of Muslim identity. "Does s/he pray or not" (*ale bè seli wa, wala a tè seli*) is the standard inquiry about an individual that plays off *seli*'s particular, local meaning against its universal significance as the ritual expression of a universal Muslim identity (1992:116; Soares 2004:206–207). The question also encapsulates the distinctive relationship between bodily practice, ethical sensibility, and emotional disposition that should inform the enactment of a Muslim's practice of piety. A person's adherence to Islam is performed and cultivated through repeated acts of prostration before God. An important implication of this conceptualization of ritual is that, as Starrett (1995) observes in contemporary Egypt, the bodily *hexis* adopted in Islamic ritual worship is not an unconscious, non-articulate expression of *doxa;* rather, it is made explicit and consciously deployed.

Questions of proper prayer posture have been repeatedly addressed in West African Muslim history. In Mali and Ivory Coast, recent decades have seen debates about whether one should pray with arms crossed or outstretched, a disagreement pitting representatives of local Islamic traditions against reform-minded Muslim activists. Here, too, tension has been at play between local, particularistic definitions of Muslim identity and participation in a global *umma* (Launay 1992, chap. 5; Brenner 1993a; Soares 2005, chap. 7). Missing in scholarly discussions of these debates and confrontations is how the debates are reformulated by women who claim a central role in articulating the essentials of ethical self-development. Mali's female supporters of Islamic renewal, while reiterating a conventional concern with proper ritual, attribute a more specific meaning to regular prayer and to its *public* enactment. In doing so, they play a role in reformulating the significance of devotional prayer to collective well-being and to the values in which the political community should be grounded. Even if their viewpoint is contested from within the movement, this recon-firms the central import of ritual worship to discursive constructions of proper Muslimhood (Bowen 1993).

Many female participants and group leaders, especially those who adopt a rule-oriented approach to ethical self-development, stress that the correct embodiment of devotion during prayer is a central tenet of the rules of Islam and a pillar on which a new society, invigorated by Islamic values, should be founded. The central importance of proper ritual conduct is evident in all the pamphlets and brochures that advise believers on the proper body posture for prayer. Sermons reveal a similar sensibility by centering on questions of correct prayer and forms of embodying a pious disposition.

Fewer female leaders and group members endorse a disposition-oriented view of the relevance of ritual. They share with those Muslim women who favor a rule-oriented approach a focus on the individual believer's relationship to God, which hints at a departure from a view of religious merit requiring the intervention of intermediaries. Their discussions reveal a view of ritual as a form of disciplinary practice designed for the creation of an inner, cognitive, and emotional disposition, in other words, of a bodily and emotional receptiveness to the divine message. Among the women who stressed the need for an inner and "deep" understanding (*a famuyali yèrè yèrè*) was Aiche, one of the leading intellectual figures in a Muslim women's group in Missira, a middle-class neigh-borhood in Bamako.[9] Inspired by Maam and her *karamògò,* Aiche stressed the centrality of embodied ritual to her pursuit of religious virtue. Regular ritual prayer, she explained, was the occasion for realizing the obligation to "work on a rightful mind" that would "enable her to understand God's word" (*k'i yèrè labèn ka se k'ala ka kuma famu*). She would pay attention to her "state of mind" at the beginning of each prayer. A similar need for constant self-examination, Aiche observed, existed during the performance of her daily chores and in interactions with her in-laws and husband. "Without your readiness to control yourself, you will always slip into disobedience towards God. You lose your capacity for endurance [*munyu*] at moments when it is demanded most of you." And she concluded, "there are people who assume that it is enough to be obedient to your seniors. But, Nanaje, this is not enough. God can tell the difference. Only if you practice obedience [*bonye*], rather than pretend it, will God appreciate your serious intention."

Aiche's explanation is noteworthy for its emphasis on perpetual self-monitoring. But it also reveals a tension. Aiche emphasizes the disciplining effects of proper ritual performance and its function in effecting an all-encompassing emotional and cognitive transformation, thereby echoing teachings of the contemporary women's mosque movement in Cairo. At the same time, by constructing the true believer in contrast to those who merely pretend, she reiterates the divide between inner attitudes and outward behavior that she and other supporters of the moral reform movement decry.

Another dimension of embodied ritual practice is the "sign function" of ritual that is manifest when Muslim women gather to pray in the presence of a larger group of observers. Although this emblematic dimension of ritual performance is not new, over the past twenty years, with the changing context of post-authoritarian state politics, collective female ritual has assumed a specific public significance. There are many occasions when women can publicly engage in this emblematic performance of ritual worship. In towns with a significant presence of Muslim women's groups, the group members often overcrowd the section reserved for female believers during Friday congregational worship. Occasions for public worship also emerge during special religious events, such as the celebration of the *mawlud*, the Prophet's birthday. The sheer number of participants in Muslim women's group meetings, and their joint prayer during sporadic mutual visits, also make their performances more visible. The gatherings in their leaders' courtyard are open to public scrutiny, and their worship can easily be viewed by men who do not withdraw to a separate section. The consequence is a temporary inversion of the conventional separation of male and female realms within the courtyard.

Another instance of the trend toward publicizing rituals, as noted in the introduction, is the effort by the UNAFEM steering committee to videotape and subsequently broadcast women's collective worship on national television. Several Muslim women's groups also made recordings of chants sung during religious ceremonies, again with the aim of "gaining public recognition," as the leader of a women's group in Mopti expressed it in 2004. After all, she added, "now that television reaches even the remotest areas of Mali," the recordings would "show to everyone what the right path for a Muslim woman is." This remark summarizes her conviction that the public act of prostration, the bodily enactment of one's total submission to God's power, also serves the interests of *da'wa,* the proclamation of faith and its propagation to those who have not yet embarked on the path to God. Certainly her interest in inviting a broader constituency to learn about the guiding role of Islam is not shared by all participants or initiators of Muslim women's groups. But among most leaders the prevailing emphasis was on the representational effects of public prayer. Many of their followers, too, were keenly aware of the symbolic meaning of public *seli,* besides its semantics of total prostration. Among them were those who, on other occasions, highlighted the positive disciplining function of prayer in creating the believer's proper attitude through the reworking of her cognitive, emotional, and bodily facilities. After some initial hesitation, however, some of them confided that they "sometimes felt uneasy about mass prayer" because, as one of them said, "it is good to convince others that they should set their mind on God and the path towards Him. But by praying before a public, one runs the risk of ostentation [*yada;* literally, "conceit"]." None of the women saw the embodiment of submission and its symbolic public function as mutually exclusive, nor did any of them consider its public recording as less authentic. The women only felt apprehensive that their leadership duties (and the attendant risk of ostentation) might conflict with their self-training in religious virtue. The women's clear recognition of the multiple meanings inherent in public ritual supports Starrett's (1995) argument that the particular significance of embodied ritual practice is created at the interface between the subjective meanings that actors attribute to it and its public and historically specific political relevance.

The significance of public prayer in Mali springs from a controversy over the relevance of religion in political life that, as illustrated in chapter 1, emerges around issues such as the reform of family law. Whereas those who defend the French model of *laïcité* view religion as a private matter and believe that demonstrations of religious faith should be banned from the public eye, activists promote proper Muslim conduct as a standard for the moral transformation of society and the self. It is not the activists' ostentatious forms of devotional practice per se that are so novel or noteworthy but rather that activists view such displays as having the utmost sociopolitical importance. This view is demonstrated by those activists who move their manifestations of embodied piety to public arenas and make them a symbol in their search for political recognition.

This points to another insight into why women stress the public significance of ritual. To explore the disciplinary practices that individuals pursue in their quest for ethical self-development is a first step toward understanding their investment in moral reform on its own terms (Mahmood 2005). By the same token, to ascertain the complex repercussions of these engagements for broader social and political processes, it is necessary to move beyond an analysis of subjective meanings and personal ethical sensibilities. Individual religiosity results from the interplay between one's quest for piety, social expectations, normative ascriptions, and a particular institutional context that is shaped by the institutions and rationalities of state power and the conditions for partaking in, or claiming one's share of, this power. With this concern in mind, I now engage questions relating to the inter-subjective creation of piety and its emblematic sociopolitical significance in contemporary Mali.

Performing Piety

While most Muslim women conceive of proper ritual conduct as an avenue toward the embodied acquisition of religious virtue, ritual simultaneously gains a symbolic function in the present political arena. This arena is shaped by secular state politics structured, among other dynamics, by the competition between various Muslim factions and a politics of cultural authenticity (Brenner 1993c; Schulz 2007a). Embodied female propriety is mobilized as a key emblem by female leaders, as well as by many male activists, in their call for an Islamic social renewal. Two points are central here. First, women's piety results from and is constitutive of the public presentation and reception of Muslim religiosity. Second, prominent representatives of Islamic renewal value the embodied forms of female piety, such as bodily conduct and a particular dress, as important signs of personal and social development. Women become both symbols *and* articulators of an Islamic normative discourse that is to be publicized to a broader constituency and bears a distinctly female imprint.

The emphasis that proponents of the moral reform movement place on publicly embodied propriety is the culminating point of a development that was initiated in the late 1930s, gained in vigor in the late 1970s, and again grew stronger in the 1990s. Explicit norms of bodily behavior have always been part of the repertory of Islamic orthopraxy in West Africa, with controversies over how to pray properly forming the core of Muslims' self-identification as believers (Launay 1992, chap. 5; Launay and Soares 1999). Written documentation is scarce on the role that women, as practitioners or symbols of propriety, played in these controversial constructions, but the reminiscences of older women and men suggest that Muslim authorities at one time gave women a certain freedom of choice regarding their apparel and obligations of worship. Starting in the 1940s, however, the authorities reformulated their views when they were confronted with the Al-Azharis and other intellectuals spurred by reformist trends in the Arab world. These influences had ambiguous effects on local female religiosity. For instance, reformists sought to enforce a stricter regulation of women's public appearance and apparel but at the same time asserted women's right to education and religious instruction (see Miran 1998).

A recent phenomenon is the specific, often feminized forms through which propriety is manifested in public.[10] As in other regions of West Africa and the modern Muslim world, questions of women's apparel and demeanor have become central to Muslim activists' mobilization of followers, especially in the wake of political liberalization.[11] Proper comportment, especially among women, is of primary importance to Muslim activists. The polyvalent significance of public prayer is one instance of this preoccupation, and another is the focus on decency and propriety in public places. These teachings illustrate the link between a renewed emphasis on correct ritual practice, individual responsibility, and the necessity to publicly practice *and* display one's faith.

In their lectures, female leaders and male teachers connect their demands regarding bodily comportment and dress with notions of respectability and decency. The different connotations of *dambe* (respect, dignity) indicate that "respectability" is constructed through the interplay between a subjective sense of dignity and the behavioral expectations of others.[12] Used in its self-referential form, *dambe* designates a woman's self-respect and sense of decorum, as reflected in her compliance with social norms. The transitive meaning of *dambe* describes the propriety manifested in social interaction: a man respects his father if he displays public signs of deference, for example, by suppressing any sign of disagreement. Similarly, a woman is said to express a sense of self-respect by her bodily demeanor.[13] By observing the requirements of decent conduct, individuals demonstrate their willingness to respect group norms. These expectations are neither uniform nor uncontested. Dress, for instance, rather than merely representing a certain behavior or moral state, plays a central role in controversial constructions of female respectability. I return to this point later.

The view of female *maloya* as a gauge of the general moral order is often spontaneously expressed by Muslim women in their activities and interactions. On a misty morning in February 1999, for instance, I accompanied Astou, a woman about forty-five years old and my closest acquaintance in the Missira Muslim women's group, to the market located next to the *Grande Mosquée* in Bamako. As we made our way through the crowds of shouting street vendors, market women, and groups of chatting women customers, I suddenly noticed how Astou's slow, dignified walk had been brought to an abrupt halt. She was looking at a teenage girl dressed in a tight T-shirt and wrap, chatting flirtatiously with several male adolescents. The girl, with a laugh, then took a 500 FCFA note from one of the boys (whom she had apparently asked for money), turned and walked away in an evocative manner as the boys stared at her and shouted their approval. At this point Astou suddenly took my arm and pulled me along. Intimidated by her grave expression (and knowing well that norms of propriety prohibit direct expressions of disapproval) I hesitated to inquire into the reasons for her annoyance. We walked in silence until we had almost reached home. The scene in the market was clearly still bothering Astou. At last I asked whether she had felt offended by the encounter, but she did not respond. I was beginning to regret my intrusiveness when she slowly turned to me and, with a visible effort at self-control, said in a faint voice:

> Scenes like the one you saw make me grieve in my heart. How can we women display a sense of self-respect, so that men treat us with respect, if our daughters have lost their (capacity to feel) shame, when they move around in front of everyone as if they forgot what their value consists in? It is difficult indeed, Nanaje, for us women who could be their older sisters or mothers, to make them understand that the first step towards self-respect is the way you walk, act, and dress. The truth is that, even if they will not laugh at us publicly, because the respect for our age forbids this, they will not take our lessons to heart. I ask you, Nanaje, how can we talk to these girls, if they refuse to accept that their true value changes if they do not act with propriety? Instead, they act and dress as if they wanted to sell what they mistakenly assume to constitute their value: their body.

Astou's somber assessment reflects her perception of bodily comportment and dress as two closely related forms of embodied respectability. It also illustrates the conviction that bodily praxis, verbal understanding, and cognition complement one another and should be reworked simultaneously. The symbolic importance of women's demeanor sheds light on some of the stakes in the Malian movement for moral renewal. Similar to developments throughout contemporary Muslim Africa and the larger Muslim world, women's embodied propriety and chastity is turned into a central metaphor for articulating Islam as a public normative discourse (see, e.g., Moghadam 1994; Hale 1997; Hodgkin 1998). The notion of female propriety is central to ethical transformation, and the nature of personal reform becomes at once social, ethical, and political.

It is significant that the representational strategies of Malian Muslim activists converge not only with those of their secularist critics and political opponents but also with traditional scholarly representations of Muslim women. Most of these representations center on the assumption that women, either as guardians of Islamic values or tradition *tout court,* or as victims of these values, can be yardsticks for measuring the status quo of political society, which is variously identified as moral or immoral, democratic or repressive (see Kandiyoti 1991b; Chatterjee 1993). What needs to be stressed, then, is that there is nothing specifically Islamic about the tendency of renewal movement supporters to feminize piety.

"En-dressing" Piety

The dress practices of Muslim women is a field in which standards of pious conduct materialize in the interplay of social norms and expectations and individual beliefs. Muslim women's identity as supporters of the moral reform movement, and their claims to religious virtue, are established and challenged in their interaction with those they refer to as "other women." Dress practices, regardless of their variability and contingent meanings, have particular significance in a given historical situation. In urban Mali, for example, Muslim women's attire assumes a specific symbolic significance; it expresses an individual believer's efforts to invite others to move closer to God. The headscarf (*musòrò*), more than any other dress item, stands for women's effort to be pious; indeed, this is reflected in the tendency among Muslim women to describe their decision to join a women's group as a matter of "attaching the (head)scarf" (*musòrò siri*). Putting on the headscarf has become the marker par excellence of a new individual and group identity, and of a woman's compliance with Islamic regulations.

Women's "veiling" (*ka muso datugu;* literally, to "close [up] a woman") is not a new practice in Mali, but only since the 1980s has it turned into the most powerful symbol of individual religiosity. *Musòrò siri* only acquired such symbolic weight because the headscarf was not standard attire. In this respect, there are strong parallels in West Africa to the politics of propriety in other regions of the Muslim world. Yet compared to the politics of Muslim dress in the Middle East, the adoption in West Africa of an Islamic dress style that resembles (what is locally seen as) "Arab fashion" bears a specific connotation of distinctiveness and cosmopolitanism.

Analyzing the personal and public significance of Muslim women's different styles of public apparel is a powerful means of demonstrating that dress, like bodily conduct, constitutes a register for the symbolic representation of women's leading role in Islamic revivalism. Dress, as social practice and meta-phor, grants Muslim women an *active* role in articulating their contribution to an Islam-inspired moral renewal of society, rather than their merely acting as symbols of a movement led by others (e.g., Kandiyoti 1991b; see Abu-Lughod 1998, 6–7). By addressing the contested significance of dress styles and fashions, another aspect of the renewal movement becomes apparent. Supporters of the moral reform movement, by calling themselves "Muslims" or "true supporters of Islam" and setting themselves apart from others who "simply pray," implic-itly assert that differences between real believers do not count. An analysis of Muslim women's diverse views and choice of proper dress allows us to question their claims to uniformity and unity, as well as their normative constructions of true believers and aberrant Muslims. Moreover, we will gain a sense of the extent to which Muslim women's differential access to an international Muslim consumer culture creates or reinforces difference among members of the moral reform movement. This will elucidate the role that clothing plays in the assertion and articulation of religious identity in urban settings where people increasingly express their identity through consumption.

To understand the meaning that "dressing as a proper Muslim" acquires in the interaction between groups and at an individual level, it is useful to keep in mind Anderson's (1982) remark that the "why" of veiling (that is, the func-tion it assumes in a particular society) does not exhaust its social significance at an individual and societal level.[14] Nor does the account of actors' personal motivations to "adopt the veil" exhaust the range of practices to which the term refers, or the significance that different actors and social groups attribute to them. Similarly insightful is Watson's (1994) suggestion to distinguish three separate levels of analysis. The first level is the scriptural/religious level, the written prescriptions for appropriate female and male dress, and the concep-tions of personhood and moral integrity dress conveys. Scriptural norms are not uniform and are open to conflicting interpretations. In urban Mali different coexisting interpretations of Islamic prescriptions of female attire open a field of dissent and conflict among actors who assert an Islamic viewpoint in public debate. On a second level, the societal norms of proper attire that are closely related to notions of morality, modesty, honor, and shame need to be consid-ered, as well as their relation to culturally specific, often inconsistent, gender ideals and roles. The third level at which Watson proposes to study motivations for donning the veil is individual choice. Individual choice, however, cannot be understood independently from the second, societal level, because personal choices and understandings of a particular mode of dress are always the product of the interaction with norms of propriety and respectability. With these caveats in mind, let us now interrogate Muslim women's sartorial preferences.

Members of Muslim women's groups do not require a specific combination of garments, but many women choose a standard combination of dress items. Whereas secularist-minded critics denounce the "oppressive" characteristics of this "Islamic dress," the women themselves do not see it as religious but rather as a decent way to cover the female body. As Hadja Bintou, the leader of the Muslim women's group in Badialan, Bamako, explained,

> There is no particular form of dress you have to wear. All that is required from a respectable Muslim is to cover yourself from head to ankles so that one cannot discern your waistline. You should cover your head and shoulders, too, and display them only to your husband. As for colors, many people feel that, because the Prophet had a special liking for white and light blue clothes, they should choose these colors, too.

Hadja's explanations illustrate that supporters of Islamic renewal associate specific cuts and colors with notions of moral integrity. A loosely cut dress protects one's dignity (*dambe*) and thus forms a variant of embodied propriety. Different codes of female and male propriety are explained by women's and men's distinct natural propensities. Whereas female attire should serve to contain the natural and potentially subversive effects of bodily exposure, male bodies need not be controlled in the same way. Instead, men must be protected from the dangerous, possibly seductive effects of female bodily exposure.[15]

Those who participate in the movement for Islamic renewal and stress that a woman's proper apparel is an important sign of her rightful disposition turn dress into a register of embodied propriety. They endow dress with a specific meaning: the return to Islamic morals. The way Muslim women discuss their choice of apparel reveals that they are fully aware of the symbolic ramifications of their apparel and self-consciously deploy it as a sign of their special status as Muslims who extend their moral call to fellow Muslims. During casual conversations among themselves, Muslim women often jokingly relate episodes to one another in which they received a special, respectful treatment on the part of "others," whether neighbors, policemen, or higher-ranking state officials, because of their apparel. As Astou once told me, tongue-in-cheek, "if you decide to take the veil, Nanaje, you will not regret it. [Because] wherever we go, people from all walks of life will pay us great respect." Her teasing brings home that the symbolic function of Muslim women's clothes is widely acknowledged both by fellow Muslim women and their social entourage.

As much as supporters of Islamic renewal agree that women's dress plays an important role in the return to a truly Islamic way of conducting one's everyday affairs, women's actual dress choices demonstrate that their views of what, exactly, this "return" implies—and in what apparel it should materialize—vary significantly, depending on the instructions they received from individual teachers and group leaders. Nevertheless, common to all their dress styles is the effort to "dress soberly" (*a sabalilen do, a b'a don fini don* ["she is reasonable, she knows what dress to wear"]) and thus to avoid forms of conspicuous consumption that "other women," as well as members of renowned religious clans, engage in. Muslim women rarely use *bazin riche*, the most prestigious and costly fabric, because its high standing in the local prestige economy does not match the ideals of equality and modesty that they promote. When a female leader wears a *bazin riche* dress during a group meeting, it is the dress she most often wears and lacks the prestige of newly purchased *bazin*.[16]

The different versions of proper Muslim apparel can be arranged along a continuum of ideal types. They often correspond to a woman's differential position in a hierarchy of age, social status, and socioeconomic and professional standing, as well as her position relative to a cosmopolitan Islam identified as "Arab Islam." The first type of dress style, preferred by many Muslim group members, is a combination of items almost identical to mainstream female attire (Schulz 2007a).[17] These are large, colorful robes (*dloki ba,* a full-length or half-length gown, or a *grand dakar,* another full-length robe), wrap-around skirts, and turbans made of imported or locally printed cotton. Women from the lower and middle social classes wear this attire for everyday life. Variations in expenditure for this type of Muslim women's dress are subtle but recognizable by fellow Muslim women.[18] As a result, although Muslim women often adopt this dress with the explicit claim that status differences among believers do not matter, they often comment on one another's apparel in ways suggesting that dress does express and reproduce differences.

Muslim women combine this outfit with a colored or plain white scarf made of low-price textile, which they drape more or less loosely over the head and shoulders. This is the scarf Muslim women refer to when they speak of their decision to don the veil (*musòrò*); it *may* serve as a "prayer shawl" (*kunabiri*), but it does not unequivocally indicate a Muslim identity. Nor does the combination of robe, turban, and headscarf have a specifically religious significance. This is because an additional scarf can be worn for purposes other than religious rituals.[19] Prior to the 1980s the draping of an additional scarf over the head, turban, and shoulders was largely a practice of older, respectable women. Wearing a *kunabiri* throughout the day signaled a woman's advanced stage of life and that she now had time to lead a life as a proper Muslim woman by meeting the Islamic ritual requirements. Nowadays, in contrast, as a result of the broader trend toward complying with Islamic precepts in everyday life, a tightly wrapped headscarf bears new meanings. Even those who agree on labeling this additional scarf a "veil" (*musòrò*) do not agree on its exact meaning. Critics of Muslim activists tend to associate a closely wrapped prayer shawl with lower-class status, illiteracy, the conservative outlook of older women, and intellectual rigidity. For those more favorable toward Muslim women's efforts for moral renewal, wearing a closely wrapped prayer shawl expresses a claim to special status based on moral disposition rather than age. Still, because additional headscarves are worn by many younger and middle-aged women for various purposes, they cannot be taken as unmistakable markers of Islamic renewal. It is the tight wrapping, rather than the mere use of a *musòrò,* that proclaims a particular view of how to live one's faith through daily practice. Moreover, depending on the particular fabric and color of a prayer shawl, it may also indicate socioeconomic standing. In many cases, it is the specific cut, value, and provenance of the robe with which the prayer shawl is *combined* that indicates a woman's piety. This polyvalent use of scarves in Mali illustrates the futility of trying to distinguish the religious or cultural significance of a dress item from its practical use (Ingham 1997). Moreover, the significance of a dress item changes over time with the social context of its use and with the particular groups of individuals it is associated with.

The key symbolic implication of "veiling" as a sign of Islamic activism or—depending on the observer—of Islamic radicalism is even more evident in the case of other headgears that Muslim women choose. In recent years the practice of combining the headscarf with other headgear, such as embroidered caps or hairnets, has become more widespread among Muslim women. Though considered a stricter version of the "veil" (and a marker of a woman's support of Islamic renewal), this headgear also offers women with little spending powers a decent way of concealing their inability to follow hair design or braiding fashions. Less frequent are black scarves that cover the entire face except for the eyes or chador-style robes covering the face and body. These types of body covers are widely considered as indications of a culturally foreign, "radical" Arab influence, and women who wear them are usually treated with polite irony or a condescending dismissal as conservative, narrow-minded, and overly submissive to their husband (implying that it is at the husband's request that women don such clothing). Even some participants in the Islamic renewal movement comment harshly on this "exaggerated" dress mode, thereby expressing their reservations, which their secularist critics share, about a greater external "Arab" influence on local society and politics.

The second type of female Muslim apparel signals a woman's endorsement of the renewal movement and comprises distinctly local, low-cost varieties of Islamic dress design that do not need to borrow from Arab style–inspired clothing or even imports. The dress consists of a large white robe cut according to local conventions (most often the *grand dakar*) and a white prayer shawl, wrapped tightly around the head, neck, and shoulders or worn in addition to a turban. Like the first style of dress, it is not the additional scarf per se that indicates a religious attitude; rather, its white color is the symbol of a woman's religiosity. Most female leaders wear this attire in their everyday public life; their disciples, in contrast, don it only for special events such as religious ceremonies, weddings, and other festivities.[20]

In contrast to the first style, which is similar to mainstream female dress, the plain white attire of Muslim women connotes a conscious decision to publicize one's own newly found faith to a broader constituency. Here, again, we see how the symbolic resonances of a specific attire are changing. Until the 1980s a woman's plain white apparel indicated her status as a "Hadja," as one who completed her pilgrimage to Mecca. Over the past fifteen years, however, white attire came to encompass a new, modest lifestyle based on the effort to position oneself socially, not by outdoing others in competing for prestigious goods but by empathy and mutual support. As a symbol of purity and simplicity, white clothing links a woman to a global community of believers (*umma*) and conveys her quest for social qualities and religious virtue. It reflects a woman's modest disposition and acceptance of the egalitarian thrust of Islam.

The color white, the common denominator of the second dress type, symbolizes Muslim women's assertion that status differences are irrelevant to their moral project. However, to a greater extent than the first type of attire, this dress style lends itself to the subtle expression of difference in accomplishment, chic, and wealth through variations in the quality and origin of the dress fabric and in degrees of ornamentation. Further, the very occasion on which a woman adopts plain white dress hints at her position in a status hierarchy. Women with less spending power wear all white clothing only when they attend a special, not necessarily religious, event. Wealthier women, in contrast, don white dress as an everyday, almost casual outfit that allows her to show her deliberate, congenial self-limitation to modest dress style and social position.

As this suggests, different colors and types of apparel play an important role in the interactions between Muslim women, as do body postures and other nonverbal forms of expressing humility and self-discipline. Slow, restrained body movements and gestures, together with all-white attire, are important ways for female leaders to convey their visions of religious virtue at group gatherings and public ceremonies. Because their clothes are plain yet clearly made of expensive, imported fabric, these leaders can subtly exhibit high prestige and spending power by wearing a dress considered more "pious" and valuable than the low-cost, colored dress of the group members. In these group meetings, then, dress serves as a means of communication in the course of which differences in status and religious prestige are established and disclaimed.

The third dress style indicates not only participation in the moral reform movement but a cosmopolitan orientation. It comprises, broadly speaking, two main variants that borrow the mode of dress, cut, ornamentation, and colors from an international, "Arab-style" fashion. One version is the *jellaba*-style dress, with either a closed front section or an embroidered front with buttons, worn with full-length wrappers or large trousers. Prestigious, high-cost versions of this apparel are imported from the Arab world (mainly Egypt, Morocco, Saudi Arabia, and Dubai) or made locally of expensive imported fabric. Elaborate patterns made with gold or silver thread make these robes a precious investment.[21] The low-cost version of this apparel, which is widely considered to be "Arab-style" dress, is sewn by local tailors and made of inexpensive material such as plain black fabric or printed, multicolored cotton produced in Malian factories. Its embroidery imitates the ornamentation of the expensive version but demands less labor and material.

Women who don the Arab-inspired fashions, especially those who can afford the high-cost versions, differ from other Muslim women in their use of accessories, including specific forms of "Arab-style" headgear, specially embroidered prayer shawls, prayer beads, shoes, and jewelry. Some accessories are costly and are imported from the Arabic-speaking world; others are low-priced imitations either locally produced or imported from Southeast Asia. They not only signal a woman's cosmopolitan orientation toward the wider world of Islam but also her affinity to revivalist trends in the Arabic-speaking world, particularly Egypt and Saudi Arabia (see LeBlanc 2000, 454). Whether imported or locally produced, this dress variety is often more costly than the first style of Muslim women's dress discussed above, especially if it integrates recent fashion trends in the Arab world and demands extra labor such as embroidery. Most women from the lower classes cannot afford such a purchase, but they sometimes receive this kind of dress as a gift from a daughter or son who returns from a business trip or pilgrimage, from an older male relative, or from their husband. Whereas poorer women would wear refined versions of this apparel only on festive occasions, many younger, married Muslim women have a strong preference for it and, if possible, would use their savings to purchase it. To them, this attire conforms with the standard of sober and modest dress demanded of Muslim women and at the same time enables its owner to position herself between the low-cost attire of older married women and the conspicuous, Western-style dress of many peers. Adopting an "Arab-style," cosmopolitan version of Muslim dress allows women to belong to a transnational community of true believers but also to be associated with a morally more acceptable mode of consumption.

Upper-class women who wear elaborate variations of this apparel downplay social distinction but simultaneously exhibit a special Muslim identity and position. This is so because high-cost versions of this dress are available through trade or travel to the Arab world and hence suggest business or family ties to an international consumer market. Female leaders, by donning Arab-style attire, subtly claim a special status and cosmopolitan orientation toward "Arab Islam" that sets them apart not only from women who refuse to adopt a Muslim identity but also (and this remains unacknowledged) from Muslim women whose lack of means and education prevents them from adopting an international Muslim outlook.

The sartorial choices of many female followers of Sharif Haidara, the leader of the Ansar Dine movement, illustrate the complex economy of religious prestige and moral distinctiveness generated by Muslim women's dress. The dress practices of Ansar Dine women demonstrate the limited ability of many Muslim women to partake in this economy of religious prestige as well as the ways in which they deal with these limitations. Most Ansar Dine members wear a low-cost variant of "Arab-style" dress consisting of a scarcely embroidered, inexpensive black fabric made into a full-length gown worn over a long wrapper or large trousers. Those who cannot afford this outfit combine industrially produced, colorful fabric with specially printed dresses and headscarves.[22] On festive occasions Ansar Dine women wear more expensive, local versions of upper-class religious dress that are affordable to lower- and lower-middle-class women with neither the opportunity nor spending power to access trade circuits with the Arab world. Distinctive about these different outfits of Ansar Dine women are prayer shawls and other dress items that bear, in green letters on a white background, the logo of the movement, as well as portraits, honorific titles, and various quotes (in French and Bamana) of their spiritual leader Sharif Haidara. Ansar Dine acolytes thus combine a cosmopolitan, religiously encoded design with local aesthetic conventions which, inspired by Western consumer emblems, materialize in items such as T-shirts, baseball caps, and scarves. These Ansar Dine dress articles are specifically local, low-cost responses to the requirements of embodying a Muslim identity. Together they constitute a commodity economy that offers Ansar Dine members a way to resolve the paradoxical tension between the renunciation of consumer culture, the need to participate in that culture in order to publicly articulate one's religious orientation, and the lack of a way to fully participate. Locally produced religious paraphernalia allow these women to renounce consumption and nevertheless express their position in a local hierarchy of respectability and piety through their attire.

In an effort to invite others to follow their moral calling, Ansar Dine women adopt an outfit that announces to a Bamanakan- and French-speaking public their devotion to their leader and his version of Islamic renewal. Another significant aspect of their dress practices is that they embody the women's attachment to a religious leader and thus are one of many religiously relevant acts through which Muslim women seek to transform their daily lives and give it new importance. Their dress practices should therefore be seen as one mode of ethical performance through which participants in the moral reform movement work to remake themselves and their society.

Articulations of a Transnational Religious Field

In an expanding and diverse consumer culture, female Muslim dress emerges as a privileged register of enacting a pious disposition and one's solidarity with equal-minded Muslims. Female dress plays a key role in realizing proper comportment in various areas of everyday life from public arenas to the more intimate domestic spheres. These dynamics are embedded in a heterogeneous religious field at the intersection of local and transnational influences.

LeBlanc (2000) argues that, in Bouaké, different local adaptations of Arabic versions of Islam are considered by many Muslims, especially younger ones, as a third option between modernity and tradition. Malian Muslim women's position within a cosmopolitan Islam, on the one hand, and local interpretive traditions, on the other, reveals parallels to, as well as differences from, the situation analyzed by LeBlanc. In urban Mali the meanings of local or cosmopolitan Muslim dress and of "Arab Islam" are highly polyvalent, contingent, and open to disagreement. Only some Muslims declare their distance from conventional, local interpretive traditions of Islam. Other participants in the moral reform movement, like their critics, consider Arab Islam and Arab-style dress a regression to a less liberal or fundamentalist Islam. Moreover, as we have seen, many lower-class Muslim women can claim respectability but not prestige based on consumption or an orientation toward cosmopolitan Arab Islam. In Mali, proper apparel offers Muslim women an opportunity to position themselves *differentially* within the landscape of Muslim activism by drawing variously on "Arab" Islamic or Western sartorial styles. The adoption of an Arab style depends on one's spending power and implication in transnational business ties and social connections, and thus remains largely restricted to more affluent women.

The version of decent dress promoted by Ansar Dine women shows that they distinguish themselves from both a Western consumer identity *and* a cosmopolitan, Arab-style Muslim identity. By choosing among a variety of decent attires, they position themselves vis-à-vis the outside world through selective borrowing. Ansar Dine women thus demonstrate the variable positions taken by female supporters of Islamic renewal to establish a third space between Western and Arab-inspired versions of modern subjectivity and morality. In their selective appropriation of various transnational consumer items and symbols, Muslim women do not differ in principle from other women who consume mainstream culture and whose limited financial means keep them from fuller participation in the world of consumerism.

Several points follow from this interpretation of religious consumption as a mode of practicing virtue. The first is that dress and other forms of embodied practice constitute a privileged space for women to place themselves in the field of competing Muslim positions and interpretations. Proper dress signals a sense of shame and respectability to which Muslim women lay claim to distance themselves from other women. Dress practices extend beyond a cultivation of religious virtue and are central to the public proclamation of a religious conviction that serves the purpose of *da'wa*. Although Muslim activists distinguish between proper, respectable dress and improper attire, and thus posit a clear contrast between themselves and others, the divisions are more complicated. Their different dress styles offer a way to assert equality and at the same time claim social distinction. In this way, hierarchies of religious prestige are established among Muslim women and between them and other women.[23] Differences between Muslim women and "other women" are often more evident, especially if the former dress in a way that identifies their affiliation with the Islamic renewal movement. The enactment of status differences within the Muslim community usually remains subtle and inexplicit. In each case, differences in social standing are realized through consumer items and attendant claims to ethical distinction. Religious consumption operates as an at once unifying and excluding mechanism.

Although dress may play a decisive role in asserting difference, we should not assume that the intent of "veiling" and other dress practices is strategic; nor is it identical for all women in a Muslim society or within a movement. Given Bourdieu's (1979) argument that consumption in contemporary society is a site where differences in prestige and social and economic capital are generated and expressed, it is time to move beyond simplistic assumptions about sartorial practices and norms, and their effects on Muslim women.

Consumption and the
Embodiment of Religious Subjectivity

Muslim women in Mali embark on a journey of ethical self-improvement that involves a changing understanding of individual responsibility, new modes of acquiring and defining religiously relevant knowledge, and an enlarged symbolic repertoire for the public expression of their ethical sensibilities. Their emphasis on individual understanding and dialogue with God has far-reaching effects that cannot be fully understood if measured by the emancipatory politics they may generate. A key implication of Muslim women's ethical impetus is that it assigns and legitimates a new religious subjectivity that is predicated on individual accountability. This insight enriches scholarly analyses of Islamic revival in Africa insofar as it highlights the ethical concerns and sensibilities that motivate women to assume leading positions in these movements. Because their daily practices and learning activities are strongly geared toward ethical self-improvement, their significance extends beyond the acquisition of Arabic literacy, knowledge about proper ritual conduct, or the adoption of a modern Muslim identity (see Alidou 2005; also see Deeb 2006).

But the specific forms in which Muslim women choose to achieve "closeness to God" hint at a paradoxical development with respect to their translocal orientations and engagements. The women's sociopolitical activities derive much of their appeal from being part of a joint transnational movement toward Islamic moral reform and from distancing themselves from Western cultural and political hegemony. Yet it is precisely women's position in a sphere of translocal Islamic influences that reinscribes hierarchies of income and prestige that lead to the weakening of women's effort to subscribe to a unifying agenda. The reproduction of difference operates to an important extent through the consumption of items of religious dress and paraphernalia.

The tension between an egalitarian orientation and the concomitant reproduction of difference is not unique to the Malian context; nor should it be seen as a recent development. Launay's (1992) analysis of changing understandings of Muslim identity in northern Ivory Coast describes the coexistence of distinct kinds of ritual practices that situate the believer in both a local, particularistic moral universe and a global community of believers (*umma*). Whereas rituals associated with the local moral community emphasize social hierarchy based on age, genealogical descent, gender, education, and status, another set of rituals articulates a decidedly universalist outlook and membership in a global community of believers. As Launay emphasizes, the meanings of these different rituals are often context-dependent and unfold in complementary areas of moral practice and belonging. Launay's insightful analysis elucidates why many Muslim women in Mali do not see a contradiction between their claims to a unitary moral project and the dress practices through which they establish and reproduce internal difference. Sartorial choice constitutes a mode of embodying piety and an opportunity to claim membership in a global community of true believers. By the same token, dress practices allow them to situate themselves and others in a local, hierarchically structured moral community. The reproduction of local social hierarchies does not invalidate the genuine nature of the universalist renewal to which they aspire. Dress practices, even if they do not form part of the ritual realm in the narrow sense, figure importantly in women's search for an ethically informed life.

The significance Muslim women attribute to dress as a mode of cultivating piety has a broader theoretical relevance for debates on consumption as a form of religious practice. Robertson (1991), for instance, argues that contrary to a central tenet of secularization theory, religion plays an important role in contemporary society that is twofold: not only has religion gained a new salience as a community-creating idiom, but it has also become a form of consumption.[24] Robertson's argument captures an important dimension of Muslim women's sartorial practices in Mali, namely, their conviction that dress is a mode of proper comportment that helps them publicize their moral quest to their social surroundings. Certain consumption practices do indeed play a greater role in their religious praxis. At the same time the consequences of the heightened significance of consumption to religiosity in urban Mali are more complicated than Robertson surmises. It is tempting to interpret the local adaptations of international, Arab-style fashion trends as signs of local creativity. However, many participants in Mali's Islamic renewal movement remain excluded from the transnational circuits through which religious dress items and paraphernalia are distributed. Consumption serves the expression of religiosity but at the same time perpetuates religious and social heterogeneity and exclusion.

These insights make Muslim women's dress practices pertinent to recent critiques of scholarship that highlight consumption as a key site of identity construction in modern society (e.g. Friedman 1994; Miller 1995). As Harvey (1989), Postone (1999), and Comaroff and Comaroff (2000) argue, authors who privilege consumption as the site of expressions of modern subjectivity reiterate an analytical bias characteristic of a neoliberal capitalist consumer ideology. This ideology could emerge only with the dislocation of sites of production from those of consumption in the current global economic order. As we have seen, for many supporters of Islamic renewal in Mali, it remains difficult, even impossible, to articulate their positions through acts of consumption, as they remain marginal in national and international consumer markets (see Ferguson 2002). Muslim women are caught in a dilemma. Although their vision of the path to God rests on renouncing Western consumerism, they also feel obliged to convince others of their moral call through proper public comportment and dress. Sartorial choice becomes a medium of religious subjectivity for Muslim women, but it also underlines their limitations rather than offering them a space for unlimited self-expression.

A shirt imprinted with Sharif Haidara's portrait. *Photo by Ute Roeschenthaler.*

A workshop run by followers of Sharif Haidara. *Photo by Ute Roeschenthaler.*

Ansar Dine paraphernalia decorate the rear window of a car. *Photo by Ute Roeschenthaler.*

SIX

"Proper Believers":
Mass-mediated Constructions of Moral Community

TO GRASP THE different facets of Islam's public prominence in Mali, we need to consider the activities, claims, and recent successes of Muslim activists in the context of worsening economic conditions, men's and women's assumption of different responsibilities, and widespread disillusion with unwarranted promises of democratization. The search for an Islamic social and moral renewal is firmly rooted in the urban middle and lower-middle classes but is by no means restricted to them. Because men are having difficulties in earning a regular income, their wives are assuming greater, sometimes exclusive, responsibility for securing the family's livelihood. Women's burden is made even greater because of their extended decision-making power. In most cases, however, men impede their wives' increased power as much as they can. Thus the mushrooming of neighborhood women's groups form part of urban Muslim women's endeavor to deal with these disruptions and the attendant financial and emotional insecurities. Their learning activities also need to be understood against the backdrop of historical transformations of religiosity that reach back to the colonial period. In recent decades these transformations are reflected in a stronger emphasis on individual understanding, the acquisition of knowledge, and greater responsibility for personal salvation. Muslim women's spiritual quest centers on personal transformation through the quotidian enactment of an Islamic morality based on patience and endurance. Women's individual motivation concurs with the aspirations of various Muslim leaders who mobilize a following through projects and institutions.

The leaders of Muslim women's groups, as well as male protagonists of the moral reform movement, ground their call for moral renewal in Islamic values and a model of political modernity which, many of them claim, differs from the government's secularist project. At the same time these actors draw on the international rhetoric of democracy and civil society as they formulate specifically Islamic norms. Moreover, as illuminated by the family law controversy, Muslim activists' constructions of political community are contested from within the Muslim community. Whereas some Muslims claim that national identity is based on Islam as the common religion, and thereby favor a kind of "religio-nationalism" (an analogy to ethno-nationalism; see Wilmsen and McAllister 1996), other activists' constructions may be closer to the governmental notion of a national community defined by its unity in (religious) diversity.

The new role of religion in public controversy raises questions about the modalities by which Islamic norms and discursive forms are rendered public. How do these modalities of intervention and publicity affect the contents and stakes of intra-Muslim debate, and how is this controversy complicated by Muslims' varying presence in the landscape of state institutions and actors? In what ways are particular media technologies conducive to these dynamics, and what role do processes of commodification and commercialization play in these changes?

To account for the relevance of commercial mass culture in Islam's move into Mali's public arenas, a useful entry point is Habermas's attention to the historical genesis and transformation of the public sphere in Western Europe. At the same time we must abandon Habermas's normative characterization of public debate to properly understand the culturally and historically specific terms on which Islam "goes public" (Lee 1993) in Mali.[1] The weight of Islam as a moral idiom in public debate calls into question Habermas's argument—as advanced in his "Structural Transformation"—that political modernity is characterized by the privatization of religion. Furthermore, the dynamic nature of intra-Muslim debate contradicts Habermas's separation of private religious faith from publicly articulated politics. Over the last decades, political controversies in Malian civil society have often been expressed in a religious idiom. Many of these controversies occur *among* Muslims, revealing not only different understandings of proper Muslim practice but also competition over religious authority and legitimacy. This chapter suggests that disagreements among Muslim activists necessitate a reassessment of Habermas's lack of attention to the stratification of the public based on structures of exclusion. By positing that internal differences and strategies of exclusion are constitutive of Muslim public debate (and do not herald its "degradation"), my analysis departs from Habermas's depiction of a unitary and homogeneous (bourgeois) public sphere in which participants exchange (private) viewpoints but do not construct embattled identities (Habermas 1990 [1962]; also see Calhoun 1997).[2] The crucial question is not *whether* identity differences can be bracketed before they are made public but *how* they are being denied or acknowledged (Fraser 1992).

One way to illuminate the dynamics of intra-Muslim debate in Mali is to address them with respect to the popular Muslim movement Ansar Dine and its spiritual leader, Sharif Ousmane Haidara, who competes with the AMUPI over public representation and leadership. An exploration of the—often mass-mediated—confrontations between Sharif Haidara and other Muslim leaders allows us to trace whose viewpoints are excluded or silenced in public debates and simultaneously to consider the broader context of mass-mediated "religious" debate (Öncü 2006; Salvatore 1999). An analysis of Haidara's enormously popular, mass-mediated interventions allows one to determine how the adoption of new media technologies affects the forms of religious debate and the subjective articulations of Islamic normativity (Hirschkind 2001a), thereby contributing to changes in the sources and forms of authority. Haidara's mass-mediated appearances shed light on several interrelated processes that are conducive to novel forms of religious experience, community, and authority. Of particular relevance are the symbolic and material dimensions of audio cassettes through which Haidara's followers recognize themselves as a "community of true believers." An examination of these forms of media engagement will reveal how specific media, such as audio recordings of sermons, reorganize the material, semantic, and discursive possibilities for generating religious community.

"Islam Goes Public": Dynamics of the Muslim Media Landscape

The growing infrastructure of proselytizing and the drive for public prominence by various Muslim actors and interest groups since 1991 marks a reconfiguration of the relationship between state and society. Contrary to Muslim activists' rhetoric of the "civil society against the state," most activists cooperate with, and are mutually dependent on, state institutions and officials. Muslim leaders who seek a following cannot afford to bypass state institutions if they want to establish a dominant position. State officials and politicians, on the other hand, despite their critical distance from protagonists of Islamic moral reform, are careful not to antagonize Muslim leaders whose mobilizing potential they recognize as a serious challenge in the present political situation. This complex picture of shifting alliances manifests in the dynamics of the recently liberalized media landscape, illustrating how access to, and control of, state resources and institutions continues to foment intra-Muslim rivalry.

Controversies among Muslim preachers, and the somewhat novel, often mass-mediated forms in which they are publicized, continue, but also significantly depart from, earlier debates over proper Muslimhood (e.g., Launay 1992, chap. 1; Launay and Soares 1999; Loimeier 2003; Kane 2003; Soares 2005, chap. 7). Some differences between current and older issues and forms of Muslim public reasoning are related to the novel political practices seen in nation-state politics and the recent spread of mass-media products embedded in commercial consumer culture. In colonial French Sudan, Muslim controversies concerned proper ritual, correct public behavior, and educational matters (Kaba 1974, 3–5; Brenner 2001, chap. 2, 3). French newspapers publicized a Muslim identity that combined universalist credentials with the particularistic identity of a modern African citizen (Soares 2005, 223–226). But these earlier, print-mediated forms of Muslim public debate had limited effects because their audience was a small French-speaking population. Mass media per se cannot induce major shifts in reasoning and consumption. To understand the effects of mass media on the dynamics of Muslim public thinking, it is important to consider the specific possibilities (and limitations) of mediating religion that individual technologies afford, possibilities determined by how the production and circulation of mass media is organized and by the forms of exclusion this organization generates (Manuel 1993; Rajagopal 2001). The liberalization of the media market in Mali since 1991 marked a new step in moving Islam into public arenas and making it an issue of public debate, as it addressed new audiences and expanded the debate to new consumer-subjects and "articulators of Islam" (Anderson 1999).

President Traoré maintained political and financial control over the most influential Muslim interest groups by granting them special privileges such as extra broadcast time on national media. Until 1991 national radio and television's Bureau des Ulema (Office de Radiodiffusion et Télévision du Mali [ORTM]) held a monopoly on religious radio and television programming, with the exception of a few weekly broadcasts from Radio Caire (Egypt) and Radio Libye.[3] Because of the close ties between the Bureau des Ulema and the AMUPI, religious programs reflected the viewpoints of the AMUPI steering committee.[4] Although this committee comprises heterogeneous views, it agrees on the rationale of maintaining the association's privileged position vis-à-vis the government.[5] Its attitude toward governmental politics, as a result, has remained unchanged since Traoré's ouster in 1991. The committee continues to influence official programming policy and exerts control over the choice of preachers on national media. But because of competition introduced by local radio stations, the Bureau des Ulema's views of Muslim religiosity have become more contested.

Although some preachers publicized their sermons on audio tapes in the 1980s, the increasing expansion of local radio stations since 1991 spurred a steady growth in the number of preachers with more or less sound religious training. In sermons and interviews on local radio, they offer advice on Islamic norms of personal conduct and collective affairs. Most of these radio preachers are teachers at local *medersa*s who have difficulty making a living because many donors from the Arabic-speaking world no longer support their school financially. The cooperation among local radio stations and preachers benefits both parties. In spite of the overwhelming popularity of local radio stations, particularly among urban women and adolescents, most stations lack the necessary financing and personnel, and suffer from a certain monotony in their programming structure (Schulz 1999a). Many directors, therefore, welcome individuals who volunteer information on legal matters and oral traditions. Broadcasting sermons is also advantageous to stations because preachers just starting out willingly pay to broadcast their sermons.[6] Once a preacher has established renown on local radio, he will draw large numbers of listeners and increase the standing of a radio station. Preachers who sermonize regularly on local radio enhance their reputation as knowledgeable *karamògòw,* and this entices parents to send their children to them and support them with alms. Regardless of their formal status as commercial or community media outlets, local radio stations reserve substantial time slots (Thursday nights and Friday mornings) for "cassette sermons" (*wajuli caseti*), thus facilitating the proliferation of diverse viewpoints on proper Muslim practice and the relevance of personal ethics to collective life.

These institutional and material changes in Mali's media landscape generate a public arena punctuated by the controversial interventions of Muslim intellectuals and freelance preachers with varying religious knowledge and oratorical skills. Some of these preachers challenge the legitimacy of the AMUPI steering committee by denouncing its close affiliation to the former government of Traoré. The two private Islamic radio stations in Bamako, Radio Islamique and Radio Dambe, support the diversification of Muslim public reasoning. The divergent positions they broadcast depend to a certain extent on the degree to which they rely on state resources. Because Radio Islamique, founded in 1994 by the AMUPI, is financed primarily through governmental funds, its choice of audio-taped sermons is limited mostly to those that express support for governmental policy (Davis 2002, 54–56). Radio Dambe, in contrast, created in 2001 by a dissenting member of the AMUPI's steering committee, publicizes views inspired by Salafi-Sunni ideas from Egypt and draws on private funding and the commercial broadcasting of sermons.

One result of this intensified struggle within the field of Muslim debate is that, in 2000, the government of Alpha Konaré created a new structure, the Haut Conseil Islamique, to accommodate certain Muslim leaders who denounced the exclusivist politics of the AMUPI. This governmental attempt at co-opting critical Muslim voices comes close to an official recognition of the potential of local radio stations and audio and video recordings to challenge official representations of Islam. Sermon audiotapes, in particular, could be interpreted as creating an oppositional or "counter" public (see Manuel 1993; Sreberny-Mohammadi and Mohammadi 1994; Hirschkind 2001a; Rajagopal 2001). Yet this interpretation would not capture the ways in which Muslim leaders and state officials in Mali are caught in a web of mutual attempts at co-optation. Moreover, Muslims who seek to promulgate their views of Islamic public norms to a broader constituency are reluctant to content themselves with using "small" media whose dissemination is not centrally controlled. These Muslims strive to access national media, as this gives them considerable advantage over their competitors. Access to, and a co-optation of, state institutions remains central in the intra-Muslim controversy.

This dynamic is manifested in the confrontation between representatives of the religious establishment and the preacher Sharif Haidara, Ansar Dine's "spiritual guide," whose interpretative and political positions on Muslims are discussed in chapter 1. Born in the early 1960s near Segou into an unimportant branch of a prestigious religious lineage,[7] Haidara, in the 1980s, started a triumphant preaching career in Ivory Coast. After his return to Mali in 1986, he settled in Bankoni, a lower-class neighborhood in Bamako, where he encountered fervent opposition from representatives of the AMUPI, who impeded his access to national media by dismissing him as a rabble-rousing upstart lacking religious knowledge.[8] In the early 1990s, after Haidara failed in his attempts to preach on national radio, he was invited to present his (already controversial) position in a televised debate with clerics closely affiliated with the AMUPI. But the videotaped controversy where, according to Haidara, "at the end, they [Haidara's opponents] no longer knew how to counter my arguments" was never broadcast because "influential members of the AMUPI intervened."[9] Confronted with these political impediments, Haidara relied even more heavily on audio and videotapes disseminated throughout southern Mali, Ivory Coast, and Guinea to gain notoriety over established Muslim leaders. Since 1994 he has preached regularly on two local radio stations in Bamako and has broadcast his audiotaped sermons on commercial radio stations in towns of southern Mali.

During the years of his exclusion, Haidara (soon to be nicknamed Wulibali Haidara, meaning "Haidara who speaks the undeniable truth [in defiance of the powerful]"), gained renown as a critic of governmental policy and of "hypocritical" religious leaders and their opportunistic relationship to the political leadership. Haidara thus profited from the enormous support afforded by a critical stance toward state officials in an atmosphere of widespread disillusion with politics. In 2001, when it became clear that Haidara's political exclusion only increased his credibility as an upright critic of self-interested politicians, Muslim leaders, and governmental policy, his opponents in the AMUPI caved in to governmental pressure and granted him access to national television and radio. They also agreed to Haidara's joining the aforementioned Haut Conseil Islamique. Haidara, however, still plays the *enfant terrible* of intra-Muslim controversy by cleverly defying eminent religious leaders in his acclaimed appearances on national media. His recent rise in official status illustrates how skillfully he capitalized on his renown as an incorruptible critic of institutional power. His success demonstrates that religious and state authorities prefer to domesticate him through accommodation rather than "let him loose" in cassette sermons and radio broadcasts. Haidara's struggle and ultimate victory over his Muslim contenders point to the continued importance of national broadcast channels as a center of symbolic mediation.[10] To those who seek to articulate Islamic norms of conduct, access to state institutions remains pivotal in establishing their interpretation as dominant. State officials, on the other hand, need to carefully straddle ideological commitments and the necessities of *realpolitik* vis-à-vis Muslim activists whose mobilizing potential they fear but also capitalize on. In a situation where officials' invocation of moral community lacks credibility, they need to consider the new conditions generated by a pluralized and commercialized media landscape. Small media, such as audio cassettes, complicate the dynamics of Muslim controversy, because they lend force to dissension enhanced by the long-standing undermining of established religious authority. Also, contrary to the assumption that proliferation of media technologies sustains critical opinion making (e.g., Eickelman and Anderson 1999; also Panos 1993), direct access to religious knowledge, facilitated by a multimedia landscape, does not necessarily invite qualified debate of religious matters. Additional attributes, such as a compelling presentational style, become factors in the public articulation of one's ethical sensibilities and convictions.

To understand why media preachers such as Haidara are so successful at evoking an alternative to the official constructions of moral community, the investigation should target the dynamics of a mass-mediated public. This requires an assessment of how the spread of a mass-mediated commercial culture and an intensifying circulation of religious media affect the means, capacities, and opportunities of Muslims to evoke "Islam" as the central reference point of moral community and collective order.

Circuits of Religious Consumption

Sermon recordings feed into modes of Muslim public thought embedded in an expanding market of religious consumption. This market follows a dynamic resulting from its location in a transnational field of competing styles of expressing one's identity as a Muslim as well as a modern consumer, and of commercial ties to the Arabic-speaking world, particularly Libya, Egypt, Saudi Arabia, and Morocco. Some of these transnational commercialization circuits have been invigorated by neoliberal economic reforms since the mid-1980s, and by opportunities for cheap transport and travel to the sites of the *hejaz* and other areas of the Muslim world. In the comparatively prosperous rural areas of Mali's south, a boost in Malian cotton production supported the spread of an urban culture of Islamic piety and religious consumer culture to the rural hinterlands. As a result of the temporary rise in the cotton prices, and the considerable remittances sent back by sons working abroad, farmers convert economic prosperity into a more lasting and redemptive currency of personal achievement. They send older family members on the *hadj* or embark on it themselves and initiate business ventures that rely on young, unemployed family members, men and women, who travel back and forth between Mali and North Africa or Saudi Arabia to purchase and resell religious paraphernalia. People from urban and rural areas capitalize on booming sectors of the economy to make their spiritual quest an integral part of their daily activities, economic and otherwise. Recent neoliberal structural changes in the national economy thus create new opportunities for Muslims in Mali to experience and express their conviction that economic success reflects and increases divine blessing, thereby validating the spiritual and economic connotations of prosperity deeply entrenched in West African Islamic traditions (Cruise O'Brien 1971; Amselle 1985; Launay 1992; Soares 2005, chap. 6). This pursuit of spiritual and financial salvation exhibits remarkable parallels with the transnational orientation and "prosperity gospel" promoted by Pentecostal movements around the globe.[11]

The new opportunities for religious enterprise and the practice of personal piety go hand in hand with a gender-specific restructuring of local markets for religious services and consumption. Muslim traders, most of them men from established merchant families with long-standing connections to the Arabic-speaking world, along with some younger women (Sanankoua 1991b), have moved into the expanding sector of religious commerce. The partial privatization of the *hadj* since the mid-1990s has stimulated an increase in the number of "*hadj* travel agencies" run by men and by a few women, who use family connections and middle men in the *hejaz*. The latter oversee the logistics of "*hadj* specials," as well as food, lodging, and transportation at the sites of the *hejaz*. The competition among the Malian *hadj* businesses over reputation and customers is seen in advertisements broadcast on national and local media and painted on the four-wheel-drive cars in which these religious entrepreneurs, and some eminent clients, parade through Mali's urban environments.

The thriving religious entrepreneurship and its awareness of the interlocking of spiritual redemption and economic success is not new to West African Islamic traditions. As Soares's account of the "prayer economy" in the Sahelian town of Nioro suggests, this economy has long-standing roots in a moral economy of religious devotion, at least in those urban areas that have been under the strong influence of clans affiliated with a Sufi path (Soares 2005, chap. 6; see Last 1988). Under current conditions of intensified trade and intellectual exchange with certain areas of the Arabic-speaking world, and an understanding that spiritual salvation is the starting point, the path to God, and the objective of the enterprise, this draws in all sorts of religious entrepreneurs, some of whom are "entrepreneurs *tout court*" (Haenni 2002, 4). Religious entrepreneurship, then, takes on new forms.

Sermons delivered on radio and audio cassettes publicize specific viewpoints on daily concerns and religious interpretations. They also use the logic and formats of commercial entertainment to reinforce their authority. Haidara, for instance, often extends his reflections on a particular topic over several recordings that need to be heard in their entirety for the sermon to be understood. On each tape he devotes some time to a summary of his earlier tapes and outlines his future teachings. This "to-be-continued" style helps listeners follow the details of his argument and encourages them to engage with his teachings over a longer period. Still, Haidara's sermons and those of other preachers should not be viewed as mere products of market competition. Nor does the inflection of styles of sermonizing through commercial consumer culture indicate that people's religious quest has been contaminated by the effort to maximize profits. Such an interpretation reiterates a crude conflict between material interests and symbolic practices, between true religiosity and superficial acts of consumption (see Schulz 2006b). My argument here is that for their enterprise of salvation to succeed, Muslim leaders, particularly those who seek a wider audience, need to respond to aspirations beyond spiritual matters. To understand the complex conditions for, and implications of, Islam's public prominence in Mali, we need to consider the intertwining of these leaders' and their listeners' heterogeneous dispositions and concerns that cannot be reduced either to the pursuit of economic profit nor to a purely ethical quest for personal improvement.

The privatization of economic and religious enterprises encourages new forms for publicizing Islam with the adoption of various (older and new) Muslim identities, such as a cosmopolitan Muslim orientation associated with reformist trends in Saudi Arabia and Egypt, or an ethically sophisticated yet "authentically African" Muslim identity (Schulz 2007a). To a greater extent than before (Amselle 1977; Launay 1992), the current culture of religious salvation revolves around consumption as a quotidian practice that uses specific religious objects to shape religious experience and engender symbolic and material ties to a global Muslim community (*umma*). The polyvalent religious significance of these products derives from their use and physical qualities. Some of them are "religious" objects because they are associated with practices of worship and the cultivation of piety. Others are religious because their fabrication involves the inscription of sacred verses (e.g., Hames 1987; see Starrett 1995). Some religious objects, such as highly valued dress items or wall decorations, are appealing because of their Arab origins and the cosmopolitan Muslim orientation they signal. Other religious commodities, such as sermon recordings in national languages, are associated with authentically local religious practices.[12] The sermon recordings are affordable and accessible, and require neither literacy skills nor sophisticated technology. Urbanites from all walks of life consume them while traveling or in the market, at home, or even during working hours.

Many listeners relate to sermon tapes not as ordinary commodities but as objects with a special capacity to sustain sociability and transfer spiritual power and benefit (see chapter 7). At first sight, this seems to support Launay's (1997) and Hirschkind's (2001a, 2006) argument that sermon tapes are not commodities in the proper sense. Although sermon tapes in Mali are treated as objects with very special qualities, however, clearly some of their features establish them as commodities. Not only is their production and consumption informed by market logic, but a sharp break marks the relationship between the producers and consumers of sermon tapes, even if the distribution of the tapes is informed by the protocols of patronage and personal obligation. Also, the circulation of sermon tapes is mediated through money. What, then, is the exact modus operandi and significance that sermon tapes develop in their role as commodities?

The making and selling of sermon tapes is not outstandingly lucrative, but they exclude the danger of unprofitable overproduction.[13] Once a master copy exists, additional copies are made on demand.[14] Those who specialize in the production of sermon tapes are often young men without a regular income who seek to make ends meet by selling religious media products. Many shops, apart from dubbing and selling various tapes, provide the technical equipment, advice, and repair skills needed to assure a normal consumption of audio- and videotapes with no disturbances. These shops (singular, *butiki*) are found in a town's central market place and, where they exist, near local radio stations. In towns' environs, sermon tapes increasingly form part of the regular merchandise offered in the small village stores specializing in the retail sale of kitchen supplies and cooking ingredients. Producers of sermon tapes usually maintain seller-client relations with the preachers whose sermons they sell. They often hold the master copy for a particular sermon because they have privileged access to the preacher's teachings sessions. The economic undertakings of these producers of sermon tapes are inspired by a conviction that promoting their guide's moral call will afford them considerable spiritual merit (*baraji*). Their attitude resonates with a broadly shared view of sermon-tape production as an activity that combines one's spiritual quest with an ethically acceptable form of enterprise. This serves as an interesting contrast to the position sermon tapes occupy in the moral economy of Islamic homiletics in Cairo, where, according to Charles Hirschkind (2001a), sermon tapes are expressly located outside the structures of commercial exchange, and preachers exhort listeners to make their sermons available to other Muslims for the sake of *da'wa* alone. In Mali, producing *wajuli caseti* is considered a perfectly acceptable response to shrinking economic resources.

Certainly no agreement among Muslims exists about the ethical value of sermon tapes and their commercial use. Several Muslim leaders, all representing established lineages of religious specialists, look at commercial sermon tapes, especially those by Sharif Haidara, with a critical eye and deplore that the entertaining effects of a preacher's "forceful speech" will displace the edifying uses of these tapes. Their criticism points to a crucial transformation in the social use of sermon tapes. It also reflects these leaders' heightened concern with the ways that certain media technologies undermine traditional religious authority by opening the field of religious debate to participants who lack scholarly erudition. Their criticism is countered by the various Muslim activists and preachers who rely on recordings and who, like their followers, do not feel a believer's vested interest in selling sermons invalidates his or her true devotion to proselytizing. Particularly striking in this respect is that, although supporters of Islamic moral renewal constantly share tapes among themselves informally, they also stress the strong moral obligation not to multiply sermons themselves but to leave the distribution of tapes to specialized vendors. In other words, those most strongly convinced of the educational and spiritual import of sermon tapes emphasize that these recordings should also serve the purpose of financially supporting fellow members of the movement. This means, then, that these acolytes not only acknowledge the commercial character of sermon tapes but highlight it as a morally acceptable, even desirable quality of these products. As commodities the sermon tapes allow their owners to provide moral and financial support. Their circulation through the structures of commerce is both a motivating force for their consumption and an end in itself. The selling, buying, and consuming of religious recordings are material evidence of a believer's genuine search for closeness to God. Sermon tapes constitute a specific type of commodity in present-day Mali inasmuch as they are part of a system of exchange dictated by the logic of commodification. This system links the "economic and technological conditions of production with the social and cultural conditions that help create and maintain the need for such production" (Morgan 1999, 17). But what are the particular social and cultural conditions that inform the consumption and demand of sermon tapes in Mali?

To most supporters of the Islamic moral reform movement, listening to their leaders' and teachers' recorded sermons is intricately related to the collective endeavor of moral reform. This close connection is felt as much in the social organization of consumption as in the kinds of experience that audio recordings generate. Although sermon tapes are always individually purchased and owned, their circulation and consumption is genuinely social. For instance, the shops where Sharif Haidara's audio- and videotaped sermons are reproduced, sold, and listened to constitute more than a business. They are informal meeting places where important insider information is passed on and their leader's most recent public presentations are debated. They are a nexus for the commercial and social networks in which followers participate and where they jointly generate the meanings of personal moral transformation and religious experience.

Supporters of Islamic moral renewal assert that their regular, joint consumption of sermon recordings allows them to grasp "that we are all united as true supporters of religion." Moral community, then, emerges not only through empathy and moral identification with a religious leader but also through the physical and sensory experiences related to the circulation and consumption of media products (Schulz 2008b). Cassette sermons pull together the community of believers to which they appeal. Their relevance transcends conventional understandings of their exchange value, which shows that once specific technologies of mediation are embedded in structures of commercialization, they do not simply broadcast a moral message to a wide audience, but they transform conventional forms of religious sociality. And, as we shall see in the next chapter, they also give rise to new kinds of religious engagement and spiritual experience. These new forms of religious experience and community are made possible through the particular quality of the medium that mediates and translates religious discourse.

Mass Mediation and the
Reconfiguration of Religious Debate

An expanding entertainment culture in Mali favors religious experience that enhances religious leaders' media appeal and community constructions. Scholarly explorations of the religious experience facilitated by various media technologies thus need to consider the structures of commercial entertainment culture within which religious discourse is embedded. In the tension-ridden interface of state media and proliferating media products, a social arena emerges in which supporters of various ethical viewpoints compete for a following and in which a preacher's style of delivery and argumentation is crucial. This development is reinforced by the spread of new media technologies that allow for specific forms of delivery and mass-mediated religious debate. This raises the question of how particular media technologies, in their capacity to mediate religious discourse, affect spiritual experience and the conditions for the establishment of religious authority. In what ways does this process of mediation transform the contents of the debate?

Different media technologies shape the nature of religious debate by infusing it with distinctive shades of publicness and by creating particular types of audience. Audio recordings and broadcasts, for instance, enable a specific listening experience that is at once public and intimate in nature and that allows preachers to create a sense of moral community with important political ramifications. This is illustrated by Haidara's invocations of moral community. His sermons often refer to the mass-mediated setting and intertextual character of his teachings. The format of his sermons echoes the "to-be-continued" pattern of television series, as previously noted; it often carries over to the next tape a topic addressed in a preceding sermon. Here is an excerpt from one of Haidara's most popular sermons in 1999 and 2000, in which he responds to questions received from his followers. This sermon from Bamako resumes a discussion initiated three weeks earlier, during Haidara's visit to Bouaké, Ivory Coast.

> I want to return to the topic of my last address to you: to the life of the Prophet. God addressed himself to the Prophet, and the Prophet addressed himself to us, of this I will talk in due course. . . . I received a letter from a man who said that . . . some of his relatives changed their behavior thanks to what I said; they abandoned their former misconduct. . . . When you believe in God, you should always continue with this belief, and if you insist in this way, believing in God and in God alone, nothing will defeat you. Someone asked me a very special question, so let me first address this question. A woman asked me about a cassette she had listened to the night before, a cassette in which I say that a woman should not quarrel with her husband. But then the tape ended and she wanted to know what other behavior I recommended. . . . Her question is very important. Today, we witness many scenes in which a woman kicks out her own husband and says "well, if it's not Jean, it will be Paul." Make sure you record well what I say, afterwards we will pass this tape on to our dear sister. The Prophet has told us what rights the man has over his wife.[15]

Haidara relies on the fact that his sermons are consumed by his followers across and beyond national borders, and thus this audio-recording technology allows him to speak to the same audience from different locales. By appealing to listeners' moral consensus, he evokes feelings of commonality. His "community of true believers" shares features with the audience of conventional Islamic sermonizing insofar as people's feelings of belonging continue to crystallize in a sense of shared moral standards. Yet Haidara's employment of audio recordings also changes the process through which a moral public is constituted. Sermon recordings allow his "moral advice" to move beyond the spatially restricted setting of sermon delivery and draw listeners from different locales into a shared realm of experience. In the process of listening to Haidara's taped speech, a new sense of community emerges that is created not by a shared locality but through the circulation of tapes.

The use of audio-recording technology allows preachers to generate a particular religious experience, as illustrated in listeners' spontaneous comments. Listeners liken the swiftness and immediacy of the spoken word to their sense of intimacy and close belonging that they experience during collective prayer. Listening to sermon tapes allows them to transpose this spiritual experience to where they live and work, and helps them in their efforts to accomplish religiously significant acts (*ibadat*) outside the ritual domain. Followers of Haidara assert that audio tapes and radio broadcasts are conducive to transmitting their leader's charismatic gifts, because these media help focus attention on the voice, which, according to local understandings, constitutes the primary medium to convey a person's extraordinary gifts (see chapter 7). Aural media technologies, by privileging sound perception, create communities of joint spiritual experience that draw on, and coexist with, conventional understandings of religious practice rather than supplanting them.

Haidara's media appearances hint at a cross-fertilization of conventional sermonizing and speech genres popularized on local radio stations since the early 1990s.[16] This process forms part of a long-standing development of partly mass-mediated, partly "live" modes of entertainment and cultural production (Schulz 2001a, chap. 6).[17] Haidara skillfully combines conventional speech conventions, such as circumlocution and framing the sermon as a dialogue (see Schulz 2001a, chap. 4), with a talk-radio format.[18] He responds to preferences for illustrative examples by interspersing numerous human-interest stories that invite empathy and identification. A further commonality between Haidara's sermons and conventional oral genres resides in his imaginative employment of paralinguistic strategies. His onomatopoeic expressions and his modeling of the tone, pitch, and melody of his voice place him on an equal footing with Mali's famous contemporary oral performers.[19]

Haidara's appearances on local radio resemble those of pop stars regularly featured on Malian national radio. Speakers introduce Haidara as "today's studio guest," mention his recent travels and successes, and ask him questions raised by listeners. The inspiration of the stylistics of broadcast entertainment is also evident in Haidara's stress on a consumer-oriented selection of topics and on the "participatory" character of his teaching sessions. The stylistic convergence of broadcast genres and conventional Islamic homiletics are part of a broader process by which diverse speech genres, whether aimed primarily at entertaining or at edifying listeners, come to occupy the same position in the field of symbolic forms that structure consumers' everyday experience (see Öncü 2006). Hence, there is no simple, unidirectional dissemination of successful preaching styles from broadcast lectures to live sermonizing. Most sermons incorporate various influences and styles of presentation.

Throughout southern Mali, preachers use their incipient careers as broadcast orators to extend their fame to rural areas and develop a preaching style adapted to nonmediated performance settings. The result is an emergent, mass-mediated culture of religious moralizing that transcends territorial boundaries and lies at the interface of various technologies and presentational styles. This is not to argue that new media technologies are a necessary precondition for the proliferation of new preaching styles. Sermons are a long-standing feature of moral education in Muslim societies in Africa, and changes in styles of sermonizing have been only partly related to technological innovation (see Hodgkin 1998, 208). Still, however, the recent adoption of new media technologies has facilitated the proliferation of new preaching formats and enhanced the success of those freelance preachers who combine live performances with those broadcast via local radio and audio recordings. This is exemplified by the preacher Sissoko, the head of the Ansar Dine branch in San. Starting his preaching career in the early 1990s, his reputation as a skillful orator soon spread to the countryside. Villagers, mostly men, flocked to his Thursday night sermons at the Grande Mosque. The sermons I attended between 1998 and 2000 reminded me of the performances given by itinerant musicians and magicians. The square in front of the mosque was crowded with people; men and women sitting in tightly arranged groups on mats and in chairs. Crowds of youth and children who had not found a place were sitting on the courtyard walls surrounding the square. Audience members observed in a matter-of-fact fashion that "those of us who do not own a television set look for something else to entertain us at night." Sissoko gradually developed a patronage relationship with one local radio station, where he now directs its Islamic programming.[20] His broadcast sermons gained him such acclaim that Sissoko is frequently invited to the surrounding villages. Dressed in jeans, undershirt, sunglasses, and a baseball cap sporting the Ansar Dine logo, Sissoko embarks on these excursions on a borrowed motor bike, together with a fellow Ansar Dine member seated behind him and carrying the loudspeaker (a donation from Haidara) on his lap.

In Sissoko's sermons, broadcast and live performances feed on each other, both in form and content. In radio sermons, he frequently resumes a topic addressed during his latest trip to the countryside. The format and topics of his sermons are akin to the ones delivered by other clerics during Friday congregational worship, but his prolific storytelling makes his sermon resemble radio entertainment with its many references to tales and fables.[21] That preachers and traditional storytellers draw on a shared expressive repertoire was brought home to me in a conversation with Sissoko's wife. When I complimented her husband's rhetorical skills, she was surprised. "Why," she finally asked, "should this be something so special? It's not difficult, you know. You just think of one story after the other so that people understand your lesson." Clearly Muslim preachers are evaluated according to the same criteria as specialists of oral performance.

Sissoko's success illustrates that audio-recording technology and radio broadcasting further the intertwining of religious and commercial culture. That he acquired popularity through live performances *and* broadcast sermons intimates that the culture of religious moralizing is constituted not on new media alone but at the interface between various technologies and settings. The inspiration that preachers like Sissoko and Haidara draw from the stylistics of broadcast entertainment and its attendant ideology of choice suggests that a commercial, mass-mediated setting does not deprive Muslim sermonizing of its ethical import. As moral edification and commercial entertainment culture intertwine, it is misleading, as pointed out repeatedly in these pages, to distill a pure religious message untainted by the logic of commerce.

A New Relevance of Islam?

In his sermons and radio interviews, Haidara repeatedly stresses the consistent and "all-encompassing nature of Islam." He claims to give "clear," "concise," and satisfactory answers in response to listeners' requests and on the basis of "what God and the prophet told us to do." Islam becomes the central formula that "regulates all domains of life, from the least detail to the largest concern."[22] Haidara's emphasis on the systematic nature of Islam seems to support the argument that mass media, along with mass education, generate a view of Islam as a systematic body of rules (e.g., Eickelman and Anderson 1999). These changes, however, do not indicate a clear-cut shift toward more rational and systematic understandings of Islam that have been supported by the adoption of new media technologies. Closer scrutiny of Haidara's sermons reveals that what has been characterized as a process of "objectification" of Islam (Eickelman 1992) does not entail an unequivocal shift toward a rational, argumentative paradigm of Islamic debate. Haidara establishes his interpretational authority to a major degree by drawing on conventional credentials rather than on rational argument (Schulz 2003a, 2006a). His citations from the Qur'an, for instance, rarely substantiate his argument. His stress on the rational character of his teachings should therefore not be taken at face value but rather as an illustration of the broader debate forming the backdrop to his interventions. This setting is one of multiple normative positions in which references to one's readiness to engage in rational argument play a role in winning support.

Although leaders stress the systematic character of Islam, their "rules of Islam" (*silameya sariaw*) are only vaguely related to the foundational texts of Islam. Most rules reflect how teachers respond to their acolytes' preoccupations and sensibilities. In 2000, for instance, a Muslim women's learning group in Bamako decided to change their regular learning module on the occasion of the upcoming fasting month (*zungalo*). They asked their teacher to advise them on "women's proper conduct during the month of Ramadan." The teacher consented; but after he elaborated on women's ritual requirements during the month of Ramadan, a delegation of women succeeded in persuading him to adjust his teachings. The instructions the women finally accepted were rules of social conduct not exclusively related to the fasting period.[23]

Similar negotiations are effected by other protagonists of Islamic moral renewal, such as those by the preacher Sissoko in San. Sissoko declined the radio director's offer to extend his speaking time on Thursday night to two hours, but he agreed to work a "question-and-answer" format into his program. As he explained to me, the "rules of Islam" that he chooses to discuss in sermons are inspired by conversations with farmers who invited him to preach. Because Sissoko's explicit objective is to adjust his teachings to life in the countryside, he usually complies with listeners' preferences. Although individual believers turn to Sissoko and other preachers in a genuine quest for spiritual guidance, the preachers' moral lessons are framed in ways that resemble the format of talk-radio programs. In both cases, the public arena is a site of competition for listeners' approval.

Whether or not we subscribe to the view of a trend toward the "objectification" of Islam, the enormous appeal of media preachers points to a neglected dimension in recent accounts of Islam's relevance to public life. It would be difficult to understand the current diversification of Islamic positions, and the new conditions on which religious authority operates, without considering the commercial consumer culture in which these developments are embedded. In the process of recording and selling live preaching events, an Islamic moral code is objectified or, in Lukacs's terms, "thingified" (*verdinglicht*): it is turned into a good that may be purchased and consumed. But believers tend to downplay this commercial dimension inherent in many acts of appropriating "the rules of Islam." This development and its intrinsic tensions are not limited to religious media products but characterize people's assessment of most products of commercial culture (Schulz 2001b).

Performing Authority, Creating Community

One way to evaluate the claims and appeal of media figures such as Sharif Haidara is to look more closely at their constructions of religious authority and moral community. This can be done by examining how Haidara defines his position as a true believer not only with respect to state politics but also in relation to competing Muslim leaders in a national arena. Chapter 1 illustrated the tension between the tendency among leaders of the Islamic moral reform movement to contrast their Islamic vision of ethical politics to a secularist one and their divergent understandings of the relevance of individual ethics to public order. The viewpoints articulated by Mali's Muslim activists in public debates on the normative foundations of the political community are characterized by their diversity, particularly regarding their grounding in Islamic doctrines and foundational texts. Representatives of the AMUPI call for an Islamic moral renewal while also supporting the government's secularist project. Recurrent in their public statements is an emphasis on the importance of uniting "all Malians as Muslims" and to suppress ritual and doctrinal differences. Still, their practices are exclusionary, such as when they publicly denounce certain religious leaders or restrict access to the national broadcast station to Muslims who support the AMUPI. Moreover, most clerics who seek representation through the AMUPI subscribe to highly exclusionary hierarchical principles of religious organization, because these allow devotees to approach their leaders only when the former dispense substantial monetary and other donations (Villalon 1995, chaps. 4, 5; Soares 2005, chap.6).

Intégristes posit a distinct Islamic political and moral order, and yet their invocation of this pristine order contrasts with the pragmatics of their political activities, that is, their engagement with party and partisan politics. Their claims to represent *ijma,* the consensus of the community of learned Muslims, conflicts with the exclusivist rhetoric with which they castigate "fake" Muslims for betraying the "authentic" teachings of Islam. They, too, tap into a "Muslim discourse of ignorance and truth" (Brenner 2001, chaps. 4, 8) and add to the highly contested public construction of a community of "proper believers."

Haidara formulates a similarly particularistic identity of a proper believer, claiming that the only true Muslims are those who support his view of personal ethics and ethical politics. Yet he is more successful than his Muslim opponents at constructing a community, partly because he integrates his effort into a forceful, mass-mediated performance of moral sharing and belonging. He frequently claims that the aim of his "scientific and sound" religious teachings is to enable his listeners to interpret and reason independently. He bolsters this claim, as well as his explanations of "the rules of Islam," by reciting passages in Arabic and paraphrasing them in Bamana. Rare are the followers who can understand the particular *sura* that he cites. Moreover, the logical connection between the cited *sura*s and his argument is often tenuous, such as when Haidara, asked to explain a woman's duties toward her husband, substantiates his explanation by reciting the *shahada* (statement of faith).[24] His followers, however, do not find this discrepancy between his claim to scientific proof and his actual practice noteworthy. To them, his authority is proven by his ability to "quote" in Arabic. As one of my neighbors in San, a young unmarried man, put it, "all he says is well founded, he always proves his argument by pointing to the exact passage of the Qur'an from which it was taken." Whether or not they understood the recited passage was not important. What mattered was that, by displaying his Arabic skill, Haidara authenticated his textual interpretation and reconfirmed his listeners' faith in his interpretive authority.

Clearly a complex process of authentication is at work here (see Stolow 2006, 76–77). By claiming to translate the Qur'an into Bamana, Haidara challenges traditional Islam in two respects. He asserts his own interpretive authority, establishing himself as a powerful competitor in the Muslim discursive arena, and he undermines the monopoly of religious specialists by claiming that everyone should have access to religious interpretation. By declaring his linguistic competencies to a constituency unable to verify his textual interpretation, he subtly enhances his authority.

Haidara's use of Arabic quotes and his concurrent emphasis on scientific argumentation is both in line and discontinuous with local uses of Arabic literacy as a source of interpretive authority. The exercise of authority through the mastery of Arabic has a long history in local Islamic traditions. In this sense Haidara's quotes perpetuate conventional modes of authenticating specific readings of the foundational texts of Islam. Yet his claim to transparent and verifiable argumentation hints at a recent restructuring of religious knowledge and its use as a source of authority. The process can be described as a trend toward the incorporation of rhetorical and symbolic registers of Western knowledge production, in this case of a rational, argumentative, discursive paradigm that allows religious leaders to reinforce interpretive authority in a competitive public arena. This trend, in turn, influences the kind of appreciation generated by a speaker's mastery of Arabic. Haidara's efforts to present a scientifically sound interpretation endows Arabic literacy with a new significance. Being able to recite in Arabic proves one's erudition, whereas its former function of conveying the immediate substance of God's Word plays a smaller role. The focus of listeners' evaluation shifts away from seeing the speaker as a mere mouthpiece of God's Word toward consideration of the speaker and his individual interpretation (also see Hirschkind 2001b).

Contrary to Haidara's claim to convince his listeners through logical argument, his sermons often lack internal consistency and references to the foundational texts of Islam. They reflect conventional, not necessarily Islamic, behavioral norms, such as the "rules of conduct" he expects from an exemplary woman and that derive from commonsensical understandings of proper relations between the sexes. On other occasions—for instance, when asked to specify his position in relation to the Tijouiyya and Qadiriyya orders, Haidara refrains from engaging in an argument about doctrinal and ritual difference. Instead, he personalizes his account by focusing on individual leaders and the incongruence between their claims and actual immoral conduct. Clearly Haidara positions himself in the landscape of competing Muslim positions by asserting ethical, not doctrinal, difference. This strategy has two advantages. First, it establishes authority on the basis of moral excellence rather than erudition. Second, because allegations of other Muslims' hypocrisy are vague and easily understood by followers who lack a thorough knowledge of Islam, these claims are difficult to refute and also assure listeners that they themselves are able to ascertain the difference between "true Muslims" and "those who pretend." It is precisely the commonsensical character of Haidara's prescriptions that contributes to their appeal. In a social situation that many urbanites perceive as a conflict between conventional norms, one ruling social interaction and the other governing the messier reality of actual struggles and renegotiations of these behavioral codes, Haidara's focus on proper conduct offers his listeners simple solutions to complex dilemmas.

Haidara's refusal to articulate clear doctrinal positions is intrinsic to his construction of a Muslim community (Schulz 2006a). His definitions of a good Muslim, of proper behavior, and of the ethical foundations of the Muslim community are not based on Islamic concepts of ethics. Instead, the blueprint for Islamic moral renewal to which Haidara appeals is defined negatively: virtue is characterized by its moral opposites: adultery, theft, and hypocrisy. His moral community includes those who respect traditional values, true Muslims and non-Muslims alike. The real threat to this community does not come from Christians and other nonbelievers but from "hypocritical" Muslims. The persuasiveness of Haidara's invocation of moral community derives from a vaguely defined notion of proper conduct that serves as a criterion for community membership and from its emotionally powerful moralizing style. Under the guise of explanation, the appeal to shared values replaces argumentation. Different religious positions and practices are presented as a matter of personal ethics and are evaluated accordingly, and Haidara repeatedly emphasizes that listeners have the moral obligation and freedom to choose the right path toward personal improvement. By stressing the importance of ethical conduct, he echoes a view articulated by a wide range of supporters of Islamic moral renewal. And by distinguishing between different kinds of Muslims according to the practices they engage in, Haidara not only adopts a common Muslim argumentative framework but follows a long-standing West African tradition of defining true Muslims in a sort of concentric movement, proceeding from relations among Muslims in the center to the periphery where rightful believers define themselves as distinct from non-Muslims (e.g. Last 1974, 1992; Brenner 1993a). Haidara's privileging of right deeds is the basis of his appeal to a heterogeneous constituency. As personal virtue becomes the decisive criterion for group membership, everyone feels included, regardless of his or her religious orientation and level of instruction. Also, because ethical conduct is open to public scrutiny, everyone risks failing the test and being declared as one who just acts. Ethical conduct, framed according to perceived Islamic norms, becomes an all-encompassing source of identity that appeals to a broad urban constituency.

Haidara is not the only preacher who defines proper Muslimhood based on a relational mode of identity construction (see Amselle 1990) that lacks a specifically Islamic normativity. During the law reform debate analyzed in chapter 1, Muslims of different persuasions claimed allegiance to an Islamic ethics. But the positions they articulated, for instance, on women's rights, tended to reflect conventional, often non-Islamic, conceptions of gender relations. Only some disagreements among these Muslims were related to interpretations of the written sources of Islam. Despite the evident parallels in how various leaders of Islamic moral reform articulate their claims to authority, Haidara differs in several respects from competing Muslim leaders, especially those who preach through the media. Whereas Haidara constructs the figure of the true believer primarily in contradistinction to the inner enemy of "hypocritical" clerics, other Muslim leaders usually refrain from such direct attacks. Because Haidara is preoccupied with the enemy within, that is, with "Muslims who only pretend," he rarely refers to a transnational *umma* of believers or to the West as an enemy. Herein resides another substantial difference in the positions formulated by, for instance, the *Intégristes* and the AMUPI leaders. A final and marked distinction resides in Haidara's explicit denunciation of the abuses of power and the politico-religious patronage of established families of religious specialists, as well as his elusive references to those he criticizes. This strategy of open criticism without naming individuals increases his popularity among followers who hail this evasiveness as a sign of prudence. By voicing his moral outrage at wealthy religious lineages, Haidara effectively portrays himself as united with his followers by the common experience of destitution. That he owns three cars and several houses does not weaken this self-portrayal in the eyes of his supporters and shows how successful he is in evoking a moral "we" as opposed to "those above."

Mass-mediated Religion and the New Articulators of Islam

People's changing views of religiosity, and the recent normative and institutional reconfigurations of public debate in Mali, need to be understood in light of changes in the relationship between the state, media, and the market. In other words, current debates over the common good and the significance of religion in personal life and public order are shaped not only by the ways in which the rationalities and institutions of modern state power reconfigure the "civilizing traditions of Islam" (Salvatore 1998). They are also constituted through commercialization and processes of mass mediation. In this process, the conditions, forms, and content of intra-Muslim debate are changing without losing their connection to local discursive traditions and notions of piety.

This development represents a process that is animating politics and personal life in much of the contemporary Muslim world and beyond (e.g., Öncü 2006; Stolow 2006); media technologies, in their intermingling with commodity exchange and consumption, play a decisive role in this process in reorganizing the discursive and semantic conditions of possibility for religious experience, argument, and authority. The complex process of authentication and authorization in which media preachers such as Sharif Haidara engage suggests that the new circumstances do not displace conventional foundations of religious authority. Instead, the new economic and technological terms of mediating religion reconfigure the material and moral conditions for creating and circulating authoritative interpretation, partly by extending the message to new interpretive publics. Media products that circulate without central control allow preachers with no particular erudition to reach a wider constituency. These preachers represent a new category of Muslim actors who base their claim to moral leadership on a combination of new and old credentials. Even if the foundations of their teachings are not sound, listeners welcome them for urging a return to authentic interpretations of Islam.

Haidara's attacks on "hypocritical" Muslims, those he excludes from the community of true believers, reveal what is at stake for those who participate in contemporary Islamic moral reform. Leaders of Islamic renewal need to attract followers and find a place in a competitive discursive field shaped, but not fully constituted, by new media. In this field, Islamic claims and morality must be presented in a compelling fashion and shown to have relevance to everyday life in order to attract followers. This substantiates my claim that, *pace* Habermas, Muslim identity does not exist prior to public debate but derives from public interaction. The results of these transformations are deeply paradoxical. As Haidara's breathtaking rise to fame illustrates, the close link between religion and commerce, between spiritual salvation and mass-mediated everyday experience, grants public prominence to actors who often lack authoritative credentials yet seek to articulate Islam as a norm of public conduct and individual civility (Salvatore 1999). In this sense, Haidara bears witness to the instrumental role of media technologies in facilitating particular modes of authority, assertiveness, and appeal. He personifies the capacity of commercial media to respond to and resonate with the aesthetic and moral sensibilities of consumers at various levels of sensual and cognitive experience. The implications of the mediation of religion via new technologies do not so much reside in the dilution of religion but rather in the transformation of its appeal, contents, and styles, and of consumers' devotional attitude (see Meyer 2004). At the same time, paradoxically, that mass-mediated argument, commercialization, and consumption are so entangled undermines these debating Muslims' claim to *ijma,* scholarly consensus, and their capacity to provide a unitary norm of public interaction and a unitary definition of collective interest. It seriously limits their chances of mounting a coherent challenge to the civilizing and nationalist project of political elites and chips away at their own exercise of moral authority.

This particular process of objectifying Islam by way of its commercialization has important implications for its community-building potential. As Islam is being integrated as a moral idiom into mainstream, mass-mediated, and commercial culture, it becomes a privileged reference point within competing community constructions. Whoever manages to mobilize the symbolic repertoire of Islam in a broadly understandable way commands an influence that politicians need to take into account and steer through carefully. At the same time, Islam's potential to appear as a viable alternative to the existing political and normative order is partly neutralized. To be sure, current religious ideals and readings can by no means be reduced to these new conditions for religious practice. Still, Haidara's popularity hints at a clear development of a novel form of asserting religious authority. Thanks to a commercialized mass-media culture, new types of religious leaders tap into a trend toward the neoliberal ideology of choice by presenting different religious practices as a matter of personal conviction. They are influenced by the tendency, characteristic of today's global capital, to frame religious conviction around cultural values and individual consumer choices (see Comaroff and Comaroff 2002). At the risk of overstatement, I suggest that many believers come to understand themselves as "consuming believers," as believers who choose a religious viewpoint and opt for particular forms of expressing, enacting, and professing it against contending positions.

SEVEN

Consuming Baraka, Debating Virtue: New Forms of Mass-mediated Religiosity

CONSIDER THE FOLLOWING three anecdotes, each conveying a distinct version of the social use of audio-recording technology in urban Mali. The three episodes, which show the close relationship between Muslims' religious practices and their consumption of media products, illustrate that there is no uniform way in which supporters of the Islamic moral reform movement in Mali use media technology or conceive of its social effects.

The first of these concerns a visit, in 1998, to my longtime friend Sekou, an outspoken defender of Islamic renewal in Segou. I found him in lively debate with two friends over a preacher who had lately started to preach on local radio, to the acclaim of many. The radio preacher, a member of a prestigious local religious clan, had recently embraced key tenets of the renewal movement. That decision had earned him the wrath of key representatives of the religious establishment—among them members of his own family—but it was not a matter of concern to Sekou and his friends. Their excitement was prompted by their anticipation of the considerable gains for the "cause of Islam" that could be derived from this media-skilled preacher's conversion to "proper Islam."

The second anecdote is about Aisee, a member of a Muslim women's group in Bamako. I asked her, in April 1999, whether she was in the possession of a year-old tape of her leader lecturing on "a Muslim woman's family duties." Not able to recall whether she owned the tape, she told her teenage daughter to fetch "all of Hadja's teachings." The daughter complied and swiftly disappeared into the family's single-room house. She emerged shortly after, carrying two plastic sacks with a potpourri of recordings, carelessly stacked in broken cases without appropriate labels. Aisee noticed my surprise at this slap-dash assortment of tapes and observed, "after all, these tapes [are] mere things, simple tools to make one's viewpoint heard by a larger audience, particularly by those who depict us [Muslim women] as conservative and backward." Then she added, in an attempt to secure my support in these matters, "Next time you go and talk to our critics, Nanaje, you should challenge them, ask whether our use of the newest technologies does not prove that we are progressive [*kodonna;* literally, "open-minded]." Whereas Aisee emphasized the purely instrumental nature of audio-recording technology, some of her fellow group members thought differently. One Friday afternoon we were listening to a "Hadja tape" and enjoying the leisure time made possible by Aisee's husband's postponed return from the Friday prayer at the *Grande Mosquee* of Bamako. Hadja had just started to enlighten us about a woman's proper performance of her ritual obligations, when one "Muslim woman," an older woman and Aisee's longtime friend, remarked on Hadja's "sober" and "sensible" character which, she felt, was made crystal-clear on the audio tapes. With a sidelong glance at me, she added, "We have followed Hadja for a long time, so we know her very well. Since the day she founded our group [in the late 1980s], week after week she has taught us the rules of Islam [*silameya sariyaw*]. But only when she started recording her teachings did her capacities fully take shape. Cassettes bring out Hadja's calling to convince others of the truth of Islam." This comment ascribes to audio-recording technology an effect that extends beyond the mere process of broadcasting: It pinpoints the technology's capacity to highlight a speaker's particular and personal qualities.

The third story concerns an occasion in October 1998, a few months after I had met the Ansar Dine women in San, when I visited Maam, a respected member of the association, and we talked about her leader's great popularity. To prove to me the great attraction Haidara held "even among people who have never seen him," Maam suggested that I listen to a sermon recorded during his recent visit to Bouaké. I happily consented and was impressed by the care with which Maam stored her leader's recordings, seemingly as a material token of her attachment to him. The tape was kept in a small metal box ornamented with stickers featuring Haidara, his wives, and his mother, and with colorful ribbons to which a rosary was attached. The box was stored in a corner of her living room that she had transformed into a sanctified space through elaborate decorations. As the tape played, Maam, listening reverently to Haidara's speech, suddenly asked me, "Can you sense it? Can you see how well his speech fits the tape?" I must have looked confused, because Maam insisted, "Don't you hear it? There is something in his voice that makes what he says compelling. It is *baraka* that gives him this power. Some people say they know nothing more impressive than being in the presence of Haidara's speech, and they travel wherever he goes. But I do not agree. Listening to his tapes will do. However forceful his speech is, it touches you with greater force when put on tape."

The first of the three episodes dramatized the hopes and aspirations that supporters of Islamic renewal attach to the broader accessibility of mass-media technologies. In contrast to other West African settings, where the suitability of new media technologies became an issue among Muslims and political authorities (e.g., Larkin 2008), Muslim activists in Mali do not consider the moral acceptability of this technology to be a controversial issue. The second anecdote hints at the dual significance of audio-recording technology: it is considered as playing a purely instrumental role, as a "tool" whose physical properties do not matter and therefore do not deserve special care; at the same time it is viewed as a technology that carries an ideology of enlightenment and progress. The third anecdote establishes an opposite view of audio-recording technology; for Maam, it brings out a speaker's hidden qualities, and thus its value extends beyond its mere capacity to disseminate media content. Haidara's recordings are seen as symbolizing the power of audio-broadcasting technology to bring out a teacher's special gifts, such as the charismatic quality of his voice. Taken together, these examples raise questions about the social implications of the technological mediation of religious experience. They intimate that some media-related activities assume the character of religious acts, thereby interlocking and remodeling existing conditions of religious subject formation. New media, in their function as technologies of translating the presence of the sacred into people's everyday reality, affect the modalities and understandings of spiritual experience.

In communications and political science research on "media and religion," questions as to the enchanting qualities of media technology are occasionally raised but are often treated in a schematic fashion in which a "disenchanted" world is re-enchanted or "re-sacralized" by broadcast media (e.g., Martin-Barbéro 1997; Murdock 1997). Underlying this narrative of Western modernity is the assumption that modern communication technologies have been instrumental in dislocating religious values, institutions, and authority. Much of this literature not only lacks detailed empirical investigation into the uses of a particular broadcast technology in culturally specific social settings, but it also appears to draw on a rather crude view of historical processes of secularization largely dispelled over the past decades (Casanova 1994, chap. 1). To be sure, recent scholarship calls into question the tendency to associate the expansion of communication technologies with processes of disenchantment. Schmidt (2000), in his study of the emergence of a post-Enlightenment religious sensibility in Western Europe, shows that scientific developments of new hearing technologies played an ambivalent role by denying while also reasserting the sacred dimension of technological mediation. Anthropologically informed studies draw attention to the genuine affinity between religion (as a form of translating the supernatural into everyday experience) and various techniques and technologies that make this translation possible and also shape what is translated and conveyed (Babb 1995; Plate 2003; Stolow 2005; Meyer and Moors 2006; see van der Veer 1995).

Other authors insist that to account for the repercussions of individual mediation technologies we should pay attention to the material and social forms through which particular media affect consumers. They explore the ideologies that individual media technologies convey and that extend their social significance beyond an exclusively technical capacity of disseminating media content (e.g., Mrazek 1997; see Ginsburg, Abu-Lughod, and Larkin 2002). Spitulnik (2000) and Larkin (2008, chaps. 1, 2), for instance, posit a close association of media technologies introduced under colonial rule with the modernist ideology of progress and a new form of cosmopolitanism. The three episodes discussed here similarly hint at an association of audio technology with an ideology of progress and enlightenment in Mali. Yet they reveal more than an affinity with Western modernity; they also point at culturally specific views of the special qualities of audio-recording technology. These views of the social effects of new broadcast technologies in contemporary Mali deserve closer scrutiny if we are to understand how they frame and inform practices and conceptions of religiosity.

Following recent critiques of Western narratives of modernity and modernization, a study of the complex intertwining of religion and media allows us to further critique the assumption that the progressive "disenchantment" of the lifeworld is reversed by a re-enchantment via media technologies.[1] The notion of re-enchantment belies the complex ways in which supporters of Islamic moral renewal in Mali engage with media products. Their mobilization of the special powers of media technologies suggests that disenchantment never fully unfolded.

Samuel Weber (2001) has suggested that religion, as an embodied practice, entails a process of mediating or translating a reality not immediately accessible to our senses (also see Stolow 2005; Meyer 2006). The question is how these forms of mediated spiritual experience, and the discourses authenticating them, are affected by the use of new technologies. Also, if, as discussed in chapter 6, mass-mediated religious discourse becomes more central to believers' constructions of themselves as true believers, one might ask these questions: How do media technologies impinge individual believers' perceptions of the spiritual, such as during their interaction with religious leaders? And what experiences of spiritual presence and of religious authority do particular media technologies facilitate, and in what embodied and sensory perceptions are these experiences grounded? To engage these questions in the Malian context, a focus on aural perception and technologies seems apposite, as audio recordings are among the most widely consumed religious media products in Mali.

Hirschkind (2006) offers a thoughtful account of sermon-tape listening practices among young men in Cairo who support Islamic revival. In exploring how listeners' engagements with mass-mediated sermons interlock with, and partly depart from, classical Islamic authoritative constructions of the link between listening and Muslim ethical conduct, Hirschkind argues strongly that these media engagements are a technique of ethical self-fashioning centered on the simultaneous remaking of mind, emotions, and body. His portrayal of the "sensible" nature of listening as a prerequisite to instill and hone dispositions for ethically correct behavior resonates strikingly with the responses and self-understandings of supporters of moral renewal in urban Mali. Significant differences exist, however, between the practices Hirschkind analyzes and the media engagements in Mali. The differences, which result partly from the different trajectories through which Islamic traditions have evolved in Egypt and in Mali's urban areas, reveal that authoritative Islamic texts have been anchored to varying degrees in the practices of common, non-erudite Malian Muslims. Other distinctions result from, as I insist, the need to pay attention to gender-specific media engagements rather than focusing on either men or women. My investigation thus reveals significant differences between media engagements of supporters of the Islamic renewal movement in Mali and cassette sermon practices in Cairo. This contrast illuminates regional differences in Islamic disciplines of ethical self-making and shows how media practices intervene in these understandings and practices.

A study of auditory perceptual processes can, potentially, critically engage authors who associate the rise of modernity with a move toward the visual as the dominant paradigm of perception, and who explore the role of media in these processes (e.g., Lowe 1982; Levin 1993). Their assumption of a sweeping shift from auditory to visual perception, with the accompanying changes in forms of cognition and patterns of social interaction, is still widely shared.[2] But some authors question the assumption that visual perception is dominant in the age of modernity and emphasize that listening, as a mode of perception, renders obsolete models of interpretation based exclusively on visual or textual appropriation. The investigation of specific cultural and social parameters shaping auditory perception in Mali follows this line of reasoning, because it insists on the persistent importance of hearing (Schmidt 2000; Drobnick 2004; Erlmann 2004).

Emphasizing the auditory as an important dimension in the mediation of spirituality does not, however, presuppose a hierarchical ordering of the senses in Malian society that would privilege hearing over vision (see McLuhan 1964; Ong 1982; Classen 1993; Howes 2004). Here I want to stress the synesthetic nature of listeners' auditory perception, a perceptiveness resembling the multi-sensorial process of viewing cinematic films (Marks 2000; Sobchack 2004). That synesthesia applies both to aural perception and visual mediation in Mali becomes apparent in the interplay between touch, hearing, and vision as it is generated by video recordings of Sharif Haidara's public appearances. For both technologies, touch plays a central role in mediating spiritual presence. The synergizing effects of the different senses, and the integral link of hearing and seeing to other senses, render futile any attempt to analyze sound, or other perceptual modality, as an autonomous realm of sensory experience.

What new forms of sociality and religious practice are generated by listeners' engagement with media? Chapter 6 demonstrated that the immersion of audio-recording technology and aural media products in a market of religious consumption contributes to the emergence of new discursive communities. These communities are articulated through a discourse on shared ethical concerns and "true Muslimhood" and have the potential to restructure Mali's public sphere from within. Largely unexplored in my discussion and in the literature on the potential of audiotapes to generate "counter-publics" (Hirschkind 2001a; Rajagopal 2001) are the social institutions and material practices that anchor these discursive communities and through which the vocation of sermon tapes, as means and emblems of mutual support, is realized. One way of grasping these material and social dimensions is to focus on the internal, gender-specific structuring of these communities and the mediating capacities inherent in the physicality of individual media products. This perspective illuminates the respective vectors along which cassette sermons (*kaseti wajuli*) circulate among female and male supporters of Islamic renewal, and contribute to new social formations or "interpretive communities" (Fish 1980; Lindlof 1988; Gaonkar and Povinelli 2003). Taking up Lee and LiPuma's (2002) insights into the intricate connection between circuits along which cultural forms circulate and the imaginaries underpinning them, we might come to understand how believers' emphasis on the edifying effect of sermon tapes relates to their particular modes of cassette circulation.

Cassette Circuits of Circulation

Sermon tapes are purchased and owned by individuals, and yet their use and circulation are associated with practices and institutions of sociability, empathy, and sharing. The link between listening to cassette sermons and the social experience is so close that, for many members, "meeting" one another has become synonymous with members listening to sermons together. Women and men sometimes listen to tapes on their own, but this tends to be discouraged as asocial. Indeed, individual listening practices bear different shades of unsociability when applied to female, as opposed to male, believers. Because women rarely own the tape recorders, they cannot take them outside the courtyard to listen to the sermons elsewhere, as many men do, and so their listening is most often confined to the courtyard. But a woman's listening will yield greater religious merit (*nafa*) if she listens to the sermons together with other women. In contrast, it is considered more acceptable for men to play a sermon tape for individual instruction during car and bus trips or in the market and in shops. Clearly the close link between sociability and sermon listening is structured by gender-specific notions of proper conduct.

Members of Muslim women's groups, as indicated earlier, use their bi-weekly gatherings or informal visits to listen to and interpret sermons together, whereas other Muslim women gather at private homes of individual group members or in a specifically designated area within the mosque's courtyard. Male listeners use sermon tapes in similar ways, for instance, to initiate debates during their learning sessions or during their daily socializing (Schulz 2002) in an individual's courtyard or in front of a particular shop in the market. During these listening sessions, which are often initiated with the explicit objective of listening to a particular preacher or a specific sermon, people interject sponta-neous remarks and expressions of enthusiastic approval. These comments mark their engagement in a dialogue with fellow listeners and the preacher, and show how the sermon registers with them at a visceral level. Recorded sermons draw speakers and listeners into a shared realm of emotional experience that is consti-tuted and mediated through words. Thus, the mass-mediated and reproducible nature of sermon tapes enhance and reproduce the forms and spirit of religious socializing in several respects. A sense of solidarity is experienced through the joint consumption of a tape. Moreover, whenever followers of a particular leader come together, their social act of listening signals a relationship of intimacy and identification that individual acolytes establish with their teacher.

That tapes constitute forms of sociability is also evident in the exchanges of tapes among supporters of moral renewal. Those who participate in the circulation, or lending, of tapes do so by drawing on an imaginary list of past and present users of particular sermon recordings.[3] The lending periods extend from two weeks to several months, and because tape circulation evolves through a chain of users, an extended temporal and social relationship of joint tape use is established. The circulation of tapes among Muslim women's groups does not foster a dyadic relationship but instead encourages a sequence of rela-tionships among group members. Women associate the passing on of sermon tapes with a sense of mutual understanding and empathy (*badenya*). "Tape relations" establish and simultaneously reflect the moral and emotional nature of group membership, which runs counter to Habermas's view that commercial, mass-mediated culture has fragmenting and degrading effects on public debate. Indeed, the expanding commercial use of sermon tapes, rather than fragmenting the public as a common body by furthering the assertion of particular identities and interpretations, actually sustains a new sense of commonality and sharing among people who come together as particular discursive communities within the public sphere.

Another factor that reinforces the capacity of cassette sermons to mediate and foster relations of sociability is their material nature; the mere fact that tapes exist as visible, palpable, and aesthetic objects enables them to reconstitute and occasionally transform believers' sociability and their imaginations of moral community (see Larkin 2008, ch. 5; also see Lefebvre 1991). The covers of the sermon audio recordings circulating among fellow believers hint at the peculiarities of their production and redistribution, and indicate what producers and users consider characteristic of individual sermons. The majority of sermon tapes have only a plain paper cover bearing the date and place where the sermon was delivered and its central topic. The covers of tapes produced at recording shops managed by followers of a specific preacher are usually decorated with an illustration, such as the preacher's picture. Some cassette sermons are so popular that people call them by special names and accord them a personality that springs as much from the preacher's persona and social standing as the sermon's topic and timeliness.[4] Here, cassette sermons are clearly treated as "impersonating" certain qualities of a preacher. Besides the personalized decorations on tape covers, they also bear traces of the tape's owners or previous users in the form of scratches and dust which hint at the tape's trajectory of circulation and therefore its biography of establishing social connectivity. Some believers are apt to decipher these physical traces of locality and comment on the reverence (or carelessness) with which the object has been treated. Indicators of community circulation are also stored in the form of remarks users scribbled on the tape covers to indicate the sections they found especially important or where a certain popular and hotly debated passage can be found. In this fashion, tapes not only indicate the moral quest of previous users but also establish common bonds reaching beyond the immediate listening event and site.

The auditory and visual imprint of a preacher's authorship, together with the traces of the tape's owner and previous users, endow the tapes with a "spirit of the gift" (Mauss 1967). They embody a sense of mutual support and connectedness, and transmit the preacher's and followers' pious disposition. These at once moral, social, and material dimensions of sermon circulation provide the institutional foundations for the "cassette communities" that, in their role as clusters of discursive exchange, come to shape and animate the broader public sphere. These moral and material investments of cassette circulation suggest a reconsideration of conventional understandings of religious experience.

The Merits of Sermon Listening

In the literature on Muslim preachers and sermonizing (e.g., Antoun 1989; Gaffney 1994; Tayob 1999), few studies examine culturally specific notions of sermon listening and how listeners receive broadcast sermons and translate them into their everyday experience. Also rare are analyses of how mass mediation affects this process of "translation" and how it may inform possibly different, gender-specific ways of relating to broadcasts. Particularly relevant here is Hirschkind's (2006) exploration of the role that Cairo's male supporters of Islamic renewal attribute to sermon listening in "opening their heart," fostering the affective disposition necessary to engage the daily challenge of acting in accordance with God's will. To them, listening does not center on cognition and rational understanding but on the full range of sensory perceptive faculties that listeners have at their disposal and that allow the divine message to fully reverberate in a believer's heart and mind. Hirschkind highlights the disciplinary endeavor implied in young men's listening practices and links it to long-standing traditions of listening to Muslim oratory as a technique of ethical self-improvement. Missing from the analysis are the material qualities of audio recording as a specific technology and their effects on sermon listening as a disciplinary practice. Against the backdrop of Hirschkind's insightful analysis, we should pursue three questions pertaining to the practice of listening to sermon tapes in Mali as part of a regionally specific tradition of Islam. The first question concerns parallels and differences between understandings of sermon-listening activities as they are formulated by supporters of Islamic renewal in urban Mali and Cairo. Because authoritative Islamic traditions have been less thoroughly anchored in the practices of the mass of believers in Mali, links to long-standing disciplinary traditions of Islam may play a comparatively limited role. Second, an analysis is required of the possibly gender-specific engagements with sermons and the perceptive processes involved in that relationship. Finally, it is important to ascertain the role that audio-recording technology plays in the eyes of supporters of Islamic renewal in mediating spiritual experience.

Three features are pervasive in the description, by believers in Mali, of the "benefits" (*nafa*) of sermon-listening practices. First, believers are urged to "scrutinize" the sermon by carefully exploring its "deep meanings" (*k'a sègèsègè k'a kòrò yèrè don*). Second, listeners do not make a formal distinction between teachings and sermons, nor do they differentiate systematically between recorded and live sermons. When asked what the differences are between the two kinds of sermons, supporters of Islamic moral renewal tended to offer a technocratic account. According to some men, the distinctive feature of cassette sermons is that they were "more useful" in that they circulated on a wider scale and had an extended use-value, as one may listen to them repeatedly. Muslim women, too, often highlighted the instrumental function of radio broadcasts and audio recordings in transcending spatial divisions established according to gender propriety. As one of them said,

> Because we women cannot leave our homes as easily as men do, we listen to the sermons at home. This is why I say that a *kaseti* is more important to a woman than to a man. Her home is the only place where she has time to listen to a *kaseti wajuli*. A woman does not just want to hear [*mèn*] a sermon. She wants to listen with attention [*k'i tlo majò a fè*] and gain benefit from learning. At home she can carefully explore [*a b'a nyanini kojugu*] the contents of a teacher's lessons, and debate [*ka baro k'a kan*] them with fellow believers. You see, women's problem is not that we lack interest or attentiveness. Our problem is a lack of means. If your husband allows you to use his radio set you can follow Hadja every Friday. But most of us cannot listen to her radio broadcasts on Friday because the men in our family take the radio with them when they go into town.

This explanation of women's limited access to learning rests on the assumption that the shortage in technical equipment constitutes an impediment to Muslim women's pursuit of virtue. The mention of women's "scrutiny" (*sègèsègèli*) and their habit of "carefully questioning" [*nyininkali kè k'a nyadon*] a speaker's teachings hints at a central tenet of their engagements with sermons. Listening to a sermon is considered a religiously significant act leading to one's embrace of God's word. Listening is contrasted to "just hearing," which is viewed as a morally neutral act without further implications.

At first sight, the notion of careful scrutiny through which teachings are appropriated appears to presuppose an argumentative spirit reminiscent of Habermas's notion of critical rational argument. Listeners insinuate this critical modality by asserting that they "learn" from sermons by discussing them (*ka baro k'a kan*) with fellow acolytes, which refers to a spectrum of conversational acts ranging from casual talk to more formalized discussions or controversies (Schulz 2002). But how far does this resemblance go, and what exactly do supporters mean when they associate sermon listening with "learning via debate"?

Several connotations are associated with Habermas's notion of "critical-rational debate," which is basic to his distinction between two different types of "public sphere" and is developed further in his "Theory of Communicative

Action." The objective of critical debate is to evolve through a series of dialogues in which controversial issues are deliberated for the purpose of ultimate agreement. Disagreements are settled according to the validity of the arguments that speakers advance, not according to their status and political power (Calhoun 1992b). The term "critical debate" pinpoints the care invested in the (allegedly power-neutral) deliberation of different viewpoints. It also refers to the political effects and potential of debate, that is, its capacity to contain the power of the state or sovereign.[5] The association with emancipatory politics implicit in Habermas's notion of debate differs from the critical scrutiny that supporters of moral renewal in Mali postulate. The latter stress the need to critically and seriously examine the teachings. Their view of critical scrutiny does not imply a fault-finding investigation with the aim of overcoming the speaker's point of view. Instead, their motivation is to "examine carefully" (*k'a lajè kossèbè*) a leader's teachings so that they can defend them against diverging viewpoints. This distinctive view of critical understanding comes across not only in self-reflexive assertions but in a range of spontaneous gestural responses. Their frequent and explicit acknowledgment of the bodily reverberations of the teachings shows that many Muslim women (and men) understand that a sermon extends beyond a purely cognitive process of appropriation. In their view, intellectual properties are not separated from a believers' embodied moral, emotional, and aesthetic sensibilities. Their conception of understanding reveals that conventional views of the need for an embodied and felt understanding are revisited by a new emphasis on individual responsibility (*no*) in defending one's personal viewpoint.

During my research I witnessed numerous occasions that, at first sight, appeared as instances of women's subversion of the existing normative order, thus seemingly supporting the view of authors who search for traces of contestation or resistance to the normative order in Muslim women's practices. Women who listen to sermons like to critically scrutinize teachings by frequently asking their teachers sensitive questions, prompting teachers to reframe issues and perspectives. But these women do not view their interventions as "critical" in the sense of challenging the teachers' authority or the validity of his interpretations. One day, on a visit to my neighbor Fatou, I interrupted a heated discussion between her and some visitors, all of whom are members of a Muslim association in one of Bamako's middle-class neighborhoods. Disagreement had arisen over a sermon their leader (*tontigi*) had delivered on a local radio station, the last part of which focused on the importance of a woman's responsibility for her family's well-being. Some of the older women (among them my host Fatou) appreciated their leader's reflections on women's responsibilities toward her family, but two younger members complained that confining women's actions to the family realm would contribute little to their search for collective renewal. "How can we make people change their minds and actions," one speaker fervently interjected, "if we content ourselves with our family's well-being?" Her question was dismissed by the older members of the group whose status as elders forbade younger opponents to challenge them. At the next group meeting in the *tontigi*'s courtyard, I waited for the discussants to consult with their leader on this issue. But nothing happened. Weeks later I learned that one of the older women had brought the disagreement to the attention of the *tontigi,* but the latter had not pursued the issue. Only once, when the group was to perform at a marriage celebration in the neighborhood, the *tontigi* mentioned, in passing (and disapprovingly), that "women who feel they should make their opinions heard in public [should] remain modest [rather than] overestimate their own importance." When I visited the *tontigi* a few days later and asked her to explain her remark, she waved her hand dismissively and said, "Some women create problems out of nothing. You should not listen to those troublemakers. Nor should you ask questions to annoy your teachers. The aim of questioning is to gain a better understanding."

The silencing of the controversy by the *tontigi*'s single authoritative gesture illustrates the nature and limits of women's critical engagement. The younger women's scrutiny did not challenge existing norms of gender propriety, such as equating a woman's virtue with her submissiveness, but aimed at understanding how they should translate these teachings into daily practice. Their proposition of a more radical reading of their *tontigi*'s teachings was silenced by the obligation to respect age and status seniority. So even if, on other occasions, some Muslim women were more successful in asserting their own viewpoints, their questioning never challenged the central tenets of the leader's teachings. Nor did they question commonsensical understandings of female propriety. Hegemonic normative ideals largely remain unquestioned in women's debate. At the same time some women, usually highly respected group members, do occasionally speak of their leader's moral exhortations in order to expose men's (double) moral standards. In one instance, some women publicly referred to their leader's call for women's uncompromising submission to their husbands in order to pressure a group member's husband and convince him to treat his different wives with greater impartiality.

Searching for signs of resistance in women's understandings obviously would not do justice to the fact that their discussions center on how to realize their ethical quest in everyday life and how to invite others to join them. Questions frequently posed to their teachers concerning the practicability of their ethical endeavor reveal their eagerness to debate and scrutinize sermons in order to establish a solid interpretation, one firm enough to withstand the attacks of contesting parties within and outside the Muslim activist camp. A female believer's primary responsibility is not to refute competing positions but to work on her own disposition and conviction. Focusing on women's questioning of authorities is thus not only misguided and mainly revelatory of the agenda of those who propose it (see Mahmood 2001; Abu-Lughod 2002), but it also fails to capture the complexity of Muslim women's motivations for debate. Consideration should be given to culturally specific notions of critical engagement that inform people's sermon-listening activities. Supporters of Islamic moral renewal in Mali scrutinize a teacher's moral lessons with the ultimate goal of translating their convictions into daily practice. Their emphasis on scrutiny as part of a continuous effort toward self-improvement reveals that religious learning is shaped by a mix of conventional forms of knowledge-acquisition and a revised view of the significance of religious learning to one's daily life.

Male Muslim activists formulate views similar to those of female activists. Fusseni, a man of about forty years of age who had been a close follower of Sharif Haidara for more than five years, explained the benefit of listening regularly to sermons:

> Listening to sermons enhances your capacity for true understanding [*famuyali*]. True understanding means that you gain insight into the logical nature of Islam [*silameya tlènen do, kènèkan ko do*]. You can try and gain this understanding by listening to what preachers and holy men say. If you listen carefully to a sermon, if you critically scrutinize a sermon, [you realize that] it is undeniable that God is the truth, that Islam is the path to this truth, and that the Qur'an extends beyond anything that a human being can produce.[6]

Fusseni's stress on the need to elucidate the "rational character" (*kènèkan ko do*) of Islam echoes Sharif Haidara's emphasis on the systematic nature of the Qur'an. Fusseni's portrayal of his consumption of sermon recordings as critical scrutiny, however, does not imply a critical attitude toward his leader's sermonizing but indicates that believers are obliged to thoroughly engage with God's word. Believers' occasional reformulation of teachings highlight a subjective dimension of the trend some authors describe as an objectification of Islam (e.g., Eickelman 1992). Along with increasing access to religious instruction, a growing number of believers pore over the "rules of Islam" (*silameya sariaw*) through the very process of discussing them. Their attempt to gain a more thorough knowledge of Islam is closely related to their recognition of the coexistence of Islam with other normative standards.

Numerous followers of Haidara, many of them men, also consider scrutiny as a way to ascertain the rational character of Islam. Others in the renewal movement, in contrast, attribute less importance to critical debate, even though many of them (such as most women organized in Muslim associations) emphasize their interest in "building their own opinion" (*k'i yèrè ka famuyali cògò la*). This means that although supporters of the movement claim unity in their quest for collective and personal moral reform, they diverge over how religiosity should be lived every day.

Many women and men would disagree with the approach to sermon listening outlined by Fusseni. Ousmane, for instance, who is married to a leading member of a Muslim women's association in Segou, underplays the cognitive process involved in listening to sermons.

> There are different ways of hearing [*mèn*] a sermon. They differ in their effect on you. You may simply hear with your ear but this will not move you to action. Only if you listen to a sermon with your heart [*ni wajuli ser'i dunsunkunna*] can you be truly moved [*a bè min k'i la*] and carried away [*a b'i miri janja*]. The action [*kèwale,* deed] triggered by a sermon must not be outwardly visible. It may remain within yourself. A sermon, once it is truly understood, opens your heart [*a b'i dunsun dayèlè*] and reaches your soul [*a bè s'i nin ma*]. It creates in you the desire to obey God's demands.

Ousmane defines "true" understanding according to the bodily perceptions it generates in the listener; true understanding occurs only if the listener's cognitive *and* emotional facilities are affected. Several Muslim women similarly highlighted the embodied responses and emotive capacities generated by sermon-listening practices. As explained by Dunsun, who leads a Muslim women's group in Bamako-Jikoroni and broadcasts her sermons regularly on an adjoining radio station:

> When I preach to women, my first goal is to grasp their attention. But the attention I seek is not an ordinary one, such as one that is needed if you walk through the street, for example, and watch out that you are not hit by a car. I seek to generate an attention that leads a woman to a better understanding of God's word. This understanding is impossible without an involvement of your heart. Unless a woman takes God's word to heart, there will be no redemption for

her. . . . My duty is to make women take God's word to heart, to make it resonate with the insight that there is no truth other than God.

Taking to heart the sermon's moral lesson involves both cognitive and emotive facilities, although supporters of Islamic moral reform do not unequivocally subscribe to this total mind-body view of engaging with sermons. They do agree, however, that listening to a sermon requires a purposeful embracing of the contents that is not predicated on a refutation of the speaker's argument. Still, even if such a refutation is not the primary objective, listeners' engagement does occasionally lead to a reformulation of a sermon's intended function.

Believers' emphatic interest in probing (*laje, sègèsègè*) the content of sermons suggests that they understand this activity involving a simultaneous reworking of the mind and body as part of their attempt to craft a particular ethical disposition (see Hirschkind 2006, chap.3). This view of "understanding" as an active appropriation is reflected in the terms by which they refer to both individual and joint practices of listening to a sermon. The verbs "to hear" and "to listen" both contain the core term *mèn,* and both refer not only to the perceptive capacity to hear (*mèn*) but also to understanding as a moral disposition and action (such as in *kaseti lamèn,* "to listen to a sermon"). A deferential attitude is expressed by the root *mèn. Ne y'a mèn* (literally, "I have heard") is commonly used to signal that one not only understands but acquiesces to the speaker's dictum. A believer may contrast his or her "listening" to a taped sermon (*ne ye kaseti wajuli lamèn*) to the process of "hearing" (*ne ye wajuliin mèn/famu*) a sermon, that is, to submitting to its central message. "Hearing" thus designates the integration of a sensory with a moral faculty. It indicates a total understanding that reflects the listener's ethical disposition and moral capacity to heed the teacher's admonitions. "Hearing" denotes deeper understanding and acceptance within a hierarchical relationship where this cognitive, bodily, and emotional process is embedded.[7]

Supporters of Islamic moral renewal in Mali associate sensory with moral capabilities in a way that parallels how young men in Cairo understand sermon-listening practices (Hirschkind 2006). For believers in Mali, listening regularly to sermons, whether taped or live, is an integral part of their daily cultivation of piety. As Oumou and Lele, two members of a Muslim women's group in a lower-class neighborhood in San, explained it in 2003:

I listen to Hadja's (audio-recorded) teachings every day, whenever I can make time. But when I have to "cope" [*jija*] because we need money very badly, I do not have time. In those situations, my mind is set on worldly things so I will not engage in sermon listening because I cannot give all my attention to Hadja's teachings. Hadja admonishes us that our hunger for money and food diverts our attention from the truth of God's word. Because listening to Hadja helps me move closer to God, I do so only when I know that I have the right state of mind. There are people who assert that we listen to tapes for the purpose of entertainment [*njanaje*]. . . . But this is wrong. Listening to a tape by a good speaker helps my mind settle on God [*ka n'hakili da ala kan*] and brings me closer to him by making my heart open to receive his word. Hadja helps me to do so, too, just by talking to me. The stories she tells us are not meant to entertain but to enlighten us. She teaches us moral lessons but she does so in a way that renders our burden lighter. Her teachings have a greater benefit than the stories broadcast on radio. She knows our problems and she knows about our deep desire to open ourselves up to God [*k'anw dunsunkun dayèlè ala ma*].

Oumou stresses the ethically purifying effects of listening to cassette sermons. Although there is an element of leisurely entertainment in the consumption of taped sermons, this does not preclude believers' emphasis on the morally superior, edifying nature of sermons compared to other mass-media products. Similar to what Hirschkind observes, earlier views of "ethical audition" have been refashioned, yet not displaced, under the influence of modes of attention and consumption shaped by various mass-media products including popular music, television entertainment, and speech genres (Hirschkind 2006, 11, chap. 3). The sermon-listening practices of supporters of Islamic renewal in Mali are informed by conventions aimed at moral edification and are refashioned by new modalities of listening to, and being entertained by, various mass-mediated genres.

Lele, my second interlocutor, focused on the cognitive effects of listening to sermons.

Listening to Hadja's sermons is an affair of the heart [*dunsun*], not of the ears [*tlo ko tè*]. The ear often cannot make a distinction between what is good [*min ka nyi*] and what is ethically correct [*min tlènèn do*]. Ears hear only words, but they do not record their true meaning [*tlo bè kuma mèn nka a t'a kòrò don*]. . . . Speech which reaches only your ears is not relevant [*a tè nafa t'u la*]. Only speech which reaches your heart can rework your mind and inner self [*min b'i*

dunsunkunna]. There are different kinds of benefits [of listening to sermons]. Some Muslims listen to sermons from
time to time because they hope to receive divine recompense [*ka nafa sòrò*]. Our objective is different. A proper
believer's mind is set on true spiritual benefit [*an'w be baraji
de nyini*]. We listen to sermons because they help us transform our inner selves, by preparing ourselves for God's
pronouncement. Listening to our leader's teachings makes
us understand the true substance of God's word and how
to work on ourselves. Only if you do this for some time
. . . can [you] distinguish between right and wrong without
even thinking about it [*a b'anw bila sira nyuman kan, hali
an'w tè miri*].

Lele contrasts "other" Muslims' strategic search for divine recompense to
the desire of proper believers to achieve a fundamental transformation of mind
and disposition. Ultimately aural sermons enhances the listener's capacity for
ethical judgment, which is the prerequisite for one's ability to "move closer to
God"—the result and precondition for the further reworking of mind and body.
Lele's emphasis on the need for a spontaneously felt moral judgment echoes the
weight many Muslim women place on self-improvement and personal accountability. Her account also resonates with central tenets of the Islamic revival in
Cairo that, as Hirschkind (2006, chap. 3) and Mahmood (2005, chap. 4) show,
revolve around the achievement of a spontaneous capacity for moral discrimination. Cairene supporters of Islamic revival view regular listening to a preacher's
teachings as intrinsic to their quotidian self-disciplinary practices. Lele's view
of the benefits of listening to recorded sermons suggests that certain elements
of Salafi-Sunni reformist thought have entered Malian arenas and inform
local formulations of proper religiosity. That Lele's approach is shared only by
some supporters of Islamic renewal in Mali demonstrates that, as in the case of
women's diverse notions of pious self-making analyzed in chapter 5, these local
reformulations of distant intellectual trends remain partial and open-ended.

Many Muslim women maintain that the benefits of sermon listening vary
with the physical environment and the listener's level of concentration. They
consider a listener's attentiveness, her receptivity for the sermon's ethically transforming qualities, as crucial for its effectiveness. By stressing that a listener's
correct attitude transforms the setting of consumption, they intimate a disparity between mundane environs (which generate little benefit) and those that,
although not sacred in the proper sense, take on a special, sanctified aura in
the process of sermon listening. They thereby portray cassette-sermon listening

differently from the instrumentalist view of media that was articulated in the second introductory anecdote. They ascribe to media technologies not only the capacity to broadcast but to bring out a speaker's special, God-granted qualities.

Recall that many supporters of Islamic moral renewal in Mali believe that understanding is predicated on a multi-sensory process of appropriation. In contrast to how critical scrutiny tends to be viewed in Western liberal political theory, these Muslims believe that "understanding" is more than just a cognitive act. Their emphasis on scrutinizing does suggest an analytical act, but they assert that listening to sermons facilitate a believer's spontaneously felt knowledge of what is right and wrong. Beyond these parallels to the ethics of sermon listening in contemporary Cairo, there are also substantial differences between the two settings, particularly in the ways that the Islamic revivalist movement affects conventional understandings of cassette sermons in these locations.

One notable distinction is the disciplinary dimension that, according to Hirschkind, male listeners in Cairo underscore when talking about their sermon-listening activities. Among supporters of Islamic moral renewal in Mali, no consensus exists about the "disciplinary effects" and ethically transforming dimensions of cassette-sermon listening. Believers such as Lele and Ousmane highlight the transformative effects of cassette sermons, but their view does not represent the understanding of the mass of participants in the movement. Another discrepancy between Islamic revival in Cairo and in urban Mali concerns the extent to which believers' ideas about the ethics of sermon listening is grounded in the written traditions of Islam. This divergence is a function of the different languages used.

In Cairo, listeners follow sermons performed in their mother tongue, whereas religious discourse in Mali is structured by considerable linguistic pluralism. In Mali Arabic literacy is a marker of inclusion and exclusion, as it regulates access to religious interpretation and authoritative discourse. Sermons in Arabic enjoy greater prestige than sermons in national languages, but few Malians understand them. Depending on the language of the sermon, Malian listeners underline the cognitive dimension of understanding to different degrees. Many believers associate Arabic with a more analytically oriented appropriation of the distinctive "rules" enumerated in a sermon. Tapes in Bamana, in contrast, are thought to speak to a listener's aesthetic and moral sensibilities.

This disparity in immediate access to Arabic has important consequences. Unlike the case in Mali, many participants in Cairo's Islamic revivalist movement seem to explicitly relate their views of the ethics of sermon listening to long-standing disciplinary Islamic traditions. In Mali, the authoritative Islamic texts have been anchored only loosely in the practices and understandings of "common," non-erudite Muslim believers. Because participants in the moral reform movement have limited Arabic literacy and interpretative knowledge, they frame their engagement with sermons in terms borrowed from conventional, not necessarily Islamic, notions of the emotive, transformative potential of listening. A final divergence from Hirschkind's analysis relates to the gender-specific structuring of access to mass-mediated sermons, and to women's and men's divergent emphasis on the cognitive dimension of "comprehending" sermons. In Mali, women and men often emphasize different dimensions in their "understanding" of sermons. Women tend to foreground the ethically enhancing, transformative capacities of sermons, whereas many men, particularly younger men, pay more attention to the argument proposed in sermons. This last disparity may result not from differences in regional Islamic traditions and their incorporation into differential social settings but instead may be owing to the differences in Hirschkind's and my analytical perspectives. Further research needs to establish whether in Cairo, too, gender-specific responses and access to mass-mediated sermons establish different trajectories of comprehension for male versus female listeners.

Cassette sermon practices in Mali clearly differ from media engagements that animate Islamic moral renewal in other areas of the Muslim world. Listeners foreground understanding and cognition, and also hint at an experience of embracing in its literal sense, meaning an act predicated on multi-sensory perception. This leaves us with a question: How does the synesthetic nature of sermon listening and individual media technologies mold, and make sense of, spiritual experience?

The Phenomenology of Listening and Spiritual Experience

What sensory processes inform sermon listening as a spiritual experience? How do these processes structure the inclusion of sermons in listeners' everyday experiences (see de Witte 2003)? Participants in the Islamic moral reform movement, both men and women, describe hearing (*men*) a sermon as a sensation that is at once auditory and tactile, regardless of whether the sermon is live or mass-mediated. Many expressions point to the tactile nature of this experience, such as "taking in" or "grasping" a sermon.[8] These words posit the intricate connection between the sensation of hearing and being touched. Aissata, a member of Hadja Bintou's women's group, described her first, inadvertent encounter with Hadja Bintou's sermonizing as an "awakening" experience that compelled her to join Hadja Bintou's group,

> When I [switched on my radio post and] heard Hadja preach,
> the mere sensation of her voice hit me as if someone lashed
> out at me. I felt the piercing truth of her lesson coming

together in her voice. . . . The sound of her voice entered me like a sword. It moved right into my heart, I could not do anything about it. I suddenly knew that I would no longer feel peace in my heart until I heeded her exhortation and moved to action.

Aissata's account of her first auditory encounter with her *tontigi* is, literally, striking. She combines the imagery of tactility and aurality to describe her existential and embodied experience of "hearing the truth." Note that Aissatta perceived the truthful nature of Hadja's moral call both in her voice and her words, thereby blurring the distinction between the sound and content of speech. The same recognition of hearing as embodied sensation, of sound as a full-bodied experience of touch, was implied in other group members' accounts of the importance of regular sermon listening. They describe hearing as a tactile experience of sound and, indeed, point to the epistemic grounding of sound in touch. They all emphasize that "comprehending the truth" is a tactile sensation: the truthful nature of speech is perceived as, and validated by, the experience of touch. This is not to suggest that listeners' stress on the constitutive link between sound and haptic perception derive from aesthetic and perceptive conventions peculiar to the sensibilities formulated by participants in the moral reform movement. Nor does this perception constitute a peculiar feature of a Malian hearing culture. The emphasis that supporters of Islamic renewal place on the touching effects of preaching should be viewed in the light of a phenomenology of hearing that begins with the embodied nature of this form of perception and aesthetic involvement (McCartney 2004; Erlmann 2004). Similar to the genuinely embodied nature of all sensory perception (Sobchak 2004), listening depends on and invokes "corpo-reality," that is, the materiality of the body (Drobnick 2004, 10).

A distinctive experience is created by the tactile dimension of sound and the forms of embodiment that it generates and is predicated upon. Aissata's mention of the "irresistible" nature of sound suggests that, to her, sound goes together with and moves beyond touch, inasmuch as it does not stop at the surface of the listener's skin but permeates the body. The capacity of sound to overcome the skin as a boundary between self and non-self seems to be one reason for the pervasive nature of hearing. As Burrows and other authors have pointed out, in contrast to sight, which perceives objects from a distance, hearing and listening create an experience of immersion in sensory perception (Burrows 1990, 16–17; also see McCartney 2004). Auditory experience surrounds and encloses listeners, resounding within the body beyond willful control. This is because sound is perceived through our tactile sense as a vibration that cannot be closed off as easily, for example, as sight can be obstructed by closing one's eyes (see Schafer 1977, 11). Aissata, for example, described a feeling of being overwhelmed by a preacher's voice, as if there were no distance between the listener and the speaker. Her account that Hadja's exhortation "moved her to action" suggests that to comprehend a sermon involves not only tactility and aurality but also kinesthesia. Moussa, a prominent representative of the Ansar Dine movement in Segou who regularly engaged in preaching activities himself, put it this way:

> You can tell the difference between a sermon full of God's truth and other sermons if you consider the effect a preacher's speech has on you, whether his words really reach and touch. But this is not a mere matter of words. It is his voice itself, its capacity to affect [literally, hit] you so that it compels you into accomplishing deeds [*kewale*] rather than just sitting and being entertained. [If it affects you in this way, then] the preacher speaks with a rightful mind and the truth of God's word is conveyed.

Moussa maintains that the auditory process generates an intimate relationship shaped by a sense of emotional rapprochement to the speaker. He characterizes a genuine listening experience by its ability to elicit an impulsive, immediate move to action, and thus stresses the combined acoustic reverberations and kinetic effects of speech. Listeners' true spiritual experience, their perception of the presence of the Divine Will in the here and now of their listening experience, is thought to manifest itself in the listeners' spontaneous movements or "gut reactions." The corpo-reality of hearing thus ensures the epistemic grounding of sound as genuine and truthful. Listening to a sermon is a religious act and provides an opportunity to be drawn into a collective spiritual experience.[9] It entails the generative possibilities of a social attachment that is registered through the senses, becomes engrained in the listener's body, and then forms an embodied form of memory and social coexistence (see McCartney 2004). These sermons come to be associated not only with the physical environment of the group meeting but with the immediate experience of being a group.

Because sermons have an immense generative potential for a participatory and performative spirituality, one may ask how particular technologies of mediation intervene. How do audio-recording technologies affect the role of the preacher's voice as the carrier of truthful speech and a facilitator of shared spiritual experience? If listening to a preacher's voice generates feelings of bonding and emotional identification, how is this perceptual experience of commonality and shared presence affected by media technologies that transport a speaker's voice across a long distance and thus generate a common experience that can no longer be perceived as being spatially shared? Exploring these questions by focusing on two technologies of mediation, audio and audio-visual recordings, is a powerful way to assess the process through which Sharif Haidara's followers confer spiritual authority on him. Although these technologies seem to establish distinct, even opposed, epistemologies of authenticating spiritual experience, they converge in their sensory effects. Essentially both technologies generate a fully synesthetic spiritual sensation.

Media Powers and/as Spiritual Powers

Haidara draws some of his acclaim by concentrating on the arguable and systematic nature of the Qur'an and the suitability of Islamic prescriptions to everyday life. The anti-hierarchical bent of his message appeals to believers from various middle- and lower-middle-class households. His focus on the unmediated communication between believers and the Divine runs counter to the Sufi emphasis on the beneficial effects of a leader acting as mediator between God and humans. But a closer look at the processes at work in Haidara's mass-mediated appearances shows that his claim is at variance with the ways he actually relates to his followers, which resemble conventional religious patronage. Haidara's ambiguous position thus illustrates the complex interweaving of credentials, old and new, on the basis of which religious leaders assert authority in Mali's public arenas. This complexity forecloses the teleological view that traditional elements of religious authority are gradually being replaced by modern credentials and styles of persuasion.

Some qualities for which Haidara's followers praise him, such as piety, devotion, erudition, and oratory skills, resonate with the qualifications of religious leadership in West African Sufi traditions, even if Haidara cannot lay claim to other conventional credentials, such as an intellectual genealogy rooted in a chain of transmission and spiritual initiation (*silsala*). Nor does he meet certain requirements that would qualify him as a "friend of God"[10] (*wali*), such as spiritual retreat (*khalwa*), visionary dreams, or the performance of miracles (see Brenner 1988; Triaud 1988b). While Haidara's opponents denounce him for lacking these credentials, his followers view the discrepancy between him and other more tradition-minded religious leaders as a sign that he has been chosen by God to show them "the right way." They contrast the genealogical prestige Haidara's opponents claim with Haidara's divinely bestowed qualities (*baraka*), especially his forceful speech and "poignant voice" (*a kan nège*) which they see as heavenly gifts granted to those with the mission of mediating between God and His subjects. Their references to *baraka* resemble the exceptional powers Weber

(1947, 358) identified as markers of charismatic authority (see Dekmejian and Wyszomirski 1972; Lindholm 1990). Although Weber's notion of charisma does not fully match the concept of *baraka,* they both illuminate an understanding of how Haidara establishes his authority in a public arena.[11] Weber's insistence on the interactive creation of charismatic leadership advances the point that Haidara's authority emerges through his relationship with individual devotees or groups of acolytes. My interest thus lies in the ways that Haidara's spiritual leadership is mediated and established through individual believers' engagements with his audio- and video-recordings.

Recent scholarship has drawn attention to the culturally specific ways that media technologies make evident the process of mediating a "supernatural" presence or, rather, dissimulate it (e.g., Babb and Wadley 1995; Meyer and Moors 2006). Morris (2002) has studied a spirit in northern Thailand that presumably refused to be embodied in a spirit medium to explore historically contingent ideas about the effects of electronic mediation. She argues that the spirit's resistance to incarnation renders problematic the association of a spirit medium with a commodified cultural authenticity. The mute spirit's refusal also hints at a new "regime of communication" made possible by video technology (ibid., 389–399). The video does not provide access to the spirit; it only defers its presence. Video technology therefore epitomizes the failure of communicating the Real (spirit) in a context of urban, commodified spirit-possession practices. Meyer's (2003) analysis of representations of magic in Ghanaian popular cinema suggests that the film medium enables a paradoxical recognition of the relevance of the occult to everyday experience. Popular movies make room for the representation of occult practices in a double sense: stories of the hero's victory over evil forces acknowledge the latter's very existence, and the films render visible what in everyday life remains arcane: they show in gruesome detail the effects of occult practices.

Haidara's followers similarly believe that individual media technologies have specific capacities for bringing out the otherwise hidden qualities of speech, and thus allow their leader's special powers to become more palpable and effective. Several men told me that the initial incentive to acquaint themselves with Haidara's teachings came with their experience of "feeling struck" by his "poignant voice," which, when broadcast on local radio, seemed to "come out of nowhere." So compelling was his voice, they said, that they "immediately felt that he spoke God's truth. Because God will only endow those with such a forceful voice who is willing to speak on his behalf." Some of Haidara's closest followers highlighted the disparity between his voice, which "obliges people to accept the truth" (*a bè mògòw diyagòya i k'a son*), and the voice of other preachers who "just speak" but do not motivate people to change. Note, here again, that voice is equated with speech. Only Haidara's voice has the ability to move and transform the heart of those in search of the truth, and touch the "feelings of everyone willing to truly understand Haidara's advice and to act accordingly." Other listeners asserted that hearing Haidara's speech "without seeing him," "touched" them so deeply that they often felt moved to tears and "purified their hearts" (*a bè n'dunsunkun sanuya*). Some young men even claimed that sensing Haidara's disembodied voice "filling" their surroundings cleansed their homes of "evil spirits" (*jinnew*).[12] Most of these unprompted observations point to the emotionally charged relationship that listeners establish with Haidara in the process of listening to his sermons. Haidara's physical absence seems to increase rather than weaken the moving effects of his voice. Many acolytes feel that Haidara's voice proves that "God bestowed extraordinary *baraka* on him" (*ala ye barika don a kuma kan na*). Others even liken their listening experience to one of spiritual awakening (*a b'i nyana k'i sara a b'i lawuli* ["he talks to you so compellingly that he can awaken you even from your deathbed"]). This subjective sense of Haidara's exceptional nature also crystallizes in the ways in which numerous acolytes relate to the material manifestations of his spiritual presence.

Haidara's followers' emphasis on the tactile and kinesthetic effects of his speech echoes their assertion that comprehending, literally "grasping" a sermon, occurs through both the sonic and haptic experience of being touched and taken in by a preacher's forceful speech. Although they attribute extraordinary qualities to his voice, this interactive generation of spiritual leadership should not be seen as unique. Rather, this view of leadership reflects a cultural framework of sensory perception in which a preacher's capacity to move listeners through sound is believed to indicate his special capacities to mediate between the here and now and an invisible world. Thus technologies that highlight a person's special emotive capacities gain importance in the interactive creation of spiritual authority.

Listeners' view of the performative qualities of Haidara's voice, and their insistence on the amplifying role of audio recordings, resonate with Hirschkind's argument that, in Egypt, the mediatization of sermons contributed to a restructuring of notions of individual agency and religious authority. In earlier traditions of sermon performance and of listening to sermons, agency was located "more in God and the disciplined ears and hearts of listeners." With the increase in mass-mediated sermons, the weight of responsibility shifts to the speaker and his capacity to convince his listeners of the truthfulness of his speech (Hirschkind 2001b, 2006, chap. 5). In Mali, however, responsibilities seem to be more equivocally distributed and do not reflect a neat historical shift. The importance that Haidara's followers attribute to his powerful speech contrasts with their emphasis on their own individual responsibility as believers.

Haidara's followers tend to accord to audio-broadcasting technologies the capacity to make his presence "im-mediate" and heighten the purifying effects of his voice. Maam's remark (reported in the third introductory anecdote to this chapter) captures this view of the special capabilities of audio broadcasting, a view that may remind us, albeit with a curious twist, of Marshall McLuhan's (1964) famous dictum that the "media is the message." McLuhan's proposition implies that a medium per se transports a certain ideological message that McLuhan assumes is universal and unchanging. The capacities attributed by Ansar Dine members to audio broadcasts suggest that, to these listeners, too, an important share of Haidara's message is conveyed by the specific media technology used. The message it conveys is not an ideology of modernism (as McLuhan suggests) but of the media's sympathetic magical capacities (see Frazer 1911–15), that is, its potential to make audible a voice's hidden qualities.

The concept of a medium's special powers reaches its striking apogee when some acolytes, in an act of "technological transference," associate the technology's powers with its physical incarnation, the technical apparatus. This shows in the ways some followers relate to the radio they use to follow their leaders' sermons. I often witnessed that, the moment Haidara's sermons would come on the local radio station, female devotees would rearrange their sitting positions and assume the posture required when the leader is physically present. Adult women immediately altered their mode of speech, talking in a low voice and deferential fashion, even advising young children to follow their example. In Ansar Dine households in San, women and girls place the tape recorder in a specific place whenever they listen to Haidara's sermons. The chosen location is usually decorated with posters depicting Haidara and his family, along with memorabilia commemorating important stages in his career. Female devotees, by carrying out their household chores in the presence of the radio, turn the consumption of his sermons into a spatially marked activity. The act of listening to his speech creates a new space for experiencing spirituality and the extraordinary. By ascribing special capabilities to audio-recording technology, devotees transform an array of practices related to Haidara's cassette sermons into religious acts.

Audio-recording technology is not the only medium that facilitates new spiritual experience. To some devotees, visual representations of Haidara and his spiritual excellence seem to have a sacrosanct character; they allow for the simultaneous experience of seeing and being seen (see Mitchell 1994; Plate 2003, 3–61; Pinney 2004, 8). I once overheard a member of the Ansar Dine women's association in San severely scolding her three- and five-year-old sons for playing with an album of photographs and memorabilia of her leader's recent visit to San. The mother was not simply concerned that her children might soil the book; that they touched a photo of Haidara was an act she clearly considered sacrilegious.

Warning them that they "should not meddle with his powers," she demanded a reverent treatment of her *karamògò*'s portraits which, she explained to me, were not to be equated with normal photographs. In a subsequent conversation with the local Ansar Dine leader and his brother and wife, I asked what they thought about this incident. They adamantly dismissed as "un-Islamic" the belief that a photograph of Haidara had the power to address the spectator and therefore deserved special treatment. Other followers, however, expressed their eagerness to obtain material tokens of their leader's charisma as a way to tap into his spiritual powers. Patently wearing dress accessories with the imprint of their leader's portrait and honorific titles implies more than articulating one's Muslim identity, contrary to what recent studies on "Islamic" dress tend to highlight. Followers who wear a baseball cap or scarf with a maxim condensing their leader's message manifest their yearning to partake in his charisma. Donning a veil with an imprint of Haidara's image allows one to embody the leader's spiritual powers and express one's emotional attachment. Even if all Haidara's followers do not share this conviction, the fact is that posters, stickers, and recorded sermons operate as media, allowing followers to enjoy an immediate, physical experience of the leader's closeness to God, an experiences that resonates with conventional modes of interacting with Sufi *shaykhs*. Similar to audio-media products, these objects facilitate both the creation and consumption of Haidara's charismatic attraction.

The special mediating powers that many participants in the Malian Islamic moral reform movement credit to audio broadcasts contrast with the effects of electronic media identified by Larkin (2008) and Spitulnik (2002) among Nigerian and Zambian media audiences. Both authors argue that audio and audiovisual media were seen as intricately connected with the ideological project of colonial modernity, and their use continues to this day to be informed by this legacy. In Muslim northern Nigeria, cinematic film became the object of controversy between proponents of Western culture and those who rejected it as moral and cultural degeneration. The Ansar Dine members' perception of the powers of audio-recording technologies suggests that these and other supporters of Islamic renewal in Mali do not classify them in a neat opposition of "modernist" orientations versus traditionalist or "preservationist" preoccupations. This also is seen in the ways that video-recording technology is sometimes used for purposes of spiritual experience. This technology enables forms of religious engagement that, while drawing on existing understandings of spiritual mediation, facilitate partly novel experiences of oneself *as* a religious subject. Video technology, distinct from audio broadcasting, is involved in important and specific ways in the sensation (and creation) of charisma. Through broader tactile engagement with visual representations of spirituality, video recordings facilitate devotees' multi-sensory and embodied experience of what one might refer to as their leader's "trickle-down" charisma.

Video Sessions:
The Sensation of "Trickle-down Charisma"

On a hot and humid Sunday morning in August 1999 I visited a well-to-do merchant in Hamdalaye, a lower-middle-class neighborhood in Bamako, who, together with his two wives, had joined the Ansar Dine movement in the early 1990s. I was surprised to find crowds of visitors—men, women, and children— sitting on mats, stools, and the few available chairs on the compound's main veranda. Although the friend who had first introduced me to the merchant and his family had praised the merchant's extraordinary hospitality, the swarm of visitors on that morning took me by surprise. His first wife, Lele, welcomed me with her usual mixture of warmth and dignified self-restraint and told me to take a chair next to some women visitors, saying that I had arrived just in time to join them in watching a video. The video was a recording of Sharif Haidara's most recent visit to San.[13] Almost an hour passed as Lele seated an endless stream of visitors in two clusters, dividing women and men and reflecting each person's position in a hierarchy of status and respectability. Finally, my host's eldest son wheeled in a cabinet covered with a cotton fabric on which a photo of Haidara looked out at us with a confidence-inspiring smile. Removal of the cover exposed the family's TV set and video recorder. The son then produced a videotape from an ornamented wooden container and inserted it into the recorder, reciting under his breath a *bissimilah* (in the name of God). The women in the audience checked their clothing, adjusted their headscarves, and admonished their children to "sit properly." An elderly woman sitting beside me observed disapprovingly that I should have brought my scarf, adding that "this definitely is not the right moment for dressing loosely. You should wear appropriate dress, and you should wear a *birifini* [an additional scarf serving as prayer shawl]." And she gravely advised my host's second wife to lend me one of her scarves.

The screening of the video started and we looked at stunning masses of people awaiting Sharif Haidara's arrival in San, reminiscent of presidential visits but more impressive because of the evident enthusiasm of the waiting crowds. I was barely able to recognize the main entry road into San, so packed was it with people in festive apparel framing the road. People of all ages, excited and smiling, waved to the camera and to one another, holding rosaries and little framed posters with photographs of Haidara and his family. Several young men carrying cameras moved in and out of the picture, smiling and inviting onlookers to have their pictures taken as a souvenir of the event. A number of serious-looking men, dressed in uniform, blue and green *pipaos*,[14] built a human barrier along the street to keep admirers from spilling over into the road. Some moments later the camera shifted to a middle-aged man whose portable loudspeaker announced Haidara's arrival. His words were immediately muted by the noisy excitement setting in, as the crowds both on television and on our veranda started cheering. At this moment three medium-sized motorcycles moved into the television screen (another resemblance to the choreography of presidential visits), steered by young men dressed smartly in jeans, sweaters, and baseball caps decorated with the Ansar Dine logo. A range rover then arrived which I identified as Haidara's "Quatre-quatre,"[15] a gift, my neighbor whispered, bestowed by a wealthy supporter to increase Haidara's comfort during his overland trips. Through the open car windows we could see Haidara, dressed in a white *pipao* with golden ribbons and a head scarf sitting next to his driver and waving to the cheering crowds with a dignified expression. All the while people in the streets, along with some of my fellow video spectators, shouted in unison "Haidara!" "Haidara!"

The closer Haidara's car moved to the location of the cameraman, the more wobbly and unstable the images became. Images bounced up and down picturing men, women, and children as they tried to bypass the guards who, in turn, were struggling to keep the crowd from obstructing the vehicle's passage. In all this pandemonium, one could intermittently discern photographers' heads bobbing up and down as they tried to photograph their religious leader and his enthusiastic entourage. To the side were people who had abandoned any hope of approaching Haidara. They touched the soil with their foreheads, some of them shouting "Haidara, *karamògò*" and "our leader, help us receive God's blessings." The hubbub on the screen continued for another ten minutes and then the images finally steadied. The next scene cut to Haidara seated on a podium. A microphone on a nearby desk was covered with a large white banner that read, in French and Bamana, "Ousmane Sharif Haidara, our spiritual guide, welcome." Photographers, bouncing in and out of view, took snapshots of Haidara and his entourage. A sudden silence fell as Haidara signaled to one of his confidants to bring the microphone closer. The camera then shifted from Haidara to the masses covering the square. Close-ups of individuals showed tense faces eagerly awaiting Haidara's voice.

This and other video screening events I attended in the course of my research are remarkable in several respects.[16] They suggest that video recordings, although less widespread and accessible than audio recordings, create opportunities for Ansar Dine members to integrate experiences of spirituality into mundane domains of the everyday and to enter into a devotional relationship with their spiritual leader. Video recordings both perpetuate and refashion conventional ways of mediating divine presence.

Like audio cassettes, video sessions give Haidara's acolytes an occasion to partake in their leader's spirituality. In their acts of reverence, they perform a hierarchical relationship of "entrusting" themselves to their spiritual guide. The screening of Haidara's videotaped appearances allows them, in a process distinct from sermon-listening practices, to sense the diminishing distance between them and their leader, and to feel bonded to him and other followers through an emotional identification. Most striking about the Ansar Dine video session is the marked difference, in emotional intensity and bodily reactions, between spectators' responses to this recording of Haidara's public appearance and their usual reactions to soap operas. The often heated, passionate debates around particular episodes or heroes of soap operas were nothing compared to the emotional pandemonium initiated by Haidara's videotaped arrival. Several men jumped up from their seats, kneeled down, and shouted "Haidara," while others (mostly women) bent at their torsos and rocked rhythmically back and forth, chanting benedictions. Haidara's presence was immediate and tangible, not just visually mediated but physically palpable in people's bodies. The atmosphere quieted down only when Haidara started his sermon and an old man (sitting to the far right of the courtyard) advised the others to be still and listen to their *karamògò*.

The screening of the videotape vividly illustrates the various intricately related opportunities that video recordings afford for the creation and experience of spiritual leadership. Haidara's video-recorded visit and its screening are moments when Haidara's followers grant him charismatic authority. Both events are predicated on the synesthetic nature of perceiving and conceiving charismatic authority. Believers' attempts to gain God's blessing by touching the figure who embodies it, the ways they kneel down, bend their heads, and touch the soil, all reveal that their veneration practices are informed by conventional notions of sainthood. Believers' engagements with audiotapes and video recordings, while demonstrating the synesthetic nature of these practices, also reveal certain differences between the spiritual experiences offered by these diverse media technologies. Clearly video technology does not portray in any simple, immediate sense the sources of Haidara's spiritual leadership. But it does bring to the fore his otherwise ephemeral powers insofar as it re-presents the effects they have on his followers, which themselves are perceived as tactile, auditory, and visual sensations. Compared to audio broadcasting, video technology adds another layer to the tactile perception of charisma, as it incites followers to touch the screen and thus actively partake in the leader's charisma. By encouraging a more agentive modality of sharing the leader's charismatic gifts, video technology reconfigures the conditions for generating and sensing religious subjectivity.

The consumption of Haidara's video recordings allows his followers to sense the touch of his spiritual powers, a transformative experience that gives a sanctified aura to mundane daily life.[17] This mode of extending Haidara's spiritual presence generates new debate over religious orthopraxy and genuine spiritual experience. As Mariam, the second wife of the merchant who hosted the video session, explained to me while walking me home,

> Some neighbors stay away when we invite them [to watch one of Haidara's video recordings]. They claim that we are not real Muslims, that we venerate a human being while we should worship God alone. This is not true. Haidara does not want us to idolize him. But indeed, when I see him, whether on video or on a visit to Bankoni, I feel how something in me changes. I leave this place and I feel transformed. I see him, I listen to his words, he touches me and I leave as another person, if only for a short while, until I get absorbed by my daily worries.

Witnessing Haidara's special, "chosen" status is central to Mariam's spiritual search. His "closeness to God" is transferred to her in the form of divine blessings. In defending against the allegation that these practices are un-Islamic, Mariam points out that her effort to move closer to God through the intermission of a spiritual leader conforms to the long-standing regional Islamic tradition of the master-disciple relationship, which is a structuring principle of the Islamic mystical traditions. Mariam's emphasis on the importance of human intercession in communicating with the Divine conflicts with the tendency among proponents of Islamic moral renewal to challenge conventional religious hierarchies and privilege independent interpretation and the cultivation of religious virtue. Yet neither Mariam nor other followers of Haidara perceive this as a significant problem. Their lack of concern is a result of Haidara simultaneously disclaiming and asserting special spiritual status (Schulz 2003a).

Mariam's recognition of Haidara's role as intercessor to the Divine is challenged by Muslims critical of Haidara, as well as by some followers. In private conversations, several members criticized what they considered "extreme manifestations" of devotion to Haidara. These critics believe that exaggerated adoration runs counter to "Haidara's true message," although, interestingly, they did not feel that consuming Haidara's broadcast sermons involved such exaggerated reactions. When I asked Haidara himself whether he thought that this veneration contradicted his message that "no one should interfere with a believer's relationship to God," he responded that he "never told people to venerate" him. "However," he continued with a smile, "people want to be guided. There is nothing wrong with people paying respect to an extraordinary personality. Their commitment to a spiritual guide reflects their seriousness toward God."

While the form and object of religious worship is contestable, people do not show much concern about the adoption of mass-mediated representations into their venerating practices. Signs of attachment and religious zest at the sight of mass-mediated images are considered part of a broader range of regular and un(re)marked religious activities. The role of video technology in mediating spirituality but also in extending it to new areas and modalities of perception is simultaneously acknowledged and minimized.

Religious media and the significance that consumers attribute to their media engagements transform their understandings and experiences of spirituality in daily life. In Mali, audiotapes have been essential in establishing interpretive communities that challenge the official public. It was not the technical capacities of these media forms that did the trick but rather the material practices, institutions, and social and cultural valuations that render their use meaningful. Although participants in the movement consider their engagements with sermons and other "religious" performances as distinct from their consumption of other broadcast genres, such as soap operas, all these media engagements form part of the emergent meta-topical space described in chapters 3 and 6, a space constituted through various media products, textualities, and modes of circulation and engagement.

The media engagements by Haidara's followers illustrate particularly well the interconnections and convergences between newly adopted media technologies and long-standing conventions of validating spiritual authority. Acolytes' appropriations of religious discourse, whether mass-mediated or im-mediate, exemplify their insistence on the presence of the supernatural in everyday life. To many, media technologies have the potential of extending, not of reinserting, spiritual experience into an array of mundane domains. This introduces problems in the analytical perspective of authors whose studies of "religion" in the era of mass media is based on a neat binary division between religious practice "before and after" new media technologies. Instead of assuming that mass-mediated religious practice generates a split from existing forms of religiosity, the challenge is to appreciate how conventional practices are inflected by the growing permeation of everyday life with mass-mediated experience. The religious subjectivity that supporters of Islamic renewal claim for themselves may be seen in their mixing of spiritual experience, "careful scrutiny," and enjoyment in their media engagements. Compared to the "textuality" (Fiske 1986) of soap operas that telespectators construct, videos generate distinctive forms of consumption centered on spiritual experience. Charismatic appeal emerges in the interaction between individual preachers and their "live" and mass-mediated audiences. These media engagements might prompt us to rethink views of the workings of "charisma" and of charismatic religious authority. The consumption of religious items turns followers of religious leaders into a distinct religious subject. Men and women physically partake in their leader's divinely granted qualities by striving to be "touched." Far from simply serving an expressive function, the attire that Ansar Dine members choose enables the sensation of a particular form of bodily mediated, trickle-down charisma. Charisma is created and experienced in the course of consumption.

The centrality of consumption practices to the spiritual experience of Haidara's followers offers a curious twist on Robertson's (1991) thesis that consumption in contemporary society replaces earlier forms of religious worship. Some media engagements by members of the moral reform movement in Mali turn into religious acts that do transform everyday experience. They do not replace conventional forms of religious expression, however, nor do they point to entirely novel conceptions of religious authority and spiritual power. It remains to be seen whether the consumption of media products and religious paraphernalia ever constitutes an all-encompassing and pervasive social dynamic. So far, the significance of consumption to religious experience in Mali is most pertinent for believers' interactions with religious leaders who, like Haidara, combine established credentials with qualities and styles of persuasion attuned to the complex demands of an urban moral topography.

Epilogue

IN DECEMBER 2009 I returned to Mali after a three-year absence. Upon visiting members of the Muslim women's group in Bamako-Missira whom I had contacted intermittently during my stay abroad, I had difficulty absorbing all the family news. Sons had left home, braving the dangers of crossing the Sahara and seeking entrance into the fortress of Europe in search of a job, leaving their parents without support and ignorant of their whereabouts. Daughters had been married off, some advantageously and to everyone's approval, others causing family disputes among new in-laws and hence chagrin for their mothers. The group leader's husband and sister had returned home after extended sojourns in Saudi Arabia and Syria, which meant that conversations during women's learning sessions now had to be conducted in a more solemn, less gossipy manner. A group member with whom I had been only loosely acquainted had left her husband and returned to his homestead only after family negotiations, in which a decisive role had been played by the *hadja*'s intervention on the woman's behalf. A close friend of mine had moved to another neighborhood, where, to everyone's delight, she founded a branch of the Muslim women's group. And Aissetou, a friend with whom I had often talked (and sometimes joked) about her unhappy marital situation, could hardly wait for me to sit down so she could gleefully show me her new acquisition, a tape recorder, sent by a dutiful nephew working in neighboring Senegal. The recorder, she said, "made her wishes complete," allowing her to follow her *hadja*'s radio lectures regularly. "This recorder," she added, to the murmuring approval of other Muslim women present, "is a sign of God's love. How else could I explain this sudden, unexpected gift from a nephew who lives far away? God sees my struggles, with my situation and my husband, and wants me to feel His presence in my life. He sent me this recorder so that I see the path that leads to Him and invite others to follow my example." Aissetou succinctly and seamlessly weaves together Islam's literally pathbreaking appeal with its mass-mediated forms, gender-specific meanings and repercussions, and role in remaking society.

Since the 1990s it has become commonplace in scholarly circles to observe that current Islamic revivalist tendencies reflect Muslims' various engagements with modernity rather than constituting signs of cultural atavism. The diverse modernist aspirations that Muslim actors articulate throughout the Muslim world mirror a historical consciousness shaped by a long-standing encounter with modern state institutions and government rationales. The crucial question, then, is not whether Muslim actors of different *couleurs* and persuasions are part of modernity but what forms their visions of modern politics and social life take. As suggested by Aissetou's remark about the tape recorder's role in mediating her access to God and facilitating her relations with her husband and social surroundings, Malian Muslims' discursive constructions of the modern self are to be understood by recognizing both their mass-mediated and gender-specific articulations.

The stress on gender as an important analytical key to Islamic renewal is not the same as exploring the effects of an allegedly conservative Islam on women. The central point here is not even the demonstration of women's agentive capacities, their capabilities to act within the parameters of Islamic reformist trends. Instead, in an expansion of Taylor's (2007) argument that religion in modern society is being reconfigured, neither disappearing nor "resurging," the main question is how the forms and meanings of Islam in Africa and beyond are changing, and where these changes have gender-specific manifestations. Islam's emotional appeal and recent move to the forefront of public debate in Mali crystallize people's efforts to come to terms with moral issues, media, and diminishing incomes. Islam's high currency in Malian politics and social life, as this book has shown, is related to its privileged representation in a feminine symbolics, and thus in a profoundly *gendered* idiom of community, modern ethics, and ethical politics. The challenge facing an ethnography of Islamic renewal in West Africa as well as its gender-specific ramifications, therefore, is not just to make up for the gaps in the documentation of Muslim women's religiosity (e.g., Boyd and Last 1985; Hodgkin 1998, 210) or the implicit equation between female Muslim religiosity and Sufi-related religious practices (e.g., Coulon 1988; Evers Rosander 1997a; see Triaud 1987). Any exploration of Islam as a discursive tradition with a significance constituted through a "political economy of meaning" (Eickelman 1979; Roff 1987) must account for gender as a source and measure of social difference. By documenting Muslim women's personal conceptions of ethical subjectivity and the forms of sociality in which their visions of a better moral order take shape, this book has offered a detailed examination of how "local forms of world religions" (Bowen 1995, 1503) emerge and change at the interface of competing discursive constructions of religious virtue, practice, and female propriety that are located in a field of transnational influences.

Over the past thirty years Islam has become a point of moral reference and identification in Mali, as well as a repertoire of symbolic and social practices through which various, sometimes conflicting aspirations and trends can be addressed and political and economic realities remade. The attraction of the "symbolic language of Islam" (Eickelman 1992) emerges from its capacity to assimilate cultural sensibilities, worries, and hopes that emerge from Malian urbanites' encounter with the dilemmas of postcolonial state politics and a changing economic order. Islam in Mali, in the form of Islamic humanitarianism and proselytizing, provides a matrix of social organization that draws on long-standing institutions of solidarity and mutual support. Islam functions as a register of morality and cultural authenticity and is also a model for social mobilization for people who feel deeply disillusioned about a political modernity fashioned on the model of the European nation-state and, more specifically, about the unfulfilled promises of democratization. Islam materializes in a conglomerate of emblems of propriety as well as in embodied manifestations of exemplary conduct. Islam becomes a vantage point and source of identity construction in a plural public arena where one's political viewpoint can be strengthened by speaking from a morally superior vantage point. As a template for spiritual experience, Islam allows for a reformulation of conceptions of religiosity and religious knowledge. Finally, as a blueprint for moral and social agency, it informs ideas of what it means to be at the same time modern and virtuous and authentically Malian/African, thus playing into people's ongoing reassessment of postcolonial subjectivity *tout court*.

What relevance for anthropological studies of Islam does this isolated case study of Islamic renewal, located in, as some might argue, a faraway place in West Africa, have for the place and public role of religion in this era of postcolonial politics? Any analysis of "fundamentalist" or "extremist" trends in religious reform movements needs to advance a historically and socially specific argument if we are to understand how people's changing perceptions are affected and mediated through ongoing social and institutional change. To move beyond the widespread scholarly preoccupation with the political aspirations of religious movements and their "threat" to secularist politics, the thriving of moralizing idioms needs to be examined in the context of a fragile urban economy, changing social institutions, and shifting responsibilities and obligations between spouses and generations. Also needed is an acknowledgment of the potentially diverse appropriations of scriptural Islam by group leaders, sponsors, and ordinary members. In Mali this diversity reveals, and emerges from, people's different positions vis-à-vis Sufi-inspired notions of religious practice and traditional lineages of religious specialists; divergences in interpretation are also often a function of the actors' different locations in a social and political institutional landscape. Exploring the appeal of Islam, in other words, implies an analysis of the ways in which abstract normative principles of Islam, their universalistic claims and transnational scope, are mediated by specific cultural understandings and social life-worlds, and how they in turn restructure the social and historical institutional context of a postcolonial polity within which they are apprehended. The emphasis on the relevance of certain brokering institutions and actors to this process of mediation echoes an argument advanced in recent debates on what should constitute the subject of an anthropology of Islam: "traditions of Islam," though, to an important extent, based on and legitimated through scriptural foundations, are always mediated through locally and historically situated practices, conventions, and norms of specific actors (Asad 1986). Malian Muslims, similar to believers and practitioners throughout the Muslim world, interpret Islamic traditions "through the lenses of their own culture and history" (Bowen 1995, 1054; 1993, chap. 14). Much is to be gained from transcending the binary approach prevalent in much earlier work on Muslim societies. That work was often caught up in an opposition between scriptural sources and "unorthodox" or "popular" religious practices that risked addressing Islam either as a "seamless essence" or as "plastic congeries of beliefs and practices" (Eickelman 1987, 18).[1] Although I agree with authors who propose to study Islam as comprised of competing claims and discourses, their perspective appears insufficient to account for the changes in, and people's challenges to, local Islamic traditions. To understand the complexity of this dynamic, an actor-oriented approach to contemporary forms of religiosity needs to be combined with an account of how broader societal processes of institutional transformation are reflected at the personal level, in the concerns, experiences, and struggles of individual women and men; and, conversely, how these struggles and efforts at personal remaking contribute to changes in the broader social and political context. The appeal of Islamic renewal evolves in a dialectical relationship between the social and political conditions of its existence, and its own potential of reconfiguring these conditions by, for instance, mobilizing people and remaking society from within.

To insist on the mutually constitutive relationship between the personal resonances and subjective ramifications of "Islam," its institutional conditions of existence, and its socially transformative effects is a powerful perspective to illuminate the tremendous appeal of Islam in contemporary Malian society. "Islam" works so compellingly as a community-evoking, moral idiom because it draws its performative power from the encounter with institutions and issues of nation-state politics in an era of multiparty democracy, and with new media technologies in a context of a commercialized entertainment culture. This perspective also sheds light on several paradoxical implications of these dynamics. Those who intervene on behalf of "Islamic morals" in public debates in Mali often reinvigorate the controlling and normative powers of state institutions and representatives. The mediating capacities of state officials are crucial to the political endeavors and survival of supporters of Islamic moral renewal. Although the initiatives of Muslim activists capitalize on the shaky foundations of a government's legitimacy, they continue to operate through important networks of political patronage and thus contribute to the partial redressing of the current political economy of state power. Various Muslim actors, activists, and religious authorities tend to frame their aspirations as a matter of civil rights; meanwhile, their recurrent claims to an alternative moral foundation diverge from these basic "Islamic" morals and social institutions as they become reconfigured by their encounter with the procedural rules and normative foundations of current nation-state politics. Muslim activists' reference to Islam as a normative resource thus entails a paradox in its simultaneously universalizing and particularizing rhetorical bent; by propagating a return to the original readings of Islam, they combine a universalizing claim to transcend ethnic particularity with a reference to a particular, "authentic" Malian culture. In their rhetoric, religion (or, more precisely, "religious orientation") occupies an equivocal position with respect to culture. Islam, then, works both as a community-building repertoire and an idiom of particularity and difference. Regardless of this paradox, the current civil rights rhetoric espoused by Muslims can be seen as a novel form of framing their claims to participation in the body politic. In their struggle to be recognized as a group in civil society, they often refer to the principles, ideals, and institutions of liberal political theory. These actors thus follow a general, international trend in which aspirations to public representation are couched as a struggle over cultural and human rights.

Aissetou's characterization of the tape recorder as a "gift of God" orienting her toward the "right path" shows the critical necessity to take into consideration the role of media technologies in facilitating and strengthening Islamic renewal. The complexity of Islamic revival and its gender-specific articulations and modes of restructuring society cannot be understood without paying proper attention to mass-mediated forms of religiosity. The key significance of mass media in personal reform and the declaration of a "religious" standpoint in public politics can be brought out by examining the dynamics of the cultural market and, more specifically, the extent to which the logic of commercialization informs the generation, consumption, and circulation of religious media products. At the same time it is important to trace the long-standing continuities between conventional and mass-mediated religious expressions and practices in order to produce a more detailed picture of the history, nature, and dynamics of a public "sphere" where religion plays a constitutive role.

The growing commercialization of both the media that generate religious experience and believers' engagement with these religious products points to a merging of genres of religious instruction and moral edification with mass-mediated popular entertainment. Islam has gained entry into mainstream culture by marketing media genres and also publicizing a particular religious standpoint. Supporting this process is not technological innovation per se but rather the broader concurrent changes in existing socioeconomic institutional arrangements. Decentralized media facilitate or reinforce long-standing tendencies in the articulation of doctrinal difference and moral exclusion among Muslims. It is not enough to be a Muslim. The important point is to adhere to a community of true believers. Rightly guided faith becomes a matter of individual conviction, personal display, social location, and the object of quotidian consumption. Islamic moral renewal, in its various material and discursive manifestations, inspires the constitutive elements of a mainstream ethical sensibility. The salience of Islam in Malian public and personal affairs resonates with trends throughout Sub-Saharan Africa, where new groups of Muslim actors effect greater public visibility and place special emphasis on the outward expression of their personal religious convictions (Kane and Triaud 1998, 20–21; Hodgkin 1998, 204–207).

The observation that Islam, as a partly commodified moral idiom, occupies a central position in public debate substantiates critiques of Habermas's historical and normative model of the public sphere. The prominence of an Islamic symbolic repertoire in broadcast genres casts doubt on Habermas's earlier view of the weakening relevance of religion and religious communication to the rise of the modern public sphere.[2] On the other hand, this confirms Taylor's (2007) observation that religion is not disappearing but is indeed prevailing in modern society through changing forms (see van der Veer 1995; Meyer 2011). As Moore (1994) points out from a historical perspective, the commercialization of religion was central to the expansion of capitalism and the emergence of the modern public sphere in the United States. Media practices by Muslims in Mali, and the forms and conceptions of religiosity to which these practices give rise show the import of religion for the structuring of social experience and the nature of "publicness" (*Öffentlichkeit*). Islam plays an eminent role in providing a blueprint for modern subjectivity and ethical practice in a historical situation in which a discourse on political modernity is increasingly intertwined with reflections on social ethics and personal accountability. Following up on a long-standing legacy in West Africa (Kane and Triaud 1998, 14, 26–27), Islam operates as a modernizing force in that it becomes crucial to Muslim activists' understandings of what it means to be modern and virtuous. For other Malians engaging with and distancing themselves from supporters of Islamic renewal, being a modern political subject also implies publicly articulating a moral position.

If modern subjectivity is notably expressed through an ethical sensibility, what modernist aspirations do its proponents articulate? And what concerns do they highlight in the aims they propose? To answer these questions, we need to consider the relevance of current revivalist trends in urban Mali in a broader, comparative perspective. Bowen recently made such a proposal, namely, to outline commonalities between contemporary reformist Muslim trends and Islamic traditions based on a framework that considers the particularity of local readings of universalistic religious normative principles. He emphasizes the "highly differentiated projects of modernist persuasions" and proposes to broadly classify them according to the specific dimensions of reform that their proponents highlight, as well as the latter's social location and political aspirations and respective social conditions (Bowen 1993, chap. 4, 1997, 175–176; also see Eickelman 1987, 15–20).[3]

The diverse and sometimes incongruent modernist persuasions formulated by Malian Muslim activists illustrate that Islamic modernism (or reformism, for that matter) cannot be defined by an essential core of values or orientations. Rather, Muslim modernist orientations in contemporary Mali are relationally constructed, that is, formed in opposition to "traditionalist" conceptions and practices of religiosity. This finding echoes Bowen's insistence on the historical, contingent, and not always coherent nature of religious forms and ideas, and highlights the need for a socially determinate and historical understanding of the changing traditions of Islam in West Africa (Bowen 1995, 1055–1056). At the same time, the contemporary surge of an Islamic moral renewal in Mali encompasses the different emphases and persuasions that, according to Bowen (1997, 176–177), allow us to compare modernist trends in the Muslim world. This is especially true in Malian urban centers such as San and Bamako, where lineages of traditional specialists do not base their influence on interpretational authority. Here a Muslim modernist outlook is less defined by content, such as actual debates on doctrinal difference, than by an emphasis on individual accountability and the necessity to publicly articulate an Islamic conviction. Characteristic of Muslims' public intervention is their stress on openly defining themselves in terms of their acts of religious virtue, as well as their effort to set themselves apart from other Muslims as true believers. Their claims to moral distinction follow long-standing regional conventions of establishing difference on the basis of ritual purity (e.g., Launay 1992). At the same time, their emphasis on the egalitarian character of Islam, as well as their integration of older and newer forms of social mobilization, downplays the existence of internal stratification along ethnic or socioeconomic divisions, and thereby appeals to a variety of urban middle- and lower-middle-class actors. Finally, most supporters of Islamic renewal emphasize individual religious virtue as the axis of society's moral transformation. Their preoccupation with total moral reform reaching beyond ritual practice reveals their strong concern with the ongoing, radical restructuring of the social and normative fabric of everyday life and, more specifically, with their inability to live up to conventional ideals of masculinity and femininity. Most remarkable, then, about the endeavor of Muslim activists, and distinguishing it from movements as various as the Tabligh-al-Jamaat in South Asia and reformist trends in the colonial French Sudan (see Metcalf 1995; Kaba 2000), is that it articulates a broad range of concern and appeals to a heterogeneous constituency.

Although contemporary Islamic revival in Mali does not fit neatly into the categories cited above, it does share a number of features with movements in other regions of the Muslim world and thus reveals similar responses to global processes that affect Muslim societies in Africa as much as in other regions of the Muslim world. Perhaps the most striking commonality between current Islamic revivalist tendencies in Mali and Muslim movements elsewhere is that, to an important extent, they are advanced by new types of actor who base their claims to leadership partly on new credentials and authoritative sources. Their rise to positions of influence reveals shifts in the basis of traditional religious authority facilitated by the greatly increased access to Western school education, by increased Arabic literacy over the last four decades, and, at least in many urban centers of the Muslim world, by the growing spread of mass media in everyday life (Eickelman 1992; Eickelman and Piscatori 1996; Hodgkin 1998; Kane and Triaud 1998, 20–21; Eickelman and Anderson 1999). As the rise of these new Muslim actors and their various reformist persuasions has been enabled by longer-standing socioeconomic and political transformations, their prominence is not specific to the contemporary moment (Kane and Triaud 1998, 26–27). This leaves us with the question of what, apart from the growing role of mass-mediation processes, distinguishes contemporary revivalist movements from their predecessors of the 1970s?

One difficulty with a circumscribed, historical argument is, of course, that it is hard to verify and even more difficult to refute. The challenge is to distinguish between different levels, kinds, and rates of historical change in the wake of changing characteristics of modernist or reformist Islamic movements and thus to consider the existence of "varied, intersecting rates of historical transformations and differences in scale at various times and places" (Eickelman 1987, 27). The ideas articulated by Muslim reformists at various times and in different places can be considered responses to, and ways of structuring, shifts in the broader political and economic formations rather than reflecting changes in actual patterns of religious faith (Eickelman and Piscatori 1996, 10–12). But a crucial question remains: Is it possible to identify the features that distinguish current Islamic movements from their historical predecessors in the 1970s and link potential differences to a changing global economic order? I am uncertain that anyone can make such a historically determinate argument. Still, by considering the political and economic institutional formations, we can ascertain the distinctive cultural forms in which current reformist trends materialize.

Consistent with the insights that may be drawn from this book, a common feature of contemporary Islamic revivalist tendencies throughout Sub-Saharan Africa and other regions of the Muslim world appears to be the political salience and power of a religious idiom as a source of moral identification and a model for restructuring social relations beyond the reach of the state. Another common feature of current Islamic revivalist trends is their espousal of a particular language and symbolism; most of the symbolic forms have a longer-standing influence on transnational and local Muslim cultural repertoires. These trends, in the current Malian context, take on a specific shape formed by the historical trajectory of the relationship between religious actors and longer-standing political and socioeconomic institutional transformations. The moralizing repertoire and symbolic forms in which such trends materialize draw their political salience from three recent developments. The first is the public prominence of Muslim actors and discourses since the late 1970s, which has been furthered by the financial support of sponsors in the Arabic-speaking world. The second development, which prompts people to translate a transnational Islamic revivalist trend into specifically local concerns, practices, and forms of self-organization, is the upsetting of conventional moral economies that was triggered in part by recent economic liberalization. The effects of the latter on urban economies, and particularly on the division of responsibilities between husband and wife and between generations, are compounded by a third trend, which is the loss in credibility of nation-state institutions and actors presently reflected in the disillusion people feel about the unfulfilled promises of multiparty democracy.

Instead of contrasting the prevalent emphasis on Islam as an ethically superior way of life to previous politically inspired movements, it is time to take the contemporary surge of ethical reform as a starting point for a comparative assessment of the high currency of morals in times of a radical restructuring of social and economic life. My point is not to advance a functionalist explanatory framework addressing the cohesive force of religion or morals in times of crisis. Rather, it is to stress the importance of considering the efforts of Malian Muslim activists and the moralizing idiom that their movement employs to articulate a *variety* of modernist aspirations and concerns. Rendering this perspective even more useful is that it allows us to make a comparative appraisal of the relationship between changing social institutions and people's culturally specific, normative mediation of the dilemmas of modern life. Such an approach does not limit itself to the Muslim world or to "religion" *tout court*. Instead, this book's investigation into the forceful prominence of an Islamic idiom in Malian politics is meant as a contribution to a comparative ethnography of moral community building and of a new politics of virtue in an era of nation-states whose internal normative and political economies are being radically restructured.

NOTES

Preface

1. Islam has enjoyed a certain presence in the area surrounding San since the early eighteenth century, but its practice remained limited to relatively few urban elite families. Even in the first two decades of French colonial rule administrators repeatedly reported on the limited number of Muslims in town. See, e.g., Archives Nationales du Mali, *Fonds Anciens, Rapports Politiques San*, 1E-67, 1903 (FA); *Politique Musulmane*, 4E-66, 1911 (FA). Starting in the 1940s Islam was gradually adopted by broader segments of the population in the region surrounding San. See Archives Nationales du Mali, *Fonds Récents*, 1E-38, *Rapports Politiques et des Tournées, Cercle de San*, 1921–1960.

2. Unless indicated otherwise, foreign terms are rendered in Bamanakan, the lingua franca of southern Mali.

3. The literal meaning of "Djenneké" is "a person from the town of Djenne." Archival documents suggest that at least in the first decades of colonial occupation of the town, administrators used the term "Djenneké" as an "ethnic" denomination. See, e.g., *Rapports sur l'islam et les confréries musulmanes*, San, 1911 (ANM FA, 4E66); Circulaire, surveillances des marabouts et personnages religieux, San, 1911 (ANM FA 4 E97).

4. These characterizations are taken from the French Colonial *Rapports Politiques* covering the period between 1897 and 1919, e.g., February and March 1898, February and December 1903 (*Archives Nationales du Mali, Fonds Anciens*, 1E-67).

Overture

1. Although some Muslim families in San were associated with the Qadiriyya, the town, like the capital Bamako and most towns of southern Mali, was never a stronghold for prestigious religious clans associated with Sufi orders as in the Sahelian and Saharan towns to the north, such as Nioro, Djenne, and Timbuktu. See ANM FA, 1E-67, Rapport Politique San, May 1903; see, too, Mann 2006, 27).

2. Conversation with the late Yero Haidara, Bamako, August 1998.

3. Certain features of the renewal movement date back to the 1930s and 1940s (see chapter 2). Since the 1980s, funding has been directed to Muslim sub-Saharan Africa by the League of the Muslim World (Rabitat al-alam al-islami), created by the regime of the al-Saud in 1962 with the aim of spreading the regime's understanding of *da'wa* (literally, "mission," "appeal," "summons") and Wahhabi doctrine (Schulze 1993, 26–29; Gresh 1983; Otayek 1993; Kane and Triaud 1998, 15).

4. In the absence of statistical data on the number of "Muslim women," I estimate that they comprise between 40 percent and 65 percent of the married, middle-aged women who live in the popular neighborhoods of Bamako, San, and other towns of southern Mali.

5. The Association Malienne pour l'Unité et le Progrès de l'Islam was created by the former president Moussa Traoré in the early 1980s to end conflicts between established families of religious specialists (often associated with Sufi practice) and those who, under

the influence of reformist trends in Egypt and Saudi Arabia, challenged the establishment for dominance. The AMUPI is run exclusively by men; only the 1996 creation of the UNAFEM extended membership to women.

6. Bamana (in Bamana, *Bamanakan;* literally, "the Bamana language") is the lingua franca of southern Mali where this ethnography is situated. Unless indicated otherwise, local expressions are rendered in Bamana.

7. Because these women link proper Muslim practice to a quest for collective and personal reform, I refer to them as "Muslim activists" or, following their self-description, as "Muslim women."

8. The other term for "religion" is *dina* (from Arabic, *din*).

9. This is so because mediation always involves, and necessitates, a reduction of the complexities and particularities of individual experience into commensurable "units" or data that are recognizable and thus communicable to others (e.g., Mazzarella 2004, 475)

10. The principal criterion for membership in a Muslim women's neighborhood group is that a woman be married.

11. This argument, articulated by Kandiyoti (1997; see Eickelman 2000) echoes the work of Abdelkar (1991), Göle (1996), and Hale (1997), and resonates with an earlier argument about the emblematic role of women in nationalist discourse (e.g., Kandiyoti 1991b; Moghadam 1994).

12. This perspective attests to the historical and cultural diversity of Islam-inspired social movements, to which the label "fundamentalism" does not do justice (see Caplan 1987; Nagata 2001).

13. This point has been addressed by Jalal (1991), Joseph (1991), and Poya (1999). See, too, Kandiyoti's (1991a) argument about the significance of the broader political and economic setting within which women's (and men's) support of Islamic revivalism needs to be understood.

14. Paradigmatic of this perspective are the works by Kaba (1974), Brenner (2001), and Soares (2005), each of them pathbreaking and fine-grained studies of (male) Muslim religiosity in colonial and post-colonial Mali. A notable exception to the focus on men is Hanretta's superb discussion of the reasons that may have led women to support the revivalist movement initiated by Yacouba Sylla in Kaedi (present-day Mauretania) in 1929 (2003, 468–473). But missing from Hanretta's account—probably because of the absence of archival and oral historical sources—is an account of the actual religious practices in which Muslim women engaged at this time.

15. Boyd's and Last's (1985) insistence on the historical role of women as "religious agents" has been bolstered by the work of Smith (1954), Boyd (1989, 2001), Sule and Starratt (1991), Asma'u (1997), Hutson (1999), and Umar (2001), but, with the exception of Smith, these works focus on leader personalities (see also Dunbar 2000, 400–404). Coulon (1988), Reveyrand-Coulon (1993), and Evers Rosander (1997a, 1998), all studying Senegal, document the significant part that female acolytes may play in Sufi orders (see Villalón 1995, 154–162; see also Constantin 1987). This perspective is important, yet one must question just how representative these women, who are organized within "holy clans" of Sufi orders, are for the mass of Muslim women in West Africa. For a general critique of the "Sufi bias" of scholarship on Islam in Africa, see Triaud 1986a, 1987.

16. As illustrated by LeBlanc (1998), Augis (2002), Umar (2004), and Alidou (2005), female educational activities constitute a key site where these local and transnational intellectual trends intertwine.

17. El Guindi (1981), Mernissi (1988), Abdelkhar (1991), Zuhur (1992), Hoodfar (1997), and Duval (1998) share this view of the emblematic significance of veiling, even if they draw different conclusions about its implications for women.

18. Other studies of this kind propose utilitarian arguments of the physical advantages of this apparel (e.g., Rugh 1986; see Lindisfarne-Tapper and Ingham 1997, 9-10).

19. The tendency to view female "veiling" as "repressive" and to take it, along with "seclusion," as an indication of women's power position can be traced back to orientalist writings (Moors 1991).

20. For work that compellingly refutes these generalizations, see Chatty 1997; Ingham 1997; and Yamani 1997.

21. "Veiling" does not necessarily have a religious connotation; nor does it always serve as a marker of (Muslim) identity (Schneider 1971; Sciama 1992; Eicher and Higgins 1992, 19–20; Schulz 2007a).

22. For like-minded attempts to move beyond a simplistic opposition between "religion" and modern (secular) politics, see, e.g., Casanova 1994; Hefner 1999; Asad 1999, 2003; Chakrabarty 2000; Scott and Hirschkind 2006; de Vries and Sullivan 2006.

23. With respect to postcolonial Africa, this argument has been succinctly formulated by Bayart (1996), Meyer and Geschiere (1999), Comaroff and Comaroff (2000), and Geschiere (2009).

24. By "liberalization" I refer to the implementation of specific economic measures and attendant political principles under international donor pressure since 1982. "Structural adjustment" in Mali meant the reduction of the state bureaucracy, the privatization of former state enterprises, the opening up of central productive sectors to foreign, often multinational, investment, and the devaluation of the Franc CFA by 50 percent. Political liberalization in Mali, particularly the introduction of multiparty democracy and administrative decentralization, complicated access to the resources of the central state, partly by adding new layers of budgetary decision making and control to the existing institutional power configurations.

25. The work by Zubaida (1989), Beinin and Stork (1997), Kepel (2000), Riesebrodt (2000), Ismail (2003), Mahmood (2005), and Deeb (2006), among others, illustrate great variation not only in the phenomenologies and different historical legacies of Islamic revivalism in different areas of the Muslim world but also in the analytical perspectives brought to bear on these movements.

26. This perspective was formulated by Launay and Soares (1999), Hoexter, Eisenstadt, and Levtzion (2002), Eickelman and Salvatore (2004), and Soares (2004). For an insightful critique of the applicability of this conception to the colonial French Sudan, see Hanretta 2003, 15 n. 11.

27. Drawing inspiration from Habermas's (1990 [1962]) account of the "public" (*Öffentlichkeit*) in nineteenth-century Western Europe, my approach differs from anthropological scholarship on religion and nation-state politics that considers Habermas's normative approach to deliberative public reasoning to be irreconcilable with the rationalities of state power in the postcolonial world (e.g., Bowen 1993; Hirschkind 2001a; Asad 2003, chap. 6). These reservations are apposite (see Calhoun 1992a, 1992b), yet they do not warrant a dismissal of Habermas's work on the "public." In some measure, this dismissal is the outcome of a reductive English translation of the term *Öffentlichkeit* as "public sphere," which privileges the spatial dimension of the term (see Mah 2000, 156). To disentangle Habermas's historical descriptive account of the

"Structural Transformation of the Public (Sphere)" from his prescriptive claims, we should first investigate, rather than assume, the norms and procedures of public debate; second, we need to recognize the key relevance of religion to Malian politics rather than assuming that modern politics are characterized by the withdrawal of religion to the private realm (Zaret 1992; see Calhoun 1992a, 35–36), an argument Habermas himself has recently revised by emphasizing the role of religious values in public deliberative politics (2005; but see Asad 2003, chap. 6).

28. Whereas the "public" is characterized by its distinctive location in nation-state politics, and the specific ideologies of communication associated with it (Warner 1990), audiences are constituted by particular media technologies, engagements, and genres (Livingstone 1998, 251; Barber 1997).

29. These four dimensions reflect the different meanings of the German notion of *Öffentlichkeit* that are not fully captured in its translation as "public sphere" (see Mah 2000, 156n4).

30. The two most important export sectors, cotton production and gold mining, were opened up for foreign investment. To date, the Compagnie Française de Développment des Textiles holds 40 percent of the former parastatal CMDT (Compagnie Malienne pour de Développement des Textiles), and more than 90 percent of gold mining and export is owned by private U.S., Canadian, and South African investors (Jeune Afrique 2000, 67–70).

31. The different conclusions drawn by Green (1989), Ghai (1991), Cornia, van der Hoeven, and Mkandawire (1992), Hoeven and Kraaj (1994), Hope (1997), and Jacques (1997) are, at least in part, the outcome of their divergent analytical perspectives. Authors who investigate the effects of liberalization on women (e.g., Commonwealth Secretariat 1989; Elson 1989; Palmer 1991) document the partial successes, and painful struggles, of women obliged to assume greater responsibility for family survival (Iken 1999; see Chant 1999).

32. By framing people's assessments as a "moral negotiation" of gender relations, I conceive of gender not as a structure of fixed relations but as the very process of structuring subjectivities (see Weston 1993; Morris 1995; see, too, Ortner and Whitehead 1981).

33. The "new" in new media is always relative (Gitelman and Pingree 2003). I use the notion of "new media technologies" in a descriptive, not analytical, sense to refer to audio and audiovisual technologies (mostly audio and visual tape recording, and radio and television) that, because of their recent adoption in the Malian context, appear to be at the origin of profound changes in social and sensuous experiences.

34. For an overview of (partly unresolved) methodological and theoretical issues in audience research, see Livingstone 1998.

35. A closely related question concerns the degree of media consumers' interpretational autonomy. Authors working along the lines of the Birmingham School of Cultural Studies emphasize the plurality of meanings of media texts and refute generalizing models of media hegemony (e.g., Abercrombie, Hill, and Turner 1980). These authors' critiques of views of an over-determining "cultural industry" (e.g., Horkheimer and Adorno 1972) are well taken, and yet their emphasis on audiences' decoding practices raises questions about how much power the media have in transporting certain representations of reality. Whereas earlier approaches suffered from a "disappearing audience" (e.g., Fejes 1984), a strong emphasis on consumers' independent "readings" of media

"texts" bears the risk of making "texts" disappear behind "active audiences'" (see Spitulnik 1993, 296–297; Livingstone 1998, 245).

36. Mass-mediated culture becomes a fetish in a double sense. Any object of cultural production "thingifies" (objectifies, *verdinglicht*) relations of social inequality. By consuming art, individuals "fetishize" art not out of an appreciation of its genuine qualities but by worshiping their own spending power.

37. With this argument, Adorno significantly departs from Benjamin's (presently more widely) cited "Artwork in the Age of Technical Reproduction."

1. "Our Nation's Authentic Traditions"

1. This remark alluded to Mali's support of the Beijing platform of September 1995.

2. Although these speakers maintained that their understandings of the nation's collective interest were based on Islamic precepts, none of them engaged in a substantive argument about the Islamic concept of *maslaha* (roughly, "common good") or to *maslaha 'amma* ("public interest"; see Zaman 2002, chaps. 1, 2).

3. The thriving of legal forms of intervention derives, as Jean and John Comaroff (2006) argue, from the Law's seeming capacity to mediate between incommensurable claims and identities, and thus to render commensurable what is irreconcilable.

4. It also manifests itself in a renewed scholarly interest in the legal domain as an area of political struggle (e.g., An Na'im 1990, 2002; Cook 1994; Risse, Ropp, and Sikkink 1999).

5. This argument does not consider that the principle of secularism, understood as the state's full neutrality toward, and equal treatment of, its citizens' diverse religious affiliations, has always been an ideal rather than a real-time achievement of Euro-American history or in the postcolonial world (Bauberot 1998; Asad 2003, 2006; Chatterjee 1993; Bhargava 1998).

6. For the French Sudan, see Kaba 1974; Brenner 2001, chaps. 3, 4; and the influential volume by Triaud and Robinson 2000. For comparative perspectives on historical shifts in the fields of Muslim religious debate, see Loimeier 1997, 2001, 2003; and Kane 2003.

7. Before the nineteenth century Islam spread in the northern regions of contemporary Mali along with the trans-Saharan trade in salt and the rise to power of families who were affiliated with the Qadiriyya order. The social organization of Islam changed, as centers of Islamic learning spread to the countryside and were integrated into pastoral ways of life. Since the redistribution of wealth was no longer closely tied to schools and mosques, religious affiliation acquired new economic and political functions (McDougall 1986; Stewart 1973).

8. With the imposition of the colonial judicial system, the former elite of Muslim legal experts was replaced by Sufi shaykhs and their spiritual leadership (Stewart 1997). On the diverse relations between colonial authorities and the lineages associated with Sufi leadership, see Triaud 1997.

9. Conversion rates in French West Africa increased rapidly after the 1920s, from 3,875,000 Muslims in 1924 to 6,241,000 in 1936 (Triaud 1997; Brenner 2001, 88n5). For conversion dynamics in the region of San, see, e.g., *Rapport annuel 1938* and *Rapport de tournée de récensement 10.-28.1.1945, of Rapports politiques et de tournées, Cercle de San, 1921–1960* (ANM, Fonds Récents, 1E38).

10. According to Mann (2006, 27), the revolts are to be understood as directed against French colonial recruitment for forced labor and military service.

11. For the history of the most notable of these uprisings, the so-called revolt of Dédougou, which emerged in the frontier zone of present-day Burkina Faso but also implicated villages in the *Cercle* of San, see Saul and Royer 2001.

12. These quotes are taken from *Rapport politique 13.5.1903*, of *Rapports Politiques et Rapports des Tournées, Cercle de San, 1897–1919* (ANM, Fonds Anciens 1E67); Rapport politique général 1918 of *Rapports Politiques et Rapports des Tournées, Cercle de San, 1921–1960* (ANM, Fonds Récents, 1E38).

13. One explanation of these conversion rates is that they reflected the radical restructuring of social hierarchies, especially those between former slaves and their masters, that resulted from the jihad waged by El Hadj Umar Tall and his successors in the region, and the fall of the "kingdom" of Macina (to the north of San, near Mopti), in the decades prior to colonial occupation. As new occupational opportunities, especially in the domain of trade and, in the colonial period, military service, opened up for people of slave descent, conversion to Islam offered a way of transcending their social origins (see Roberts 1988; Mann 2003, 76; 2006, chap.1). It is difficult, however, to ascertain the exact percentage of converts of slave origin because they usually bore the patronymic or family name (*jamu*) of their free-born masters.

14. See *Rapport annuel 1910, Rapports Janvier 1910, Avril 1910* of *Rapports Politiques, San, 1897–1919* (ANM, Fonds Anciens 1E-67); *Politique musulmane—Rapport annuel sur l'islam et les confréries musulmanes, Cercle de San, 1911* (ANM, Fonds Anciens, 4E66); *Rapport Politique, 1928*, 3ème trimestre (ANM, Fonds Anciens, 1E38).

15. See *Rapport Juillet 1928* of *Rapports politiques et de tournées, Cercle de San, 1921–1960* (ANM, Fonds Récents, 1E38); *Rapports de tournées, Cercle de San, 1932–1935* (ANM, Fonds Récents, 1E71); and *Monographie du Cercle de San, 1933* (ANM, Fonds Anciens, 1D54).

16. For an insightful discussion of a controversy over proper Muslim practice that reveals long-standing fissures within the Muslim religious field, see Brenner 2001, chap.4; see, too, Launay and Soares 1999.

17. For the ways in which colonial French policy toward Islam played out in the French Sudan, see Robinson 1988, 1992; Stewart 1997; Triaud 1997; Launay and Soares 1999; and Brenner 2001. For an illustration of the form in which these directives were transmitted to, and adopted by, local administrators, see *Politique Musulmane, Circulaire numéro BCII du gouverneur du Haut Sénégal Niger, 12.8.1911 aux commandants de regions et de cercles* (ANM, Fonds Anciens, 4E-97); and *Police Musulmane, Cerle de San* (ANM, Fonds Anciens, 4E125).

18. For several cases, see *Rapports Politiques, Segou, 1940–1959 II* (ANM, Fonds Récents, 1E40); Rapports Février 1912, Mars 1913, Décembre 1914, Janvier 1915 of *Rapports Politiques, San, 1897-1919* (ANM, Fonds Anciens, 1E67).

19. *Rapport Aôut 1914* of *Rapports Politiques, San, 1897–1919* (ANM, Fonds Anciens 1E67); *Renseignements sur les marabouts et personnages religieux, Segou, 1900–1916* (ANM, Fonds Anciens, 4E92); *Rapports annuels 1935, 1938* of *Rapports Politiques, Segou, 1935–1939* (ANM, Fonds Anciens, 1E40,I); see Harrison 1988, chaps 5, 8; Soares 2005, 57–58.

20. This argument is based on Kaba (1974), Triaud (1997), and Brenner (2001, chap. 4), and on oral testimony by I. Togola and S. Kulubali, Segou, August 1998;

B. Traoré, San, June 1999; S. Dembele, San, February 2002—all of them men aged sixty-five and older. I was unable to locate detailed archival accounts of sermons delivered in San and its surrounding region; administrators, preoccupied with the attitude of individual preachers toward the colonial powers, reported on the contents of sermons only in passing. See, e.g., *Rapport annuel 1912, Rapport Mars 1913, Rapport Avril 1913* of *Rapports politiques, San, 1897–1919* (ANM, Fonds Anciens, 1E67); *Rapport Mars 1928* of *Rapports politiques et de tournées, Cercle de San, 1921–1960* (ANM, Fonds Récents, 1E38).

21. Supporters of the doctrine view themselves as Salafi—that is, as those who abide to an ideal model of an original Islam lived by the "revered elders" (*al-salaf al-salih*) and untainted by the compromises of later generations of Muslims (Kaba 1974, chap. 4; Triaud 1986b).

22. Although the counter-reformers argued that their norms of public conduct, based on a modern African Muslim identity, ran counter to the understandings articulated by Al-Azhari proponents of educational reform, their respective understandings of Muslim subjectivity emerged in a mutually constitutive relationship (Brenner 2001, chap. 3).

23. Key elements of this symbolism is the vestimentary code and (for men) beard common in Saudi Arabia, and the folding of arms across the chest during prayer (Triaud 1986b, 164–166), a posture decried in the popular Malian nickname *bòlòminénaw* ("those who pray with crossed arms").

24. Soares (2005, chap. 7) argues that the last decades of French colonial rule witnessed a "standardization" of forms of Muslim religious practice and the emergence of a supra-local Muslim identity. I remain skeptical about the first part of his argument. Because many people only converted to Islam in these years, and thus learned about proper Muslim ritual practice for the first time, it is not evident how their religious activities could have undergone a process of adaptation to standard Muslim practice.

25. See *Rapports mensuels, Avril, Mai, Août, Septembre 1957, Janvier 1958* of *Rapports politiques et rapports de tournées, Cercle de San, 1921–1960* (ANM, FR 1E38); and Mann (2006, 53–54). For an informed discussion of the struggles over understandings of masculinity and male family authority on which Ousmane Sidibé's teachings reflected, see Mann (2003).

26. Following Bauberot (1990, 1998), I use the term *laïcité* to point to the distinctiveness of French *laïcité* that resulted from the historically determinate conditions of its emergence since the late seventeenth century.

27. Soares (2005, chap. 8) argues that in the 1950s French Sudanese witnessed an emergent Islamic public sphere that manifested itself in publications by Muslim intellectuals in *Le Soudan Francais,* a newspaper owned and produced by a French resident of Bamako. In my view, the reach of this form of mass-mediated public discourse should not be overestimated. Advertisements and articles on Mali's "cultural traditions" published in the newspaper illustrate that its readership was limited to a small reading elite of *assimilés,* that is, the new political elites and those considered French citizens.

28. A military committee (Comité Militaire de la Libération Nationale [CMLN]) ruled the country until 1979, when single-party rule was introduced by the UDPM (Union Démocratique du Peuple Malien). Under Traoré's presidency, the country gradually shifted from its earlier socialist leanings to alliances with the Western capitalist world.

29. The official rationale for the creation of the AMUPI was to reconcile the Muslim establishment and the "Sunni" merchants, and to put an end to the open hostilities and occasionally violent confrontations between these factions (Amselle 1985; Brenner 1993a, 65–71; 1993b).

30. The movement represented the segments of the elite who, as a consequence of the Structural Adjustment Programs' radical reduction of posts in state bureaucracy since the mid-1980s, felt excluded from the resources of the central state.

31. The term derives from their claim to be "integral Sunni," that is, to subscribe to "orthodox" Islam (Triaud 1985, 273).

32. There were, however, several occasions on which leading AMUPI representatives clashed with these governments. The first confrontation occurred in 1991, during the Gouvernement de Transition under Colonel Toumani Touré whose military coup had put an end to Moussa Traoré's single-party rule and who organized the country's first multi-party electoral campaign. Representatives of the national Muslim association (AMUPI) publicly denounced Touré's transition government for its refusal to order the closing of bars and dance halls during the month of Ramadan, a policy Traoré's government had adopted. In a demonstration in the city center of Bamako, they implored the government to respect "the Malian people's religious sensibilities." When police forcefully ended the demonstration, the critics viewed this as further proof of the new government's irreligious orientation. Another clash between the defenders of Islam and of *laïcité* occurred in late 1995, when President Konaré's government, in support of the platform issued by the United Nations Fourth World Conference on Women in Beijing, initiated a campaign against female circumcision (Hock 1998, chap. 5). In each case, the government succeeded in tempering the conflict by isolating the most vociferous Muslim critics.

33. These Sunni intellectuals maintain close informal ties to the government, even while publicly criticizing the government for accepting measures dictated by the International Monetary Fund and the World Bank.

34. The French colonial legal code was created two years before the principle of *laïcité* (Bauberot 1990) was established in the French constitution (Sarr and Roberts 1991, 136–137).

35. What colonial administrators applied as "customary" law only gradually emerged from an interplay between the (changing) agenda of French colonial administration and alliances between the colonial judiciary and (older) men from the local population who presented those regulations as customary law to the colonial authorities that served their own interests (Roberts 1991; see Chanock 1985). As Roberts (2006) illustrates in his analysis of litigation patterns at civil courts between 1905 and 1912, the application of "customary" law supported changes in the relations between powerful clans and their former slaves. It also limited women's opportunities for getting their grievances approved, and thus substantially enforced patriarchal and gerontocratic power relations within the family (see Cooper 1997, chaps. 6, 7).

36. Courts existed at the district and province level. The highest instance was the Court of Appeal in St. Louis.

37. Although not unique to societies in the postcolonial world, the gap is arguably more marked in states whose legal system has resulted from a combination of an imported judicial model and diverse local norms. Predicaments of contemporary African legal systems also emerged from bilateral cooperation in post-independent legal reform and from competition between different segments of the political elite (LeRoy 1995, 35–36).

38. The constitution of 1960 had already made women full citizens with equal civil and political rights. The *CMT* expanded colonial legislation of family life laid down in the *Decréts* Jacquinot and Mendel (1932, 1939) which prohibited the custom of levirate marriage and made marriage conditional upon the spouses' mutual consent. The *CMT* was slightly revised on January 23, 1963, and through a decree issued on May 30, 1975.

39. The *Concertations Régionales* took place in the national capital of Bamako and in the different regional capitals of Mali. At the request of the international donor organizations that sponsored the reform, the debates were designed as a platform for popular participation in the reform project.

40. Among these intellectuals are high-school teachers, journalists, and state officials. Most of them initially supported the *Mouvement pour la Démocratie* from which the ADEMA party emerged but grew critical of President Konaré's government and the culture of corruption it allegedly facilitated.

41. Under President Traoré, women in leading governmental positions had been trained in the national or other West African educational systems. The new female elite, in contrast, benefited from higher educational degrees in Europe or North America.

42. They were represented by NGOs that offer women legal assistance (*Cliniques Juridiques*) in divorce and inheritance matters.

43. In private conversations, members of the AMUPI steering committee asserted that they needed to contravene what they considered President Konaré's efforts to instigate conflicts between Muslim interest groups and within the AMUPI.

44. For a detailed analysis of the arguments generated by the 2000 draft law, see Schulz 2003b, 146–157).

45. These disputes often pit the sons of the deceased against their father's younger brother, who, according to customary regulations, becomes the head of the family and is entitled to his older brother's property.

46. State law (based on the *Code Napoléon*) would be applied if the deceased had not specified whether to apply customary, Islamic, or state law.

47. The legislation affects relations between wife and husband, and between generations, because they set the brothers of the deceased in opposition to his sons and daughters. Although the initial *CMT* (1962) already defined the nuclear family as the basic unit of social life, it accommodated the gap between the state-defined nuclear family and social regulations that enforce the prerogatives of the extended family.

48. Journalists and government officials (all of them men) cautioned that legal enforcement would neither halt this practice nor bridge the gap between positive law and actual social practice.

49. The *CMT* stipulates a woman's submission to her husband in exchange for his protection. The husband's exclusive responsibility for the family implies his right to choose the site of the family residence.

50. Female lawyers in charge of the draft law, in anticipation of male resistance, had prepared the proviso to void the obedience clause of its original substance. Yet, although the proviso limits the prerogatives of husbands and in-laws, its vague formula leaves considerable discretionary power to individual judges, and thus may not ensure women's equal rights in marriage. The proviso also primarily benefits urban women who have the means to pursue their case in court.

51. For instance, UNAFEM spokeswomen were the only ones to point out that malpractices related to bride-price payments required different solutions in remote rural regions than in urban areas.

52. Jalal (1991), Molyneux (1991), Hatem (1994), Dennerlein (1999), and Moors (1999) come to surprisingly similar conclusions in their analyses of law reforms in other Muslim-majority countries.

2. Times of Hardship

1. For the effects of the Structural Adjustment Programs on the Malian labor market, see Amselle 1985; Lachaud 1994.

2. Most of the families are long-term migrants, having arrived in the town over the past fifteen years (see Traoré 1979; Vaa, Findley, and Diallo 1989).

3. I view gender as a processual subjectivity emerging in a social field structured by lines of power and conflict that are embedded in socioeconomic processes. Gender is constituted and transformed in a generative tension between actors' individual experiences and practices of signification, and a historically determinate political-economic context that enables, yet does not determine, practices of social inequality.

4. I follow Beneria and Roldán's (1987, chap. 6) conception of the household as being composed of different (power) relations and dynamics that together constitute the household at a particular moment in time and space (see Guyer 1981; Vaughan 1983).

5. The following analysis occasionally distinguishes between "middle" and "lower-middle" class background, but the distinction is a loose one (see Lachaud 1994). Similarly, it is impossible to establish a clear dividing line between the informal and formal sectors of the economy (e.g., Marfaing and Sow 1999).

6. Bamako has a high proportion of migrants who moved to the capital since the years of severe drought in the mid-1980s. Since then, the proportion of female migrants has grown significantly ((RMUAO 1992/1993; Vaa, Findley, and Diallo 1989; Findley 1994).

7. Of the sixty-two married women I interviewed in Bamako, forty-four indicated that they had migrated to town over the past fifteen years. This percentage is not representative, but it gives a sense of the high proportion of migrant families in the neighborhoods where I conducted my research.

8. Working on urban Australia, Connell emphasizes class-related distinctions between masculinities. In Mali, different masculinity ideals range on an urban-rural continuum of family forms. For a critique of Connell's approach to masculinity, see MacInnes (1998, 55–64); also see Cornwall and Lindisfarne (1994); Ghoussoub and Sinclair Webb (2000).

9. Because the second, third, and fourth wife is generally chosen by the husband himself, there are definite advantages to entering a polygamous marital arrangement.

10. This criticism often refers to conflicts between senior women and their daughters-in-law over their respective financial responsibilities.

11. Although being a bachelor has certain economic advantages, many male adolescents experience their situation as a setback and struggle with their inability to achieve full adult status. Their opportunities to engage in premarital sex without parental obligations clearly put them in a different situation than girls, for whom the postponement or failure of marriage forecloses social adulthood.

12. Of my closest twenty-four female acquaintances from Muslim women's groups, seventeen lived in a household where a woman was the principal breadwinner. A 1992 survey of two low-income Bamako neighborhoods similarly documented a rising

percentage of female household heads (Yero Haidara, personal communication, Bamako, September 2000).

13. A 1993 survey shows that 64.4 percent of the women who work in the informal economy engage in commerce (as opposed to 26.5 percent of the men). The size of the informal economy has grown from comprising 61 percent of the population (not active in agriculture) in 1985 to 66.7 percent in 1989, and to 74.2 percent of the population in 1993 (Gouvernorat du District de Bamako 1994).

14. Financial input ranges from between 15,000 and 30,000 FCFA per day (1,000 FCFA = U.S.$2.20).

15. Their profit ranges from between 25 and 750 FCFA per day, with 250 FCFA needed for 1 kg of rice; a family of ten requires 3 kg of rice.

16. To save on daily expenses, they limit the number of meals to one. At night the children eat leftovers from lunch. Other family members need to "cope" (*k'i jija*) and find their own food.

17. More than 60 percent of the women I interviewed relied on staple food they received from their rural kin, and sometimes also depended on urban relatives.

18. Aissata lives, together with her husband and her co-wife's family, in extremely poor conditions in a large courtyard in San.

19. For instance, all women interviewed by Vaa and colleagues (1989) had the necessary funds to create *pari* groups and exchange gifts, the value of which generally ranged between 200 and 1,000 FCFA.

20. In other francophone African countries, the French term *tontine* is used more widely (e.g., Mayoukou 1994).

21. Monthly fees range from 500 to 5,000 FCFA.

22. Women implicitly distinguish between "gifts" that are deemed obligatory, such as donations given to relatives on the occasion of family ceremonies, and "free gifts" offered irregularly to good friends. The circulation of these two types of gifts follows different rules of moral obligation and frequency.

23. I met Modibo, a man in his early fifties and the father of seven children, in 1998, shortly after he had lost his job as a driver for a development project.

3. Family Conflicts

1. With this focus on consumption, Miller (1994, 1995a) and Friedman (1994) follow the now classic work of Baudrillard (1970), Douglas and Isherwood (1979), Barthes (1983), and Bourdieu (1979). See, also, Appadurai (1986); Featherstone (1987).

2. According to Anderson, along with print capitalism emerged a print-mediated view of collectivity that replaced earlier views of face-to-face communication and community. Habermas (1990 [1962]) posits the emergence of a "critical-rational" bourgeois public sphere from earlier forms of presentational publicity, and the subsequent transformation of this site for critical discourse into a modern mass-mediated public whose members uncritically "consume" politics. Mass-mediated consumer culture in fully industrialized societies thus rests upon a new ideology of public intervention.

3. For critiques of discourse-centered conceptualizations of public subjectivity, see Freitag (2001) and Pinney (2004); also Appadurai and Breckenridge (1988); Baker (1994). For a critical assessment of these critiques, see Schulz (2006b).

4. Hall (1980, 1994), Morley (1980), and Fiske (1989) question the portrayal of mass-media consumers as passive and uncritical, and argue that even under conditions of capitalist marketing some space remains for divergent interpretation, contestation, and transformation.

5. Sreberny-Mohammadi and Mohammadi (1994) use the term "small media" to emphasize that because they are not centrally controlled, they operate outside the purview of the state. I prefer to describe them as "decentralized media." Whereas a distinctive feature of these media is the decentralized trajectory of their production and distribution, the social organization of their use differs from one political economic setting to another. In Mali, they are distributed partly through market, partly through informal networks of lending.

6. According to Morley and Silverstone (1990, 33–38), "media consumption" involves not only engagements with media content but also with the material qualities and ideologies of individual media.

7. Television consumption is not correlated with ownership of a television set. In San and the lower-middle-class neighborhoods of Bamako where I conducted research between 1998 and 2006, less than twenty percent of households own a television set, but many more people watch television at their friends' or neighbors' homes.

8. Other broadcast music includes international African and American-style pop music. The programs featuring national music are mainly followed by middle-aged women and adolescents.

9. In 1999 the American soap opera *Amoureusement vôtre* (whose primary audience were youth and younger women) was broadcast every weekday night; two other telenovelas, the Brazilian *Femmes de sable* and the Mexican *Rose Sauvage* (each attracting an age- and gender-diverse audience), were broadcast once a week.

10. To respond to the challenge, a second national radio channel (*Chaîne Deux*) was created in 1992.

11. The only exception was the (enormously popular) serial *Walaha,* produced by Malian national television and broadcast in 2005, which spanned only five episodes.

12. Although this perspective only relegates the problem of interpretation to another analytical level, I believe that exploring viewers' responses as a matter of "guesswork" is more realistic—and more honest—than boasting an objective and representative analysis that, in fact, cannot be realized.

13. Discrepancies between male viewers cannot be related consistently to educational and age differences.

14. Whereas *Femme de Sable* and *Rose Sauvage* revolve around women as integrating figures, in *Amoureusement vôtre* two female protagonists are seductresses, and the third plays the role of the good, naïve girl.

15. Most wedding videos are produced in the two largest cities of Mali, Bamako and Segou; in smaller towns like San, few can afford the costs of a wedding video. Prices range between 10,000 and 25,000 FCFA (between U.S.$8.00 and U.S.$20.00), a substantial amount of money compared to the monthly salary of a primary-school teacher (65,000 FCFA).

16. The ethics of conventional patronage gives a *jeli* singer leverage to request enormous sums of money from powerful sponsors, and a patron has little power to refuse to "give a gift" (Schulz 1998, 1999a).

17. The videos extensively cover scenes in which *jeliw* interact with important guests and give them an opportunity to show (off) their wealth and social power through generous gifts.

18. Comments on the groom's family reflect a concern with its spending power and thus its social success.

4. Practicing Humanity

1. Its underlying normative assumptions are deeply anchored in a particular strand of Western, liberal, and secularist discourse that draws on a specific ideal of liberty (Skinner 1998).

2. Some spokesmen of the AMUPI invoke the "age-old Islamic tradition" of providing support for the poor and needy, but few refer to Islamic concepts of religiously motivated charity. Historically, religious endowments known as *awqaf* (singular, *waqf*) have been rare in this area of West Africa.

3. As mentioned earlier, the political role played by Sufi orders in Senegal since French colonial rule contrasts with their situation in Mali, where their political influence is restricted to towns such as Segou, Djenne, Timbuktu, and Nioro.

4. That younger Muslim activists also mobilize through political patronage networks appears paradoxical, because they claim to defend orthodox Islamic doctrine and challenge established Sufi clans for their condoning of practices of human intercession such as saint veneration. Nevertheless, their support of patronage networks illustrates that they share broader assumptions about the legitimate nature of religious patronage.

5. From Arabic, Ancâr ud-Dîn, the "supporters of religion," a term referring to the Prophet's community of followers.

6. The classical Qur'anic concept of *da'wa* (Arabic, "summons" or "invitation" to Islam) refers to the responsibility of Muslims to invite fellow believers to practice greater piety in all domains of life, and to engage in the required rituals. The meaning of *da'wa* has been expanded in modern times to refer to social and educational activities aimed at fellow Muslims, but it can be directed at non-Muslims as well (Otayek 1993; Schulze 1993; see Mendel 1995). In Mali, understandings of *da'wa* are strongly shaped by the missionary efforts of Muslim actors with intellectual ties to Saudi Arabia and Egypt. Most Muslim women do not use the term but describe their endeavor as inviting "other Muslims" to join their search for "closeness to God."

7. The mixed organizational repertoire of Muslim activism is mirrored in the fact that, although Muslim activists openly denounce the pro-Western governments of Presidents Alpha Konaré and Amadou Touré for their subservience to foreign donors, they draw on the same rhetoric of democratic participation to validate their own political aspirations.

8. To purchase his land, located in the irrigated rice cultivation zone of the Office du Niger near Segou, Kunta benefited from his connections to the regime of the former president Moussa Traoré.

9. To do so, committee members asked for the help of influential relatives, most of them merchants with close ties to party members whom they had sponsored during the previous presidential campaign.

10. Political observers interpreted Bâ Konaré's conference participation in this light and surmised that, in return, she might have claimed support for the ruling party ADEMA in the upcoming presidential elections.

11. Muslim activists' relations to the traditional families of religious specialists range from mutual tolerance and respect to distrust and (sometimes personalized) attacks. It is also important to note that some leading representatives of Muslim activism come from influential families of religious specialists.

12. Boyd and Last's argument about the "lop-sided" nature of this scholarship still applies, even if important studies on women's religious activities have been published since then (e.g., Coulon 1988; Dunbar 1991; Echard 1991; Sule and Starratt 1991; Mack and Boyd 1997; Hutson 1999; Boyd 2001; Umar 2001).

13. Triaud contends that these "agents religieux" had modest Arabic literacy skills and scholarly erudition, yet were crucial in spreading Muslim religious practice and identity.

14. Written documentation of female religious organization and practice in this area of French colonial Africa is scarce. My historical reconstruction is based on Sanankoua (1991b), oral historical research, and conversations with older members of the UNAFEM steering committee.

15. This, at least, is what the comparative literature on West Africa suggests. See, e.g., Dunbar (1991); Cooper (1995); Villalon (1995); Glew (1996); Loimeier (1997, 2001); Reichmuth (1996).

16. Practices of mismanagement by local recipients of these donations played a role in the drying up of funds. Forms of long-distance funding existed already in colonial times, but they never reached the scope of the money remittances of the 1980s.

17. Some long-distance sponsoring, mostly from Saudi Arabia, Libya, and Iran, is still effective.

18. For reasons of etiquette and respect, group members cannot oversee the *tontigi*'s handling of financial matters. This lack of accountability occasionally prompts gossip about a leader's alleged mismanagement of funds.

19. Reluctant to ask their *tontigi* for help, they mostly rely on the (weaker) financial support of other group members.

20. That women leaders refer to these sponsors in much the same fashion as ordinary group members do, as someone who offers support or "hope" (*jigi*) in times of distress, indicates that their activities are embedded in the same moral matrix of patronage as are other institutions of Islamic moral reform in Mali.

21. Future research is needed to explore the inculcation and reproduction of physically engrained norms of decency through female education in Muslim societies in Africa (see Boddy 1989; also see Comaroff and Comaroff 1992, chaps. 3, 9).

22. *Mori kalan,* the term for primary education in traditional Qur'anic schools, points to the mnemonic techniques conventionally employed in this kind of learning. For the long-standing association of writing and Islamic schooling with notions of progress in West Africa, see Wilks 1968 and Hamès 1997.

23. The complex legacy of women's learning groups signals the coexistence of overlapping paradigms of learning and relevant knowledge (Reichmuth 1994; Brenner 2001, chaps. 3, 4).

24. Sending out disciples to collect money and food has become widespread among teachers in town who no longer receive regular support (alms) from sponsors (see Tamari 1996; Hamès 1997; Loimeier 2002).

25. Incentives for attending "modern" school have changed from the prospect of upward mobility in colonial times to the present situation in which state education no longer guarantees employment in the public sector. As a consequence, many parents consider Islamic education a valuable alternative to Western schooling.

26. In Islamic higher-educational institutions in Morocco in the 1930s, peer learning was combined with knowledge transmission along master-disciple ties (Eickelman 1978, chaps. 3–5).

27. Eickelman (1978, 493) argues that this (popular and scholarly) norm contrasts with actual changes in the corpus of religious texts over time.

28. Muslim women's emphasis on intellectual improvement also contrasts with female religious socializing in Senegal that is structured by allegiances to a Sufi *shaykh*. As women are often not allowed to make a vow of obedience, their activities are oriented toward venerating and receiving blessings (*baraka*) from the *shaykh,* in exchange for their regular monetary support (Evers Rosander 1997).

29. Interviews with Aissatta Traoré Kulibali, San, August 1998; Fanta Diallo Tall, Segou, August 1999; Hadja Bintou Traoré Diakité, Segou, March 2000; and Hadja Nene Dia, Kayes, 2003.

30. Hanretta (2003) and Mann (2003) mention examples of reform-minded Muslim preachers who, in the late 1930s and late 1950s, respectively, explicitly addressed the issue of women's ritual practices. Both examples seem to suggest that women's participation in religious ritual was limited at that time. See Hanretta 2003, 2, 471–488; Mann 2003.

31. Eickelman (1978) similarly stresses the networking dimension of schooling activities that facilitated students' later professional careers.

32. A central element of modest appearance is the additional prayer shawl wrapped around a woman's head and shoulders that helps to conceal that she cannot afford to braid her hair. Newcomers, who appear at the first meeting in a *dloki ba,* a prestigious style of urban apparel, are usually (subtly) reprimanded for their alleged effort to rise above others.

33. Other Muslim women's groups are invited for dance and song performances during religious holiday, such as the Prophet's birthday (*mawlud*). The songs recount the life and deeds of the Prophet or laud the conduct of exemplary Muslim women.

34. Whereas in other groups, funds are administered by a specifically designated member, Hadja herself manages the "alms" her group receives. I received contradictory accounts of the ways Hadja used the collected money. According to Hadja, it was used to buy technical equipment for the group's musical activities and to support women in situations of crisis. Some group members, in contrast, observed that this was not the case but that there was always a chance that in the future, Hadja would "show pity," that is, use the funds to support them.

5. *Alasira,* the Path to God

1. Women frequently stress "their own responsibility to become a true Muslim" (*n'no do ko ne ka kè silame ye)* and that "nobody forced them" to embark on the "path to God" (*mògò si man n'diyagoya ka kè silame ye, a diara ne yèrè de ye k'ala sira ta*).

2. Interviews with F. Diallo, Bamako-Korofina, August 1998; N. S. Tall, Segou, March 2001; C. M. Kulubali, Segou, August 2002; R. C. Traore, San, April 2003.

3. Whereas men's songs are associated with the realm of Qur'anic schools, it is women's task to elevate the devotees' spiritual attitude during religious ceremonies. This

repartition of tasks follows a common classification of gender-specific performance genres (Schulz 2001a).

4. The proper translation of "unlawful innovation" is *bid'a makrûha,* but people in Mali refer to it simply as *bid'a.* In doing so they echo Ibn Taymiyya, the intellectual forerunner of twentieth-century revivalist trends in Egypt and Saudi Arabia who indiscriminately rejected all innovation rather than distinguishing between unlawful and "good innovation" (*bid'a hasanna*).

5. Mahmood herein draws on Asad's conceptualization of ritual as a disciplinary practice (Asad 1993, 62–79).

6. Although reluctant to openly criticize a teacher's authoritarian approach, the students ventured that a more useful course was to encourage women to assume responsibility for trying to "render one's mind receptive to the word of God" (*k'i hakili dayèlè k'ala ka kuma lamèn*).

7. Compared to Badialan 1 (where Hadja's group is located), the general standard of living is higher in Missira.

8. S*eli* denotes the ritual act of worship, in contrast to the supplicatory prayer *duwa* (Arabic, *du'a*).

9. Aiche's intellectualism is certainly related to her training as a midwife and to her present occupation as a secretary of a Malian nongovernmental organization.

10. Soares (2004) mentions itinerant preachers and their sermons but does not cite concrete examples of these sermons. I collected oral histories covering the period from the 1950s to the 1960s that report on preachers whose sermons on women's proper conduct won them a significant female clientele.

11. For Senegal and Niger, this point is forcefully demonstrated by Augis (2002); Alidou (2005); and Masquelier (2009). For studies on Egypt, Turkey, and Iran that reach similar conclusions, see El Guindi (1981, 1999); Olson (1985); MacLeod (1991, 1992); Moghadam (1991); Badran (1994); Saktanber (1994); Taraki (1995); Göle (1996); Karam (1997); and Ismail (2001, 37–38, 2003).

12. Teachers offer detailed descriptions of appropriate bodily demeanor, such as addressing seniors with downcast eyes and walking discreetly to avoid "attracting the attention [desire] of onlookers" (*ka na mogow lajarabi la*).

13. A typical expression one hears is *musoin kika de ye* ("this woman is complete").

14. Muslim women's dress is closely linked to notions of proper bodily conduct. "Dress" includes various aspects and modifications of the outer appearance, such as accessories, headdress, hairstyle, and bodily *habitus* and expression (Barnes and Eicher 1992). It is not the shape of a particular dress item per se but the way it is used to decorate and cover the body that is decisive for its significance in specific settings (see Hendrickson 1996).

15. With the spread of Islam during the colonial period, Islamic notions of decency gradually superseded and transformed conventional norms of bodily coverage. Pre-Islamic female dress codes did not require women to cover the upper part of the body. Under the influence of Islam, women *and* men covered the body more thoroughly. Today no neat distinctions exist between Islamic and other local conceptions of respectable dress.

16. New *bazin riche,* the high-prestige fabric par excellence, has a shimmering quality that fades with repeated washings. Middle- or upper-class Muslim women wear loosely cut robes made of *bazin riche* but not the three piece combination (*dloki ba*) that

demands more cloth and expenditure, and therefore reflects one's greater spending powers. Lower-class women who wear *bazin riche* usually received it as a present from relatives or friends.

17. A scarf wrapped as a turban around the head to cover a woman's hair and a skirt covering the legs beyond the knee are indicators of a more advanced age and married status (see Le Blanc 2000). But there are also a growing number of single mothers who wear this attire and thereby "stretch the limits" of its significance as a marker of marital status.

18. Costs depend on the price and origin of the fabric (locally produced or imported from Europe or Southeast Asia) and on the dress items with which they are combined, such as shoes and prayer shawls.

19. Younger or middle-aged women, when they travel in a bus or ride a motorcycle, wear such a "prayer shawl" draped lightly over the shoulders and head to protect themselves from dust and exhaust.

20. The social distribution of white attire also changes over time, with shifting fashion trends. When I began my research in 1998, white dress was worn mostly by female leaders and wealthier Muslim women. By 2002 the fashion had trickled down to the lower ranks of the renewal movement.

21. The cost of the prestigious version of the *jellaba*-style dress ranges between 120,000 and 150,000 FCFA (1,000 FCFA = U.S.$2.20).

22. The attire of male Ansar Dine members is less uniform. Many men wear a button or a cap or use stickers but male clothing with Ansar Dine emblems are less widespread than female clothes with this kind of decoration.

23. This does not preclude that many Muslim women strive for self-improvement and seek to show empathy toward "other women" whose straying from the right path they deplore.

24. Somewhat unclear is whether Robertson posits that consumption becomes a form of religious practice or that consumption is loaded with a quasi-religious meaning; he argues the latter in Garett and Robertson (1991).

6. "Proper Believers"

1. Calhoun (1992b, 4–6, 40) notes that Habermas's account oscillates between a historical analysis and a normative argument. The following refutes some of Habermas's normative assumptions.

2. Thus, *pace* Habermas, I do not assume that the "invasion" of public debate by interest groups is inimical to a diverse, "democratic" public.

3. The Bureau des Ulema was created in 1975 by Colonel Yusuf Touré, a member of the ruling military committee (Sanankoua 1991a, 139–140). Located in the national broadcast station, its primary function was to supervise religious programs in Arabic and national languages on national radio and, since September 1983, on television.

4. Regular radio and television programs include debates among Muslim intellectuals (e.g., "Causerie religieuse") and lectures on special topics (e.g., "Connaissance de l'Islam," "Les Règles de l'Islam," and "L'Islam et la vie"); special radio programs broadcast on Islamic holidays include "Spécial Ramadan" and "Rencontre avec les Ulema" (Sanankoua 1991a, 132–138).

5. The members of the Bureau des Ulemas are designated by the Ministry of Information, in deliberation with the leading representatives of AMUPI. Bureau

members thus benefit from their close relations to the AMUPI leadership (personal communication by members of the Bureau, Bamako, January 2004; see Sanankoua 1991a, 139).

6. Depending on the radio station, the fees ranged between 500 FCFA and 1,250 FCFA in 2006 (1,000 FCFA = U.S. $2.20). Preachers often seek the support of admirers to cover the broadcasting fee.

7. The patronymic Haidara claims descent from the Prophet Muhammad.

8. By denouncing his lack of scholarly erudition, these critics allude—more or less overtly—to the fact that Haidara quit the prestigious reformed Qur'anic school of Saad Oumar Touré in Segou after only a few years of enrollment.

9. Interviews with Sharif Haidara, Bankoni (Bamako), September 1998, March 2000 and January 2004.

10. Although some leading protagonists of Islamic renewal are vociferous critics of governmental policy, one should not underestimate their eagerness to seek occasional governmental support.

11. See, e.g., Larkin and Meyer 2006; on the historical specificity of the Pentecostal "prosperity gospel," see Marshall-Fratani 1998; Marshall 2009; Maxwell 1998; J. Comaroff and J. L. Comaroff 2002; and Meyer 2004.

12. Among them are decorative items in hand-woven cloth, brass, and paper, locally made dress items and accessories, bumper stickers, posters, prayer beads, and framed Qur'anic verses.

13. In 2003 prices for sermon tapes ranged from 750 to 1,250 FCFA, depending on the renown of the preacher, the locale, and the season. Prices usually increase immediately before and during the fasting month and religious holidays, when most sermons are sold.

14. Most shops keep one copy of each recorded sermon and make additional copies when requested to do so.

15. From the audio tape "Cè hakè muso kan" ("A husband's rights over his wife").

16. Haidara is not the only preacher to use these framing devices, but his sermons are among the most elaborate examples of this "hybrid" style.

17. The following argument is based on my comparison of sermons delivered by several media preachers who are currently very popular; the sermon recordings were collected by Louis Brenner during his research in the mid- and late 1980s. I thank him for generously sharing this invaluable information with me.

18. The dialogical principle works at different levels. For instance, in the sermon Kunkòlòkòrò ("skull"), recorded in 1999, Haidara sets up an imaginary dialogue with his listeners while also reporting on God's imaginary dialogue with the Prophet Mohammed and other protagonists, and, finally, on Issa's (Jesus) conversation with a skull.

19. According to local aesthetic perceptions, Haidara is sharp, witty, and "quick" in his talk. He employs concise expressions, characterizes situations and personalities quite accurately, and displays his vast store of proverbs, a skill particularly appreciated as a sign of the speaker's knowledge of "authentic" traditions.

20. Sissoko initially preached live every week. But since 1999, because of his rising popularity, his schedule has become so tight that he often asks the radio staff to broadcast one of Haidara's or his own recorded sermons. Sissoko does not pay a fee for broadcasting his sermons, but he has occasionally provided substantial financial assistance to the radio station.

21. According to a number of young men who listen to Sissoko's sermons whenever they can, Sissoko "tells good stories" that are often "much more interesting than what other radio speakers offer."

22. Interview with Sharif Haidara, Bamako-Bankoni, September 1998.

23. The rules offered advice to guide one's behavior, such as "Do not eat at public places so as not to aggravate poor people who might envy you"; "Do not stare at people who pass by the courtyard, and do not talk about them"; "Do not speak badly about other people"; "Be patient and forbearing with quarrelsome co-wives"; and "Make sure that you greet people respectfully."

24. From the audiotape " Cè hakè muso kan."

7. Consuming *Baraka,* Debating Virtue

1. Anthropological literature that offers a critical reassessment of the modernization paradigm is vast. Among the works most relevant to my argument here are Comaroff and Comaroff (1993); Geschiere (1995); Luig and Behrend (1999); Behrend (2003); and Meyer (2003).

2. Ong (1982) and McLuhan (1964) posit a fundamental difference between oral and literate societies by arguing that culturally specific hierarchies of sensual perception generate distinct analytical capacities. Although their ontologizing views of a "natural" link between forms of perception and modalities of cognition is problematic, their insistence on culturally specific modes of perception is useful for an exploration of the synesthetic nature of media engagements in Mali.

3. Whenever a woman wants to listen (or rehearse) a particular tape, she will visit the woman currently listening to the sermon recording and either borrow the tape or listen to it with the other woman.

4. Listeners who ascribe a personality to individual sermons tend to choose tapes based on the preacher's identity. Purchasing the sermon tape of a particular preacher becomes part of the listener's affiliation with him.

5. A similar privileging of a critical-cum-emancipatory agenda is evident in studies which assume that "gaining a voice" allows women to liberate themselves from oppressive power structures (e.g., Wright 1993; Weix 1998; but see Abu-Lughod 1990). It is important to avoid ontologizing assumptions about the emancipatory effects of "speech" and "voice," an assumption that is implied in Habermas's approach to debate (see Postone 1993, chap. 6).

6. Interview in Bamako-Bankoni, September 1999.

7. The expression "God has heard my request" (*n'ka delili lamèna ala fè*), for example, indicates God's acceptance of one's supplication.

8. Other frequent responses to a compelling sermon are "this really entered me" or "his speech entered my heart" (*a ye dunsun don*).

9. A similar point was made by Mai, a member of a Muslim women's group in Bamako-Missira who, in describing how she was affected by her *tontigi*'s sermons, associated the sonic and haptic experience of "being touched" with a sensation of locality constituted as a shared realm of perception.

10. *Wali* is sometimes translated as "saint," but the more apt meaning is "friend of God" (Cruise O'Brien and Coulon 1988).

11. Whereas charisma refers to a person's special powers that are a "gift of grace" (*Gottesgnadentum;* Weber 1947, 360), *baraka* is a "benign force of divine origin" that,

inherited within certain lineages, may manifest itself in the working of miracles (Cruise, O'Brien, and Coulon 1988; Triaud 1988b, 53–54; Otayek 1988, 93–95).

12. This view, however, is dismissed by other Ansar Dine members as "un-Islamic."

13. The hosts were among few families in the neighborhood who owned a television set and a video recorder. The merchant and Lele, both natives of San, often act as contacts between Ansar Dine members in San and Bamako.

14. A *pipao* is a plain one-piece robe for men that is considered a "sober," modest dress style.

15. A "four-wheel-drive," the ultimate symbol of affluence, is associated with wealthy merchants and expatriates.

16. Video screenings similar to the one described here are also held in Segou (Kimberley Davis, personal communication, May 2001).

17. This observation applies not only to Muslims who consider themselves Haidara's followers. Many Muslims who do not belong to a Sufi order share the assumption that some people's "special gifts" or genealogical descent qualifies them for spiritual leadership.

Epilogue

1. A central question that emerged from this binary approach was how to study the relationship between the universalistic principles of Islam (which are largely based on and legitimized through reference to scripture), on one side, and, on the other, the diverse, often competing or conflicting ways in which believers and practitioners throughout the Muslim world "read," adopt, and integrate guiding normative principles into ritual practice and worldly matters.

2. As mentioned in the introduction, Habermas (2005) has recently revised his earlier argument, emphasizing the role of religious values in public deliberative politics, a view that, if we follow Asad (2003) and Taylor (2007), does not go far enough.

3. Bowen distinguishes between modernist trends that place great emphasis on (publicly displayed) distinctions (from other Muslims and non-Muslims); movements that oppose existing social and religious hierarchies and "underscore the egalitarian . . . messages of 'scripturalism'"; and, finally, movements that, in a context of strong gender polarization, stress the importance of personal reform rather than the reworking of specific liturgical practices (1997, 176–177).

REFERENCES

ARCHIVAL MATERIALS

Archives Nationales du Mali, Bamako (ANM)

PUBLISHED MATERIALS

Abdelkah, Fariba. 1991. *La révolution sous le voile.* Paris: Karthala.

Abercrombie, N., S. Hill, and B. Turner. 1980. *The Dominant Ideology Thesis.* London: Allen and Unwin.

Abu-Lughod, Lila. 1986. *Veiled Sentiments. Honor and Poetry in a Bedouin Society.* Berkeley: University of California Press.

———. 1990. "The Romance of Resistance: Tracing Transformations of Power through Bedouin Women." *American Ethnologist* 17: 41–55.

———. 1995. "The Objects of Soap Opera: Egyptian Television and the Cultural Politics of Modernity." In *Worlds Apart: Modernity through the Prism of the Local,* ed. Daniel Miller, 190–210. London: Routledge.

———. 1998. "Feminist Longings and Postcolonial Conditions." In *Remaking Women: Feminism and Modernity in the Middle East,* ed. Lila Abu-Lughod, 3–31. Princeton, NJ: Princeton University Press.

———. 2002. "Do Muslim Women Really Need Saving? Anthropological Reflections on Cultural Relativism and Its Others." *American Anthropologist* 104 (3): 783–790.

———. 2005. "Dramas of Nationhood. The Politics of Television in Egypt. Chicago and London: University of Chicago Press.

Adorno, Theodor W. 1938. *Über den Fetischcharakter der Musik und die Regression des Hörens. Zeitschrift für Sozialforschung* 7: 321–356.

Afshar, Haleh, and Stephanie Barrientos. 1999. *Women, Globalization, and Fragmentation in the Developing World.* New York: St. Martin's.

Ahmed, Leila. 1992. *Women and Gender in Islam.* New Haven, CT: Yale University Press.

Alidou, Ousseina. 2005. *Engaging Modernity: Muslim Women and the Politics of Agency in Postcolonial Niger.* Madison: University of Wisconsin Press.

Allen, Richard. 1995. *To Be Continued . . . Soap Operas around the World.* London: Routledge.

Alliman, Mahamane. 1984–85. *Le mouvement wahhabite à Bamako (origine et evolution).* Mémoire de fin d'études. Ecole Normale Supérieure.

Allor, M. 1988. "Relocating the Site of the Audience." *Critical Studies in Mass Communication* 5 (3): 217–233.

al-Mughni, Haya. 1996. "Women's Organizations in Kuwait." *Middle East Report* 198: 32–35.

Amin, Samir. 1970. *L'accumulation à l'échelle mondiale; critique de la théorie du sous-développement.* Dakar: IFAN.

Amselle, Jean-Loup. 1977. *Les Négociants de la Savane.* Paris: Éditions anthropos.

———. 1985. "Le Wahhabisme à Bamako (1945–1985)." *Canadian Journal of African Studies* 19 (2): 345–357.

———. 1990. *Logiques métisses.* Paris: Éditions Payot.

Anderson, Benedict. 1991[1983]. *Imagined Communities: Reflections on the Origins and Spread of Nationalism.* London: Verso.

Anderson, Jon. 1982. "Social Structure and the Veil: Comportment and the Composition of Interaction in Afghanistan." *Anthropos* 77 (3–4): 397–420.

———. 1999. "The Internet and Islam's New Interpreters." In *New Media in the Muslim World,* ed. Dale Eickelman and Jon Anderson. Bloomington: Indiana University Press.

Ang, Ien. 1985. *Watching "Dallas": Soap Opera and the Melodramatic Imagination.* New York: Methuen.

———. 1994. "In the Realm of Uncertainty: The Global Village and Capitalist Postmodernity. In *Communication Theory Today,* ed. D. Mitchell and D. Crowell, 193–213. Cambridge: Polity.

An-Na'im, Abdullahi A. 1990. *Human Rights in Africa. Cross Cultural Perspectives.* Washington, DC: Brookings Institution.

———. 2002. *Cultural Transformation and Human Rights in Africa.* London: Zed.

Antoun, Richard. 1989. *Muslim Preacher in the Modern World. A Jordanian Case Study in Contemporary Perspective.* Princeton, NJ: Princeton University Press.

Appadurai, Arjun. 1986. *The Social Life of Things. Commodities in Cultural Perspective.* Cambridge: Cambridge University Press.

———. 1990. "Topographies of the Self: Praise and Emotion in Hindu India. In *Language and the Politics of Emotion,* ed. Lila Abu-Lughod and Catherine Lutz, 92–112. Cambridge: Cambridge University Press.

———. 1996. *Modernity at Large: Cultural Dimensions of Globalization.* Minneapolis: University of Minnesota Press.

Appadurai, Arjun, and Carol Breckenridge. 1988. "Why Public Culture?" *Public Culture* 1 (1): 5–10.

Ardener, Shirley, and Sandra Burman. 1995. *Money-Go-Rounds: The Importance of Rotating Savings and Credit Associations for Women.* Oxford: Berg.

Armbrust, Walter. 1996. *Mass Culture and Modernism in Egypt.* Cambridge: Cambridge University Press.

Asad, Talal. 1986. "The Idea of an Anthropology of Islam." Georgetown University, Center for Contemporary Arab Studies Occasional Papers Series.

———. 1993. *Genealogies of Religion.* Baltimore: John Hopkins University Press.

———. 1999. "Religion, Nation-State, Secularism." In *Nation and Religion: Perspectives on Europe and Asia.* ed. Peter van der Veer and Lehmann Hartmut, 178–192. Princeton, NJ: Princeton University Press.

———. 2003. *Formations of the Secular.* Stanford, CA: Stanford University Press.

———. 2006. "Trying to Understand French Secularism." In *Political Theologies: Public Religions in a Post-Secular World,* ed. Hent de Vries, 494–526. New York: Fordham University Press.

Ask, Karin, and Marit Tjomsland. 1998. *Women and Islamization: Contemporary Dimensions of Discourse on Gender Relations.* New York: Berg.

Askew, Kelly. 1999. "Female Circles and Male Lines: Gender Dynamics along the Swahili Coast." *Africa Today* 46 (3–4): 66–102.

Asma'u, Nana. 1997. *Collected Works of Nana Asma'u, Daughter of Usman dan Fodio.* Edited by Jean Boyd and Beverly Mack. East Lansing: Michigan State University Press.

Augis, Erin. 2002. *Dakar's Sunnite Women: The Politics of Person.* Ph.D. dissertation, University of Chicago.

Babb, Lawrence, and Susan Wadley. 1995. *Media and the Transformation of Religion in South Asia.* Philadelphia: University of Pennsylvania Press.

Badran, Margot. 1994. "Gender Activism: Feminists and Islamists in Egypt. In *Identity Politics and Women,* ed. V. Moghadam, 202–227. Boulder, CO: Westview.

Baker, Houston. 1994. "Critical Memory and the Black Public Sphere." *Public Culture* 7 (1): 3–33.

Barber, Karin. 1997. "Preliminary Notes on Audiences in Africa." *Africa* 67 (3): 347–362.

Barnes, Ruth, and Joanne Eicher. 1992. "Introduction." In *Dress and Gender: Making and Meaning,* ed. Ruth Barnes and Joanne Eicher, 1–7. Oxford: Berg.

Barthes, Roland. 1983. *The Fashion System.* New York: Hill and Yang.

Bauberot, Jean. 1990. "La laicité, quel heritage? De 1789 a nos jours." Geneva: Labor and Fides.

———. 1998. "Two Thresholds of Laicization." In *Secularism and Its Critics,* ed. Rajeev Bhargava, 94–136. Delhi: Oxford University Press.

Baudrillard, Jean. 1970. *La société de consommation.* Paris: Gallimard.

Bausinger, H. 1984. "Media, Technology, and Daily Life." *Media, Culture, and Society* 6: 43–51.

Bayart, Jean-Francois. 1989. L'État en Afrique. La politique du ventre. Paris: Fayard.

———. 1993. *Religion et modernité politique en Afrique noire. Dieu pour tous et chacun pour soi.* Paris: Karthala

———. 1996. *L'illusion identitaire.* Paris: Fayard.

———. 2000. "Africa in the World: A History of Extraversion." *African Affairs* 99: 217–267.

Behrend, Heike. 2003. "Photomagic." *Journal of Religion in Africa* 33 (2): 129–145.

Beinin, Joel, and Joe Stork. 1997. *Political Islam. Essays from Middle East Report.* London: Tauris.

Beneriá, Lourdes, and Shelley Feldman. 1992. Unequal Burden: Economic Crises, Persistent Poverty, and Women's Work. Boulder, CO: Westview.

Beneriá, Lourdes, and Martha Roldán. 1987. *The Crossroads of Class and Gender.* Chicago: University of Chicago Press.

Bennett, Tony, Colin Mercer, and Janet Woollacott. 1986. *Popular Culture and Social Relations.* Philadelphia: Open University Press.

Berkey, Jonathan. 1992. *The Transmission of Knowledge in Medieval Cairo: A Social History of Islamic Education.* Princeton, NJ: Princeton University Press.

Bernal, Victoria. 1994. "Gender, Culture, and Capitalism: Women and the Remaking of 'Islamic' Tradition in a Sudanese Village." *Comparative Studies in Society and History* 36 (1): 36–67.

Bhargava, Rajeev. 1998. "What Is Secularism For?" In *Secularism and its Critics,* ed. Rajeev Bhargava, 486–542. Delhi: Oxford University Press.

Boddy, Janice. 1989. *Wombs and Alien Spirits: Women and the Zar Cult in Northern Sudan.* Madison: University of Wisconsin Press.

———. 1992. "Bucking the Agnatic System: Status and Strategies in Rural Northern Sudan." In *In Her Prime: New Views of Middle-Aged Women,* ed. Victoria Kerns, 141–153. Urbana: University of Illinois Press.

Bourdieu, Pierre. 1979. *La distinction. Critique sociale du jugement.* Paris: Éditions du Minuit.

Bowen, John. 1989. Salat in Indonesia: The Social Meaning of an Islamic Ritual. *Man* 24 (4): 600–619.

———. 1992. "On Scriptural Essentialism and Ritual Variation: Muslim Sacrifice in Sumatra and Morocco." *American Ethnologist* 19: 656–671.

———. 1993. *Muslims through Discourse: Religion and Ritual in Gayo Society.* Princeton, NJ: Princeton University Press.

———. 1995. "The Forms Culture Takes: A State-of-the-Field Essay on the Anthropology of Southeast Asia." *Journal of Asian Studies* 54 (4): 1047–1078.

———. 1997. "Modern Intentions: Reshaping Subjectivities in an Indonesian Muslim Society." In *Politics and Religious Renewal in Muslim Southeast Asia,* ed. Robert Hefner, 157–182. Honolulu: University of Hawaii Press.

Boyd, Jean. 1989. *The Caliph's Sister: Nana Asma'u (1793–1865), Teacher, Poet, and Islamic Leader.* London: Cass.

———. 2001. "Distance Learning from Purdah in Nineteenth-Century Northern Nigeria: The Work of Asma'u Fodio." *Journal of African Cultural Studies* 14 (1): 7–22.

Boyd, Jean, and Murray Last. 1985. "The Role of Women as 'Agents Religieux' in Sokoto." *Canadian Journal of African Studies* 19 (2): 283–300.

Brand, Saskia. 2001. *Mediating Means and Fate: A Socio-Political Analysis of Fertility and Demographic Change in Bamako, Mali.* Leiden: Brill.

Brenner, Louis. 1988. "Concepts of Tariqa in West Africa: The Case of the Qadiriyya." In *Charisma and Brotherhood in African Islam,* ed. Donal B. Cruise O'Brien and Christian Coulon, 33–52. Oxford: Clarendon.

———. 1992. "The Jihad Debate between Sokoto and Borno: An Historical Analysis of Islamic Political Discourse in Nigeria." In *People and Empires in African History: Essays in Memory of Michael Crowder,* ed. J. F. Ade Ajayi, and J. D. Y. Peel, 21–44. London: Longman.

———. 1993a. "Constructing Muslim Identities in Mali." In *Muslim Identity and Social Change in Sub-Saharan Africa,* ed. Louis Brenner, 59–78. Bloomington: Indiana University Press.

———. 1993b. "La culture arabo-islamique au Mali." In *Le radicalisme islamique au sud du Sahara,* ed. René Otayek, 161–195. Paris: Karthala.

———. 1993c. "Two Paradigms of Islamic Schooling in West Africa." In *Modes de transmission de la culture religieuse en Islam,* ed. Hassan Elboudrari, 160–197. Le Caire: Institut Français d'Archéologie Orientale du Caire.

———. 1997. "Becoming Muslim in Soudan Français." In *Le temps des marabouts. Itinéraires et stratégies islamiques en Afrique occidentale française, v. 1880–1960,* ed. David Robinson and Jean-Louis Triaud, 467–492. Paris: Karthala.

———. 2000. "Sufism in Africa." In *African Spirituality. Forms, Meanings, and Expressions,* ed. Jacob K. Olupona, 324–349. New York: Crossroad.

———. 2001. *Controlling Knowledge: Religion, Power, and Schooling in a West African Muslim Society.* Bloomington: Indiana University Press.

Brenner, Louis, and Murray Last. 1985. "The Role of Language in West African Islam." *Africa* 55 (4): 433–446.

Brink, Judy, and Joan Mencher. 1997. *Mixed Blessings: Gender and Religious Fundamentalism.* New York: Routledge.

Brod, Harry, and Michael Kaufman. 1994. *Theorising Masculinities.* Thousand Oaks, CA: Sage.

Bunwaree, Sheila. 2004. "Neoliberal Ideologies, Identity, and Gender: Managing Diversity in Mauritius." In *Rights and the Politics of Recognition in Africa,* ed. Harry Englund and Francis Nyamnjoh, 148–168. New York: Palgrave.

Burrows, David. 1990. *Sound, Speech, and Music.* Amherst: University of Massachusetts Press.

Cairoli, M. Laetitia. 1998. "Factory as Home and Family: Female Workers in the Moroccan Garment Industry." *Human Organization* 57: 181–189.

Calhoun, Craig, ed. 1992a. *Habermas and the Public Sphere.* Cambridge, MA: MIT Press.

———. 1992b. "Introduction." In *Habermas and the Public Sphere,* ed. Craig Calhoun, 1–50. Cambridge, MA: MIT Press.

———. 1997. "Nationalism and the Public Sphere." In *Public and Private in Thought and Practice: Perspectives on a Grand Dichotomy,* ed. Jeff Weintraub and Krishan Kumar, 75–102. Chicago: University of Chicago Press.

―――. 1998. "The Public Good as a Social and Cultural Project." In *Private Action and the Public Good,* ed. Walter W. Powell and Elisabeth Stephanie Clemens, 20–35. New Haven, CT: Yale University Press.

Callaway, Barbara, and Lucy Creevey. 1994. *The Heritage of Islam: Women, Religion, and Politics in West Africa.* Boulder, CO: Lynne Rienner.

Campbell, Bonnie, and John Loxley. 1989. *Structural Adjustment in Africa.* London: Macmillan.

Caplan, Lionel. 1987. "Introduction: Popular Perceptions of Fundamentalism." In *Studies in Religious Fundamentalism,* ed. Lionel Caplan, 1–24. Albany: State University of New York Press.

Casanova, José. 1994. *Public Religions in the Modern World.* Chicago: University of Chicago Press.

Castells, Manuel. 1996. *The Power of Identity: Information Age, Economy, Society, and Culture.* Malden, MA: Blackwell.

Chakrabarty, Dipesh. 2000. *Provincializing Europe: Postcolonial Thought and Historical Difference.* Princeton, NJ: Princeton University Press.

Chanock, Martin. 1985. *Law, Custom, and Social Order: The Colonial Experience in Malawi and Zambia.* Cambridge: Cambridge University Press.

Chant, Sylvia. 1999. "Women-Headed Households: Global Orthodoxies and Grassroots Realities." In *Women, Globalization, and Fragmentation of the Developing World,* ed. Haleh Afshar and Stephanie Barrientos, 91–130. New York: St. Martin's.

Chatterjee, Partha. 1993. *The Nation and Its Fragments: Colonial and Postcolonial Histories.* Princeton, NJ: Princeton University Press.

Chatty, Dawn. 1997. "The Burqa Face Cover: An Aspect of Dress in Southeastern Arabia." In *The Language of Dress in the Middle East,* ed. Nancy Lindisfarne-Tapper and Bruce Ingham, 127–148. Richmond, UK: Curzon.

Chatty, Dawn, and Annika Rabo. 1997. *Organizing Women: Formal and Informal Women's Groups in the Middle East.* Oxford: Berg.

Cissé, Seydou. 1992. *L'enseignement islamique en Afrique Noire.* Paris: Éditions l'Harmattan.

Classen, Constance. 1993. *Worlds of Sense: Exploring the Senses in History and across Cultures.* New York: Routledge.

Coles, Catherine, and Beverly Mack. 1991. *Hausa Women in the Twentieth Century.* Madison: University of Wisconsin Press.

Comaroff, Jean, and John L. Comaroff. 1993. *Modernity and Its Malcontents: Ritual and Power in Postcolonial Africa.* Chicago: University of Chicago Press.

―――. 2000. "Millenial Capitalism: First Thoughts on a Second Coming." *Public Culture* 12 (2): 291–344.

―――. 2002. "Second Comings: Neoprotestant Ethics and Millenial Capitalism in South Africa, and Elsewhere." In *2000 Years and Beyond: Faith, Identity, and the Common Era,* ed. Paul Gifford, with David Archard, Trevor A. Hart, and Nigel Rapport, 106–126. London: Routledge.

———. 2004. "Criminal Obsessions, after Foucault: Postcoloniality, Policing, and the Metaphysics of Disorder." *Critical Inquiry* 30: 800–824.

Comaroff, John L. 1987. "Sui Genderis: Feminism, Kinship Theory, and Structural 'Domains.'" In *Gender and Kinship: Toward a Unified Analysis,* ed. Jane Collier and Sylvia Yanagisako, 53–85. Stanford: Stanford University Press.

———. 1998. "Reflections on the Colonial State, in South Africa and Elsewhere: Factions, Fragments, Facts and Fictions." *Social Identities* 4 (3): 321–361.

Comaroff, John L., and Jean Comaroff, eds. 1992. *Ethnography and the Historical Imagination.* Boulder, CO: Westview.

———. 1999. "Introduction." In *Civil Society and the Political Imagination in Africa: Critical Perspectives,* ed. John L. Comaroff and Jean Comaroff, 1–43. Chicago: University of Chicago Press.

———. 2004. "Criminal Justice, Cultural Justice: The Limits of Liberalism and the Pragmatics of Difference in the New South Africa." *American Ethnologist* 31 (2): 188–204.

———. 2006. "Law and Disorder in the Postcolony. An Introduction." In *Law and Disorder in the Postcolony,* ed. Jean Comaroff and John L. Comaroff, 1–56. Chicago: University of Chicago Press.

Commonwealth Secretariat. 1989. *Engendering Adjustment for the 1990s: Report of a Commonwealth Expert Group on Women and Structural Adjustment.* London: Commonwealth Secretariat.

Connell, Robert. 1995. *Masculinities.* Cambridge: Polity.

Constantin, Francois. 1987. "Condition féminine et dynamique confrérique en Afrique orientale." *Islam et Sociétés au Sud du Sahara* 1: 58–69.

Cook, Rebecca. 1994. *Human Rights of Women: National and International Perspectives.* Philadelphia: University of Pennsylvania Press.

Cooper, Barbara. 1995. "The Politics of Difference and Women's Associations in Niger: Of 'Prostitutes,' the Public, and Politics." *Signs* 20 (4): 851–882.

———. 1997. *Marriage in Maradi: Gender and Culture in a Hausa Society in Niger (1900–1989).* Portsmouth, NH: Heinemann.

Corner, J. 1995. *Television Form and Public Address.* London: Arnold.

Cornia, Giovanni A., Rolph van der Hoeven, and Thandika Mkandawire. 1992. *Africa's Recovery in the 1990s: From Stagnation and Adjustment to Human Development.* London: Macmillan.

Cornwall, Andrea, and Nancy Lindisfarne. 1994. Dislocating Masculinity. Gender, Power, and Anthropology." In *Dislocating Masculinity,* ed. Andre Cornwall and Nancy Lindisfarne, 11–47. London: Routledge.

Coulon, Christian. 1983. *Les musulmans et le pouvoir en Afrique noire: Religion et contre-culture.* Paris: Karthala.

———. 1988. "Women, Islam, and Baraka." In *Charisma and Brotherhood in African Islam,* ed. Donal B. Cruise O'Brien and Christian Coulon, 113–133. Oxford: Clarendon.

Coulon, Christian, and Odile Reveyrand-Coulon. 1990. "L'Islam au féminin: Sokhna Magat Diop Cheikh de la Confrérie Mouride (Senegal)." Centre d'Etudes d'Afrique Noire, Travaux et Document 25.

Crary, Jonathan. 1999. *Suspensions of Perception: Attention, Spectacle, and Modern Culture.* Cambridge, MA: MIT Press.

Cruise O'Brien, Donal. 1971. *The Mourides of Senegal: The Political and Economic Organisation of an Islamic Brotherhood.* Oxford: Clarendon.

Cruise O'Brien, Donal, and Christian Coulon. 1988. *Charisma and Brotherhood in African Islam.* Oxford: Clarendon.

Das, Veena. 1995. "On Soap Opera: What Kind of Anthropological Object Is It? In *Worlds Apart: Modernity through the Prism of the Local,* ed. Daniel Miller, 169–189. London: Routledge.

Dasgupta, Sudeep. 2001. "Hindu (Trans)Natlionalism: The Aura of Modernity and the Promises of Globalization." Paper presented at the conference "Religion, Media, and the Public Sphere," Amsterdam, December.

Davis, Kimberley. 2002. "Preaching to the Converted: Charismatic Leaders, Performances, and Electronic Media in Contemporary Islamic Communities." Master's thesis, Concordia University.

de Jorio, Rosa. 1997. "Female Elites, Women's Formal Associations, and Political Practices in Urban Mali, West Africa." Ph.D. dissertation, University of Illinois.

———. 2007. "Between Dialogue and Contestation: Gender, Islam, and the Challenges of a Malian Public Sphere." *Journal of the Royal Anthropological Institute* (n.s.): 95–111.

de Miras, Claude. 1987. "De l'accumulation de capital dans le secteur informel." *Cahiers des Sciences Humaines* 23 (1): 49–74.

de Vries, Hent. 2001. "In Medias Res: Global Religion, Public Spheres, and the Task of Contemporary Religious Studies." In *Religion and Media,* ed. Hent de Vries and Samuel Weber, 3–45. Stanford, CA: Stanford University Press.

de Vries, Hent, and Lawrence Sullivan. 2006. *Political Theologies: Public Religions in a Post-Secular World.* New York: Fordham University Press.

de Vries, Hent, and Samuel Weber, eds. 2001. *Religion and Media.* Stanford, CA: Stanford University Press.

de Witte, Marleen. 2003. "Altar Media's Living Word: Televised Charismatics in Ghana." *Journal of Religion in Africa* 33 (2): 172–202.

Deeb, Lara. 2006. *An Enchanted Modern: Gender and Public Piety in Shi'i Islam.* Princeton, NJ: Princeton University Press.

Dekmejian, Richard, and Margaret Wyszomirski. 1972. "Charismatic Leadership in Islam: The Mahdi of the Sudan." *Comparative Studies in Society and History* 14 (2): 193–214.

Dennerlein, Bettina. 1999. "Changing Conceptions of Marriage in Algerian Status Law." In *Perspectives on Islamic Law, Justice, and Society.* ed. R. S. Khare, 123–141. Lanham, MD: Rowman and Littlefield.

Diallo, Tidiane. 1988. "Pouvoir et marabouts en Afrique de l'Ouest." *Islam et Sociétés au Sud du Sahara* 2: 7–10.

Dilger, Hansjoerg, and Ute Luig, eds. 2010. *Morality, Hope, and Grief: Anthropologies of Aids in Africa.* Oxford: Berghahn Books.

Diouf, Made Bandé. 1981. "Les restauratrices de la zone industrielle de Dakar, ou La guerre des marmites." *Cahiers d'études africaines* 81–83 (21, 1–3): 237–250.

Douglas, Mary, and Baron Isherwood. 1979. *The World of Goods: Towards an Anthropology of Consumption.* London: Routledge.

Drobnick, Jim, ed. 2004. *Aural Cultures.* Banff, Alberta, Canada: YYZ Books.

Dunbar, Roberta Ann. 1991. "Islamic Values, the State, and "the Development of Women": The Case of Niger." In *Hausa Women in the Twentieth Century,* ed. Catherine M. Coles and Beverly Mack, 69–89. Madison: University of Wisconsin Press.

———. 2000. "Muslim Women in African History." In *The History of Islam in Africa,* ed. Nehemia Levtzion, and Randall L. Pouwels, 397–417. Athens: Ohio University Press.

Duval, Soroya. 1998. "New Veils and New Voices: Islamist Women's Groups in Egypt." In *Women and Islamization: Contemporary Dimensions of Discourse on Gender Relations,* ed. Karin Ask and Marit Tjomsland, 45–72. Oxford: Berg.

Echard, Nicole. 1991. "Gender Relationships and Religion: Women in the Hausa Bori of Niger." In *Hausa Women in the Twentieth Century,* ed. Catherine Coles and Beverly Mack, 207–220. Madison: University of Wisconsin Press.

Ehteshami, Anoushiravan, and A. Salam Sidahmed. 1996. *Islamic Fundamentalism.* Boulder, CO: Westview.

Eicher, Joanne B., and Mary Ellen Roach-Higgins. 1992. "Definition and Classification of Dress: Implications for Analysis of Gender Roles." In *Dress and Gender: Making and Meaning,* ed. Ruth Barnes and Joanne B. Eicher, 8–28. Providence, RI: Berg.

Eickelman, Dale. 1978. "The Art of Memory: Islamic Education and Its Social Reproduction." *Comparative Studies in Society and History* 20 (4): 485–516.

———. 1987. "Changing Interpretations of Islamic Movements." In *Islam and the Political Economy of Meaning: Comparative Studies of Muslim Discourse,* ed. William R. Roff, 13–30. Berkeley: University of California Press.

———. 1992. "Mass Higher Education and the Religious Imagination in Contemporary Arab Societies." *American Ethnologist* 19 (4): 643–655.

Eickelman, Dale, and Jon Anderson. 1999. "Redefining Muslim Publics." In *New Media in the Muslim World,* ed. Dale Eickelman and Jon Anderson, 1–18. Bloomington: Indiana University Press.

Eickelman, Dale, and James Piscatori. 1996. *Muslim Politics.* Princeton, NJ: Princeton University Press.

Eickelman, Dale, and Armando Salvatore. 2004. *Public Islam and the Common Good.* Leiden: Brill.

El Guindi, Fadwa. 1981. "Veiling Infitah with Muslim Ethic: Egypt's Contemporary Islamic Movement." *Social Problems* 28 (4): 465–485.

———. 1999. *Veil: Modesty, Privacy, and Resistance.* Oxford: Berg.

Elson, Diane. 1989. "The Impact of Structural Adjustment on Women: Concepts and Issues." In *The IMF, the World Bank, and the African Debt.* Vol. 2, *The Social and Political Impact,* ed. Bade Onimode, 56–74. London: Zed.

EMMU. 1992/1993. *Enquête Malienne sur les Migrations et l'Urbanisation, Rapport National Descriptif.* Bamako: Réseau Malien sur les Migrations et l'Urbanisation.

Englund, Harri. 2003. "Christian Independency and Global Membership: Pentecostal Extraversions in Malawi. *Journal of Religion in Africa* 33 (1): 83–111.

Englund, Harri, and Francis Nyamnjoh. 2004. *Rights and the Politics of Recognition in Africa.* London: Zed.

Erlmann, Veit. 2004. *Hearing Cultures. Essays on Sound, Listening, and Modernity.* Oxford: Berg.

Esposito, John. 1998 [1984]. *Islam and Politics.* Syracuse, NY: Syracuse University Press.

Evers Rosander, Eva. 1997. "Le dahira de Mam Diarra Bousso de Mbacké." In *Transforming Female Identities: Women's Organizational Forms in West Africa,* ed. Eva Evers Rosander, 160–174. Uppsala: Nordiska Afrikainstitutet.

———. 1998. "Women and Muridism in Senegal: The Case of the Mam Diarra Bousso Daira in Mbacké." In *Women and Islamization: Contemporary Dimensions of Discourse on Gender Relations,* ed. Karin Ask and Marit Tjomsland, 147–176. Oxford: Berg.

Fabian, Johannes. 1978. "Popular Culture in Africa: Findings and Conjectures." *Africa* 48 (4): 315–334.

Fall, Abdou Salam. 1995. "Relations à distance des migrants et reseaux d'insertion à Dakar." In *La ville à guichets fermés? Itinéraires, réseaux et insertion urbaine,* ed. Philippe Antoine and Diop Abdoulaye Bara, 257–275. Dakar, Senegal: IFAN/ORSTOM.

Fay, Claude. 1995. "La démocratie au Mali, ou le pouvoir en pâture." *Cahiers d'Etudes Africaines* 137 (35, 1): 19–53.

Featherstone, Mike. 1987. "Consumer Culture, Symbolic Power, and Universalism." In *Mass Culture, Popular Culture, and Social Life in the Middle East,* ed. Sami Zubaida and Georg Stauth, 17–46. Boulder, CO: Westview.

———. 1991. "Consumer Culture, Postmodernism, and Global Disorder." In *Religion and Global Order,* ed. Roland Robertson and William R. Garrett. 182–198. New York: Paragon House.

Fejes, Fred. 1984. "Critical Mass Communications Research and Media Effects: The Problem of the Disappearing Audience." *Media, Culture, and Society* 6: 219–232.

Ferguson, James. 2002. "Of Mimicry and Membership: Africans and the 'New World Society.'" *Cultural Anthropology* 17 (4): 551–569.

———. 2006. *Global Shadows: Africa in the Neoliberal World Order.* Durham, NC: Duke University Press.

Findley, Sally. 1994. "Does Drought Increase Migration? A Study of Migration from Rural Mali during the 1983–1985 Drought." *International Migration Review* 28 (3): 539–553.

Fischer, Michael, and Mehdi Abedi. 1990. *Debating Muslims.* Madison: University of Wisconsin Press.

Fish, Stanley. 1980. *Is There a Text in This Class.* Cambridge, MA: Harvard University Press.

Fiske, John. 1986. "Television: Polysemy and Popularity." *Critical Studies in Mass Communication* 3 (4): 391–408.

———. 1987. *Television Culture.* London: Methuen.

———. 1989. "Moments of Television: Neither the Text nor the Audience. In *Remote Control: Television Audiences and Cultural Power,* ed. Ellen Seiter, Hans Borchers, Gabriele Keutzner, and Eva-Maria Warth, 56–87. London: Routledge.

———. 1994. Media Matters. Everyday Culture and Political Change. Minneapolis: University of Minnesota Press.

Fortier, Corinne. 1997. "Mémorisation et audition: L'enseignement coranique chez les Maures de Mauritanie." *Islam et Sociétés au Sud du Sahara* 11: 85–105.

Fourchard, Laurent, André Mary, and René Otayek, eds. 2005. *Entreprises religieuses transnationales en Afrique de l'Ouest.* Paris: Karthala.

Fraser, Nancy. 1992. "Rethinking the Public Sphere: A Contribution to the Critique of Actually Existing Democracy." In *Habermas and the Public Sphere,* ed. Craig Calhoun, 109–142. Cambridge, MA: MIT Press.

Frazer, James. 1911–1915. *The Golden Bough. A Study in Magic and Religion.* London: Macmillan.

Freitag, Sandra. 2001. "Visions of the Nation: Theorizing the Nexus between Creation, Consumption, and Participation in the Public Sphere." In *Pleasure and the Nation,* ed. Rachel Dwyer and Christopher Pinney, 35–75. New York: Oxford University Press.

Friedman, Jonathan. 1994. "Introduction." In *Consumption and Identity,* ed. Jonathan Friedman, 1–22. London: Harwood Academic Press.

Fuglesang, Minou. 1994. *Veils and Videos: Female Youth Culture on the Kenyan Coast.* Stockholm: Stockholm Studies in Social Anthropology.

Gaffney, Patrick 1994. *The Prophet's Pulpit: Islamic Preaching in Contemporary Egypt.* Berkeley: University of California Press.

Gaonkar, Dilip Parameshwar. 1999. "On Alternative Modernities." *Public Culture* 11 (1): 1–18.

Gaonkar, Dilip Parameshwar, and Elizabeth Povinelli. 2003. "Technologies of Public Forms: Circulation, Transfiguration, Recognition." *Public Culture* 15 (3): 385–397.

Geraghty, C. 1991. *Women and Soap Opera: A Study of Prime Time Soaps.* Cambridge: Polity.

Gerami, Shahin, and Melodye Lehnerer. 2001. "Women's Agency and Household Diplomacy: Negotiating Fundamentalism." *Gender and Society* 15 (4): 556–573.

Geschiere, Peter. 1995. *Sorcellerie et politique en Afrique. La viande des autres.* Paris: Karthala.

———. 2009. *The Perils of Belonging: Autochthony, Citizenship, and Exclusion in Africa and Europe.* Chicago: University of Chicago Press.

Ghai, Dharam. 1991. *The IMF and the South: The Social Impact of Crisis and Adjustment.* London: Zed.

Ghoussoub, Mai, and Emma Sinclair-Webb. 2000. *Imagined Masculinities: Male Identity and Culture in the Modern Middle East.* London: Saqi Books.

Gifford, Paul. 1995. *The Christian Churches and the Democratisation of Africa.* Leiden: Brill.

———. 1998. *African Christianity: Its Public Role.* Bloomington: Indiana University Press.

Gillespie, Marie. 1995. *Television, Ethnicity, and Cultural Change.* London: Routledge.

Ginsburg, Faye, Lila Abu-Lughod, and Brian Larkin, eds. 2002. *Media Worlds: Anthropology on New Terrain.* Berkeley: University of California Press.

Gitelman, Lisa, and Geoffrey Pingree, eds. 2003. *New Media, 1740–1915.* Cambridge, MA: MIT Press.

Glew, Robert. 1996. "Islamic Associations in Niger." *Islam et Sociétés au Sud du Sahara* 10: 187–204.

Göle, Nilüfer. 1996. *The Forbidden Modern: Civilization and Veiling.* Ann Arbor: University of Michigan Press.

———. 2002. "Islam in Public: New Visibilities and New Imaginaries." *Public Culture* 14 (1): 173–190.

Gomez-Perez, Muriel. 1991. "Associations Islamiques à Dakar." *Islam et Sociétés au Sud du Sahara* 5: 5–19.

———. 2005. "Généalogies de l'islam reformiste au Sénégal: figures, savoirs et réseaux." In *Entreprises religieuses transnationales en Afrique de l'Ouest,* ed. Laurent Fourchard, André Mary, and René Otayek, 193–222. Paris: Karthala.

Gouvernorat du District de Bamako . 1994. *Monographie du District de Bamako.* Bamako: Gouvernorat, Cellule Technique du District.

Green, Reginald Herbold. 1989. "The Broken Pot: The Social Fabric, Economic Disaster, and Adjustment in Africa." In *The IMF, the World Bank, and the African Debt.* Vol. 2, *The Social and Political Impact,* ed. Bade Onimode, 31–55. London: Zed.

Gresh, A. 1983. L'Arabie saoudite en Afrique non arabe. *Politique Africaine* 10 (June): 55–74.

Grosz-Ngaté, Maria. 1986. "Bambara Men and women and the Reproduction of Social Life in Sana Province, Mali." Ph.D. dissertation, University of Michigan.

Gunter, Barrie. 1988. "Finding the Limits of Audience Activity." In *Communication Yearbook,* ed. Jon Anderson, 11: 108–126. Newbury Park, CA: Sage.

Gurevitch, Michael, Tony Benner, James Curran, and Janet Woollacott, eds. 1982. *Culture, Society, and the Media.* London: Methuen.

Guyer, Jane. 1981. "Household and Community in African Studies." *African Studies Review* 24 (2/3): 87–137.

Guyer, Jane, and Karen Tranberg Hansen. 2001. "Introduction: Markets in Africa in a New Era." *Africa* 71 (2): 197–201.

Habermas, Jürgen. 1990 [1962]. *Strukturwandel der Öffentlichkeit. Untersuchungen zu einer Kategorie der bürgerlichen Gesellschaft.* 2nd ed. Frankfurt am Main: Suhrkamp.

———. 2005. "Religion in the Public Sphere." *European Journal of Philosophy* 14 (1): 1–25.

Haenni, Patrick. 2002. "Les nouveaux prêcheurs égyptiens." *Religioscope* (November): 1–15.

Hagberg, Sten. 2004. "Ethnic Identification in Voluntary Associations: The Politics of Development and Culture in Burkina Faso." In *Rights and the Politics of Recognition in Africa,* ed. Harry Englund and Francis Nyamnjoh, 195–218. New York: Palgrave.

Hale, Sondra. 1997. *Gender Politics in Sudan: Islamism, Socialism, and the State.* Boulder, CO: Westview.

Hall, Stuart. 1977. "Culture, the Media, and the "Ideological Effect." In *Mass Communication and Society,* ed. James Curran, Michael Gurevitch, and Janet Woollacott, 315–348. London: Edward Arnold.

———. 1980. "Cultural Studies: Two Paradigms." *Media, Culture, and Society* 2: 57–72.

———. 1994. "Reflections on the Encoding/Decoding Model." In *Viewing, Reading, Listening: Audiences and Cultural Reception,* ed. Jon Cruz and Justin M. Lewis, 253–274. Boulder, CO: Westview.

Hamès, Constant. 1980. "Deux aspects du fondamentalisme islamique. Sa signification au Mali actuel et chez Ibn Taimîya." *Archives des Sciences Sociales des Religions* 50 (2): 177–190.

———. 1987. "*Taktub* ou la magie de l'écriture islamique. Textes Soninké à usage magique." *Arabica* 34: 305–325.

———. 1997. "L'Enseignement Islamique en Afrique de l'Ouest (Mauritanie)." In *Madrasa. La transmission du savoirs dans le monde musulman,* ed. Nicole Grandin and Marc Gaborieau, 219–228. Paris: Éditions Arguments.

Hanretta, Sean. 2003. "Constructing a Religious Community in French West Africa: The Hamawi Sufis of Yacouba Sylla." Ph.D. dissertation, Department of History, University of Wisconsin, Madison.

Hansen, Karen Tranberg, and Mariken Vaa. 2004. *Reconsidering Informality: Perspectives from Urban Africa.* Uppsala: Nordiska Afrikainstitutet.

Hansen, Thomas Blom, and Finn Stepputat. 2005. "Introduction." In *Sovereign Bodies: Citizens, Migrants, and States in the Postcolonial World,* ed. Thomas Blom Hansen and Finn Stepputat, 1–36. Princeton, NJ: Princeton University Press.

Hanson, John. 1996. *Migration, Jihad, and Muslim Authority in West Africa.* Bloomington: Indiana University Press.

Harrison, Christopher. 1988. *France and Islam in West Africa, 1860–1960.* Cambridge: Cambridge University Press.

Harvey, David. 1989. *The Condition of Postmodernity: An Enquiry into the Origins of Cultural Change.* Cambridge, MA: Blackwell.

———. 2006. *Global Capitalism. Towards a Theory of Uneven Geographical Development.* London: Verso.

Hatem, Mervat. 1994. "Egyptian Discourses on Gender and Political Liberalization: Do Secularist and Islamist Views Really Differ?" *Middle East Journal* 48 (4): 661–676.

Haynes, Jonathan, and Onookome Okome. 2000. "Evolving Popular Media: Nigerian Video Films." In *Nigerian Video Films.* ed. Jonathan Haynes, 51–88. Athens: Ohio University Center for International Studies.

Hebdige, Dick. 1979. *Subculture: The Meaning of Style.* London: Methuen.

Hefner, Robert W. 1997. "Islam in an Era of Nation-States." In *Islam in an Era of Nation-States: Politics and Religious Renewal in Muslim Southeast Asia,* ed. Robert W. Hefner and Patricia Horvatich, 3–42. Honolulu: University of Hawaii Press.

Hendrickson, Hildi. 1996. "Introduction." In *Clothing and Difference. Embodied Identities in Colonial and Post-Colonial Africa,* ed. Hildi Hendrickson. 1–16. Durham, NC: Duke University Press.

Hirschkind, Charles. 2001a. "Civic Virtue and Religious Reason: An Islamic Counterpublic." *Cultural Anthropology* 16 (1): 3–34.

———. 2001b. "Hearing Modernity: Egypt, Islam, and the Pious Ear." Paper presented at the Conference "Media, Religion, and the Public Sphere," University of Amsterdam, December.

———. 2006. *The Ethical Soundscape: Cassette Sermons and Islamic Counterpublics.* New York: Columbia University Press.

Hock, Carsten. 1998. "Muslimische Reform und staatliche Autorität in der Republik Mali seit 1960." Ph.D. dissertation, University of Bayreuth.

Hodgkin, Elizabeth. 1998 [1990]. "Islamism and Islamic Research in Africa." In *Islam et islamismes au sud du Sahara,* ed. Ousmane Kane and Jean-Louis Triaud, 197–254. Paris: Karthala.

Hodgson, Dorothy, and Sheryl McCurdy. 2001. *"Wicked" Women and the Reconfiguration of Gender in Africa.* Portsmouth, NH: Heinemann.

Hoeven, Rolph van der, and Fred van der Kraaij. 1994. *Structural Adjustment and Beyond in Sub-Saharan Africa.* London: James Currey.

Hoexter, Miriam, Shmuel Eisenstadt, and Nehemia Levtzion, eds. 2002. *The Public Sphere in Muslim Societies.* Albany: State University of New York Press.

Hoodfar, Homa. 1997. "The Veil in Their Minds and on Our Heads: Veiling Practices and Muslim Women." In *The Politics of Culture in the Shadow of Capital,* ed. Lisa Lowe and David Lloyd, 248–279. Durham, NC: Duke University Press.

Hoover, Stewart, and Knut Lundby. 1997. *Rethinking Media, Religion, and Culture.* Thousand Oaks, CA: Sage.

Hope, Kempe Ronald. 1997. *Structural Adjustment, Reconstruction, and Development in Africa.* Aldershot: Ashgate.

Horkheimer, Max, and Theodor W. Adorno. 1972. *Dialectic of Enlightenment.* New York: Seabury.

Horsfield, Peter, Mary Hess, and Adan Medrano. 2004. *Belief in Media: Cultural Perspectives on Media and Christianity.* Aldershot: Ashgate.

Howes, David. 1991. *The Varieties of Sensory Experience. A Sourcebook in the Anthropology of the Senses.* Toronto: University of Toronto Press.

———. 2004. "Sound Thinking." In *Aural Cultures,* ed. Jim Drobnick, 240–251. Toronto: YYZ Books.

Hutson, Alaine. 1999. "The Development of Women's Authority in the Kano Tijaniyya, 1894–1963." *Africa Today* 46 (3/4): 48–64.

Iken, Adelheid. 1999. *Women-Headed Households in Southern Namibia: Causes, Patterns, and Consequences.* Frankfurt: IKO-Verlag für Interkulturelle Kommunikation.

Ilumoka, Adetoun. 1994. "African Women's Economic, Social, and Cultural Rights— Toward a Relevant Theory and Practice." In *Human Rights of Women: National and International Perspectives,* ed. Rebecca Cook 307–324. Philadelphia: University of Pennsylvania Press.

Ingham, Bruce. 1997. "Men's Dress in the Arabian Peninsula: Historical and Present Perspectives." In *The Language of Dress in the Middle-East,* ed. Nancy Lindisfarne-Tapper and Bruce Ingham, 40–54. Richmond, Surrey: Curzon.

Institut des Sciences Humaines. 1984. *Exode des femmes du Mali: Main-d'oeuvre domés-tique féminine à Bamako et Segou.* Bamako: Institut des Sciences Humaines.

Ismail, Salwa. 2001. "The Paradox of Islamist Politics." *Middle East Report* 221: 34–39.

———. 2003. *Rethinking Islamist Politics: Culture, the State, and Islamism.* London: Tauris.

Jacquemot, Pierre, and Elsa Assidon. 1988. *Exchange Rate Policy and Adjustment in Africa: The Experience of 16 Countries in Africa South of the Sahara and in the Indian Ocean.* Paris: Ministry of Cooperation and Development.

Jacques, Gloria. 1997. "Structural Adjustment and the Poverty Principle in Africa." In *Structural Adjustment, Reconstruction, and Development in Africa,* ed. Ronald Hope Kempe Sr., 107–121. Aldershot: Ashgate.

Jalal, Ayesha. 1991. "The Convenience of Subservience: Women and the State of Pakistan." In *Women, Islam, and the State,* ed. Deniz Kandiyoti, 77–114. London: Macmillan.

Jameson, Fredric. 1984. "Postmodernism, or the Cultural Logic of Late Capitalism." *New Left Review* 146: 59–92.

Janson, Marloes. 2008. "Renegotiating Gender: Changing Moral Practice in the Tabligh Jamaat in the Gambia." *Journal for Islamic Studies,* special issue: *Reconfiguring Gender Relations in Muslim Africa,* ed. Marloes Janson and Dorothea Schulz, 28: 9–36.

Jeune Afrique. 2000. "Mali-Une république à part." *L'Intelligent* 2083 (December): 12–18.

Joseph, Suad. 1991. "Elite Strategies for State Building: Women, Family, Religion, and the State in Iraq and Lebanon." In *Women, Islam, and the State,* ed Deniz Kandiyoti, 176–200. London: Macmillan.

———. 1997. "Gender and Civil Society (interview with Joe Stork)." In *Political Islam: Essays from Middle East Report,* ed. Joel Beinin and Joe Stork, 64–82. London: Tauris.

Joseph, Terri Brint. 1980. "Poetry as a Strategy of Power: The Case of Riffian Berber Women." *Signs* 5 (3): 418–434.

Kaba, Lansiné. 1974. *The Wahhabiyya: Islamic Reform and Politics in French West Africa.* Evanston, IL: Northwestern University Press.

———. 1976. "The Politics of Quranic Education among Muslim Traders in the Western Sudan: The Subbanu Experience." *Revue Canadienne des Etudes Africaines/Canadian Journal of African Studies* 10 (3): 409–421.

———. 2000. "Islam in West Africa: Radicalism and the New Ethic of Disagreement, 1960–1990." In *The History of Islam in Africa,* ed. Nehemia Levtzion and Randall L. Pouwels, 189–208. Athens: Ohio University Press.

Kamalkhani, Zahra. 1998. "Reconstruction of Islamic Knowledge and Knowing: A Case of Islamic Practices among Women in Iran." In *Women and Islamization: Contemporary Dimensions of Discourse on Gender Relations,* ed. Karin Ask and Marit Tjomsland, 177–194. Oxford: Berg.

Kandiyoti, Deniz. 1988. "Bargaining with Patriarchy." *Gender and Society* 2 (3): 274–290.

———. 1991a. "Introduction." In *Women, Islam, and the State,* ed. Deniz Kandiyoti, 3–21. London: Macmillan.

———. 1991b. "End of Empire: Islam, Nationalism, and Women in Turkey." In *Women, Islam, and the State,* ed. Deniz Kandiyoti, 22–48. London: Macmillan.

———. 1994. "The Paradoxes of Masculinity: Some Thoughts on Segregated Societies." In *Dislocating Masculinities,* ed. Andrea Cornwall and Nancy Lindisfarne, 197–213. London: Routledge.

———. 1997. "Beyond Beijing: Obstacles and Prospects for the Middle East." In *Muslim Women and the Politics of Participation: Implementing the Beijing Platform.* Mahnaz Afkhami and Erika Friedl, 3–10. Syracuse, NY: Syracuse University Press.

Kane, Ousmane. 1997. "Muslim Missionaries and African States." In *Transnational Religion and Fading States,* ed. Susanne H. Rudolph and James Piscatori, 47–62. Boulder, CO: Westview.

———. 2003. *Muslim Modernity in Postcolonial Nigeria: A Study of the Society for the Removal and the Reinstatement of Tradition.* Leiden: Brill.

Kane, Ousmane, and Jean-Louis Triaud. 1998. "Introduction." In *Islam et islamismes au sud du Sahara,* ed. Ousmane Kane and Jean-Louis Triaud 5–30. Paris: Karthala.

Karam, A. 1997. "Women, Islamisms, and the State: Dynamics of Power and Contemporary Feminisms in Egypt." In *Muslim Women and the Politics of*

Participation: Implementing the Beijing Platform, ed. Mahnaz Afkhami and Erika Friedl, 18–28. Syracuse, NY: Syracuse University Press.

Kepel, Gilles. 2000. *Jihad: Expansion et déclin de l'Islamisme.* Paris: Gallimard.

Kerns, Victoria, and Judith Brown. 1992. *In Her Prime: New Views of Middle-Aged Women.* Urbana: University of Illinois Press.

Kintz, Linda, and Julia Lesage. 1998. *Media, Culture, and the Religious Right.* Minneapolis: University of Minnesota Press.

Kleiner-Bosaller, Anke, and Roman Loimeier. 1994. "Radical Muslim Women and Male Politics in Nigeria." In *Gender and Identity in Africa,* ed. M. Reh and G. Ludwar-Ene 61–69. Hamburg: LIT.

Kuenyehia, Akua. 1994. "The Impact of Structural Adjustment Programs on Women's International Human Rights: The Example of Ghana." In *Human Rights of Women: National and International Perspectives,* ed. Rebecca Cook, 422–436. Philadelphia: University of Pennsylvania Press.

———. 1998. *Women and Law in West Africa: Situational Analysis of Some Key Issues Affecting Women.* Legon: University of Ghana.

Lachaud, Jean-Pierre. 1994. *Pauvreté et marché du travail urbain en Afrique subsaharienne: analyse comparative.* Geneva: International Institute for Labour Studies.

Lamarre, Jules, and Marc Miller. 2000. "Une approche organisationelle de la pauvrété." *Travail, capital et société* 33 (1): 76–106.

Lambek, Michael. 1992. "Motherhood and Other Careers in Mayotte (Comoro Islands)." In *In Her Prime: New Views of Middle-Aged Women,* ed. Virginia. Kerns and Judith K. Brown, 77–92. Urbana: University of Illinois Press.

———. 1993. *Knowledge and Practice in Mayotte: Local Discourses of Islam, Sorcery, and Spirit Possession.* Toronto: University of Toronto Press.

Lambert, Agnès. 1993. "Les commerçantes maliennes du chemin de fer Dakar-Bamako." In *Grands Commerçants d'Afrique de l'Ouest,* ed. Grégoire Emmanuel and Labazée Pascal 37–70. Paris: Karthala.

Lambert de Frondeville, Agnès. 1987. "Une alliance tumultueuse: les commerçantes maliennes du Dakar-Niger et les agents de l'État." *Cahiers des Sciences Humaines* 23 (1): 89–103.

Lamphere, Louise, Patricia Zavella, Felipe Gonzalez, and Peter Evans. 1993. *Sunbelt Working Mothers: Reconciling Family and Factory.* Ithaca, NY: Cornell University Press.

Landes, Joan. 1995. "The Public and the Private Sphere." In *Feminists Read Habermas: Gendering the Subject of Discourse,* ed. Johanna Meehan, 91–116. New York: Routledge.

Larkin, Brian. 1997. "Indian Films and Nigerian Lovers: Media and the Creation of Parallel Modernities." *Africa* 67 (3): 419–440.

———. 2008. *Signal and Noise: Media, Infrastructure, and Urban Culture in Nigeria.* Durham, NC: Duke University Press.

Larkin, Brian, and Birgit Meyer. 2006. "Pentecostalism, Islam, and Culture: New Religious Movements in West Africa." In *Themes in West African History*, ed. Emmanuel Akyeampong, 286–311. Oxford: James Currey.

Last, Murray. 1974. "Reform in West Africa: The Jihad Movements of the Nineteenth Century." In *History of West Africa*, ed. J. F. A. Ajayi and M. Crowder, 2:1–27. London: Longman.

———. 1988. "Charisma and Medicine in Northern Nigeria." In *Charisma and Brotherhood in African Islam*, ed. Christian Coulon and Donal Cruise O'Brien, 179–198. Oxford: Clarendon.

———. 1992. "'Injustice' and Legitimacy in the Early Sokoto Caliphate." In *People and Empires in African History: Essays in Memory of Michael Crowder*, ed. J. F. A. Ayaji and John Peel, 45–58. London: Longman.

Launay, Robert. 1992. *Beyond the Stream: Islam and Society in a West African Town*. Berkeley: University of California Press.

———. 1997. "Spirit Media: The Electronic Media and Islam among the Dyula of Northern Côte d'Ivoire." *Africa* 67 (3): 441–453.

Launay, Robert, and Benjamin Soares. 1999. "The Formation of an 'Islamic sphere' in French Colonial West Africa." *Economy and Society* 28 (3): 467–489.

LeBlanc, Marie-Nathalie. 1998. "Youth, Islam, and Changing Identities in Bouaké, Côte d'Ivoire." Ph.D. dissertation, University of London.

———. 1999. "The Production of Islamic Identities through Knowledge Claims in Bouaké, Côte d'Ivoire." *African Affairs* 98 (393): 485–509.

———. 2000. "Versioning Womanhood and Muslimhood: 'Fashion' and the Life Course in Contemporary Bouaké, Côte d'Ivoire." *Africa* 70 (3): 442–481.

Lee, Benjamin, and Edward LiPuma. 2002. "Cultures of Circulation. Imaginations of Modernity." *Public Culture* 14 (1): 191–213.

LeRoy, Etienne. 1995. "Thirty Years of Legal Practice in the Shadow of the State: The Taming of Leviathan." In *State and Society in Francophone Africa since Independence*, ed. Anthony Kirk-Greene and Daniel Bach, 34–45. Oxford: St. Martin's.

Lee, Benjamin. 1993. "Going Public." *Public Culture* 5: 165–178.

Lee, Benjamin, and Edward LiPuma. 2002. "Cultures of Circulation: The Imaginations of Modernity." *Public Culture* 14 (1): 191–213.

Lemarchand, Réné. 1992. "Uncivil States and Civil Societies: How Illusion Became Reality." *Journal of Modern African Studies* 30 (2): 177–191.

Levin, David. 1993. *Modernity and the Hegemony of Vision*. Berkeley: University of California Press.

Levtzion, Nehemia. 1986a. "Rural and Urban Islam in West Africa: An Introductory Essay." *Asian and African Studies* 20: 7–26.

———. 1986b. "Merchants versus Scholars and Clerics in West Africa: Differential and Complementary Roles." *Asian and African Studies* 20: 27–43.

————. 2000. "Islam in the Bilad al-Sudan to 1800." In *History of Islam in Africa,* ed. Nehemia Levtzion and Randall Pouwels, 63–92. Athens: Ohio University Press.

Liebes, Tamar, and Elihu Katz. 1990. *The Export of Meaning: Cross-Cultural Readings of "Dallas."* Oxford: Oxford University Press.

Lindholm, Charles. 1990. *Charisma.* Cambridge, MA: Blackwell.

Lindisfarne-Tapper, Nancy, and Bruce Ingham. 1997. "Approaches to the Study of Dress in the Middle East." In *The Language of Dress in the Middle East,* ed. Nancy Lindisfarne-Tapper and Bruce Ingham, 1–39. Richmond, Surrey: Curzon.

Lindlof, Thomas. 1988. "Media Audiences as Interpretive Communities." In *Communication Yearbook,* ed. Jon Anderson, 11:81–107. Newbury Park, CA: Sage.

Lindsay, Lisa, and Stephan Miescher. 2003. *Men and Masculinities in Modern Africa.* Portsmouth, NH: Heinemann.

Lipschutz, Ronnie. 1992. "Reconstructing World Politics: The Emergence of Global Civil Society." *Millenium: Journal of International Studies* 2 (3): 391–410.

Little, Kenneth. 1965. *West African Urbanization: A Study of Voluntary Associations in Social Change.* Cambridge: Cambridge University Press.

Livingstone, Sonia. 1998. "Relationships between Media and Audiences: Prospects for Audience Reception Studies." In *Media, Ritual, and Identity,* ed. T. Liebes and J. Curran, 237–255. London: Routledge.

Locoh, Thérèse. 1988. "Le rôle des familles dans l'accueil des migrants vers les villes africaines." In *Dakar: L'insertion urbaine des migrants en Afrique,* ed. P. S. C. Antoine, 21–33. Paris: ORSTOM.

————. 1995. *Familles africaines, population et qualité de la vie.* Paris: INED-CEPED.

Logan, Ikubolajeh Bernard, and Kidane Mengisteab. 1993. "IMF-World Bank Adjustment and Structural Transformation in Sub-Saharan Africa." *Economic Geography* 69 (1): 1–24.

Loimeier, Roman. 1997. *Islamic Reform and Political Change in Northern Nigeria.* Evanston, IL: Northwestern University Press.

————. 2001. *Säkulärer Staat und islamische Gesellschaft. Die Beziehungen zwischen Staat, Sufi-Bruderschaften und islamischer Reformbewegung in Senegal im 20.* Hamburg: LIT Verlag.

————. 2002. "Je veux etudier sans mendier: The Campaign against the Qur'anic Schools in Senegal." In *Social Welfare in Muslim Societies,* ed. H. Weiss, 118–137. Stockholm: Nordiska Afrikainstitutet.

————. 2003. "Patterns and Peculiarities of Islamic Reform in Africa." *Journal of Religion in Africa* 33 (3): 237–262.

Loizos, Peter. 1994. "A Broken Mirror: Masculine Sexuality in Greek Ethnography." In *Dislocating Masculinity,* ed. Andre Cornwall and Nancy Lindisfarne, 66–81. London: Routledge.

Lomnitz, Larissa Adler. 1977. *Networks and Marginality: Life in a Mexican Shantytown.* New York: Academic Press.

Lowe, Donald. 1982. *History of Bourgeois Perception.* Chicago: University of Chicago Press.

Luig, Ute, and Heike Behrend. 1999. *Spirit Possession, Modernity, and Power in Africa.* Madison, WI: University of Wisconsin Press.

Lukács, Georg. 1968. *Geschichte und Klassenbewußtsein. Studien über marxistische Dialektik.* Berlin, Neuwied: Luchterhand.

MacInnes, John. 1998. *The End of Masculinity: The Confusion of Sexual Genesis and Sexual Difference in Modern Society.* Philadelphia: Open University Press.

Mack, Beverly, and Jean Boyd. 1997. *A Woman's Jihad. Nana Asma'u, Scholar and Scribe.* Bloomington: Indiana University Press.

MacLeod, Arlene Elowe. 1991. *Accommodating Protest.* Cairo: American University in Cairo Press.

———. 1992. "Hegemonic Relations and Gender Resistance: The New Veiling as Accommodating Protest in Cairo." *Signs* 17 (3): 533–557.

Mah, Harold. 2000. "Phantasies of the Public Sphere: Rethinking the Habermas of the Historians." *Journal of Modern History* 72: 153-182.

Mahmood, Saba. 2001. "Feminist Theory, Embodiment, and the Docile Agent: Some Reflections on the Egyptian Islamic Revival." *Cultural Anthropology* 16 (2): 202–236.

———. 2005. *Politics of Piety: The Islamic Revival and the Feminist Subject.* Princeton, NJ: Princeton University Press.

Mamdani, Mahmood. 1996. *Citizen and Subject: Contemporary Africa and the Legacy of Late Colonialism.* London: James Currey.

———. 2000. *Beyond Rights Talk and Culture Talk: Comparative Essays on the Politics of Rights and Culture.* Cape Town: David Philip.

———. 2004. *Good Muslim, Bad Muslim: America, the Cold War, and the Roots of Terror.* New York: Pantheon Books.

Mankekar, Purnima. 1999. *Screening Culture, Viewing Politics: An Ethnography of Television, Womanhood, and Nation in Postcolonial India.* Durham, NC: Duke University Press.

Manley, Andrew. 1997. "The Sosso and the Haidara: Two Muslim Lineages in Soudan français, 1890–1960." In *Le temps des marabouts. Itinéraires et stratégies islamiques en Afrique occidentale française v. 1880–1960,* ed. David Robinson and Jean-Louis Triaud, 319–336. Paris: Karthala.

Mann, Gregory. 2003. "Old Soldiers, Young Men: Masculinity, Islam, and Military Veterans in Late 1950s Soudan Français (Mali)." In *Men and Masculinities in Modern Africa,* ed. Lisa Lindsay and Stephan Miescher, 69–81. Portsmouth, NH: Heinemann.

———. 2006. *Native Sons: West African Veterans and France in the Twentieth Century.* Durham, NC: Duke University Press.

Mansbridge, Jane. 1998. "On the Contested Nature of the Public Good." In *Private Action and the Public Good,* ed. Walter W. Powell and Elisabeth Stephanie Clemens, 3–19. New Haven, CT: Yale University Press.

Manuel, Peter. 1993. *Cassette Culture*. Chicago: University of Chicago Press.

Marfaing, Laurence, and Mariam Sow. 1999. *Les operateurs économiques au Senegal: Entre le formel et l'informel, 1930–1996*. Paris: Karthala.

Marks, Laura. 2000. *The Skin of Film: Intercultural Cinema, Embodiment, and the Senses*. Durham, NC: Duke University Press.

Marshall, Ruth. 2009. *Political Spiritualities. The Pentecostal Revolution in Nigeria*. Chicago: University of Chicago Press.

Marshall, Susan. 1984. "Paradoxes of Change: Culture Crisis, Islamic Revival, and the Reactivation of Patriarchy." *Journal of Asian and African Studies* 19 (1–2): 1–17.

Marshall-Fratani, Ruth. 1998. "Mediating the Global and the Local in Nigerian Pentecostalism." *Journal of Religion in Africa* 28 (3): 27–315.

Martín-Barbero, Jesus. 1997. "Mass Media as a Site of Resacralization of Contemporary Cultures." In *Rethinking Media, Religion, and Culture*, ed. Stewart M. Hoover and Knut Lunby, 102–116. Thousand Oaks, CA: Sage.

Marty, Martin, and R. Scott Appleby. 1993a. *Fundamentalisms and Society: Reclaiming the Sciences, the Family, and Education*. Chicago: University of Chicago Press.

———. 1993b. *Fundamentalisms and the State: Remaking Politics, Economies, and Militance*. Chicago: University of Chicago Press.

Masquelier, Adeline. 1999. "Debating Muslims, Disputed Practices: Struggles for the Realization of an Alternative Moral Order in Niger." In *Civil Society and the Political Imagination in Africa: Critical Perspectives*, ed. John L. Comaroff and Jean Comaroff, 218–250. Chicago: University of Chicago Press.

———. 2009. *Women and Islamic Revival in a West African Town*. Bloomington: Indiana University Press.

Mauss, Marcel. 1967. *The Gift: Forms and Functions of Exchange in Archaic Societies*. New York: Norton.

Maxwell, David. 1998. "'Delivered from the Spirit of Poverty': Pentecostalism, Prosperity and Modernity in Zimbabwe." *Journal of Religion in Africa* 28 (3): 350–373.

Mayoukou, Célestin. 1994. *Le système des tontines en Afrique. Un système bancaire informel. Le cas du Congo*. Paris: Éditions l'Harmattan.

Mazzarella, William. 2004. "Internet X-Ray: E-Governance, Transparency, and the Politics of Immediation in India." *Public Culture* 18 (3): 473–505.

Mbembe, Achilles. 1992. "The Banality of Power and the Aesthetics of Vulgarity in the Postcolony." *Public Culture* 4 (2): 1–30.

Mbow, Penda. 1997. "Les femmes, l'Islam et les associations religieuses au Senegal." In *Transforming Female Identities*. Eva Evers Rosander, 148–159. Uppsala: Nordiska Afriainstituet.

McCartney, Andra. 2004. "Soundscape Works, Listening, and the Touch of Sound." In *Aural Cultures*, ed. Jim Drobnick, 179–185. Toronto: YYZ Books.

McCormick, Dorothy. 1996. "Women in Business: Class and Nairobi's Small and Medium-Sized Producers." In *Courtyards, Markets, City Streets*, ed. Kathleen Sheldon, 193–211. Boulder, CO: Westview.

McDannell, Colleen. 1995. *Material Christianity: Religion and Popular Culture in America.* New Haven, CT: Yale University Press.

McDougall, Ann. 1986. "The Economics of Islam in the Southern Sahara: The Rise of the Kunta Clan." *Asian and African Studies* 20: 45–60.

McLuhan, Marshall. 1964. *Understanding Media. The Extensions of Man.* New York: McGraw-Hill.

Meillassoux, Claude. 1968. *Urbanization of an African Community: Voluntary Associations in Bamako.* Seattle: University of Washington Press.

Mendel, Milos. 1995. "The Concept of 'ad-Da'wa al-Islamiya': Towards a Discussion of the Islamic Reformist Religio-Political Terminology." *Archív Orientální* 63: 286–304.

Mendieta, Eduardo, ed. 2005. *The Frankfurt School on Religion: Key Writings by the Major Thinkers.* New York: Routledge.

Mengistaeb, Kidane, and B. Ikubolajeh Logan, eds. 1995. *Beyond Economic Liberalization in Africa: Structural Adjustment and the Alternatives.* London: Zed.

Mernissi, Fatima. 1988. "Muslim Women and Fundamentalism." *Middle East Report* (July–August): 8ff.

Messick, Brinkley. 1987. "Subordinate Discourse: Women, Weaving, and Gender Relations in North Africa." *American Ethnologist* 14 (2): 210–225.

Metcalf, Barbara. 1995. "Islam and Women: The Case of the Tablighi Jama'at." *Stanford Humanities Review* 5 (1): 51–59.

Meyer, Birgit. 1998. "The Power of Money: Politics, Occult Forces, and Pentecostalism in Ghana." *African Studies Review* 41 (3): 16–38.

———. 2003. "Ghanaian Popular Cinema and the Magic in and of Film." In *Magic and Modernity: Interfaces of Revelation and Concealment,* ed. Birgit Meyer and Peter Pels, 200–221. Stanford: Stanford University Press.

———. 2004. "'Praise the Lord': Popular Cinema and Pentecostalite Style in Ghana's New Public Sphere." *American Ethnologist* 31 (1): 92–110.

———. 2006. "Religious Revelation, Secrecy, and the Limits of Representation." *Anthropological Theory* 6 (4): 631–653.

———. 2011. "Going and Making Public: Some Reflections on Pentecostalism as Public Religion in Ghana." In *Christianity and Public Culture in Africa,* ed. Harri Englund, 148–163. Athens: Ohio University Press.

Meyer, Birgit, and Annelies Moors. 2006. "Introduction." In *Religion, Media, and the Public Sphere,* ed. Birgit Meyer and Annelies Moors, 1–25. Bloomington: Indiana University Press.

Meyer, Birgit, and Peter Geschiere. 1999. *Globalization and Identity: Dialectics of Flow and Closure.* Malden, MA: Blackwell.

Miescher, Stephan. 2005. *Making Men in Ghana.* Bloomington: Indiana University Press.

Miller, Daniel. 1992. "The Young and the Restless in Trinidad: A Case of the Local and the Global in Mass Consumption." In *Consuming Technologies,* ed. Roger Silverstone and Eric Hirsch. 152–181. London: Routledge.

———. 1994. *Modernity: An Ethnographic Approach.* Providence, RI: Berg.

———. 1995a. *Worlds Apart: Modernity through the Prism of the Local.* London: Routledge.

———. 1995b. Introduction: Anthropology, Modernity, Consumption. In *Worlds Apart: Modernity through the Prism of the Local,* ed. D. Miller, 1–22. London: Routledge.

———. 1995c. "Consumption as the Vanguard of History: A Polemic by Way of Introduction." In *Acknowledging Consumption: A Review of New Studies,* ed. D. Miller, 1–57. London: Routledge.

Mir-Hosseini, Ziba. 1999. *Islam and Gender.* Princeton, NJ: Princeton University Press.

Miran, Marie. 1998. "Le Wahhabisme à Abidjan: Dynamisme urbain d'un islam reformiste en Côte d'Ivoire contemporaine (1960–1996)." *Islam et sociétés au Sud du Sahara* 12: 5–74.

———. 2005. "D'Abidjan à Porto Novo: Associations islamiques et culture religieuse réformiste sur la Côte de Guinée." In *Entreprises religieuses transnationales en Afrique de l'Ouest,* ed. Laurent Fourchard, André Marty, and René Otayek, 43–72. Paris: Karthala.

Mirza, Jasmin. 2002. *Between Chaddor and the Market.* Oxford: Oxford University Press.

Mitchell, Jolyon. 1999. *Visually Speaking: Radio and the Renaissance of Preaching.* Louisville, KY: Westminster John Knox Press.

Mitchell, W. J. Thomas. 1994. *Picture Theory: Essays on Verbal and Visual Representation.* Chicago: University of Chicago Press.

Moghadam, Valentine. 1991. "Islamist Movements and Women's Responses in the Middle East." *Gender and History* 3 (3): 268–284.

———. 1992. "Revolution, Islam, and Women: Sexual Politics in Iran and Afghanistan." In *Nationalisms and Sexualities,* ed. Andrew Parker, Mary Russo, and Patricia Yaeger, 424–446. New York: Routledge.

———. 1994. *Gender and National Identity: Women and Politics in Muslim Societies.* Atlantic Highlands, NJ: Zed.

Molyneux, Maxine. 1991. "The Law, the State, and Socialist Policies with Regard to Women: The Case of the People's Republic of Yemen, 1967–1990." In *Women, Islam, and the State,* ed. Deniz Kandiyoti, 237–271. London: Macmillan.

Mommersteeg, Geert. 1991. "L'education coranique au Mali: Le pouvoir des mots sacrés." In *L'enseignement islamique au Mali,* ed. Louis Brenner, 44–61. Bamako: Jamana.

Monteil, Vincent-Monsour. 1980. *L'Islam Noir: Une religion à la conquête de l'Afrique.* Paris: Éditions du Seuil.

Moore, Laurence. 1994. *Selling God: American Religion in the Marketplace of Culture.* New York: Oxford University Press.

Moors, Annelies. 1991. "Women and the Orient: A Note on Difference." In *Constructing Knowledge: Authority and Critique in Social Sciences,* ed. Lorraine Nencel and Peter Pels, 114–122. London: Sage.

————. 1999. "Debating Islamic Family Law: Legal Texts and Social Practices." In *Social History of Women and Gender in the Modern Middle East,* ed. Margaret Meriwether and Judith Tucker, 141–176. Boulder, CO: Westview.

Morgan, David. 1999. *Protestants and Pictures: Religion, Visual Culture, and the Age of American Mass Production.* Oxford: Oxford University Press.

Morley, David. 1980. *The Nationwide Audience: Structure and Decoding.* London: British Film Institute.

————. 1986. *Family Television: Cultural Power and Domestic Leisure.* London: Comedia.

Morley, David, and Roger Silverstone. 1990. "Domestic Communication: Technologies and Meanings." *Media, Culture, and Society* 12 (1): 31–55.

Morris, Rosalind. 1995. "All Made Up: Performance Theory and the New Anthropology of Sex and Gender." *Annual Review of Anthropology* 24: 567–592.

2002. "A Room with a Voice: Mediation and Mediumship in Thailand's Information Age." In *Media Worlds: Anthropology on New Terrain,* ed. Faye D. Ginsburg, Lila Abu-Lughod, and Brian Larkin, 383–397. Berkeley: University of California Press.

Mrázek, Rudolf. 1997. "Let Us Become Radio Mechanics: Technology and National Identity in Late-Colonial Netherlands East Indies." *Comparative Studies in Society and History* 39 (1): 3–33.

Murdock, Graham. 1997. "The Re-enchantment of the World: Religion and the Transformations of Modernity." In *Rethinking Media, Religion, and Culture,* ed. Stewart M. Hoover and Knut Lunby, 85–101. Thousand Oaks, CA: Sage.

Nagata, Judith. 2001. "Beyond Theology: Toward an Anthropology of Fundamentalism." *American Anthropologist* 103 (2): 481–498.

Nageeb, Salma Ahmed. 2004. *New Spaces and Old Frontiers: Women, Social Space, and Islamization in Sudan.* Lanham, MD: Lexington Books.

Navaro-Yashin, Yael. 2002. *Faces of the State: Secularism and Public Life in Turkey.* Princeton, NJ: Princeton University Press.

Negt, Oskar, and Alexander Kluge. 1993. *The Public Sphere and Experience.* Minneapolis: University of Minnesota Press.

Niezen, R. W. 1990. "The 'Community of Helpers of the Sunna': Islamic Reform among the Songhay of Gao (Mali)." *Africa* 60 (3): 399–424.

Norval, Aletta. 1996. "Thinking Identities: Against a Theory of Ethnicity." In *The Politics of Difference: Ethnic Premises in a World of Power,* ed. Edwin N. Wilmsen and Patrick McAllister, 59–70. Chicago: University of Chicago Press.

Olson, Emelie. 1985. "Muslim Identity and Secularism in Contemporary Turkey: 'The Headscarf Debate.'" *Anthropological Quarterly* 58 (4): 161–169.

Öncü, Ayse. 2006. "Becoming 'Secular Muslims': Yasar Nuri Öztürk as a Supersubject on Turkish Television." In *Religion, Media, and the Public Sphere,* ed. Birgit Meyer and Annelies Moors, 227–550. Bloomington: Indiana University Press.

Ong, Aihwa. 1987. *Spirits of Resistance and Capitalist Discipline: Factory Women in Malaysia.* Albany: State University of New York Press.

———. 1990. "State versus Islam: Malay Families, Women's Bodies, and the Body Politic in Malaysia." *American Ethnologist* 17 (2): 258–276.

Ong, Walter. 1982. *Orality and Literacy: The Technologizing of the World.* London: Routledge.

Ortner, Sherry, and Harriet Whitehead, eds. 1981. *Sexual Meanings: The Cultural Construction of Gender and Sexuality.* Cambridge: Cambridge University Press.

Otayek, René. 1988. "Muslim Charisma in Burkina Faso." In *Charisma and Brotherhood in African Islam,* ed. Donal B. Cruise O'Brien and Christian Coulon, 91–112. Oxford: Clarendon.

———. 1993. *Le radicalisme islamique au sud du Sahara.* Paris: Karthala.

Ouzgane, Lahoucine, and Robert Morell. 2005. *African Masculinities: Men in Africa from the Late Nineteenth Century to the Present.* New York: Palgrave Macmillan.

Palmer, Ingrid. 1991. *Gender and Population in the Adjustment of African Economies: Planning for Change.* Geneva: International Labor Office.

Panos Institute. 1993. *Radio Pluralism in West Africa: A Survey Conducted by the Panos Institute in Paris and l'Union des Journalistes d'Afrique de l'Ouest.* Vol. 3. Paris: Institut Panos and L'Harmattan.

Parry, Jonathan, and Maurice Bloch. 1989. *Money and the Morality of Exchange.* Cambridge: Cambridge University Press.

Penacchioni, Irene. 1984. "The Reception of Popular Television in Northeast Brazil." *Media, Culture, and Society* 6: 337–341.

Pinney, Christopher. 2004. *Photos of the Gods: The Printed Image and Political Struggle in India.* London: Reaktion Books.

Piscatori, James. 1996. *Islam in a World of Nation-States.* Cambridge: Cambridge University Press.

Plate, Brent. 2003. "Introduction. Filmmaking, Mythmaking, Culture Making." In *Representing Religion in World Cinema: Filmmaking, Mythmaking, Culture Making,* ed. S. Brent Plate, 1–18. New York: Palgrave Macmillan.

Postone, Moishe. 1992. "Political Theory and Historical Analysis." In *Habermas and the Public Sphere,* ed. Craig Calhoun, 164–180. Cambridge, MA: MIT Press.

———. 1993. *Time, Labor, and Social Domination: A Reinterpretation of Marx's Critical Theory.* Cambridge: Cambridge University Press.

———. 1999. "Contemporary Historical Transformations: Beyond Postindustrial Theory and Neo-Marxism." *Current Perspectives in Social Theory* 19: 3–53.

Potash, Betty. 1986. *Widows in African Societies: Choices and Constraints.* Stanford: Stanford University Press.

Poya, Mariam. 1999. *Women, Work, and Islamism: Ideology and Resistance in Iran.* London: Zed.

Projet Urbain du Mali (PUM). 1984. *Etude du Développement Urbain de Bamako. Programmation Décennale des Investissements.* Bamako: Ministère de l'Interieur, Direction du Projet Urbain du Mali.

Rajagopal, Arvind. 2001. *Politics after Television: Religious Nationalism and the Reshaping of the Public in India.* Cambridge: Cambridge University Press.

Randeria, Shalini. 2007. "The State of Globalization: Legal Plurality, Overlapping Sovereignties, and Ambiguous Alliances between Civil Society and the Cunning State in India." *Theory, Culture, and Society* 24 (1): 1–33.

Rassam, Amal. 1980. "Women and Domestic Power in Morocco." *International Journal of Middle East Studies* 12 (2): 171–191.

Rebhun, Linda Ann. 1999. *The Heart Is Unknown Country: Love in the Changing Economy of Northeast Brazil.* Stanford, CA: Stanford University Press.

Reichmuth, Stefan. 1994. "Islamic Learning and 'Western Education' in Nigeria: Concepts, Institutions, and Conflicts." In *Échanges Franco-Allemands sur l'Afrique,* ed. János Riesz and Helene d'Almeida-Topor, 175–184. Bayreuth: Bayreuth African Studies Series.

———. 1996. "Education and the Growth of Religious Associations among Yoruba Muslims—The Ansar-ud-Deen Society in Nigeria." *Journal of Religion in Africa* 26 (4): 364–405.

———. 2000. "Islamic Education and Scholarship in Sub-Saharan Africa." In *The History of Islam in Africa, ed.* Nehemia Levtzion, and Randall L. Pouwels, 419–440. Athens: Ohio University Press.

Renders, Marleen. 2002. "An Ambiguous Adventure: Muslim Organisations and the Discourse of 'Development' in Senegal." *Journal of Religion in Africa* 32 (1): 61–82.

Reveyrand-Coulon, Odile. 1993. "Les énoncés féminins de l'Islam." In *Religion et modernité politique en Afrique Noire. Dieu pour tous et chacun pour soi,* ed. Jean-François Bayart, 63–100. Paris: Karthala.

Ridd, Rosemary. 1994. "Separate but More Than Equal: Muslim Women at the Cape." In *Muslim Women's Choices: Religious Belief and Social Reality,* ed. Camilla Fawzi El-Solh and Judy Mabro, 85–107. Providence, RI: Berg.

Riddel, Barry. 1992. "Things Fall Apart Again: Structural Adjustment Programmes in Sub-Saharan Africa." *Journal of Modern African Studies* 30 (1): 53–68.

Riesebrodt, Martin. 2000. *Die Rückkehr der Religionen. Fundamentalismus und der "Kampf der Kulturen."* Munich: Beck.

Risse, Thomas, Stephen Ropp, and Kathryn Sikkink. 1999. *The Power of Human Rights: International Norms and Domestic Change.* Cambridge: Cambridge University Press.

Robbins, Joel. 2007. "Continuity Thinking and the Problem of Christian Culture: Belief, Time, and the Anthropology of Christianity." *Current Anthropology* 48 (1): 5–38.

Roberts, Richard. 1988. "The End of Slavery in the French Sudan, 1905–1914." In *The End of Slavery in Africa,* ed. Suzanne Miers and Richard Roberts, 282–306. Madison: University of Wisconsin Press.

———. 1991. "The Case of Faama Mademba Sy and the Ambiguities of Legal Jurisdiction in Early Colonial French Sudan." In *Law in Colonial Africa,* ed. Richard L. Roberts and Kristin Mann, 185–204. Portsmouth, NH: Heinemann.

———. 2006. *Litigants and Households: African Disputes and Colonial Courts in the French Sudan, 1895–1912.* Portsmouth, NH: Heinemann.

Robertson, Roland. 1991. "Globalization, Modernization, and Postmodernization: The Ambiguous Position of Religion." In *Religion and Global Order*, ed. Roland Robertson and William R. Garrett, 281–291. New York: Paragon House.

Robins, Kevin 1996. *Into the Image. Culture and Politics in the Field of Vision.* London: Routledge.

Robinson, David. 1985. *The Holy War of Umar Tal: The Western Sudan in the Mid-Nineteenth Century.* Oxford: Clarendon.

———. 1988. "French 'Islamic' Policy and Practice in Late Nineteenth-Century Senegal." *Journal of African History* 29 (3): 415–435.

———. 1992. "Ethnography and Customary Law in Senegal." *Cahiers d'Etudes Africaines* 136 (32, 3): 221–237.

———. 2000. "Revolutions in the Western Sudan." In *History of Islam in Africa*, ed. Nehemia Levtzion and Randall Pouwels, 131–152. Athens: Ohio University Press.

Robinson, David, and Jean-Louis Triaud. 1997. *Le temps des marabouts. Itinéraires et strategies islamiques en Afrique occidentale française, v. 1880–1960.* Paris: Karthala.

Roff, William. 1987. *Islam and the Political Economy of Meaning: Comparative Studies of Muslim Discourse.* Berkeley: University of California Press.

Rondeau, Chantal. 1989. "Les restauratrices de la nuit à Bamako (Mali)." *Travail, capital et société* 22 (2): 262–286.

Roost Vischer, Lilo. 1997. *Muetter zwischen Herd und Markt: das Verhaeltnis von Mutterschaft, sozialer Elternschaft und Frauenarbeit bei den Moose (Mossi) in Ouagadougou/Burkina Faso.* Basel: Ethnologisches Seminar der Universitaet und Museum der Kulturen.

Roth, Claudia. 1994. *Und sie sind stolz: Zur Ökonomie der Liebe. Die Geschlechtertrennung bei den Zara in Bobo-Dioulasso, Burkina Faso.* Frankfurt am Main: Brandes and Apsel.

Roy, Olivier. 1994. *The Failure of Political Islam.* Cambridge, MA: Harvard University Press.

Rugh, Andrea. 1986. *Reveal and Conceal: Dress in Contemporary Egypt.* Syracuse, NY: Syracuse University Press.

Saktanber, Ayse. 1994. "Becoming the "Other" as a Muslim in Turkey: Turkish Women vs. Islamist Women." *New Perspectives on Turkey* 11: 99–134.

Salam Sidahmed, and Anourshiravan Ehteshami. 1996. *Islamic Fundamentalism.* Boulder, CO: Westview.

Salama, P. 1998. "Des pauvrétés en général et de la pauvreté en particulier dans le tiers-monde: évaluations et mésures." In *L'insoutenable misère du monde*, ed. Richard Poulin and Pierre Salama, 35–64. Hull, Québec: Éditions Vents d'Ouest.

Salvatore, Armando. 1998. "Staging Virtue: The Disembodiment of Self-Correctness and the Making of Islam as Public Norm." *Yearbook of the Sociology of Islam* 1: 87–120.

———. 1999. "Global Influences and Discontinuities in a Religious Tradition: Public Islam and the 'New' Sari'a." In *Dissociation and Appropriation: Responses to Globalization in Asia and Africa,* ed. Katja Füllberg-Stolberg, Petra Heidrich, and Ellinor Schöne, 211–234. Berlin: Das Arabische Buch.

Salvatore, Armando, and Dale Eickelman. 2004. *Public Islam and the Common Good.* Leiden: Brill.

Sanankoua, Bintou. 1985. "Les ecoles 'coraniques' au Mali: Problèmes actuels." *Canadian Journal of African Studies* 19 (2): 359–367.

———. 1991a. "L'enseignement islamique à la radio et la television au Mali." In *L'enseignement islamique au Mali,* ed. Bintou Sanankoua, 127–142. Bamako: Éditions Jamana.

———. 1991b. "Les associations féminines musulmanes à Bamako." *In L'enseignement islamique au Mali,* ed. Bintou Sanankoua, 105–126. Bamako: Éditions Jamana.

Sarr, Dominique, and Richard Roberts. 1991. "The Jurisdiction of Muslim Tribunals in Colonial Senegal, 1857–1932." In *Law in Colonial Africa,* ed. Richard L. Roberts and Kristin Mann 131–145. Portsmouth, NH: Heinemann.

Sassen, Saskia. 1996. *Losing Control? Sovereignty in an Age of Globalization.* New York: Columbia University Press.

Saul, Mahir, and Patrick Royer. 2001. *West African Challenge to Empire: Culture and History in the Volta-Bani Anticolonial War.* Athens: Ohio University Press.

Schafer, Murray. 1977. *The Tuning of the World.* Toronto: McClelland and Stewart.

Schildkrout, Enid. 1983. "Dependence and Autonomy: The Economic Activities of Secluded Hausa Women in Kano." In *Female and Male in West Africa,* ed. Christine Oppong, 107–126. London: George Allen.

Schmidt, Leigh E. 2000. *Hearing Things: Religion, Illusion, and the American Enlightenment.* Cambridge, MA: Harvard University Press.

Schneider, Jane. 1971. "Of Vigilance and Virgins: Honor, Shame, and Access to Resources in Mediterranean Societies." *Ethnology* 10 (1): 1–24.

Schulz, Dorothea E. 1998. "Morals of Praise: Broadcast Media and the Commoditization of Jeli Praise Performances in Mali." *Research in Economic Anthropology* 19: 117–133.

———. 1999a. "Pricey Publicity, Refutable Reputations: *Jeliw* and the Economics of Honour in Mali." *Paideuma* 45: 275–292.

———. 1999b. "In Pursuit of Publicity: Talk Radio and the Imagination of a Moral Public in Mali." *Africa Spectrum* 99 (2): 161–185.

———. 2000. "Communities of Sentiment: Local Radio Stations and the Emergence of New Spheres of Public Communication in Mali." In *Neue Medien und Öffentlichkeiten. Politik und Tele-Kommunikation in Asien, Afrika, und Lateinamerika,* ed. S. Brühne, 2:36–62. Hamburg: Übersee Institut.

———. 2001a. *Perpetuating the Politics of Praise: Jeli Praise Singers, Radios, and Political Mediation in Mali.* Cologne: Rüdiger Köppe.

———. 2001b. "Music Videos and the Effeminate Vices of Urban Culture in Mali." *Africa* 71 (3): 325–337.

———. 2002. "'The World is Made by Talk': Female Fans, Popular Music, and New Forms of Public Sociality in Urban Mali." *Cahiers d'etudes africaines* 68 (42[2]): 797–829.

———. 2003a. "'Charisma and Brotherhood' Revisited: Mass-Mediated Forms of Spirituality in Urban Mali. *Journal of Religion in Africa* 33 (2): 146–171.

———. 2003b. "Political Factions, Ideological Fictions: The Controversy over the Reform of Family Law in Democratic Mali." *Islamic Law and Society* 10 (1): 132–164.

———. 2005. "Love Potions and Money Machines: Commercial Occultism and the Reworking of Social Relations in Urban Mali." In *Wari Matters: Ethnographic Exploration of Money in the Mande World,* ed. Stephen Wooten, 93–115. Hamburg: LIT.

———. 2006a. "Morality, Community, 'Public-ness': Shifting Terms of Debate in the Malian Public." In *Religion, Media, and the Public Sphere,* ed. Birgit Meyer and Annelies Moors, 132–151. Bloomington: Indiana University Press.

———. 2006b. "Promises of (Im)mediate Salvation. Islam, Broadcast Media, and the Remaking of Religious Experience in Mali." *American Ethnologist* 33 (2): 210–229.

———. 2007a. Competing Sartorial Assertions of Femininity and Muslim Identity in Mali." *Fashion Theory* 11 (2/3): 253–280.

———. 2007b. "Drama, Desire, and Debate: Mass-Mediated Subjectivities in Urban Mali." *Visual Anthropology* 20 (1): 19–39.

———. 2008a. "Piety's Manifold Embodiments: Muslim Women's Quest for Moral Renewal in Mali." *Journal for Islamic Studies* 28: 66–90.

———. 2008b. "'Channeling' the Powers of God's Word. Audio-Recordings as Scriptures in Mali." *Postscripts* 4 (2): 135–156.

Schulze, Reinhard. 1993. "La da'wa saoudienne en Afrique de l'Ouest." In *Le radicalisme islamique au sud du Sahara,* ed. R. Otayek, 21–35. Paris: Karthala.

Sciama, Lidia. 1992. "Lacemaking in Venetian Culture." In *Dress and Gender: Making and Meaning,* ed. Ruth Barnes and Joanne B. Eicher, 121–144. Providence, RI: Berg.

Scott, Alan. 1997. *The Limits of Globalization. Cases and Arguments.* London: Routledge.

Scott, David, and Charles Hirschkind. 2006. *Powers of the Secular Modern: Talal Asad and His Interlocutors.* Stanford, CA: Stanford University Press.

Seaman, William. 1992. "Active Audience Theory: Pointless Populism." *Media, Culture, and Society* 14: 301–311.

Seesemann, Rüdiger. 1999. "'Where East Meets West.' The Development of Qur'anic Education in Darfur." *Islam et Sociétés au Sud du Sahara* 13: 41–61.

Segal, L. 1993. "Changing Men: Masculinities in Context." *Theory and Society* 22: 625–641.

Seidler, Victor. 1991. *Recreating Sexual Politics: Men, Feminism, and Politics.* London: Routledge.

————. 1992. *Men, Sex, and Relationships.* London: Routledge.

Shaheed, F. 1995. "Networking for Change: The Role of Women's Groups in Initiating Dialogue on Women's Issues." In *Faith and Freedom: Women's Human Rights in the Muslim World,* ed. M. Afkhami, 78–103. London: Tauris.

Sheldon, Kathleen, ed. 1996. *Courtyards, Markets, City Streets: Urban Women in Africa.* Boulder, CO: Westview.

Shivji, Issa. 1999. "Constructing a New Rights Regime: Promises, Problems, and Prospects." *Social and Legal Studies* 8: 253–276.

Simone, Abdou Maliq. 2003. "Reaching the Larger World: New Forms of Social Collaboration in Pikine, Senegal." *Africa* 73 (2): 226–250.

Skinner, Quentin. 1998. *Liberty before Liberalism.* Cambridge: Cambridge University Press.

Smith, Mary. 1954. *Baba of Karo: A Woman of the Muslim Hausa.* New Haven, CT: Yale University Press.

Soares, Benjamin. 2004. "Islam and Public Piety in Mali." In *Public Islam and the Common Good,* ed. Armando Salvatore and Dale F. Eickelman, 205–226. Leiden: Brill.

————. 2005. *Islam and the Prayer Economy: History and Authority in a Malian Town.* Ann Arbor: University of Michigan Press.

————. 2006. "Islam in Mali in the Neoliberal Age." *African Affairs* 105: 77–95.

Soares, Benjamin, and Réné Otayek. 2007. *Islam and Muslim Politics in Africa.* New York: Palgrave Macmillan.

Sobchack, Vivian. 2004. *Carnal Thoughts: Embodiment and Moving Image Culture.* Berkeley: University of California Press.

Sottas, Beate, and Lilo Roost Vischer. 1995. *Überleben im afrikanischen Alltag: Improvisationstechniken im ländlichen und städtischen Bereich.* Bern: Peter Lang.

Spitulnik, Debra. 1993. "Anthropology and Mass Media." *Annual Review of Anthropology* 22: 293–315.

2002. "Mobile Machines and Fluid Audiences: Rethinking Reception through Zambian Radio Culture." In *Media Worlds: Anthropology on New Terrain,* ed. Faye Ginsburg, Lila Abu-Lughod, and Brian Larkin, 337–354. Berkeley: University of California Press.

————. 2000. "Media Connections and Disconnections: Radio Culture and the Public Sphere in Zambia." Book manuscript.

Sreberny, Annabelle. 2000. "The Global in the Local in International Communications." In *Mass Media and Society,* ed. James Curran and Michael Gurevitch, 93–119. London: Edward Arnold.

Sreberny-Mohammadi, Annabelle, and Ali Mohammadi. 1994. *Small Media, Big Revolution: Communication, Culture, and the Iranian Revolution.* Minneapolis: University of Minnesota Press.

Starrett, Gregory. 1995. "The Hexis of Interpretation: Islam and the Body in the Egyptian Popular School." *American Ethnologist* 22 (4): 953–969.

Stewart, Charles. 1973. *Islam and Social Order in Mauritania.* Oxford: Clarendon.

———. 1997. "Colonial Justice and the Spread of Islam in the Early Twentieth Century." In *Le temps des marabouts. Itinéraires et strategies islamiques en Afrique occidentale francaise, v. 1880–1960,* ed. David Robinson and Jean-Louis Triaud, 53–66. Paris: Karthala.

Stitcher, Sharon, and Jane Parpart. 1988. *Patriarchy and Class: African Women in the Home and the Workforce.* Boulder, CO: Westview.

Stolow, Jeremy. 2005. "Religion and/as Media." *Theory, Culture, and Society* 22 (4): 119–145.

———. 2006. "Communicating Authority, Consuming Tradition: Jewish Orthodox Outreach Literature and Its Reading Public." In *Religion, Media, and the Public Sphere,* ed. Birgit Meyer and Annelies Moors, 73–90, Bloomington: Indiana University Press.

Stout, Daniel, and Judith Buddenbaum. 1996. *Religion and Mass Media.* Thousand Oaks, CA: Sage.

Stowasser, Barbara. 1994. *Women in the Qur'an, Traditions, and Interpretation.* New York: Oxford University Press.

Strobel, Margaret. 1976. "From Lelemama to Lobbying: Women's Associations in Mombasa, Kenya." In *Women in Africa: Studies in Social and Economic Change,* ed. Nancy J. Hafkin and Edna G. Bay, 185–211. Stanford, CA: Stanford University Press.

———. 1979. *Muslim Women in Mombasa, 1890–1975.* New Haven, CT: Yale University Press.

Sule, Barbara, and Priscilla Starratt. 1991. "Islamic Leadership Positions for Women in Contemporary Kano Society." In *Hausa Women in the Twentieth Century,* ed. Catherine M. Coles and Beverly Mack, 29–49. Madison: University of Wisconsin Press.

Tamari, Tal. 1996. "L'exegese coranique (tafsir) en milieu Mandingue. Rapport preliminaire sur une recherche sur le terrain." *Islam et Sociétés au Sud du Sahara* 10: 43–79.

———. 2003. "Islamic Higher Education in West Africa: Some Examples from Mali." In *Islam in Africa,* ed. Thomas Bierschenk and George Stauth, 91–128. Hamburg: LIT.

Taraki, Lisa. 1995. "Islam Is the Solution: Jordanian Islamists and the Dilemma of the 'Modern Woman.'" *British Journal of Sociology* 46 (4): 643–661.

Taussig, Michael. 1980. *The Devil and Commodity Fetishism in South America.* Chapel Hill: University of North Carolina Press.

Taylor, Charles. 1992. *Multiculturalism and the "Politics of Recognition."* Princeton, NJ: Princeton University Press.

———. 2002. "Modern Social Imaginaries." *Public Culture* 14 (1): 91–124.

———. 2007. *A Secular Age.* Cambridge, MA: Harvard University Press.

Tayob, Abdulkader. 1999. *Islam in South Africa: Mosques, Imams, and Sermons.* Gainesville: University Press of Florida.

Teltscher, Susanne. 1992. "Small Trade and the World Economy: Informal Vendors in Quito, Equador." *Economic Geography* 70 (2): 167–187.

Thomas-Emeagwali, Gloria. 1995. *Women Pay the Price: Structural Adjustment in Africa and the Carribean.* Trenton, NJ: Africa World Press.

Tomasevsky, Katarina. 1993. *Development Aid and Human Rights: A Study for the Danish Center of Human Rights.* London: Pinter.

Traoré, Alpha Boubacar. 1979. "Réinsertion d'un quartier spontané de Bamako au Mali. Mémoire de maîtrise." Masters thesis, University of Paris VIII.

Trevor, Jean. 1975. "Western Education and Muslim/Fulani Women in Sokoto, Northern Nigeria." In *Conflict and Harmony in Education in Tropical Africa,* ed. Godfrey J. Brown and Mervyn Hiskett, 247–270. London: Allen and Unwin.

Triaud, Jean-Louis. 1985. "Les agents religieux islamiques en Afrique tropicale: réflexions autour d'un thème." *Canadian Journal of African Studies* 19 (2): 271–282.

———. 1986a. "Le thème confrérique en Afrique de l'ouest. Essai historique et bibliographique." In *Les ordres mystiques dans l'Islam. Cheminements et situation actuelle,* ed. Alexandre Popovic and Gilles Veinstein, 271–282. Paris: Éditions de l'EHESS.

———. 1986b. "Abd al-Rahman l'Africain (1908–1957), pionnier et precurseur du wahhabisme au Mali." In *Radicalismes islamiques,* ed. Olivier Carré and Paul Dumont 2: 162–180. Paris: Harmattan.

———. 1987. "Les chemins de l'islamologue." In *Les voies de l'islam en Afrique Orientale,* ed. François Constantin, 9–17. Paris: Karthala.

———. 1988a (after Fodé Doumbia). "Bamako, la ville aux deux cents mosquées, ou la victoire du 'secteur informel' islamique." *Islam et Sociétés au Sud du Sahara* 2 (1): 166–177.

———. 1988b. *Khalwa and the Career of Sainthood: An Interpretative Essay.* In *Charisma and Brotherhood in African Islam,* ed. Donal B. Cruise O'Brien and Christian Coulon, 53–66. Oxford: Clarendon.

———. 1997. "Introduction." In *Le temps des marabouts. Itinéraires et strategies islamiques en Afrique occidentale française, v. 1880–1960,* ed. David Robinson and Jean-Louis Triaud, 11–29. Paris: Karthala.

———. 2000. "Islam in Africa under French Colonial Rule." In *History of Islam in Africa,* ed. Nehemia Levtzion and Randall Pouwels, 169–189. Athens: Ohio University Press.

Triaud, Jean-Louis, and David Robinson, ed. 2000. *La Tijaniyya: une confrerie musulmane à la conquête de l'Afrique.* Paris: Karthala.

Umar, Muhammad S. 2001. "Education and Islamic Trends in Northern Nigeria, 1970s–1990s." *Africa Today* 48 (2): 127–150.

———. 2004. "Mass Islamic Education and the Emergence of Female Ulama in Northern Nigeria: Background, Trends, and Consequences." In *The Transmission of Learning in Islamic Africa,* ed. Scott S. Reese, 99–120. Leiden: Brill.

Vaa, Mariken, Sally Findley, and Assitan Diallo. 1989. "The Gift Economy: A Study of Women Migrants' Survival Strategies in a Low-Income Bamako Neighborhood." *Travail, capital et société* 22 (2): 234–260.

Van der Veer, Peter. 1995. "The Secular Production of Religion." *Etnofoor* 8 (2): 5–14.

Vaughan, Megan. 1983. "Which Family? Problems in the Reconstruction of the History of the Family as an Economic and Cultural Unit." *Journal of African History* 24: 275–283.

Vicor, Knut. 2002. "Sufism and Social Welfare in the Sahara." In *Social Welfare in Muslim Societies in Africa,* ed. H. Weiss, 80–97. Stockholm: Nordiska Afrikainstituet.

Villalón, Leonardo. 1995. *Islamic Society and State Power in Senegal: Disciples and Citizens in Fatick.* Cambridge: Cambridge University Press.

Warner, Michael. 1990. *The Letters of the Republic.* Cambridge, MA: Harvard University Press.

———. 2002. "Publics and Counterpublics." *Public Culture* 14 (1): 49–90.

Watson, Helen. 1994. "Women and the Veil: Personal Responses to Global Process. In *Islam, Globalization, and Postmodernity,* ed. Akbar S. Ahmed and Hastings Donnan, 141–159. London: Routledge.

Weber, Max. 1947. *The Theory of Social and Economic Organization.* Edited by Talcott Parsons. New York: Oxford University Press.

Weber, Samuel. 2001. "Religion, Repetition, Media." In *Religion and Media,* ed. Hent de Vries and Samuel Weber 43–55. Stanford, CA: Stanford University Press.

Weintraub, Jeff, and Krishan Kumar. 1997. *Public and Private in Thought and Practice: Perspectives on a Grand Dichotomy.* Chicago: University of Chicago Press.

Weiss, Brad. 1996. *The Making and Unmaking of the Haya Lived World: Consumption, Commoditization, and Everyday Practice.* Durham, NC: Duke University Press.

Weiss, Holger. 2002. "Reorganising Social Welfare among Muslims: Islamic Voluntarism and Other Forms of Communal Support in Northern Ghana." *Journal of Religion in Africa* 32 (1): 83–109.

Weix, Gretchen G. 1998. "Islamic Prayer Groups in Indonesia: Local Forums and Gendered Responses." *Critique of Anthropology* 18 (4): 405–420.

Wendl, Tobias. 2004. *Africa Screams: Das Böse in Kino, Kunst, und Kult.* Wuppertal: Peter Hammer.

Werbner, Pnina, and Helene Basu. 1998. *Embodying Charisma: Modernity, Locality, and the Performance of Emotion in Sufi Cults.* London: Routledge.

Werbner, Richard. 2004. *Reasonable Radicals and Citizenship in Botswana: The Public Anthropology of Katanga Elites.* Bloomington: Indiana University Press.

Westerlund, David. 1997. "Reaction and Action: Accounting for the Rise of Islamism." In *African Islam and Islam in Africa: Encounters between Sufis and Islamists,* ed. Eva Evers Rosander and David Westerlund, 308–334. London: Hurst.

Weston, Kath. 1993. "Lesbian/Gay Studies in the House of Anthropology." *Annual Review of Anthropology* 22: 339–367.

Wikan, Unni. 1982. *Behind the Veil in Arabia: Women in Oman.* Baltimore, MD: Johns Hopkins University Press.

———. 1996. *Tomorrow, God Willing: Self-Made Destinies in Cairo.* Chicago: University of Chicago Press.

Wilk, Richard. 2002. "Television, Time, and the National Imagery in Belize." In *Media Worlds: Anthropology on New Terrain,* ed. Faye Ginsburg, Lila Abu-Lughod, and Brian Larkin, 171–188. Berkeley: University of California Press.

Wilks, Ivor. 1968. "The Transmission of Islamic Learning in the Western Sudan." In *Literacy in Traditional Societies,* ed. J. Goody 162–197. Cambridge: Cambridge University Press.

Willemse, Karin. 2001. *"One Foot in Heaven": Narratives on Gender and Islam in Darfur, West-Sudan.* Leiden: Colofon.

Williams, Raymond. 1991. "Base and Superstructure in Marxist Cultural Theory." In *Rethinking Popular Culture: Contemporary Perspectives in Cultural Studies,* ed. Chandra Mukerji and Michael Schudson, 407–423. Berkeley: University of California Press.

Willis, John. 1979. *Studies in West African Islamic History.* Vol. 1, *The Cultivators of Islam.* London: Cass.

Wilmsen, Edwin, and Patrick McAllister. 1996. *The Politics of Difference: Ethnic Premises in a World of Power.* Chicago: University of Chicago Press.

Wolf, Diane. 1992. *Factory Daughters: Gender, Household Dynamics, and Rural Industrialization in Java.* Berkeley: University of California Press.

Worby, Eric. 1998. "Tyranny, Parody, and Ethnic Polarity: Ritual Engagements with the State in Northwestern Zambia." *Journal of Southern African Studies* 24: 561–578.

Wright, Marcia. 1993. *Strategies of Slaves and Women: Life Stories from East/Central Africa.* New York: Barber.

Yamani, Mai. 1997. "Changing the Habits of a Lifetime: The Adaptation of Hejazi Dress to the New Social Order." In *The Language of Dress in the Middle East,* ed. Nancy Lindisfarne-Tapper and Bruce Ingham, 55–66. Richmond, Surrey: Curzon.

Yazbeck Haddad, Yvonne, and John Esposito. 1998. *Islam, Gender, and Social Change.* New York: Oxford University Press.

Zaman, Muhammad Quasim. 2002. *The Ulema in Contemporary Islam: Custodians of Change.* Princeton, NJ: Princeton University Press.

Zaret, David. 1992. "Religion, Science, and Printing in the Public Spheres in Seventeenth-Century England." In *Habermas and the Public Sphere,* ed. Craig Calhoun, 212–235. Cambridge, MA: MIT Press.

Zubaida, Sami. 1989. *Islam, the People, and the State: Essays on Political Ideas and Movements in the Middle East.* London: Tauris.

Zuhur, Sherifa. 1992. *Revealing Reveiling: Islamist Gender Ideology in Contemporary Egypt.* Albany: State University of New York Press.

INDEX

Page numbers in italics refer to illustrations.

suras and, 120, 141; Muslim elite consciousness and, 138; Muslim women's groups and, 5, 110, 115–116, 118, 142; of religious brokers, 250n13; sermon listening and, 213, 214; as source of interpretive authority, 191; spread of, 122–123

Arabic-speaking world, 111, 146; commercial ties to, 179; exchange with, 27; fashion accessories imported from, 165; financial support from, 13, 236; institutions of higher learning in, 33, 138; intellectual trends in, 109, 122; Malian women in, 150; Mali's history of engagement with, 46; Muslim activists of Mali and, 34–35; radio preachers and, 176; reactionary influences from, 24; Salafiyya reformist discourse in, 29; trade connections to, 114, 180

Asad, Talal, 130, 256n2

Association of the Servants of God (Association Serviteurs d'Allah), 106

audiences, 15, 16, 240n35; diversity of responses from, 79; media theory and, 85; "strong model" of activity by, 84

audio cassettes, xii, xiii, 2, 77; Haidara's sermons on, 175; interpretive communities and, 226; sermons delivered on, 181

audio-recording technologies, 196–197, 198, 199, 201, 221, 228; charisma and, 224; common experience and, 216–217; spiritual experience facilitated by, 220

authenticity, cultural, 46, 89, 156, 218, 230; law reform and, 43, 45; policing of women and, 137

Bamako, city of, x, 111, 133, 237n1 (chap 1); Badialan neighborhood, 62, 98, 126, 131, 136, 142, 161, 252n7; in colonial period, 28; Grand Mosque, 157, 187, 197; Hamdalaye neighborhood, 98, 197; history of Islamic renewal in, xi; Lafiabougou neighborhood,

98; lifestyle of television serials and, 82; low-income neighborhoods, 62, 64–65; on map, *xvi;* middle-class neighborhoods, 13, 206, 222; migrants in, 48, 246nn6,7; Missira neighborhood, 147, 153, 157, 228, 252n7, 255n9; Muslim women's groups in, xiii, 189, 196, 209, 228; promise of easier life in, 50; public visibility of Islam in, 2; *Radio Islamique,* 39; radio stations, 177, 178; rural-urban migration in, 49; television reception in, 76

Bamana (Bamanakan) language, xiii, 152, 166, 223, 237n2 (preface), 238n6; Qur'an translated into, 190–191; sermon tapes in, 213

Bamana people, 28

baraji (spiritual merit), 141, 152, 182

baraka (divine blessing), 141, 197, 217–218, 219, 255n11

Baudrillard, Jean, 95

Bayart, Jean-François, 101

bazin riche fabric, 162, 252n16

Beijing platform, 24, 244n32

Benin, 60

bid'a (unlawful innovation), 30, 140, 252n4

Binta Sall, Haja, 111–112

birth control, 120–121

"Black Islam," 29

Bobo people, xii, 28

body, the: bodily coverage of dress, 252n15; disciplining of, 144, 156, 158, 252n14; listening and corporeality (materiality) of, 126, 215

Bollywood movies, 73

Bourdieu, Pierre, 168

Bowen, John, 234, 256n3

Boyd, Jean, 110, 134

bride-price payments, 37, 245n51

Bureau des Ulema, 176, 253nn3,5

Burkina Faso, x

Burrows, David, 215

Cairene mosque movement, 129, 146–147, 151, 152, 154

Calhoun, Craig, 26

capitalism, 12, 18, 248n4; commercialization of religion and, 233; consumer culture and, 74, 75, 170; Traoré regime and, 243n28

cassette sermons. *See* sermon cassette tapes (*kaseti wajuli*)

Castells, Manuel, 80

Catholic Church, xii, 67

charisma, 217–218, 221–227, 255n11

charity, 105, 106–107, 249n2

children, xiii, 52, 55, 59, 222; economic hardship and, 63, 64, 247n16; fathers' authority and, 54; migrant, 50; sent to ask favors, 51; women entrepreneurs and, 61; women's status and, 52

Christians/Christianity, 33, 100, 113, 192; extraversion strategies of, 101; missionaries, xii; Pentecostal movements, 180; religion and material interest, 129–130

cinema, 200, 218

circumcision, female, 34, 38, 244n32

civil liberties, xiii, 2, 34

civil rights, 232

civil society, 12, 26, 41; AMUPI and, 45; gender equality and, 43; "global civil society," 108; imported ideal of, 95; Islamic renewal and rhetoric of, 173; law reform debate and, 46; Muslim women's groups as part of, 110; secularism and, 100; state divided from, 135, 175

class distinctions, 43, 163, 164, 167, 246n8, 253n20. *See also* middle classes

clothing. *See* dress style

Code de Procedure Civile, Commerciale et Sociale (CPCCS), 37

Code du Mariage et de la Tutelle (CDT), 24, 36–37, 44, 245n38

Code Napoleon, 36, 245n46

colonial rule, French: Bamako's importance and, xi; "civilizing" mission of, xi, 101; conversion to Islam under, x, xii, 2, 123, 243n24; judicial system, 36, 244n35; Muslim reformers

in period of, 117; resistance to, 28, 242nn10,11; state and interest groups under, 26–33; Sufi orders and, 103. *See also* Sudan, French (*Soudan Français*)

Comaroff, Jean, and John L. Comaroff, 170

commodification, 17, 183, 218

communications research, 84

Concertations Régionales, 37–38, 39, 245n39

Connell, Robert, 54

consumer culture, 17, 18, 23, 75; female Muslim dress and, 166, 167; fragmentary nature in Mali and Africa, 95; global circulation of American culture, 73; passivity and activity of consumers, 88; personal experience and, 74; rejection of, 138, 166, 170; sermonizing and, 181; social inequality and, 78

consumption, 17, 61, 76; blanket denunciations of, 79; circuits of religious consumption, 179–184; cultural homogenization and, 73; dress style and, 162, 165; essentialist views of, 16; Habermas's view of, 75; ideals of common good and, 88; identity expressed through, 160; marginal position in world of, 82; production and, 89, 93; of religious discourse / media products, 18, 232; religious subjectivity embodied in, 168–170, 227; scholarship on, 74; sermon listening as, 212; social organization of, 183–184; social/economic capital expressed in, 168; of television serials, 77, 83, 88

corruption, 38, 105, 245n40

cosmopolitanism, 199

cotton production, 179–180

courtyard (*da*), as women's place, 51, 52

co-wives, 52, 53, 57, 255n23

credit savings associations, 65, 102, 126, 128

culture industry, 18, 76, 240n35

customary law, 36, 40, 244n35

Dallas (television series), 83

dance, 98–99

da'wa (Islamic proselytizing), 106, 113, 134, 237n3 (chap 1), 249n6; dress practices and, 168; public acts of prostration and, 155; sermon tapes and, 183. *See also* learning groups, Muslim women's; *medersa* schools

debate, intra-Muslim, 174, 177, 194, 231, 253n4; Haidara and, 178–179; sermon cassette tapes and, 205–206; state institutions and, 177–178; in women's groups, 206–208

democracy/democratization, 2, 11, 106; Christian churches and, 100; introduction of, xii; Islamic renewal and rhetoric of, 173; law and, 25; legal reform and, 45; performative power of "Islam" and, 231; Touré government and, 35; unfulfilled promises of, xii–xiii, 230, 236

Dialectics of Enlightenment (Adorno and Horkheimer), 88

dignity, 54, 55, 92, 157

discourse, 12, 17–18, 29; on civility and knowledge transmission, 31; of human rights, 38; of ignorance and truth, 190; mass-mediated and immediate, 226

Divine, the, 4, 17, 19, 140, 225

Djenné, town of, x, xi, 28, 237n3 (preface); on map, *xvi;* Sufi orders in, 249n3

donor organizations, Western, 24, 26; credibility of, 34; exchange with, 150; Muslim activism compared with, 106–107; organizational terminology of, 113; women's rights NGOs and, 38

draft law debate (2000), 40–44, 104

dress style, xiv, 2, 139, 142, 222, 252n14; "Arab" style, 163, 165–166, 167, 170; class distinctions and, 163, 164, 167, 253n20; global community of believers and, 169; piety expressed through, 159–167; prayer controversies and, 157; white attire, significance of, 163–164, 253n20

economy/economic conditions, 11, 145, 236; currency devaluation, 47; extraversion strategies and, 101; hardship and, 47; informal economy, 60, 247n13; Islamic way of trading, 129–133; parallel economy, 102–103, 108; spiritual connotations of prosperity, 180. *See also* liberalization, economic; merchants

education, 5, 68, 117; as means of self-advancement, 7; paradigms of learning, 117–123; peer learning, 119, 251n26; Western, 118, 119, 152, 235; women's right to, 157

Egypt (Cairo), 5, 8, 109, 145, 238n5; apparel imported from, 165; Al-Azhar University, 30; Cairene mosque movement, 146–147, 151, 152, 154; cassette sermon practices in, 199–200; commercial ties to, 179; cosmopolitan Muslim orientation and, 181; *da'wa* concept and, 249n6; intellectual and institutional trends in, 123, 139; intellectuals' ties to, 35; Islamic discursive traditions in, 18; local re-readings of reformist thought from, 150; modernism in, xi; radio broadcasts from, 176; Salafi-Sunni ideas from, 177; sermon tape listening in, 204, 210, 212, 213–214, 219; Sunni reformists in, 30; television soap operas in, 77, 78

Eickelman, Dale, 122, 251n31

Englund, Harri, 101

entrepreneurship, 60–62, 102–103

Europe, Western, 51, 76, 95, 228, 230

everyday life, xiii, 8, 21, 217, 225, 234; competing allegiances and conflicts in, 86; domestic conflicts in, 56; ethical quest in, 207; gender and research in, xiv; gender-specific power relations in, 17; inter-medial topical sites and, 90; mass-mediated culture and, 88; mediatization of, 15; Muslim dress style in, 162; permeation by mass media, 9, 226, 235; private realm in, 51; relevance of Qur'anic *suras* to, 142; religious knowledge and practice in, 126; sign and signified in, 95; supernatural in, 23, 226; tension between autonomy and responsibility, 80

extraversion, 101, 113, 135

faantanya (sorrow and shame of poverty), 62, 64, 65, 69

Fabian, Johannes, 90

family: economic changes and, 13–14; home economic circumstances and, 49–51; nuclear family model, 36, 40, 44, 78, 245n47; public-private distinction and, 51; soap operas and, 84–87; women's place in, 3

family law, 20, 24, 36–37, 173

femininity, 14, 49, 71, 234

feminism, 48, 145

Femmes de sable (telenovela), 248nn9,14

filimu (soap operas), 76, 80–86, 224, 226; consumerism displayed in, 81; Islamic renewal supporters as viewers of, 83, 87; meanings ascribed to by spectators, 80; organization of daily life and, 77; spectators' moralizing analysis of, 87; viewers as debating subjects, 88; women's engagement with, 82. *See also* telenovelas

Fiske, John, 85

France, 60, 82; Ansar Dine followers in, 133; Malian expatriate communities in, 91, 150; television broadcasts from, 76

Frankfurt school theorists, 75, 76, 88, 94

French language, xiii, 34, 166, 223; incomplete knowledge of, 139; Muslim public debate in, 176

friendship, female, 58

Fulbe families, xi, 28, 103

"fundamentalism," 6, 7, 230, 238n12; Muslim associations criticized for, 102; religious parties and, 11; secular politics in conflict with, 109

funerals, 3, 15, 140, 141

gaa (veranda), 50, 51

Gambia, 138

Gao, town of, *xvi*, 28, 36, 112

gèlèya (heaviness, difficulty), 47, 55

gender, ix, 229, 246n3; anthropology of, 48–49; inequality within moral reform movement, 114; moral economy of, 20; segregation by, xiii–xiv

gender relations, 9, 21; economic liberalization and, 58–59; marital division of responsibilities, 51–53, 173, 236; men's discursive regulation of, 66–71; moral negotiation of, 13–14, 240n32; "proper," 25

gender studies, 71

generations, 13, 53, 70, 94, 245n47; conflicts between, 61, 70, 81, 84, 86; divisions of responsibility between, 14, 53, 230, 236; masculinity and rural relations between, 54; of Muslim reformists, 5, 32, 123; obligations between, 20, 56, 64, 230

Geraghty, C., 85, 86

Ghana, 60, 91, 93, 218

Gifford, Paul, 101

gifts, obligations and, 63, 66, 247n22; poverty and inability to reciprocate, 62; praise singers (*jeliw*) at weddings, 91, 92, 248n16

globalization, cultural, 80

Gramsci, Antonio, 85

grand dakar robe, 162, 164

Guinea, 76

Habermas, Jürgen, 74, 87, 88, 90, 256n2; "critical-rational debate" concept, 205–206; pessimistic view of mass-mediated subjectivity, 75; on public debate, 174, 194, 202, 253nn1,2; public sphere in theory of, 174, 205, 233, 239n27, 247n2; subjectivities in theory of, 94

hademadenya, 126, 127

Hadith, 30

Haidara, Shaykh Sharif Ousmane Madani, xii, 22, 35, 45, 195, 201; AMUPI's opposition to, 178; *baraka* (blessing) and, 197, 219; charismatic quality of voice, 197, 198, 217–220; *Concertations Régionales* and, 39–40; conflicts with other Muslim leaders, 174–175; female acolytes of, 133, 166, 220; government policy toward, 178–179; images of, *171*, 220–221; media technology used by, 185–186; moral community invoked by, 185, 190–194; patronage and, 104; shops selling sermons of, 184; speech conventions used by, 186, 254nn16,19; "Sufi Islam" and, 141; on systematic nature of Islam and the Qur'an, 188–189, 208, 217; "to-be-continued" style of preaching, 181; "trickle-down" charisma of, 221, 222–226; workshops run by followers of, *171*

Hall, Stuart, 84
Hamawiyya, 141
hardship, economic, 47, 48, 49–51
Harvey, David, 74, 170
Haut Conseil Islamique, 177, 178
hearing, sense of, 215–216
hegemony, media, 85
hejaz, xi, 31, 179, 180. *See also* Middle East
"hip wrap power" (*taafe fanga*), 52–53
Hirschkind, Charles, 18, 204, 211, 212, 214; on agency and mediatized sermons, 219; on audition practices and Islamic discourse, 17; on disciplinary dimension of sermon listening, 213; on media engagements as ethical self-fashioning, 199–200; on sermon tapes and commercial exchange, 182–183
Horkheimer, Max, 77, 88
human rights discourse, 38

identity: consumption and, 74, 78, 160, 170; national, 173–174; public debate and, 174; Western consumer, 167
identity, Muslim, 33, 122, 138, 153; Arab, 138; charismatic authority and, 221; competing styles of, 179; cosmopolitan and traditional, 138; dress style and, 162, 165–166; economic privatization and, 181; ethical self-improvement and, 169; in French Sudan, 176; performance of worship and, 152; public debate and, 194–195; relational mode of identity construction, 193; Western consumerism combined with, 167
identity politics, religious/cultural, 8, 10, 137
ijma (community of scholarly consensus), 29, 190, 195
imperialism, 106
India, 77, 78
inheritance, 36, 37, 40, 41, 43, 44, 245n45
in-laws, 114, 128, 154, 245n50; family disputes with, 228; obedience to, 143; power relations and, 53; reluctance to ask help from, 64; respectful demeanor toward, 52, 144; support from, 57, 59, 60, 63
intégristes ("integral Sunnis"), 34, 35, 40, 44, 190, 244n31. *See also* Sunnism
intellectuals, 6, 27–28, 157, 253n4; Islamic code of civility and, 33; law reform and, 38; Sunni reformers, 29–30; Wahhabi doctrine and, 31; Western-oriented/educated, 34, 39, 106
interest groups, 2, 24, 26–36; AMUPI and, 245n43; divisions among, 34; ritual performance and, 124; state power and prerogatives of, 45; Traoré regime and, 33, 176
International Monetary Fund (IMF), 244n33
International Women's Day, 58
intimacy, public, 89
Iran, 122, 250n17
Islam, 2, 26, 110, 230–231; "Arab Islam," 123, 162, 166; as blueprint for personal ethics, 13; civilizing traditions of, 194; cosmopolitan, 167; cultural authenticity and, 45, 46; discursive traditions of, 17, 18, 231; doctrinal controversy within, 27;

egalitarianism and, 164, 234; foundational texts of, 18, 30, 189, 190, 191, 192; French colonial administrators and, 31; gender roles and, 13–14; Mali's traditional culture and, 24; mass mediation and new articulators of, 194–195; as modernizing force, 233; moral foundations of nation and, 25; mystical traditions, 225; national identity and, 173–174; "objectification" of, 188, 189, 208; pan-Islamism, 28; politics and, 26, 46; public role or face of, 10–13, 135; "rational character" of, 208, 209; relevance to public life, 188–189; return to original teachings of, 141, 232; spread in West Africa, 130, 252n15; "submission" as literal meaning of, 5; symbolic language of, 6, 230; universalistic conception of, 29, 31, 231, 256n1. *See also* Muhammad, Prophet; Muslims; Qur'an; "rules of Islam" (*silameya sariyaw*); Sufism/ Sufi orders; Sunnism
"Islam," 7, 12, 23, 132, 179, 231
Islam, conversion to, xiv, 28, 32, 242n13; in colonial period, x, xii, 2, 123, 243n24; since early twentieth century, 18, 36, 241n9
Islamic renewal (*tajdid*), x, 2, 6, 11, 99, 237n3 (chap 1); consumer culture and, 73; critics of, 129; dialectic with social/political conditions, 231; discrepant trends within, 7; dress style and, 163, 168; established religious specialists and, 30; ethnography of, 229; ideals of common good in media consumption and, 88; individual responsibility and, 124; male supporters of, 83; media technologies and, 17, 197–198; mediation and, 4; pathways chosen by supporters of, 3, 5, 19; prayer controversies and, 153; radio programs and, 89; sermon listening and, 212; social and historical contexts of, 100–110, 235; spiritual experience mixed with enjoyment,

226; television serial viewing and, 87; waves of, 138; women's contribution to, 3, 110; as worldwide movement, 9
Ivory Coast, 60, 122, 150; Haidara in, 178, 185; Muslim identity in, 169; prayer controversies in, 153

Jameson, Fredric, 74
jeliw (praise singers), 91–94, 98, 132, 248n16, 249n17
jellaba-style dress, 165, 253n21
jihad, 27, 242n13
judiciary system, 24, 36, 38–39, 241n8, 244n37
justice, God as, 47

Kamalkhani, Zahra, 122
Kandiyoti, Deniz, 54, 55
Kankan, town of, 111
karamògòw (spiritual leaders/teachers), 115, 117–118, 142, 150, 153; Haidara as *karamògò*, 221, 223, 224; radio preachers as, 177
Katz, Elihu, 84
Kayes, town of, *xvi*, 112
Keita, Modibo, 32, 33
Kenedugu (Sikasso), "kingdom" of, xi
kin, 57, 64, 65, 125, 129; authority based in networks of, 44; elder authority and, 37; foreign sponsors accessed through, 114; male kin and proper Muslim woman, 124; membership in women's group and, 128; support network and, 53, 59, 62, 63, 64, 247n17; wealth redistribution among, 31; woman's ability to provide for, 66
kinesthesia, 216, 219
Kita, town of, xiv, *xvi*
knowledge, 22, 126; as conduit to moral renewal, 6; debate and, 121; esoteric, 140; hierarchy of, 142; memorization, 119–120, 121; paradigms of, 122; ritual, 5, 116; transmission of, 31, 117; of worship obligations, 123–124
Konaré, Adam Bâ, 109, 250n10
Konaré, Alpha Oumar, xii, 6, 34, 103, 249n7; campaign against female

circumcision, 34, 244n32; corruption and, 245n40; Haut Conseil Islamique and, 177; Muslim activists and government of, 108, 249n7

Koutiala, town of, *xvi*, 133

Kunta, Al-Bekkaye, 106–107, 249n8

Kunta clan, 130

labor migration, seasonal, 37

laïcité, 243n26, 244n32; colonial state's sacrifice of, 31, 32; constitution of French Sudan and, 33; draft law (2000) debate and, 41, 43; in French constitution, 244n34; religion as private matter, 155; state's failure to establish, 26–27; Touré regime and, 34. *See also* secularism

languages, local, 77

Larkin, Brian, 87, 199, 221

Last, Murray, 110, 134

Latin America: female propriety norms in, 67; telenovelas from, 73, 87

Launay, Robert, 169, 182

law: customary law, 36, 40, 244n35; family law, 20, 24, 36–37, 173; state law, 37, 40, 245n46

learning groups, Muslim women's, 21, 50, 119, 250n23; Arabic literacy and, 123; relevancies of learning, 115–117; "rules of Islam" and, 89; widening access to religious knowledge and, 5. *See also* Muslim women's groups (*silame musow tonw*)

LeBlanc, Marie-Nathalie, 122, 123, 167

Lee, Benjamin, 201

liberalization, economic, 7, 11–12, 20, 236, 239n24, 240n30; female responsibility and, 71; patriarchal authority undermined by, 70; religion invigorated in era of, 129; revision of marital obligations and, 58–59; social transformations and, 13; urban survival and, 48; women's peer support networks and, 66. *See also* neoliberalism; Structural Adjustment Programs

liberalization, political, 11, 111, 133, 239n24

Libya, 35, 176, 179, 250n17

Liebes, Tamar, 84

Lipschutz, Ronnie, 108

LiPuma, Edward, 201

literary theory, 84

lower classes, 43, 45

Lukács, Georg, 75, 189

MacLeod, Arlene Elowe, 129

Maghreb, 115, 151

Mahmood, Saba, 129, 130, 146, 149, 212

Mali, 4, 19, 219, 227; Arabic-speaking world and, 46; "authentic" culture of, 232, 243n27; Cairo movement compared with, 210, 212, 213–214; conflicts in everyday life, 86; constitution of, 35; *da'wa* (Islamic proselytizing) in, 113; entertainment culture in, 184; female religious praxis in, 8; "home" videos in, 91–92; independence (1960), xii, 32, 33; Islamic proselytizing in, 230; Islam's public prominence in, 19, 99, 173, 229; legalistic culture in, 26; map of, *xvi*; media practices in urban areas, 16, 18, 75–78; north and south of, x–xi, 18, 28, 241n7; political landscape, 11; public debate in, 194, 229, 231; public sphere of, 26, 201; religious patronage in, 103–104; secular constitution of, 6, 33; Senegal compared with, 111, 151–152, 251n28

maloya (humility, modesty, shame), 62, 69, 143; as gauge of moral order, 157. *See also* shame

marabouts (religious leaders), 29

Marka families, xi, 28

marriage/weddings, 131–132, 140; civil marriage registration, 41; co-wives, 52, 53, 57, 255n23; family law and, 36–37, 245n38; full adult status and, 56, 246n11; as locus of family conflicts, 48; wedding videos, 91–94, 248n15

Marty, Martin, 129

masculinity, 14, 49, 54, 57, 234, 246n8

Mauretania, xiv, 238n14

McLuhan, Marshall, 220

Mecca, pilgrimage to (*hadj*), 111, 112, 131, 164, 180

medersa schools, 103, 104–105, 117, 120, 176

media, mass, technologies of, x, 2, 5, 174, 188, 196; common experience and, 216–217; dynamics of Muslim media landscape, 175–179; essentialist views of, 16; everyday life permeated by, 9, 226, 235; media powers as spiritual powers, 217–222; modernity and religion in relation to, 198–199; new technologies, 15, 23, 226, 240n33; religious debate and, 175, 184–188; religious experience/practice and, 14–19, 22, 23, 226; traditional religious authority undermined by, 183; Western institutions/values associated with, 76. *See also* audio-recording technologies; radio; television; video technology

media, small (decentralized media), 76, 178, 179, 233, 248n5

media engagements, 21, 23, 75; as ethical self-fashioning, 200; metatopical space and, 226; as non-discursive practices, 90

media landscape (mediascape), 81, 94, 175, 177, 179

mediation, 4–5, 14–19, 184–188, 218, 238n9

medicine, Islamic, 140

men, Muslim, 14, 21, 101; AMUPI run by, 238n5; beards, 243n23; conduct standards and, 54–55; *da'wa* (Islamic proselytizing) and, 113; discursive regulation of gender relations, 66–71; dress style, 223, 252n15, 253n22, 256n14; Haidara followers, 222–223, 224; marital/family authority of, 37, 42, 245n49; married status of, 56, 57, 246n11; Muslim religiosity in Mali, 8, 238n14; outside (*kènèma*) associated with, 51; sermon tape listening

by, 202, 204–205, 208, 209; "shortage of men," 57, 67; soap operas deplored by, 81, 83; television serials and, 82–83; wives' increased power and, 173; women's support networks and, 128. *See also* gender relations; masculinity

menopause, 5, 142

merchants, xi, 5, 31, 222, 225; integration of Muslim practices in local culture and, 130; political parties and, 32, 33, 244n29

metatopical space, 87–88, 95, 226

Meyer, Birgit, 101, 218

middle classes, 3–4, 5, 13, 76, 246n5; dress style, 162; egalitarian character of Islam and, 234; in francophone West Africa, 151; gender and intergenerational relations in, 20; Haidara followers among, 217; hardship and, 47; husband's authority in family, 42; income generation patterns in, 49, 50; Islamic renewal rooted in, 173; kin reliance in, 63; Malian Muslim associations and, 34; neoliberal reform and, 134; television advertisements and, 78

Middle East, 9, 10, 27; pan-Arabic movement in, 29; "patriarchal bargain" in, 55; politics of Muslim dress in, 159. See also *hejaz*

migrants, 48, 102, 246n2

Ministry of Women, Children, and the Family, 24, 38, 39, 109

miracles, performance of, 217, 256n11

missionary effort, transnational, 111

modernism, Muslim, xi, 5, 229, 234

modernity, 7, 73, 167, 229; colonial, 145, 221; ethics and, 233; Muslim associations and, 102, 116; parallel modernities, 87; privatization of religion and, 174; religion and broadcast media, 198; visual perception associated with, 200

"modest dress," 10, 143, 251n32

Moore, Laurence, 233

Mopti, town of, *xvi*, 28, 112

Morocco, 76, 106; apparel imported from, 165; commercial ties to, 179; Islamic learning in, 120, 122, 251n26

Morris, Rosalind, 218

mosques, xii, 15, 104, 187

mother-daughter relationships, 57, 64, 228

motherhood, 52

Mouvement pour la Démocratie, 34, 245n40

Muhammad, Prophet, 30, 99, 185, 254n7; birthday (*mawlud*), 115, 123, 125, 140, 154, 251n33; community of followers of, 116, 249n5; direct relationship to, 141; veneration of, 140; wives of, 143

munyu (patience, endurance), 55, 143, 145

music, popular, 76, 77, 78, 211, 248n8; female performers and audiences, 88–89; Haidara compared with pop stars, 186

Muslim associations, 34, 99, 209; as bridge between state and nonstate actors, 108; dress norms for women, xiv; in economy of patronage and trade, 102–103; emergence in West Africa, 111; grassroots mobilization and, 101; material interests and, 115, 135; patterns of sociality in, 106; rural male youth and, 104

Muslim women's groups (*silame musow tonw*), 2, 110–115, 202; *hadjas* of, 112, 147, 151, 210–211, 228; paradigms of learning, 117–123; political associations criticized by, 105–106; prayer ritual in, 153–154, 154–155; social hierarchies in, 113. *See also* learning groups, Muslim women's; *tontigiw* (women's group leaders, *présidentes*)

Muslims, xiv, 6, 160; colonial rule and, 27–28; community of true or proper believers, 190, 192, 194, 233, 234; cultural interpretation of Islamic traditions by, 231; democracy and, 11; legitimate representation of, 40; as minority in southern Mali, xi; modernity and, 228–229; pathways to God and, 19; "proper Muslims," 127, 128, 133; public debates among, 174, 253n4; "traditionalist," 117, 123

naming ceremonies, 140, 141

nasòngo ("price of the sauce"), 48, 53, 56, 57

National Union of Muslim Women of Mali. *See* UNAFEM (Union Nationale des Femmes Musulmanes du Mali)

nationalism, 137

nation-state, politics of, 7, 137, 138, 175, 239n27, 240n28; institutions' loss of credibility, 236; Malian law reform and, 25; modernity based on model of, 230; weakening significance of, 11

neoliberalism, 12, 26, 45, 100, 170; currency devaluation and, 47; transnational commercial circuits and, 179. *See also* liberalization, economic

Niger, x, 111, 130

Nigeria, 28, 87, 111, 138; cinema in, 221; merchant women in, 130; video-film industry in, 91

Nioro, town of, x, 28; on map, *xvi*; "prayer economy" in, 180; Sufi orders in, 141, 249n3

nongovernmental organizations (NGOs), 25, 38, 39, 45, 245n42

North Africa, 30, 61, 119, 122, 180

North America, 51, 95

"obedience" clause, 42, 245n50

pathway to God (*alasira*), 3–4, 7, 136; introduction to, 142–152; learning and, 135; media technologies and, 15; moralizing endeavor of Muslim women as, 6; Muslim identity and, 22; mutual assistance joined with spirituality, 105; public piety and, 8; ritual and, 124; understanding of religiosity and, 19

patriarchy, ix, 6, 13, 72; decline of, 48; female submissiveness and, 145; norms of female propriety and, 52;

"patriarchal bargain," 53–54, 55, 59; resistance to, 121; soap operas and, 85; Western-educated female elite and, 42; women's learning groups and, 115

patronage, political/religious, 102, 103, 105, 114, 135, 193; conventional, 217; female and male networks, 133; Muslim women's groups and, 115, 250n20; parallel economy and, 108; reciprocity and, 107

peers, exchange networks among, 64–66

piety, xiii, 13, 136, 152; demonstrative acts of, 148; dress practices and, 159–167; elements of, 145; Haidara praised for, 217; inter-subjective meanings of, 137; performance of, 156–159; personal quest for, 9, 22, 152; public practice of, x, 8, 10; studies of female public piety, 16; symbols of, 2, 125; Wahhabi doctrine and, 31; women as models of, 139, 140

politics, 11–12, 24, 44; "Arab" influence on, 163; consumption of, 247n2; market-mediated, 75; multiparty, xii, 34; nation-state, 137, 138, 175, 231; public-private distinction and, 51; secular, 11, 12, 13, 230; single-party rule, 33, 34, 99

polygamy, 56, 246n9

Postone, Moishe, 74, 170

poverty, 48, 62, 71

power relations, 17, 37, 42, 53, 110

prayer, 96, 118, 124–125, 197, 252n8; controversies involving, 145, 152–156; direct relationship to the Prophet through, 141; as path to God, 148; proper performance of, 143

prayer shawls, 162–163, 165, 222, 253nn18,19

PRODEJ (Promotion de la Démocratie et de la Justice), 24, 37–40, 46

progress, ideology of, 7, 16, 198, 199

Prophet, the. *See* Muhammad, Prophet

propriety, 10, 43, 48, 56–57, 230

propriety, female, 54–55, 70, 71, 229; in Catholic societies, 67; debates in

women's groups and, 207; double standard and, 52; dress style and, 159, 165; economic liberalization and, 71; entrepreneurs and, 61; ethical transformation and, 158; "patriarchal bargain" and, 55; prayer controversies and, 156–157; "return" to tradition and, 125; rules of conduct for Muslim women, 144

"prosperity gospel," 180

Protestants, xii

PSP (Parti Soudaniste Progressiste), xii, 32

public sphere, 22, 26, 232, 239n27; in French Sudan, 243n27; Habermas's conception of, 174, 205, 233, 247n2; as metatopical space, 87–88; restructured from within, 201; sermon tape circulation and, 203

publicity, 12, 58, 247n2

public/publicness, notion of, 12–13, 22, 233, 239n27, 240nn28,29

punishment, divine, 120, 146, 147, 149, 152

Qadiriyya, 27, 28, 130, 192, 237n1 (chap 1), 241n7. *See also* Sufism/Sufi orders

Qur'an, 121, 217; Arabic literacy in reading, 118; distortions of original teachings of, 30; Haidara's citations from, 188, 191, 208; recitation of, 4. See also *suras,* Qur'anic

Qur'anic schools/studies, 111, 117, 250n22; disciples sent to beg, 119, 250n24; gender and, 251n3; in Iran, 122; of Saad Oumar Touré, 254n8

radio, ix, 2, 58, 196; Bureau des Ulema and, 176, 253n3; debates among Muslims on, 253n4; Haidara's use of, xii, 178; illiterate population reached by, 34; market competition and, 78; national radio of Mali, 24, 150–151; as new media technology, 240n33; public subjectivity and, 89; Radio Islamique, 39, 177; sermons on, 3,

143, 181, 209; spatial divisions of gender propriety and, 205; talk-radio programs, 89, 90, 94, 186, 189; wide appeal of, 77

Ramadan, 67, 189, 244n32

religion, 26, 236; consumer culture and, 18, 233; as form of consumption, 170; gains in African politics since 1980s, 100; interpretive authority, 23; mediation and, 4, 15, 194–195; modernity and, 174, 198; politics and, 11–12, 24

religiosity, xiii, 4, 20, 209; changed understandings of, 7, 194; Christian, 129; consumption and, 170; conventional understanding of, x, 8, 22; dress style and, 164; female propriety and, 157; mass-mediated forms of, 232; of men, 8, 238n14; "pathway" notion and, 19; public demonstrations of, 125, 137, 156; Sufism and female religiosity, 229; "traditionalist," 234; "unlawful innovation" (*bid'a*), 30, 140, 252n4; veiling and, 9

resistance agency, 7

responsibility, individual/personal, 7, 22, 31–32, 124, 168

reward, divine, 146, 147, 152

rites of passage, 140

ritual, 123–126, 139, 152–153, 156, 169

Robertson, Roland, 170, 227, 253n24

robes, 162

Rose Sauvage (telenovela), 71, 248nn9,14

Roy, Olivier, 125

"rules of Islam" (*silameya sariyaw*), 121, 141, 147, 197, 208; commercial culture and, 189; Haidara's invocation of, 190; Muslim identity and, 138; prayer ritual and, 153

rural society: draft law debate and, 42; economic liberalization and, 13; inheritance issues in, 40; kin solidarity in, 63, 64; masculinity in, 54; migration to urban areas, 49; Muslim activists and, 35; networking activities, 104; "patriarchal bargain" and, 53; state corruption and, 34; urban Islamic piety spread to, 179–180

saints, veneration of, 140, 224

Salafiyya/Salafism, 29, 30, 146, 149, 212, 243n21

salat (act of worship), 152

San, town of, ix, 58; Ansar Dine in, 117, 128, 133, 187, 197, 220; conversions to Islam in colonial period, 28; economic achievement indicators in, 49–50; Haidara in, 222; historically marginal position of Islam in, xi, 237n1 (preface); Islam's history in, 2, 237n1 (chap 1); low-income neighborhoods, 62, 64–65; on map, *xvi;* middle-class neighborhoods, 13; migrants in, xii, 48; multiethnic composition of, xi; Muslim women's groups in, xiii; radio in, 68; television viewing in, 73, 77, 248n7; Wahhabi doctrine in, 31

Sanankoua, Bintou, 131, 132

Saudi Arabia, 2, 61, 109, 145, 180, 238n5; apparel imported from, 165; capital and influence from, 106; commercial ties to, 179; cosmopolitan Muslim orientation and, 181; *da'wa* concept and, 249n6; dress code in, 31, 243n23; "fundamentalism" and money from, 6; funding for Muslim women's groups from, 250n17; intellectual and institutional trends in, 5, 123, 139; intellectuals' ties to, 35; local rereadings of reformist thought from, 150; Malians in, 228; sponsorship of Arabic schools in Mali, 103; Sunni reformists in, 30; television broadcasts from, 76

scholars, Muslim, 27, 29, 31, 36, 110, 116

secularism, 6, 11, 173; conflict with religious values, 46; as ideal, 44, 241n5; Islamic renewal and, 13; law reform debate and, 45; nation-state politics, 7, 138; paradigm of personal success and, 119; *politiki,* 105–106, 109, 126; religious movements as "threat" to, 230; women as measure of political society and, 159. See also *laïcité*

Segou, town of, xi, 28, 133, 178, 196;
    Ansar Dine in, 216; on map, *xvi;*
    Silame jama in, 112; Sufi orders in,
    249n3
self-improvement, ethical, 122, 168, 169,
    204
seli (public worship), 139, 152, 155
Senegal, 28, 76, 111, 138, 228; Muslim
    women in, 151–152; power of reli-
    gious clans in, 104; Sufi orders in,
    103, 113, 130, 140, 249n3
sensory perception, 199, 214, 215, 219
sermon cassette tapes (*kaseti wajuli*), 3,
    17, 18, 177, 183, 201; audition prac-
    tices, 17, 18; circulation circuits of,
    201–203; cognitive effects of listening
    to, 211–212; as commodities, 182–183;
    community of believers and, 184,
    185–186; Haidara and, 179; "hearing"
    and "listening" to, 210; listeners'
    engagements with, 199–200; merits
    of listening to, 204–214; oppositional
    culture and, 177; phenomenology of
    listening as spiritual experience, 214–
    217; popular entertainment media
    and, 17; preachers' personalities and,
    203, 255n4; prices for, 182, 254n13;
    sharing (social consumption) of, 183,
    184, 201–202; sold in shops, 182, 184,
    254n14; speech genres and, 186–187
sexuality, 51, 52, 246n11; female pro-
    miscuity, 52, 67, 69; on television
    serials, 83
shahada (testimony of faith), 118, 124,
    191
shame, 126, 144; Catholic honor/shame
    complex, 52; erosion of patriarchal
    authority and, 70; intergenerational
    conflict and, 158; modest dress and,
    143; norms of attire and, 160; poverty
    and, 62, 65, 69
shari'a (Islamic law), 34, 35, 36, 40
siblings, half and full, 86
Sidibé, Ousmane, 32
Silame jama, 111–112
Simone, Abdou Maliq, 104
simulacrum, thesis of the, 95

Sissoko, 187–188, 189, 254n20, 255n21
slavery, 36, 242n13
soap operas. See *filimu* (soap operas)
Soares, Benjamin, 141, 180, 252n10
social imaginary, 87
social security networks, 43, 48
socialism, 33, 243n28
songs, religious, 140, 251n3
specialists, religious, 5, 119; absence
    of, xi; Haidara's challenge to, 183,
    191, 193; interpretational authority
    and, 234; politics and, xii, 109, 141;
    reformist intellectuals opposed by,
    30, 31; traditional lineages of, 230.
    See also Sufism/Sufi orders
speech, 211, 220; "forceful speech," 18,
    183, 197, 217, 219; hidden qualities of,
    218; Islamic homiletics and speech
    genres, 186–187; kinesthetic effects
    of, 216, 219; sense perception and,
    215; voice equated with, 219
Spitulnik, Debra, 79–80, 199, 221
Starrett, Gregory, 152, 155
state, the, 11, 12, 134, 230, 236; civil
    society against, 41, 135, 175; debate
    among Muslims and, 177–178; inter-
    action with officials of, 12; interest
    groups and, 26–36; law and, 37, 38,
    44; media controlled by, 22; Muslim
    activists and, 108, 249n7; Muslims'
    presence in institutions of, 174;
    shrinking resources of, 13; sover-
    eignty and coercive powers of, 38
Structural Adjustment Programs, 14, 48,
    102, 244n30. *See also* liberalization,
    economic
"Structural Transformation" (Haber-
    mas), 174
subjectivity, x, 10, 145, 243n22; actor-
    oriented account of, 12; capitalist
    marketing and, 77; changing notions
    of, 22; consumer culture and, 75,
    170; dress style and, 167; education
    as battleground and, 119; ethical sen-
    sibility and, 233; gender and, 246n3;
    in Habermas model, 94; mass-
    mediated, 73–75; media technologies

of, 1–3, 7, 8, 9, 10, 12; Qur'anic schooling and, 121; steering committee, 150, 154; video recording of conference, 14–15
"understanding," of sermons, 208, 209, 210, 213, 214
unemployment, 59, 64, 86
United States, 76, 87, 91, 133, 233
urban (town) society, 104, 200; economic liberalization and, 13, 70; "envy" in, 66; Islamic piety spread to rural areas from, 179–180; media practices in, 75–78; patriarchal authority in, 70; veiling in, 10
urbanization, 13
US-RDA (Union Soudaniste du Rassemblement Démocratique), xii, 32–33, 36

Vaa, Mariken, 65
veil, donning or taking the, 1, 2, 168, 239n21; as either-or decision, 8–9; Haidara's image and, 221; headgear and, 163; history in Mali, 159; as mark of dedication to Islam, 2; as "modest dress," 143–144; public practice of piety and, 10; scarf, 162–163, 222; symbolism of, 9; variety of dress modes, 9–10; women's subjugation associated with, 9, 239n19
video technology, xiii, 1, 2, 90; charisma and, 221–226; doubling of agency and perspective in screenings, 92–94; "home" videos, 91–92; recorders, 77, 222; shops and, 182; spiritual presence and, 218; wedding videos, 91–94, 248n15
Villalon, Leonardo, 103, 111
virtue, 53, 139, 193, 205, 229, 236; bodily comportment and, 144; Cairene mosque movement and, 146; interaction with "other women" and, 159; negative definition of, 192; religious consumption and, 168; ritual and, 153, 155, 156; submissiveness equated with, 207; white clothing and, 164
vision, sense of, 215–216

Wahhabis/Wahhabi doctrine, 30, 31, 32, 237n3 (chap 1)
wali ("friend of God"), 217, 255n10
Warner, Michael, 20
Watson, Helen, 160
Weber, Max, 218
Weber, Samuel, 199
wedding videos, 91–94, 248n15
welfare organizations, Islamic, 2, 13
West, the, 138, 193; consumer culture of, 73, 74; humanitarian aid from, 106; mass media consumption in, 84; political dependence on, 2, 46; public subjectivity in, 75
West Africa, x, 3, 101, 229; charity and agricultural labor in, 107; divisions among Muslims, 40; female religious praxis in, 8, 110; grassroots mobilization in, 101; history of controversies among Muslim scholars, 27; Islamic proselytizing in, 29; Malian expatriate communities in, 91; media practices in, 87; pathways to God in, 15; prayer controversies in, 156; religious education in, 119; women entrepreneurs in, 60; women's associations, 127. *See also* Africa
Westerlund, David, 116
Williams, Raymond, 85
women, Muslim, 1, 2, 5–7, 238n7; as breadwinners, 59, 127, 246n12; continuity and change in religious practice, 139–142; debates among, 206–208, 209; dress practices of, 159–167, 252n14; entrepreneurs, 60–62; extraversion strategies and, 101, 135; family law reform and, 24, 36–37, 245n38; female friendship, 58; gender relations and, 14; gendered division of responsibilities and, 51–53; in informal economy, 60, 247n13; learning groups, 21, *96–97;* male supporters of moral reform and, 137; married status of, 5, 10, 42, 43, 56, 139, 238n10, 253n17; men's response to greater autonomy of, 66–71; middle classes, 3–4; migrants,

50, 246n7; mixed blessings of greater female responsibility, 71–72; motivations to join renewal movement, ix–x; as "pawns" in hands of male leaders, 6, 99; pop star fan culture and, 89; reasoning capacities (*hakili*), 149; as religious agents, 8, 238n15; religious song and dance of, 98–99; ritual and, 123–126, 251n30; rules of conduct for, 143–152, 189, 196, 255n23; search for security, 62–64; secularism criticized by, 109; senior, 55, 246n10; sermon tape listening by, 201–202, 205–214, 255n3; social networks of, 51, 53, 65–66; support networks of, 126–129; televised dramas and, 74, 81; trade activities of, 130–131. *See also* femininity; gender relations; learning groups, Muslim women's; Muslim women's groups (*silame musow tonw*)

World Bank, 244n33

youth, xii, 101, 138; Arabic literacy of, 5; female, 81; male, 48, 68, 81, 104; talk-radio programs and, 89; television dramas watched by, 81, 88

Zaire, 90
Zambia, 221

DOROTHEA E. SCHULZ is Professor in the Department of Cultural and Social Anthropology at the University of Cologne.